150 LEADING CASES

Obligations:
CONTRACT LAW

150 Leading Cases

Obligations:
Contract Law

Consultant Editor: Lord Templeman
Editor: D G Cracknell
LLB, of the Middle Temple, Barrister

Old Bailey Press

OLD BAILEY PRESS
200 Greyhound Road, London W14 9RY

ISBN 1 85836 273 3

British Library Cataloguing-in-Publication

A catalogue record for this book is available from the British Library.

Printed and bound in Great Britain

Contents

Acknowledgements   *vii*

Preface   *ix*

Table of Cases   *xi*

1   Offer and Acceptance   *1*

2   Consideration   *13*

3   Certainty and Form of Contract   *27*

4   Contents of Contracts   *38*

5   Misrepresentation   *56*

6   Exclusion Clauses   *66*

7   Incapacity   *75*

8   Mistake   *80*

9   Duress and Undue Influence   *92*

10 Privity of Contract   *106*

11 Illegality   *113*

12 Frustration   *120*

13 Discharge of the Contract   *126*

14 Remedies for Breach of Contract – Damages   *139*

15 Remedies for Breach of Contract – Equitable Remedies   *155*

16 Quasi-Contract   *168*

17 Agency   *173*

18 Sale of Goods, Consumer Credit and Supply of Goods and Services   *178*

19 Assignment   *190*

Acknowledgements

The publishers and author would like to thank the Incorporated Council of Law Reporting for England and Wales for kind permission to reproduce extracts from the Weekly Law Reports, and Butterworths for their kind permission to reproduce extracts from the All England Law Reports.

Preface

Old Bailey Press Casebooks are intended as companion volumes to the Textbooks but they are also invaluable reference tools in themselves. Their aim is to supplement and enhance a student's understanding and interpretation of a particular area of law and provide essential background reading. Companion Revision WorkBooks and Statutes are also published.

The *Obligations: Contract Law* casebook is designed for use by any undergraduates who have Contract Law within their syllabus. It will be equally useful for all CPE/LLDip students who must study Contract Law as one of the 'core' subjects.

In reducing to 150, or thereabouts, the number of cases included in this book, an attempt has been made to include cases which make clear the underlying principles within a particular area. Extracts from judgments have been selected with a view also to identifying, and in some cases explaining, earlier decisions where a similar point arose.

Decisions of the House of Lords added to the text include *Malik* v *Bank of Credit and Commerce International SA* [1997] 3 All ER 1 (damages for stigma), *Co-operative Insurance Society* v *Argyll Stores (Holdings) Ltd* [1997] 3 All ER 297 (specific performance) and *Investors Compensation Scheme Ltd* v *West Bromwich Building Society* [1998] 1 All ER 98 (interpretation of contractual documents).

Cases reported up to May 1998 have been taken into consideration.

Table of Cases

Cases in bold type are the leading cases. Page numbers in bold indicate the main references to them.

Adams v Lindsell (1818) B & Ald 681   8

Addis v Gramophone Co Ltd [1909] AC 488   46, 47, **139**, 147, 153

Adler v Dickson [1955] 1 QB 158   110

Afovos Shipping Co SA v Pagnan (The Afovos) [1983] 1 WLR 195; [1983] 1 All ER 449 **126**

Aiken v Short (1856) 1 H & N 210   **168**, 169, 171, 195

Ailsa Craig Fishing Co Ltd v Malvern Fishing Co [1983] 1 WLR 964; [1983] 1 All ER 101 **66**, 67

Al-Nakib Investments (Jersey) Ltd v Longcroft [1990] 3 All ER 321   74

Al Saudi Banque v Clark Pixley [1989] 3 All ER 361   74

Albazero, The [1977] AC 774; [1976] 3 All ER 129   191

Alder v Moore [1961] 2 QB 57; [1961] 2 WLR 426   **140**, 143

Alexander v Rayson [1936] 1 KB 169   **113**

Ali v Christian Salvesen Food Services Ltd [1997] 1 All ER 721   **38**

Allcard v Skinner (1887) 36 Ch D 145   **92**, 95, 102

Amalgamated Investment and Property Co Ltd v John Walker & Sons Ltd [1977] 1 WLR 164; [1976] 3 All ER 509   **80**, 120

Amsprop Trading Ltd v Harris Distribution Ltd [1997] 2 All ER 990   107

Antaios Cia Naviera SA v Salen Rederierna AB, (The Antaios) [1984] 3 All ER 229   193

Archbolds (Freightage) Ltd v S Spanglett Ltd [1961] 1 QB 374; [1961] 2 WLR 170; [1961] 1 All ER 417   118

Argy Trading Development Co Ltd v Lapid Developments Ltd [1977] 1 WLR 444   **13**, 15, 18

Ashbury Railway Carriage & Iron Co v Riche (1875) LR 7 HL 653   75

Ashington Piggeries Ltd v Christopher Hill Ltd, Christopher Hill Ltd v Norsildmel [1972] AC 441; [1971] 1 All ER 847   188

Associated Japanese Bank (International) Ltd v Credit du Nord SA [1989] 1 WLR 255; [1988] 3 All ER 902   **82**

Associated Portland Cement Manufacturers [1900] Ltd v Houlder Brothers & Co Ltd (1917) 86 LJKB 1495   49

Astley v Reynolds (1731) 2 Stra 915   24

Atari Corp (UK) Ltd v Electronic Boutique Stores (UK) Ltd [1998] 1 All ER 1010 **178**

Atlantic Barron, The see North Ocean Shipping v Hyundai Construction

Atlas Express Ltd v Kafco (Importers and Distributors) Ltd [1989] 3 WLR 389; [1989] 1 All ER 641   14, 19, **93**

Avon Finance Co Ltd v Bridger [1985] 2 All ER 281   91

B & S Contracts and Design Ltd v Victor Green Publications Ltd [1984] ICR 419   94

Bailey v Bullock [1950] 2 All ER 1167   153

Balfour v Balfour [1919] 2 KB 571   **27**, 28, 32, 34

Banco Exterior Internacional v Mann [1995] 1 All ER 936   98, 104

Bank Line Ltd v Arthur Capel & Co [1919] AC 435   123

Bank of Baroda v Rayarel [1995] 2 FLR 376 98

Bank of Credit and Commerce International SA v Aboody [1989] 2 WLR 759; [1992] 4 All ER 955   93, **94**, 96–97, 98, 103

Bank of Montreal v Stuart [1911] AC 120   95

Barber v NWS Bank plc [1996] 1 All ER 906   42, 44, **179**

Barclays Bank Ltd v W J Simms Son & Cooke (Southern) Ltd [1980] QB 677; [1979] 3 All ER 522   86, 168, 170, 195

Barclays Bank plc v O'Brien [1993] 3 WLR 786; [1993] 4 All ER 417   **96**, 98, 99, 103, 104, 194

Barclays Bank plc v Thomson [1997] 4 All ER 816   96, **98**, 104

Barton *v* Armstrong [1976] AC 104; [1975] 2
    WLR 1050   *24, 99*
Beale *v* Taylor [1967] 1 WLR 1193; [1967] 3 All
    ER 253   *181*
Behn *v* Burness (1863) 3 B & S 751   *49, 54*
Behzadi *v* Shaftesbury Hotels Ltd [1991] 2 All ER
    477   *129*
Bell *v* Lever Bros [1932] AC 161   *82*
Bendall *v* McWhirter [1952] 2 QB 466   *7*
Bentley (Dick) Productions Ltd *v* Harold
    Smith (Motors) Ltd [1965] 1 WLR 623
    39, 52
Bentsen *v* Taylor Sons & Co [1893] 2 QB 274
    43
Beresford *v* Royal Insurance Co Ltd [1938] 2 All
    ER 602   *114*
Berry *v* Berry [1929] 2 KB 316   *14*
Beswick *v* Beswick [1968] AC 58; [1967] 3 WLR
    932; [1967] 2 All ER 1197   *106, 107, 110,
    112, 155, 190*
Bettini *v* Gye (1876) 1 QBD 183   *40*
Binions *v* Evans [1972] Ch 359; [1972] 2 WLR
    729   *7*
Birch *v* Paramount Estates Ltd (1958) 167 EG 396
    51, 52
Birmingham and District Land Co *v* London and
    North Western Ry Co (1888) 40 Ch D 268
    15
Bisset *v* Wilkinson [1927] AC 177   *56*
Blackpool & Fylde Aero Club Ltd *v* Blackpool
    Borough Council [1990] 1 WLR 1195   *1*
Bliss *v* South East Thames Regional Health
    Authority [1985] IRLR 308; [1987] ICR 700
    140, 147, 153
Bolton *v* Mahadeva [1972] 2 All ER 1322
    127, 130, 135
Bolton Partners *v* Lambert (1889) 41 Ch D 295
    173
Boone *v* Eyre (1779) 1 Hy Bl 273n   *48*
Braddon Towers Ltd *v* International Stores Ltd
    (1979) [1987] 1 EGLR 209   *155*
Branca *v* Cobarro [1947] KB 854; [1947] 2 All
    ER 101   *2*
Bremer Handelsgesellschaft mbH *v* J H Rayner &
    Co Ltd [1978] 2 Lloyd's Rep 73   *41*
Bremer Handelsgesellschaft mbH *v* Vanden
    Avenne-Izegem PVBA [1978] 2 Lloyd's Rep
    109   *42*
Bridge *v* Campbell Discount Co [1962] AC 600;
    [1962] 2 WLR 439   *143*
Briggs *v* Oates [1991] 1 All ER 407   *119*
Brikom Investments Ltd *v* Carr [1979] QB 467;
    [1979] 2 WLR 737; [1979] 2 All ER 753   *15*

Brinkibon Ltd *v* Stahag Stahl und
    Stahlwarenhandelsgesellschaft mbH [1983] 2
    AC 34; [1982] 2 WLR 264; [1982] 1 All ER
    293   *6*
British and Commonwealth Holdings plc *v*
    Quadrex Holdings Inc [1989] 3 WLR 723
    128
British Westinghouse Electric and Manufacturing
    Co *v* Underground Electric Railways Co of
    London Ltd [1912] AC 673   *149, 190*
Brocklehurst, Re, Hall *v* Roberts [1978] Ch 14;
    [1978] 1 All ER 767   *93, 95*
Brogden *v* Metropolitan Railway Co (1877) 2 App
    Cas 666   *3*
Brown *v* Raphael [1958] Ch 636   *57, 62*
Bunge Corporation *v* Tradax SA [1981] 1 WLR
    711; [1981] 2 All ER 513   *41, 44, 180*
Burgess *v* Purchase & Sons (Farms) Ltd [1983] 2
    All ER 4   *28*
Burnett *v* Westminster Bank Ltd [1966] 1 QB 742;
    [1965] 3 All ER 81   *6, 72*
Buttery *v* Pickard (1946) 174 TLR 144   *14*
Byrne & Co *v* Leon Van Tienhoven & Co (1880)
    5 CPD 344   *8*

CTN Cash and Carry Ltd *v* Gallaher Ltd
    [1994] 4 All ER 714   *100, 105*
Cammell Laird & Co Ltd *v* Manganese Bronze
    and Brass [1934] AC 402   *186*
Campbell *v* Edwards [1976] 1 WLR 403   *28*
Campbell Discount Co Ltd *v* Bridge [1962] 1 All
    ER 385   *164*
Canada Steamship Lines Ltd *v* R [1952] AC 192
    66
Candler *v* Crane Christmas & Co [1951] 1 All ER
    426   *72*
Carlill *v* Carbolic Smoke Ball Co Ltd [1893] 1
    QB 256   *2, 14*
Carlisle and Cumberland Banking Co *v* Bragg
    [1911] 1 KB 489   *91*
Casey's Patents, Re [1892] 1 Ch 104   *23*
Central London Property Trust Ltd *v* High
    Trees House Ltd [1947] 1 KB 130   *13, 14,
    16, 17*
Chandelor *v* Lopus (1603) Cro Jac 4   *50, 52*
Chapleton *v* Barry Urban District Council
    [1940] 1 KB 532   *5, 12, 67, 68*
Chaplin *v* Leslie Frewin (Publishers) Ltd [1966]
    Ch 71; [1965] 3 All ER 764   *76*
Chappell & Co Ltd *v* The Nestlé Co Ltd [1959]
    3 WLR 168   *16*
Charrington & Co Ltd *v* Wooder [1914] AC 21
    55

Charter *v* **Sullivan** [1957] 2 QB 117; [1957] 2
WLR 528   *141, 181, 189*
Chesnau *v* Interhome Ltd (1983) 134 NLJ 341
    63
Citibank NA *v* **Brown Shipley & Co Ltd** [1991]
2 All ER 690   *83*
Clarke *v* Urquhart [1930] AC 28   *59, 60*
Clements *v* London and North Western Railway
[1894] 2 QB 482   *76*
Clydebank Engineering and Shipbuilding Co *v*
Castaneda [1905] AC 6   *141, 142, 143*
Combe *v* **Combe** [1951] 2 KB 215   *13, 15, 16*
Co-operative Insurance Society *v* **Argyll Stores
(Holdings) Ltd** [1997] 3 All ER 297   *ix,
155*
Cornish *v* Midland Bank plc [1985] 3 All ER 513
    103
Couchman *v* Hill [1947] KB 54; [1947] 1 All ER
103   *51*
Craven-Ellis *v* **Canons Ltd** [1936] 2 KB 403
    168
Crosse *v* Gardner (1689) Carth 90   *50*
Cumber *v* Wane (1721) 1 Stra 425   *21, 22*
Cundy *v* Lindsay (1878) 3 App Cas 459   *84, 86*
Curlewis *v* Clark (1849) 3 Exch 375   *21*
Curtis *v* **Chemical Cleaning & Dyeing Co Ltd**
[1951] 1 KB 805   *58, 67*
Cutter *v* **Powell** (1795) 6 Term Rep 320; (1795) 2
Smith LC 1   *48, 127, 129*

D *v* M [1996] IRLR 192   *119*
D & C Builders Ltd *v* **Rees** [1966] 2 QB 617;
[1966] 2 WLR 288; [1966] 3 All ER 837
18, 19, 22, 25, 94
Dakin (H) & Co Ltd *v* Lee [1916] 1 KB 566
127, 128
Darlington Borough Council *v* **Wiltshier
Northern Ltd** [1995] 1 WLR 68   *190*
Davis Contractors Ltd *v* Fareham Urban District
Council [1956] AC 696; [1956] 3 WLR 37
    81
Decro-Wall International SA *v* **Practitioners in
Marketing Ltd** [1971] 1 WLR 361   *44, 49,
130, 138, 156, 157*
Denny, Mott & Dickson Ltd *v* James B Fraser &
Co Ltd [1944] AC 265   *81*
Dick Bentley Productions Ltd *v* Harold Smith
(Motors) Ltd *see* Bentley (Dick) Productions
Ltd *v* Harold Smith (Motors) Ltd
Dickinson *v* Dodds (1876) 2 Ch D 463   *9*
Doyle *v* Olby (Ironmongers) Ltd [1969] 2 QB
158; [1969] 2 All ER 119   *59, 60, 61, 63*
Doyle *v* **White City Stadium Ltd** [1935] 1 KB
110   *75*

Drive Yourself Hire Co Ltd *v* Strutt [1954] 1 QB
250; [1953] 2 All ER 1475   *112*
Dunbar *v* **Plant** [1997] 4 All ER 289   *113*
Dunk *v* George Waller & Son [1970] 2 QB 163;
[1970] 2 WLR 1241   *140*
Dunlop *v* Higgins (1848) 1 HL Cas 381   *8*
Dunlop *v* Lambert (1839) 6 Cl & Fin 600   *191*
Dunlop Pneumatic Tyre Co Ltd *v* **New
Garage & Motor Co Ltd** [1915] AC 79
141, 142
Dunlop Pneumatic Tyre Co Ltd *v* Selfridge & Co
Ltd [1915] AC 847   *109, 190*

East *v* **Maurer** [1991] 2 All ER 733   *58, 65*
Economides *v* **Commercial Union Assurance
Co plc** [1997] 3 All ER 636   *61*
Edwards *v* **Carter** [1893] AC 360   *76*
Edwards *v* **Skyways Ltd** [1964] 1 WLR 349
27, 28
Elder, Dempster & Co *v* Paterson Zochonis & Co
[1924] AC 522   *109, 110*
Elpis Maritime Co Ltd *v* **Marti Chartering Co
Inc (The Maria D)** [1991] 3 All ER 785
30
Engell *v* Fitch (1868) LR 3 QB 314   *139*
Entores *v* **Miles Far East Corporation** [1955] 2
QB 327; [1955] 3 WLR 48   *6*
Errington *v* **Errington and Woods** [1952] 1 KB
290   *6*
Esso Petroleum Co Ltd *v* Mardon [1976] QB 801;
[1976] 2 All ER 5   *57*
Eurymedon, The *see* New Zealand Shipping Co
Ltd *v* A M Satterthwaite & Co
Evans *v* London and Provincial Bank (1917) 3
LDAB 152   *146*
Evans (J) & Son (Portsmouth) Ltd *v* Andrea
Merzario Ltd [1976] 1 WLR 1078   *40*

Farrow *v* **Wilson** (1869) LR & CP 744   *191*
Fawcett *v* Smethurst (1914) 84 LJKB 473   *78*
Fenner *v* Blake [1900] 1 QB 426   *14*
Fercometal Sarl *v* **Mediterranean Shipping Co
SA (The Simona)** [1988] 3 WLR 200; [1988]
2 All ER 742   *131, 136*
Ferguson *v* **Davies** [1997] 1 All ER 315   *19,
22, 25, 133*
Finnish Government (Ministry of Food) *v* H V
Ford & Co Ltd (1921) 6 Ll LR 188   *49*
Fisher *v* Bell [1961] 1 QB 394; [1960] 3 All ER
731   *10*
Fitch *v* **Dewes** [1921] 2 AC 158   *116*
Fleming *v* Bank of New Zealand [1900] AC 577
    173

Foakes *v* Beer (1884) 9 App Cas 605   *19, 20,*
    25, 26
Foley *v* Classique Coaches [1934] 2 KB 1   *33*
Forthright Finance Ltd *v* Carlyle Finance Ltd
    [1997] 4 All ER 90   *182*
Foster *v* Mackinnon (1869) LR 4 CP 704   *91*
Foster *v* Robinson [1951] 1 KB 149; [1950] 2 All
    ER 346   *7*
Freeth *v* Burr (1874) LR 9 CP 208   *134*
Frost *v* Knight (1872) LR 7 Ex 111   *133*

Gaisberg *v* Storr [1950] 1 KB 107   *17*
Gallie *v* Lee *see* Saunders *v* Anglia Building
    Society
Gardner *v* Marsh and Parsons [1997] 3 All ER 871
    154
General Billposting Co Ltd *v* Atkinson [1909]
    AC 118   *118, 133*
Gibbons *v* Westminster Bank Ltd [1939] 2 KB
    882; [1939] 3 All ER 577   *143, 146, 147*
Giles (C H) & Co Ltd *v* Morris [1972] 1 WLR
    307; [1972] 1 All ER 960   *156, 159, 160,*
    161
**Glencore Grain Rotterdam BV *v* Lebanese
    Organisation for International Commerce**
    [1997] 4 All ER 514   *183*
Goddard *v* O'Brien (1882) 9 QBD 37   *21*
Gosling *v* Anderson [1972] EGD 709   *63*
Gould *v* Gould [1970] 1 QB 275; [1969] 3 WLR
    490   *27, 31*
Grant *v* Australian Knitting Mills Ltd [1936] AC
    85   *181*
Gray *v* Barr [1971] 2 QB 554; [1971] 2 All ER
    949   *114, 115*
Griffiths *v* Peter Conway Ltd [1939] 1 All ER 685
    187
Grist *v* Bailey [1967] Ch 532; [1966] 2 All ER
    875   *82*
Groom *v* Cocker [1938] 2 All ER 394   *153*
Guinness Mahon & Co Ltd *v* Kensington and
    Chelsea Royal London Borough Council
    [1998] 2 All ER 272   *75*

Hadley *v* Baxendale (1854) 9 Exch 341   *59,*
    144, 146, 148
Halifax Mortgage Services (formerly BNP
    Mortgages Ltd) *v* Stepsky [1996] 2 All ER
    277   *98*
Halkett *v* Earl of Dudley [1907] 1 Ch 390   *161*
Hall's Estate, Re, Hall *v* Knight [1914] P 1   *114*
Hardwick *v* Johnson [1978] 1 WLR 683   *7*
Hardy & Co *v* Hillerns & Fowler [1923] 2 KB 490
    179

Hare *v* Murphy Bros Ltd [1974] ICR 331; affd
    [1974] 3 All ER 940   *123*
Harling *v* Eddy [1951] 2 KB 739; [1951] 2 All ER
    212   *51*
**Harlingdon & Leinster Enterprises Ltd *v*
    Christopher Hull Fine Art Ltd** [1990] 1 All
    ER 737   *184*
Harris *v* Great Western Railway (1876) 1 QBD
    515   *70*
Harris *v* Nickerson (1873) LR 8 QB 286   *7*
Harris *v* Watson (1791) Peake 72   *24*
Harris *v* Wyre Forest District Council [1989] 2
    WLR 790; [1989] 2 All ER 514   *68, 72*
Hayes *v* James and Charles Dodd [1990] 2 All ER
    815   *154*
Heilbut, Symons & Co *v* Buckleton [1913] AC 30
    39, 50, 51, 52
Helby *v* Matthews [1895] AC 471   *183*
Henderson *v* Stevenson (1875) LR 2 Sc & Div 470
    70
Henthorn *v* Fraser [1892] 2 Ch 27   *8*
Herne Bay Steam Boat Company *v* Hutton [1903]
    2 KB 683   *124*
Heron II, The *see* Koufos *v* C Czarnikow
Hill *v* C A Parsons & Co Ltd [1972] Ch 305;
    [1971] 3 WLR 995   *156*
Hillas & Co Ltd *v* Arcos (1932) 147 LT 503
    32
Hobbs *v* London and Southwestern Rly Co (1875)
    LR 10 QB 111   *153*
Hochster *v* De la Tour (1853) 2 El & Bl 678
    133
Hoenig *v* Isaacs [1952] 2 All ER 176   *128*
Hollier *v* Rambler Motors (AMC) Ltd [1972] 2
    QB 71; [1972] 2 WLR 401   *69*
Holwell Securities Ltd *v* Hughes [1974] 1 WLR
    155   *9*
**Hong Kong Fir Shipping *v* Kawasaki Kisen
    Kaisha** [1962] 2 QB 26; [1962] 2 WLR 474;
    [1962] 1 All ER 474   *41, 42, 48, 130, 180*
Household Fire and Carriage Accident Insurance
    Co *v* Grant (1879) 4 Ex D 216   *8*
Howatson *v* Webb [1907] 1 Ch 537; affirmed
    [1908] 1 Ch 1   *91*
Hoyle, Re, Hoyle *v* Hoyle [1893] 1 Ch 84   *31*
Hughes *v* Metropolitan Railway Co (1877) 2 App
    Cas 439   *15, 18*
Hyman *v* Hyman [1929] AC 601   *17, 163*

Imperial Land Co of Marseilles, Re, Harris' Case
    (1872) 7 Ch App 587   *8*
Ingram *v* Little [1961] 1 QB 31; [1960] 3 WLR
    505   *84, 87, 88, 89*

Interfoto Picture Library Ltd *v* Stiletto Visual Programmes Ltd [1988] 1 All ER 348   *12, 73*

Interoffice Telephones Ltd *v* Robert Freeman Co Ltd [1957] 3 All ER 479   *189*

Investers Compensation Scheme Ltd *v* West Bromwich Building Society [1998] 1 All ER 98   *ix, 53, 55, 145, 157, **192***

Jackson *v* Horizon Holidays [1975] 1 WLR 1468   ***107, 108, 145***

Jackson *v* Union Marine Insurance (1873) LR 10 CP 125   *43*

Jarvis *v* Swan Tours Ltd [1973] 2 QB 233; [1973] 1 All ER 71   *63, 153*

Jerome *v* Bentley & Co [1952] 2 All ER 114   *176*

Jones (R E) Ltd *v* Waring & Gillow Ltd [1926] AC 670   *85, 86*

Jorden *v* Money (1854) 5 HL Cas 185   *14, 15*

Joseph Constantine Steamship Line Ltd *v* Imperial Smelting Corp Ltd (The Kingswood) [1942] AC 154   *123*

K (deceased), Re [1985] 1 All ER 403   *115*

Karflex *v* Poole [1933] 2 KB 251   *180*

Keighley, Maxsted & Co *v* Durant [1901] AC 240   ***173***

Kemble *v* Farren (1829) 6 Bing 141   *142*

King, Re (1858) 3 De G & J 63   *78*

Kings Norton Metal Co Ltd *v* Edridge, Merrett & Co Ltd (1897) 14 TLR 98   *88*

Kingswood, The *see* Joseph Constantine Steamship Line Ltd *v* Imperial Smelting Corp Ltd

Kish *v* Taylor [1912] AC 604   *44*

Kleinwort Benson Ltd *v* Malaysia Mining Corp Bhd [1989] 1 WLR 379; [1989] 1 All ER 785   *30, **33***

Koufos *v* C Czarnikow Ltd (The Heron II) [1967] 3 WLR 1491; [1967] 3 All ER 686   *145, 148*

Kpohraror *v* Woolwich Building Society [1996] 4 All ER 119   *140, 143, **145***

Krell *v* Henry [1903] 2 KB 740   ***120, 124***

Lake *v* Simmons [1927] AC 487   *84, 85, 86*

Lampleigh *v* Braithwait (1615) Hob 105   *22*

Larner *v* London County Council [1949] 2 KB 683   *168, **169**, 171*

Lawson *v* Hosemaster Machine Co Ltd [1966] 2 All ER 944   *173*

Lazenby Garages Ltd *v* Wright [1976] 2 All ER 770   *189*

Leaf *v* International Galleries [1950] 2 KB 86; [1950] 1 All ER 693   *50, 185*

Legione *v* Hateley (1983) 152 CLR 406   *165*

Leslie (R) Ltd *v* Sheill [1914] 3 KB 607   ***77***

L'Estrange *v* Graucob [1934] 2 KB 394   *68*

Lewis *v* Averay [1972] 1 QB 198; [1971] 3 WLR 603   *84, **87**, 186*

Linden Gardens Trust *v* Lenesta Sludge Disposals Ltd [1994] 1 AC 85   *191*

Liverpool City Council *v* Irwin [1976] 2 All ER 39   *38*

Living Designs (Home Improvements) Ltd *v* Davidson [1994] IRLR 69   *119*

Lloyds *v* Harper (1880) 16 Ch D 290   *107, 108, 190*

Lloyds Bank Ltd *v* Bundy [1975] QB 326   *102*

Lord Elphinstone *v* Monkland Iron and Coal Co (1886) 11 App Cas 332   *143*

Lumley *v* Wagner (1852) 1 De GM & G 604   ***157, 166***

Lyus *v* Prowsa Developments Ltd [1982] 2 All ER 953   *161*

McCausland *v* Duncan Lawrie Ltd [1996] 4 All ER 995   *37, **44***

McConnel *v* Wright [1903] 1 Ch 546   *59*

McCutcheon *v* David MacBrayne Ltd [1964] 1 WLR 125   *11, **68**, 172*

McRae *v* Commonwealth Disposals Commission (1950) 84 CLR 377   *82*

Mahkutai, The [1996] 3 All ER 502   *110*

Majik Markets Pty Ltd *v* S & M Motor Repairs Pty Ltd (No 1) (1987) 10 NSWLR 49   *136*

Malik *v* Bank of Credit and Commerce International SA [1997] 3 All ER 1   *ix, **45**, 140, 149*

Mannai Investment Co Ltd *v* Eagle Star Life Assurance Co Ltd [1997] 3 All ER 352   *179, 193*

Maredelanto Compania Naviera SA *v* Bergbau-Handel GmbH *see* The Mihalis Angelos

Maria D, The *see* Elpis Maritime Co Ltd *v* Marti Chartering Co Inc

Maritime National Fish Ltd *v* Ocean Trawlers Ltd [1935] AC 524   *122*

Maskell *v* Horner [1915] 3 KB 106   *24*

Massey *v* Midland Bank plc [1995] 1 All ER 929   *98, 104*

Maw *v* Jones (1890) 25 QBD 107   *139*

Medina *v* Stoughton (1700) 1 Salk 210   *50*

Meritt *v* Meritt [1970] 1 WLR 1211   *27, 32*

Mersey Steel and Iron Co Ltd *v* Naylor, Benzon & Co Ltd (1884) 9 App Cas 434   *48, 130, 134*

Mertens *v* Home Freeholds Co [1921] 2 KB 526
  122, 123
Metropolitan Coal Consumers' Association, Re,
  Karberg's Case [1892] 3 Ch 11   *56*
Midland Bank plc *v* Serter [1995] 1 FLR 1034
  98
Midland Bank plc *v* Shephard [1988] 3 All ER 17
  103
Mihalis Angelos, The [1971] 1 QB 164; [1970] 3
  WLR 601; [1970] 1 All ER 673   *44,* **48,**
  130, 133
Mitchell (George) (Chesterhall) Ltd *v* Finney
  Lock Seeds Ltd [1983] 3 WLR 163   *67*
Monarch Steamship Co Ltd *v* Karlshamns (AB)
  Oljefabriker [1949] 1 All ER 1   *146*
Moore & Co and Landauer & Co, Re [1921] 2 KB
  519   *54*
Morgan *v* Ashcroft [1938] 1 KB 49   *168, 169,*
  170
Morris *v* Baron [1918] AC 1   *45*
Morris *v* Redland Bricks [1970] AC 652; [1969] 2
  All ER 576   *156*
Mutual Finance Ltd *v* John Wetton & Sons Ltd
  [1937] 2 All ER 657   *101*

Nash *v* Inman [1908] 2 KB 1   *78*
National Carriers *v* Panalpina (Northern) Ltd
  [1981] AC 675; [1981] 2 WLR 45   ***121,***
  124
National Westminster Bank plc *v* Morgan
  [1985] AC 686; [1985] 2 WLR 588; [1985] 1
  All ER 821   *93, 95,* **101**
Naughton *v* O'Callaghan [1990] 3 All ER 91
  64
New York Star, The *see* Port Jackson Stevedoring
  v Salmond and Spraggon
New Zealand Shipping Co Ltd *v* AM Satterthwaite
  & Co Ltd (The Eurymedon) [1975] AC 154;
  [1974] 2 WLR 865; [1974] 1 All ER 1015
  4, 23, 108, 110, 111
North Ocean Shipping Co Ltd *v* Hyundai
  Construction Co Ltd (The Atlantic Baron)
  [1979] QB 705; [1978] 3 All ER 1170   *24,*
  94
Norwich and Peterborough Building Society *v*
  Steed (No 2) [1993] 1 All ER 330   *91*
Nutbrown *v* Thornton (1804) 10 Ves 159   *36*

Occidental Worldwide Investment Corp *v* Skibs
  A/S Avanti (The Siboen and The Sibotre)
  [1976] 1 Lloyd's Rep 293   *24, 25, 94*
O'Laoire *v* Jackel International Ltd [1991] IRLR
  170   *140*

O'Laoire *v* Jackel International Ltd (No 2) [1991]
  ICR 718   *47*
Oliver *v* Davis [1949] 2 KB 727   *17*
Olley *v* Marlborough Court Ltd [1949] 1 KB 532
  12
Oscar Chess Ltd *v* Williams [1957] 1 WLR 370
  40, **49**
O'Sullivan *v* Management Agency and Music Ltd
  [1985] 3 All ER 351   *103*

PCW Syndicates *v* PCW Reinsurers [1996] 1 All
  ER 774   *62*
Paal Wilson & Co A/S *v* Partenreederei Hannah
  Bluementhal [1983] 1 AC 843   *123*
Page One Records *v* Britton [1968] 1 WLR 157;
  [1967] 3 All ER 822   *158*
Palatine Graphic Arts Co Ltd *v* Liverpool City
  Council [1986] 1 All ER 366   *150*
**Pan Ocean Shipping Co Ltd *v* Creditcorp Ltd
  (The Trident Beauty)** [1994] 1 All ER 470
  195
Pao On *v* Lau Yiu Long [1980] AC 614; [1979]
  AC 614; [1979] 3 WLR 435; [1979] 3 All ER
  65   **22,** *26, 94, 100, 103*
Parker *v* South Eastern Railway Co (1877) 2
  CPD 416   *5, 11, 69,* **70**
Parry *v* Cleaver [1969] 1 All ER 555   *150*
Parsons (H) (Livestock) Ltd *v* Uttley Ingham &
  Co Ltd [1977] 3 WLR 990; [1978] 1 All ER
  525   *145, 149*
Pasley *v* Freeman (1789) 3 Term Rep 51   *50*
Patel *v* Ali [1984] 2 WLR 690; [1984] 1 All ER
  978   ***158***
Payzu *v* Saunders [1919] 2 KB 581   *149*
Pearce *v* Brooks (1866) LR 1 Ex 213   ***117***
Penn *v* Bristol and West Building Society
  [1997] 3 All ER 470   ***174***
Pettit *v* Pettit [1970] AC 777   *27,* **34**
**Pharmaceutical Society of Great Britain *v*
  Boots Cash Chemists (Southern) Ltd** [1953]
  1 QB 401; [1953] 1 All ER 482; [1952] 2 All
  ER 456   *9*
Philips *v* Ward [1956] 1 WLR 471   *152, 153*
Phillips *v* Brooks Ltd [1919] 2 KB 243   *84, 87,*
  88, 89
Photo Production Ltd *v* Securicor Transport Ltd
  [1980] AC 827   *67, 126, 176*
Pilkington *v* Wood [1953] Ch 770   *145*
Pinnel's Case (1602) 5 Co Rep 117a   *19, 21,* **25**
Pioneer Shipping Ltd *v* BTP Tioxide Ltd [1982]
  AC 724   *122*
Planché *v* Colburn (1831) 8 Bing 14   *134, 135,*
  171

Pollock (W & S) & Co *v* Macrae 1922 SC (HL) 192   *66*

Poosathurai *v* Kannappa Chettiar (1919) LR 47 Ind App 1   *102*

Pordage *v* Cole (1669) 1 WMS Saund 319   *134*

Port Jackson Stevedoring *v* Salmond and Spraggon (The New York Star) [1981] 1 WLR 138   *110*

Posner *v* Scott-Lewis [1986] 3 WLR 531   *159*

Post Chaser, The *see* Société Italo-Belge pour le Commerce et l'Industine SA *v* Palm and Vegetable Oils (Malaysia) Sdn Bhd

Poussard *v* Spiers and Pond (1876) 1 QBD 410 *41*

Prenn *v* Simmonds [1971] 1 WLR 1381; [1971] 3 All ER 237   *52, 192*

Price *v* Strange [1977] 3 WLR 943; [1977] 3 All ER 371   *160, 163*

Public Works Commissioner *v* Hills [1906] AC 368   *142*

R *v* Clarke (1927) 40 CLR 227   *10*

Rae *v* Yorkshire Bank plc [1988] BTLC 35 *146, 147*

Reardon Smith Line Ltd *v* Yngvar Hansen-Tangen [1976] 1 WLR 989; [1976] 3 All ER 570   *53, 134, 192*

Record *v* Bell [1991] 1 WLR 853   *35, 37, 161*

Reynell *v* Sprye (1852) 1 De GM & G 660   *99*

Richmond Gate Property Co Ltd [1964] 3 All ER 936   *169*

Robertson *v* Minister of Pensions [1949] 1 KB 227   *17*

Rock Refrigeration Ltd *v* Jones [1997] 1 All ER 1   *118, 134*

Rose & Frank Co *v* J R Crompton & Bros Ltd [1925] AC 445; [1923] 2 KB 261   *28*

Routledge *v* McKay [1954] 1 WLR 615   *51, 52*

Royal Bank of Scotland plc *v* Etridge [1997] 3 All ER 628   *99, 103*

Royscott Trust Ltd *v* Rogerson [1991] 3 WLR 57; [1991] 3 All ER 294   *61, 62*

Rust *v* Abbey Life Insurance Co [1979] 2 Lloyd's Rep 334   *136*

Ryan *v* Mutual Tontine Westminster Chambers Association [1893] 1 Ch 116   *159*

Ryder *v* Wombwell (1868) LR 3 Exch 90   *79*

St Albans City and District Council *v* International Computers Ltd [1996] 4 All ER 481   *55, 72, 149, 186*

St Martin's Property Corp Ltd *v* Sir Robert McAlpine & Sons Ltd [1994] 1 AC 85   *191*

Salisbury *v* Gilmore [1942] 1 All ER 457   *15*

Samuel Sanday & Co *v* Keighley, Maxted & Co (1922) 91 LJKB 624   *49*

Santa Clara, The *see* Vitol SA *v* Norelf Ltd

Saunders *v* Anglia Building Society [1970] 3 WLR 1078   *87, 89*

Scandinavian Trading Tanker Co AB *v* Flota Petrolera Ecuatoriana (The Scaptrade) [1983] 2 All ER 763   *164*

Scaptrade, The *see* Scandinavian Trading Tanker Co AB *v* Flota Petrolera Ecuatoriana

Scorer *v* Seymour Johns [1966] 3 All ER 347 *117*

Scruttons *v* Midland Silicones Ltd [1962] AC 446; [1962] 2 WLR 186   *108, 110, 111, 190*

Selectmove, Re [1995] 2 All ER 531   *22, 26*

Shepherd (F C) & Co Ltd *v* Jerrom [1986] 3 WLR 801   *122*

Shiloh Spinners Ltd *v* Harding [1973] 2 WLR 28; [1973] 1 All ER 90   *159, 164*

Siboen, The and The Sibotre *see* Occidental Worldwide Investment Corp *v* Skibs A/S Avanti

Sibree *v* Tripp (1846) 14 M & W 23   *21*

Sikes *v* Wild (1861) 1 B & S 587   *140*

Simona, The *see* Fercometal SARL *v* Mediterranean Shipping Co SA

Skeate *v* Beale (1840) 11 Ad & El 983   *24*

Sky Petroleum *v* VIP Petroleum Ltd [1974] 1 WLR 576; [1974] 1 All ER 954   *162*

Slater *v* Finning Ltd [1996] 3 All ER 398   *186*

Smith *v* Chadwick (1882) 20 Ch D 27   *56*

Smith *v* Eric S Bush [1989] 2 WLR 790; [1989] 2 All ER 514   *72*

Smith *v* Land and House Property Corporation (1884) 28 Ch D 7   *56, 58, 62*

Smith *v* UMB Chrysler (Scotland) Ltd 1978 SC (HL) 1   *66*

Société Italo-Belge pour le Commerce et l'Industrie SA *v* Palm and Vegetable Oils (Malaysia) Sdn Bhd (The Post Chaser) [1982] 1 All ER 19   *15*

Solle *v* Butcher [1950] 1 KB 671; [1949] 2 All ER 1107   *50*

Southern Water Authority *v* Carey [1985] 2 All ER 1077   *110*

Spellman *v* Spellman [1961] 2 All ER 498   *27*

Spencer *v* Harding (1870) LR 5 CP 561   *8*

Spiro *v* Glencrown Properties [1991] 2 WLR 931   *36, 45*

Spurling (J) Ltd *v* Bradshaw [1956] 1 WLR 461; [1956] 2 All ER 121   *12*

Staffordshire Area Health Authority *v* South Staffordshire Waterworks Co [1978] 1 WLR 1387   *55*

Steadman *v* Steadman [1976] AC 536; [1974] 3
   WLR 56   *163*
Steedman *v* Drinkle [1916] 1 AC 275   *165*
Stern *v* McArthur (1988) 165 CLR 489
   165
Stevenson, Jacques & Co *v* McLean (1880) 5
   QBD 346   *8*
Steward *v* Rapley [1989] 1 EGLR 159   *153*
Stilk *v* Myrick (1809) 2 Camp 317; (1809) 6 Esp
   129   *24, 26*
Stocks *v* Wilson [1913] 2 KB 235   *78*
Strange (S W) Ltd *v* Mann [1965] 1 All ER 1069
   117
Strutt *v* Whitnell [1975] 2 All ER 510   *149*
Sumpter *v* Hedges [1898] 1 QB 673   ***134***
Sutton *v* Sutton [1984] 2 WLR 146; [1984] 1 All
   ER 168   *119, 161, **162***
Syros Shipping Co SA *v* Elaghill Trading Co
   [1981] 3 All ER 189   *18*

Tamplin *v* James (1880) 15 Ch D 215   *158*
Taylor *v* Caldwell (1863) 3 B & S 826   *120,*
   123
Taylor *v* Oakes Roncoroni & Co (1922) 12 LT
   267   *184*
Thomas *v* Hammersmith Borough Council [1938]
   3 All ER 203   *172*
Thompson *v* London, Midland and Scottish
   Railway Co [1930] 1 KB 41   *5, 11*
**Thompson (W L) Ltd *v* R Robinson
   (Gunmakers) Ltd** [1955] Ch 177; [1955] 2
   WLR 185   *152, 182, **188***
Thorne *v* Motor Trade Association [1937] 3 All
   ER 157   *101*
Thornton *v* Shoe Lane Parking Ltd [1971] 2 QB
   163; [1971] 2 WLR 585   ***11**, 74*
Tinline *v* White Cross Insurance Association Ltd
   [1921] 3 KB 327   *114*
Tinsley *v* Milligan [1993] 3 All ER 65   *113*
Tito *v* Waddell (No 2), Tito *v* A-G [1977] 2 WLR
   496   *160*
Tool Metal Manufacturing Co Ltd *v* Tungsten
   Electric Co Ltd [1955] 1 WLR 761; [1955] 2
   All ER 657   *18*
Toteff *v* Antonas (1952) 87 CLR 647   *60*
Trident Beauty, The *see* Pan Ocean Shipping Co
   Ltd *v* Creditcorp Ltd
Trollope & Colls Ltd *v* North West Metropolitan
   Regional Hospital Board [1973] 2 All ER 260
   152
**Tsakiroglou & Co Ltd *v* Noblee and Thorl
   GmbH** [1962] AC 93; [1961] 2 WLR 633;
   [1961] 2 All ER 179   ***124***

Turnbull (Peter) & Co Pty Ltd *v* Mundas Trading
   Co (Australasia) Pty Ltd [1954] 2 Lloyd's Rep
   198   *41*
Tweddle *v* Atkinson (1861) 1 B & S 393   *26,*
   *109, 110, **111**, 112*

Union Eagle Ltd *v* Golden Achievement Ltd
   [1997] 2 All ER 215   *135, **164***
United Scientific Holdings *v* Burnley Borough
   Council [1978] AC 904   *41*
**Universe Tankships Inc of Monrovia *v*
   International Transport Workers'
   Federation (The Universe Sentinel)** [1982] 2
   WLR 803; [1982] 2 All ER 67   *94, 101, **104***

Varley *v* Whipp [1900] 1 QB 513   *185*
Victoria Laundry (Windsor) Ltd *v* Newman
   Industries Ltd [1949] 2 KB 528   *145*
Vitol SA *v* Norelf Ltd [1996] 3 WLR 107; [1996]
   3 All ER 193   *133, **135***

Wallis *v* Smith (1892) 21 Ch D 243   *141, 143*
Wallis, Son & Wells *v* Pratt & Haynes [1911] AC
   394; [1910] 2 KB 1003   *48*
Ward *v* Byham [1956] 1 WLR 496   *26*
Warlow *v* Harrison (1859) 1 E & E 309   *8*
Warman *v* Southern Counties Car Finance Corp
   (W J Ameris Car Sales, third party) [1949] 1
   All ER 711   *180*
Warner Bros Pictures Inc *v* Nelson [1937] 1 KB
   209; [1936] 3 All ER 160   *158, 166*
Warren *v* Mendy [1989] 3 All ER 103   *158,*
   165
Watkins *v* Rymill (1883) 10 QBD 178   *11*
Watteau *v* Fenwick [1893] 1 QB 346   ***175***
Watts *v* Morrow [1991] 1 WLR 1421   ***152***
Watts *v* Spence [1976] Ch 165; [1975] 2 All ER
   528   *63*
White and Carter (Councils) Ltd *v* MacGregor
   [1962] AC 413; [1962] 2 WLR 17   ***137**,*
   138, 154
Wickham, Re (1917) 34 TLR 158   *14*
Wigan *v* English and Scottish Law Life Assurance
   Association [1909] 1 Ch 298   *17*
William Porter & Co Ltd, Re [1937] 2 All ER 361
   14
Williams *v* Carwardine (1833) 5 Car & P 566;
   (1833) 4 B & Ad 621   *3, 11*
**Williams *v* Roffey Bros & Nicholls
   (Contractors) Ltd** [1990] 2 WLR 1153   *25*
Williams *v* Williams [1957] 1 WLR 148   *26*
Wilson *v* Best Travel Ltd [1993] 1 All ER 353
   189

Wilson *v* United Counties Bank Ltd [1920] AC 102   *146*

Winter Garden Theatre (London) Ltd *v* Millenium Productions Ltd [1947] 2 All ER 336; [1946] 1 All ER 280   *7*

Withers *v* General Theatre Corp Ltd [1933] 2 KB 536   *46*

Withers *v* Reynolds (1831) 2 B & Ad 882   *131*

Wolverhampton Corp *v* Emmons [1901] 1 KB 515 *156*

Wood *v* Fenwick (1842) 10 M & W 195   *76*

Wood Factory Pty Ltd *v* Kiritos Pty Ltd [1985] 2 NSWLR 105   *136*

Woodar Investment Development Ltd *v* Wimpey Construction UK Ltd [1980] 1 WLR 277; [1980] 1 All ER 571   *107–108, 112, 190*

Wroth *v* Tyler [1974] Ch 30; [1973] 2 WLR 405 *145*

Yasuda Fire & Marine Insurance Co of Europe Ltd *v* Orion Marine Insurance Underwriting Agency Ltd [1995] 2 WLR 49 *176*

Yianni *v* Edwin & Sons [1981] 3 All ER 592 *74*

Young *v* Schuler (1883) 11 QBD 651   *30*

1   Offer and Acceptance

Blackpool & Fylde Aero Club Ltd* v *Blackpool Borough Council [1990] 1 WLR 1195 Court of Appeal (Stocker, Bingham and Farquharson LJJ)

- *Tenders – failure to consider*

Facts
The defendant local authority owned the local airport for which it granted concessions for the operation of scenic and pleasure flights. On the expiry date of the current concessions it invited the plaintiffs and seven other companies to tender for the new concession. The plaintiffs currently held the existing pleasure flight concession. The invitation to submit tenders was accompanied by a condition that no tender received after a certain date/time would be considered. The plaintiffs' tender was posted by hand in the town hall letterbox, before the expiry date, but unfortunately the box was not cleared regularly and the town clerk received the tender, which was higher than any of the others submitted, after the deadline. The local authority announced that they were not considering it because it was too late.

Held
Where invitations are issued to specified parties to submit tenders, and the submission procedure is clearly laid down, along with a fixed date for submission, then if an invitee complied with the submission procedure and submitted his tender within the deadline, he had not just a moral but a contractual right to be considered. Although an invitation to tender was normally no more than an offer to consider bids, circumstances could exist whereby it gave rise to binding contractual obligations. While the invitation did not

specifically state this, a careful examination of what the parties said, and did, established a clear intention on the part of the defendants to be bound to examine, and give equal consideration to, all tenders submitted within the deadline. Since the plaintiffs had submitted on time, they were entitled to expect their tender to be considered in conjunction with all the other tenders. As it had not been so considered, they were entitled to damages for breach of contract.

Bingham LJ:

'It is of course true that the invitation to tender does not explicitly state that the council will consider timely and conforming tenders. That is why one is concerned with implication ... I readily accept that contracts are not to be lightly implied. Having examined what the parties said and did, the court must be able to conclude with confidence both that the parties intended to create contractual relations, and that the agreement was to the effect contended for.'

Stocker LJ:

'The format of the invitation to tender document itself suggests in my view that a legal obligation to consider a tender applied ... to any operator ... who complied with its terms and conditions ... I therefore agree that in all the circumstances of this case there was an intention to create binding legal obligations if and when a tender was submitted in accordance with the terms of the invitation to tender, and that a binding contractual obligation arose that the club's tender would be before the officer or committee by whom the decision was to be taken for consideration before a decision was made or any tender accepted. This would not preclude or inhibit the council from deciding not to accept any tender or to

1

award the concession, provided the decision was bona fide and honest, to any tenderer. The obligation was that the club's tender would be before the deciding body for consideration before any award was made.'

Branca v *Cobarro* [1947] KB 854 Court of Appeal (Lord Greene MR, Tucker and Asquith LJJ)

- *Effect of 'provisional' agreement*

Facts
A document signed by both parties made provision for the sale and purchase of a mushroom farm and concluded: 'This is a provisional agreement until a fully legalised agreement drawn up by a solicitor and embodying all the conditions herewith stated is signed.' Denning J decided that 'provisional' meant 'tentative' and therefore that the parties were not bound by the agreement contained in the document. The vendor, who was resisting the purchaser's claim for the return of his deposit, appealed.

Held
The appeal would be allowed.

Lord Greene MR:

'My reading of this document is that both parties were determined to hold themselves and one another bound. They realised the desirability of a formal document as many contracting parties do, but they were determined that there should be no escape for either of them in the interim period between the signing of this document and the signature of a formal agreement, and they have used words which are exactly apt to produce that result and do not, in my opinion, suggest that the fully legalised agreement is in any sense to be a condition to be fulfilled before the parties are bound, because, as I have said, the word "until" is certainly not the right word to import a condition or a stipulation as to the event referred to. In my judgment, if the parties never signed a fully legalised agreement, the event putting an

end to the provisional operation of this agreement would never occur and this document would continue to bind the parties.'

Comment
Any contract for the sale of land must now satisfy the requirements of s2 of the Law of Property (Miscellaneous Provisions) Act 1989.

Carlill v *Carbolic Smoke Ball Co* [1893] 1 QB 256 Court of Appeal (Lindley, Bowen and A L Smith LJJ)

- *Offer to the world – acceptance*

Facts
The defendants issued a newspaper advertisement in which they said they would pay £100 to any person who contracted influenza after using one of their smoke balls in a specified manner for a specified period. They also stated that they had deposited £1,000 with a named bank, to show their sincerity in the matter. The plaintiff, believing the accuracy of the advertisement, purchased one of the balls at a chemist's in Oxford Street and used it as directed – but she caught 'flu nevertheless! She sued to recover the £100.

Held
She was entitled to succeed.

Lindley LJ:

'The first observation I would make upon this is that we are not dealing with any inference of fact. We are dealing with an express promise to pay £100 in certain events. There can be no mistake about that at all. Read this how you will, and twist it about as you will, here is a distinct promise, expressed in language which is perfectly unmistakeable, that £100 reward will be paid by the Carbolic Smoke Ball Co to any person who contracts influenza after having used the ball three times daily, and so on. One must look a little further and see if this is intended to be a promise at all; whether it is a mere puff – a sort of thing which means nothing. Is that the meaning of it? My answer to that question is "No" and I base my answer upon this passage: "£1,000 is deposited with the Alliance Bank, Regent Street, showing our sincerity in the matter". What is that money deposited for? What is that passage put in for, except to negative the suggestion that this is a mere puff, and means nothing at all? The deposit is called in aid by the advertisers as proof of their sincerity in the matter. What do they mean? It is to show their intention to pay the £100 in the events which they have specified. I do not know who drew the advertisement, but he has distinctly in words expressed that promise. It is as plain as words can make it.

Then it is said that it is a promise that is not binding. In the first place it is said that it is not made with anybody in particular. The offer is to anybody who performs the conditions named in the advertisement. Anybody who does perform the conditions accepts the offer. I take it that if you look at this advertisement in point of law, it is an offer to pay £100 to anybody who will perform these conditions, and the performance of these conditions is the acceptance of the offer. That rests upon a string of authorities, the earliest of which is that celebrated advertisement case of *Williams* v *Carwardine* (1833) 4 B & Ad 621, which has been followed by a good many other cases concerning advertisements of rewards. But then it is said: "Supposing that the performance of the conditions is an acceptance of the offer, that acceptance ought to be notified". Unquestionably as a general proposition when an offer is made, you must have it not only accepted, but the acceptance notified. But is that so in cases of this kind? I apprehend that this is rather an exception to the rule, or, if not an exception, it is open to the observation that the notification of the acceptance need not precede the performance. This offer is a continuing offer. It was never revoked, and if notice of acceptance is required (which I doubt very much, for I rather think the true view is that which is as expressed and explained by Lord Blackburn in *Brogden* v *Metropolitan Rail Co* (1877) 2 App Cas 666), the person who

makes the offer receives the notice of acceptance contemporaneously with his notice of the performance of the conditions. Anyhow, if notice is wanted, he gets it before his offer is revoked, which is all you want in principle. But I doubt very much whether the true view is not, in a case of this kind, that the person who makes the offer shows by his language and from the nature of the transaction that he does not expect and does not require notice of the acceptance apart from notice of the performance.

We have, therefore, all the elements which are necessary to form a binding contract enforceable in point of law subject to two observations. First of all, it is said that this advertisement is so vague that you cannot construe it as a promise; that the vagueness of the language, to which I will allude presently, shows that a legal promise was never intended nor contemplated. No doubt the language is vague and uncertain in some respects, and particularly in that the £100 is to be paid to any person who contracts influenza after having used the ball three times daily, and so on. It is said, "When are they to be used?" According to the language of the advertisement no time is fixed, and construing the offer most strongly against the person who has made it, one might infer that any time was meant, I doubt whether that was meant, and I doubt whether that would not be pushing too far the doctrine as to construing language most strongly against the person using it. I doubt whether business people, or reasonable people would understand that if you took a smoke ball and used it three times daily for the time specified – two weeks – you were to be guaranteed against influenza for the rest of your life. I do not think the advertisement means that, to do the defendants justice. I think it would be pushing their language a little too far. But if it does not mean that, what does it mean? It is for them to show what it does mean; and it strikes me that there are two reasonable constructions to be put on this advertisement, either of which will answer the purpose of the plaintiff. Possibly there are three.

It may mean that the promise of the

reward is limited to persons catching the increasing influenza, or any colds, or diseases caused by taking colds, during the prevalence of the epidemic. That is one suggestion. That does not fascinate me, I confess. I prefer the other two. Another is, that you are warranted free from catching influenza, or cold, or other diseases caused by taking cold, while you are using this preparation. If this is the meaning, then the plaintiff was actually using the preparation when she got influenza. Another meaning – and the one which I rather think I should prefer myself – is becoming diseased within a reasonable time after having used the smoke ball. Then it is asked: "What is a reasonable time?" And one of my brothers suggested that that depended upon the reasonable view of the time taken by a germ in developing? I do not feel pressed by that. It strikes me that a reasonable time may be got at in a business sense, and in a sense to the satisfaction of a lawyer in this way. Find out what the preparation is. A chemist will tell you that. Find out from a skilled physician how long such a preparation could be reasonably expected to endure so as to protect a person from an epidemic or cold. In that way you will get a standard to be laid before a court by which it might exercise its judgment as to what a reasonable time would be. And it strikes me, I confess, that the true construction of this is that £100 will be paid to anybody who uses this smoke ball three times daily, for two weeks according to the printed directions, and who gets influenza, or a cold, or some other disease caused by taking cold, within a reasonable time after so using it. I think that that is the fair and proper business construction of it. If that is the true construction, it is enough for the plaintiff. Therefore, I say no more about the vagueness of the document.

I come now to the last point, which I think requires attention, ie, the question of the consideration. Counsel for the defendants has argued with great skill that this is a nudum pactum – that there is no consideration. We must apply to that argument the usual legal tests. Let us see whether there is no advantage to the defendants. Counsel says it is no advantage to them how much the ball is used. What is an advantage to them and what benefits them is the sale, and he has put the ingenious case that a lot of these balls might be stolen, and that it would be no advantage to them if the thief or other people used them. The answer to that I think is this. It is quite obvious that, in the view of the defendants, the advertisers, a use of the smoke balls by the public, if they can get the public to have confidence enough to use them, will react and produce a sale which is directly beneficial to them, the defendants. Therefore, it appears to me that out of this transaction emerges an advantage to them which is enough to constitute a consideration. But there is another view of it. What about the person who acts upon this and accepts the offer? Does not that person put himself to some inconvenience at the request of the defendants? Is it nothing to use this ball three times daily at the request of the defendants for two weeks according to the directions? Is that to go for nothing? It appears to me that that is a distinct inconvenience, if not a detriment, to any person who uses the smoke ball. When, therefore, you come to analyse this argument of want of consideration, it appears to me that there is ample consideration for the promise …

It appears to me, therefore, that these defendants must perform their promise, and if they have been so unguarded and so unwary as to expose themselves to a great many actions, so much the worse for them. For once in a way the advertiser has reckoned too much on the gullibility of the public. It appears to me that it would be very little short of a scandal if we said that no action would lie on such a promise as this, acted upon as it has been.'

Comment

Applied in *New Zealand Shipping Co Ltd* v *A M Satterthwaite & Co Ltd* [1974] 2 WLR 865.

Chapelton v *Barry Urban District Council* [1940] 1 KB 532 Court of Appeal (Slesser, MacKinnon and Goddard LJJ)

• *Hire of deck chair – condition on ticket*

Facts

Beside deck chairs stacked on a beach was a notice: 'Barry Urban District Council ... Hire of chairs, 2d per session of 3 hours ...' The plaintiff took two of the chairs and he received from the attendant two tickets which he put in his pocket without reading the statement printed on the back that 'The Council will not be liable for any accident or damage arising from hire of chair'. The canvas of the plaintiff's chair gave way and he suffered injury.

Held

He was entitled to damages since he was not bound by the conditions printed on the ticket.

MacKinnon LJ:

'If a man does an act which constitutes the making of a contract, such as taking a railway ticket, or depositing his bag in a cloakroom, he will be bound by the terms of the documents handed to him by the servant of the carriers or bailees, as the case may be. If, however, he merely pays money for something, and receives a receipt for it, or does something which may clearly only amount to that, he cannot be deemed to have entered into a contract in the terms of the words which his creditor has chosen to print on the back of the receipt, unless, of course, the creditor has taken reasonable steps to bring the terms of the proposed contract to the mind of the man. In this case there is no evidence at all upon which the county court judge could find that the defendants had taken any steps at all to bring the terms of their proposed contract to the mind of the plaintiff. In those circumstances, I am satisfied that the defendants could not rely upon the words on the back of the ticket issued to the plaintiff, and, having admittedly been negligent in regard to the condition of the chair, they had no defence to the plaintiff's cause of action.'

Slesser LJ:

'I do not think that this document was in the nature of a term of a contract at all, and I find it unnecessary really to refer to the different authorities which were cited to us, save that I would just mention a passage in the judgment of Mellish LJ, in *Parker* v *South Eastern Ry Co* (1877) 2 CPD 416, where he points out that it may be that a receipt or ticket may not contain terms of the contract at all, but may be a voucher. He says, at p422:

"For instance, if a person driving through a turnpike-gate received a ticket upon paying the toll, he might reasonably assume that the object of the ticket was that by producing it he might be free from paying toll at some other turnpike-gate, and might put it in his pocket unread."

I think that the object of the giving and the taking of this ticket was that the person taking it might have evidence at hand by which he could show that his obligation to pay 2d for the use of the chair for three hours had been duly discharged, and I think that, in the absence of any qualification of liability in the notice put up near the pile of chairs, it is altogether inconsistent to attempt to read into it the qualification contended for. In my opinion, this ticket is no more than a receipt, and it is entirely distinguishable from a railway ticket which contains upon it the terms upon which the railway company agree to carry the passenger. This, therefore, is not, I think, as counsel for the respondents has argued, a question of fact for the county court judge. I think that the county court judge as a matter of law has misconstrued this contract, and, looking at all the circumstances of the case, he has assumed that this condition on the ticket, or the terms upon which the ticket was issued, has disentitled the plaintiff to recover. The class of case with which Sankey LJ dealt in *Thompson* v *London, Midland and Scottish Ry Co* [1930] 1 KB 41, which seems to have influenced the county court judge in his decision, is a class of case different from that which we have to consider in the present appeal.'

Comment
Applied in *Burnett* v *Westminister Bank Ltd* [1965] 3 All ER 81 (notice on cheque book cover not binding on bank's customer).

Entores Ltd v *Miles Far East Corporation* [1955] 3 WLR 48 Court of Appeal (Denning, Birkett and Parker LJJ)

• *Contract – telex place of acceptance*

Facts
An English company in London was in communication with a Dutch company in Amsterdam by telex. The English company received an offer of goods from the Dutch company and made a counter offer which the Dutch company accepted – all by telex. For purposes of jurisdiction, where was the contract made?

Held
In London, where the English company received the acceptance.

Birkett LJ:

'I am of opinion that in the case of telex communications (which do not differ in principle from the cases where the parties negotiating a contract are actually in the presence of each other) there can be no binding contract until the offeror receives notice of the acceptance from the offeree. Counsel for the defendants submitted that the proper principle to be applied to a case like the present could be thus stated: "If A makes an offer to B, there is a concluded contract when B has done all that he can do to communicate his acceptance by approved methods." He further submitted that great difficulties would arise if telex communications were treated differently from acceptances by post or telegram.

In my opinion the cases governing the making of contracts by letters passing through the post have no application to the making of contracts by telex communications. The ordinary rule of law, to which the special considerations governing contracts by post are exceptions, is that the acceptance of an offer must be communicated to the offeror and the place where the contract is made is the place where the offeror receives the notification of the acceptance by the offeree. If a telex instrument in Amsterdam is used to send London the notification of the acceptance of an offer, the contract is complete when the telex instrument in London receives the notification of the acceptance (usually at the same moment that the message is being printed in Amsterdam) and the acceptance is then notified to the offeror, and the contract is made in London.'

Comment
Approved by the House of Lords in *Brinkibon Ltd* v *Stahag Stahl und Stahlwarenhandelsgesellschaft mbH* [1982] 2 WLR 264.

Errington v *Errington and Woods* [1952] 1 KB 290 Court of Appeal (Somervell, Denning and Hodson LJJ)

• *Offer – implied revocation*

Facts
A father bought a house for his son and daughter-in-law to live in. The father put down £250 and borrowed £250 from a building society on the security of the house, repayable at 15s per week. He took the house in his own name and was responsible for the repayments. However, he told his daughter-in-law that the £250 was a present to them but left the couple to make the repayments. He told them that the house would be theirs when the mortgage was repaid and that he would transfer the house into their names. They duly paid the instalments, although they never contractually bound themselves to do so.

Held

In these circumstances, so long as the couple went on paying the instalments, the father's promise was irrevocable.

Denning LJ:

'The father's promise was a unilateral contract – a promise of the house in return for their act of paying the instalments. It could not be revoked by him once the couple entered on performance of the act, but it would cease to bind him if they left it incomplete and unperformed ...

... it seems to me that, although the couple had exclusive possession of the house, there was clearly no relationship of landlord and tenant. They were not tenants at will, but licensees. They had a mere personal privilege to remain there, with no right to assign or sub-let. They were, however, not bare licensees. They were licensees with a contractual right to remain. As such they have no right at law to remain, but only in equity, and equitable rights now prevail. I confess, however, that it has taken the courts some time to reach this position. At common law a licence was always revocable at will, notwithstanding a contract to the contrary ... The remedy for a breach of the contract was only in damages. That was the view generally held until a few years ago ... The rule has, however, been altered owing to the inter-position of equity. Law and equity have been fused for nearly eighty years, and since 1948 it has become clear that, as a result of the fusion, a licensor will not be permitted to eject a licensee in breach of a contract to allow him to remain: see *Winter Garden Theatre (London) Ltd* v *Millennium Productions Ltd* [1946] 1 All ER 680 *per* Lord Greene MR, [1947] 2 All ER 336 *per* Viscount Simon; nor in breach of a promise on which the licensee has acted, even though he gave no value for it: see *Foster* v *Robinson* [1950] 2 All ER 346, where Sir Raymond Evershed MR said that as a result of the oral arrangement to let the man stay, he "was entitled as licensee to occupy the cottage without charge for the rest of his days ..." This infusion of equity means that contractual licences now have a

force and validity of their own and cannot be revoked in breach of the contract. Neither the licensor nor anyone who claims through him can disregard the contract except a purchaser for value without notice.'

Comment

Applied in (inter alia) *Binions* v *Evans* [1972] 2 WLR 729, *Bendall* v *McWhirter* [1952] 2 QB 466 and *Hardwick* v *Johnson* [1978] 1 WLR 683.

Harris v *Nickerson* (1873) LR 8 QB 286 Queen's Bench (Blackburn, Quain and Archibald JJ)

- *Advertisement of sale a contract?*

Facts

The defendant auctioneer advertised for sale by auction, inter alia, office furniture. The plaintiff travelled to the sale, intending to bid for the office furniture, but these lots were withdrawn from the sale. He sued to recover for two days' loss of time.

Held

His action could not succeed.

Quain J:

'To uphold the judge's decision [that the defendant was liable] it is necessary to go to the extent of saying that when an auctioneer issues an advertisement of the sale of goods, if he withdraws any part of them without notice, the persons attending may all maintain actions against him. In the present case, it is to be observed that the plaintiff bought some other lots; but it is said he had a commission to buy the furniture, either the whole or in part, and that therefore he has a right of action against the defendant. Such a proposition seems to be destitute of all authority; and it would be introducing an extremely inconvenient rule of law to say that an auctioneer is bound to give notice of withdrawal or to be held liable to everybody attending the sale. The case is certainly of the first impression.

When a sale is advertised as without reserve, and a lot is put up and bid for, there is ground for saying, as was said in *Warlow* v *Harrison* (1859) 1 E & E 309, that a contract is entered into between the auctioneer and the highest bona fide bidder; but that has no application to the present case; here the lots were never put up and no offer was made by the plaintiff nor promise made by the defendant, except by his advertisement that certain goods would be sold. It is impossible to say that that is a contract with everybody attending the sale, and that the auctioneer is to be liable for their expenses if any single article is withdrawn. *Spencer* v *Harding* (1870) LR 5 CP 561 which was cited by the plaintiff's counsel, as far as it goes, is a direct authority against his proposition.'

Comment

As to auction sales generally, see s57 of the Sale of Goods Act 1979.

Henthorn v *Fraser* [1892] 2 Ch 27
Court of Appeal (Lord Herschell, Lindley and Kay LJJ)

* *Offer – acceptance by post*

Facts

The plaintiff, who lived in Birkenhead, was handed a note at the defendants' office in Liverpool, giving him an option to purchase certain property within fourteen days. The next day, the defendants posted a letter withdrawing the offer, which did not reach Birkenhead until 5.00 pm. Meanwhile, the plaintiff had posted a letter at 3.50 pm accepting the offer. That letter was delivered after the defendants' office was closed and was opened the following morning.

Held

A valid contract had been concluded at 3.50 pm.

Lord Herschell:

'If the acceptance by the plaintiff of the defendants' offer is to be treated as complete at the time the letter containing it was posted, I can entertain no doubt that the [defendants'] attempted revocation of the offer was wholly ineffectual. I think that a person who has made an offer must be considered as continuously making it until he has brought to the knowledge of the person to whom it was made that it is withdrawn. This seems to me to be in accordance with the reasoning of the Court of King's Bench in *Adams* v *Lindsell* (1818) 1 B & Ald 681, which was approved by the Lord Chancellor in *Dunlop* v *Higgins* (1848) 1 HL Cas 381, and also with the opinion of Mellish LJ in *Re Imperial Land Co of Marseilles, Harris' Case* (1872) 7 Ch App 587. The very point was decided in *Byrne & Co* v *Leon Van Tienhoven & Co* (1880) 5 CPD 344 by Lindley LJ, and his decision was subsequently followed by Lush J in *Stevenson, Jaques & Co* v *McLean* (1880) 5 QBD 346.

The grounds upon which it has been held that the acceptance of an offer is complete when it is posted have, I think, no application to the revocation or modification of an offer. These can be no more effectual than the offer itself, unless brought to the mind of the person to whom the offer is made. But it is contended on behalf of the defendants that the acceptance was complete only when received by them, and not on the letter being posted.

It cannot, of course, be denied, after the decision in *Dunlop* v *Higgins* in the House of Lords, that, where an offer has been made through the medium of the post, the contract is complete as soon as the acceptance of the offer is posted; but that decision is said to be inapplicable here, inasmuch as the letter containing the offer was not sent by post to Birkenhead, but handed to the plaintiff in the defendants' office at Liverpool. The question therefore arises, in what circumstances the acceptance of an offer is to be regarded as complete as soon as it is posted.

In *Household Fire and Carriage Accident Insurance Co* v *Grant* (1879) 4 Ex D 216 Baggallay LJ said that he thought that the principle established in *Dunlop* v *Higgins* is limited in its application to cases in which, by reason of general usage, or of the relations between the parties to any particular transactions, or of the terms in which the offer is made, the acceptance of such offer by a letter through the post is expressly or impliedly authorised. And in the same case Thesiger LJ based his judgment on the defendant having made an application for shares under circumstances from which it must be implied that he authorised the company, in the event of their allotting the shares applied for, to send the notice of allotment by post. The facts of that case where, that the defendant had, in Swansea, where he resided, handed a letter of application to an agent of the company, their place of business being situate in London. It was from these circumstances that the lords justices implied an authority to the company to accept the defendant's offer to take shares through the medium of the post.

Applying the law thus laid down by the Court of Appeal, I think in the present case an authority to accept by post must be implied. Although the plaintiff received the offer at the defendants' office in Liverpool, he resided in another town, and is must have been in contemplation that he would take the offer, which by its terms was to remain open for some days, with him to his place of residence, and those who made the offer must have known that it would be according to the ordinary usages of mankind, that if he accepted it he should communicate his acceptance by means of the post.

I am not sure that I should myself have regarded the doctrine that an acceptance is complete as soon as the letter containing it is posted as resting upon an implied authority by the person making the offer to the person receiving it to accept by those means. It strikes me as somewhat artificial to speak of the person to whom the offer is made as having the implied authority of the other party to send his acceptance by post. He needs no authority to transmit the acceptance through any particular channel; he may select what means he pleases, the Post Office no less than any other. The only effect of the supposed authority will obviously be implied only when the tribunal

considers that it is a case in which this result ought to be reached. I should prefer to state the rule thus: Where the circumstances are such that it must have been within the contemplation of the parties that, according to the ordinary usages of mankind, the post might be used as a means of communicating the acceptance of an offer, the acceptance is complete as soon as it is posted. It matters not in which way the proposition be stated; the present case is in either view within it.

The learned Vice-Chancellor [in the court below] appears to have based his decision to some extent on the fact that before the acceptance was posted the defendants had sold the property to another person. *Dickinson* v *Dodds* (1876) 2 Ch D 463 was relied upon in support of that defence. In that case, however, the plaintiff knew of the subsequent sale before he accepted the offer, which, in my judgment, distinguishes it entirely from the present case.'

Comment
Distinguished in *Holwell Securities Ltd* v *Hughes* [1974] 1 WLR 155 where the Court of Appeal decided that 'the artificial posting rule' (per Russell LJ) did not apply where (as in that case) it was an express term of the offer that acceptance had to reach the offeror. Today, any contract for the sale of land must satisfy the requirements of s2 of the Law of Property (Miscellaneous Provisions) Act 1989.

Pharmaceutical Society of Great Britain v *Boots Cash Chemists (Southern) Ltd* [1953] 1 QB 401
Court of Appeal (Somervell, Birkett and Romer LJJ)

• *Supermarket – when contract of sale concluded*

Facts
Statute required that sales of certain poisons should be supervised by a registered pharma-

cist. A customer took one such poison off the shelf of a 'self-service' shop or supermarket and the transaction was supervised by a pharmacist at the cash desk.

Held
No offence had been committed because there had been no sale until the customer's money had been taken at the cash desk.

Somervell LJ:

'I agree entirely ... that in the case of the ordinary shop, although goods are displayed and it is intended that customers should go and choose what they want, the contract is not completed until the customer has indicated the article which he needs and the shopkeeper or someone on his behalf accepts that offer. Not till then is the contract completed, and, that being the normal position, I can see no reason for drawing any different inference from the arrangements which were made in the present case ...

I can see no reason for implying from this arrangement any position other than that ... it is a convenient method of enabling customers to see what there is for sale, to choose and, possibly, to put back and substitute, articles which they wish to have, and then go to the cashier and offer to buy what they have chosen. On that conclusion the case fails, because it is admitted that in those circumstances there was supervision in the sense required by the Act and at the appropriate moment of time.'

Romer LJ:

'The Lord Chief Justice observed [in the court below] that if, on the footing of the plaintiff society's contention, a person picked up an article, once having picked it up he would never be able to put it back and say he had changed his mind, for the shopkeeper could say that the property had passed and the customer would have to pay. If that were the position in this and similar shops, and that was known to the general public, I should imagine the popularity of such shops would wane a good deal. I am satisfied that that is not the position, and that

the articles, even though they are priced and put in shops like this, do not represent an offer by the shopkeeper which can be accepted merely by the picking up of the article in question.'

Comment
In *Fisher* v *Bell* [1960] 3 All ER 731 Lord Parker CJ said:

'It is clear that, according to the ordinary law of contract, the display of an article with a price on it in a shop window is merely an invitation to treat. It is in no sense an offer for sale the acceptance of which constitutes a contract. That is clearly the general law of the country. Not only is that so, but it is to be observed that, in many statutes and orders which prohibit selling and offering for sale of goods, it is very common, when it is so desired, to insert the words "offering or exposing for sale", "exposing for sale" being clearly words which would cover the display of goods in a shop window.'

R v *Clarke* (1927) 40 CLR 227 High Court of Australia (Isaacs ACJ, Higgins and Starke JJ)

• *Offer – information given for other reasons*

Facts
A reward had been offered for information leading to the arrest and conviction of the murderer of two police officers. Clarke, who knew of the offer and was himself suspected of the crime, gave such information. He admitted that he had done so only to clear himself of the charge and at the time he gave the information, all thought of the reward had passed out of his mind.

Held
He was not entitled to the reward.

Higgins J:

'Clarke had seen the offer, indeed; but it was not present to his mind – he had forgotten it, and gave no consideration to it, in his intense excitement as to his own danger. There cannot be assent without knowledge of the offer; and ignorance of the offer is the same thing, whether it is due to never hearing of it or to forgetting it after hearing it.'

Isaacs ACJ:

'Instances easily suggest themselves where precisely the same act done with reference to an offer would be performance of the condition, but done with reference to a totally distinct object would not be such a performance. An offer of £100 to any person who should swim a hundred yards in the harbour on the first day of the year, would be met by voluntarily performing the feat with reference to the offer, but would not in my opinion be satisfied by a person who was accidentally or maliciously thrown overboard on that date and swam the distance simply to save his life, without any thought of the offer. The offeror might or might not feel morally impelled to give the sum in such a case, but would be under no contractual obligation to do so.'

Comment

This decision may be compared with *Williams* v *Carwardine* (1833) 5 C & P 566 where a woman was held to be entitled to a reward of which she knew, even though she had supplied the information 'from stings of conscience'.

Thornton v *Shoe Lane Parking Ltd*
[1971] 2 WLR 585 Court of Appeal (Lord Denning MR, Megaw LJ and Sir Gordon Willmer)

• *Automatic car park – notice – ticket – exemption clause*

Facts

A notice displayed at the entrance to a car park stated 'All cars parked at owners risk'. The plaintiff approached the car park, took a ticket dispensed by an automatic machine and entered. The ticket stated that it was 'issued subject to the conditions of issue as displayed on the premises'. These conditions, displayed inside the car park, purported to exempt the defendants from liability for damage to cars, or any injury to the customer howsoever caused. When the plaintiff went to collect his car he was injured in an accident, partly caused by the defendants' negligence.

Held

The exemption clause was not a term of the contract and it did not, therefore, enable the defendants to escape liability.

Lord Denning MR:

'We have been referred to the ticket cases of former times from *Parker* v *South Eastern Ry Co* (1887) 2 CPD 416 to *McCutcheon* v *David MacBrayne Ltd* [1964] 1 WLR 125. They were concerned with railways, steamships and cloakrooms, where booking clerks issued tickets to customers who took them away without reading them. In those cases, the issue of the ticket was regarded as an offer by the company. If the customer took it and retained it without obligation, his act was regarded as an acceptance of the offer: see *Watkins* v *Rymill* (1883) 10 QBD 178 and *Thompson* v *London, Midland and Scottish Ry Co* [1930] 1 KB 41. These cases were based on the theory that the customer, on being handed the ticket, could refuse it and decline to enter into a contract on those terms. He could ask for his money back. That theory was, of course, a fiction. No customer in a thousand ever read the conditions. If he had stopped to do so, he would have missed the train or the boat.

None of those cases has any application to a ticket which is issued by an automatic machine. The customer pays his money and gets a ticket. He cannot refuse it. He cannot get his money back. He may protest to the machine, even swear at it; but it will remain unmoved. He is committed beyond recall. He was committed at the very moment when he put his money into the machine. The contract was concluded at that time. It can be translated into offer and acceptance in this way. The offer is made when the proprietor of the machine holds it out as being ready to receive the money. The acceptance takes place when the customer puts his money into the slot. The terms of the offer are contained in the notice placed on or near the machine, stating what is offered for the money. The customer is bound by those terms as long as they are sufficiently brought to his notice beforehand, but not otherwise. He is not bound by the terms printed on the ticket if they differ from the notice, because the ticket comes too late. The contract has already been made: see *Olley* v *Marlborough Court Ltd* [1949] 1 KB 532. The ticket is no more than a voucher or receipt for the money that has been paid (as in the deckchair case, *Chapelton* v *Barry Urban District Council* [1940] 1 KB 532), on terms which have been offered and accepted before the ticket is issued. In the present case, the offer was contained in the notice at the entrance, giving the charges for garaging and saying, 'At owners' risk', ie at the risk of the owner so far as damage to the car was concerned. The offer was accepted when the plaintiff drove up to the entrance and, by the movement of his car, turned the light from red to green and the ticket was thrust at him. The contract was then concluded and it could not be altered by any words printed on the ticket itself. In particular, it could not be altered so as to exempt the company from liability for personal injury due to their negligence.

... the customer is bound by the exempting condition if he knows that the ticket is issued subject to it; or, if the company did what was reasonably sufficient to give him notice of it. Counsel for the defendants admitted here that the defendants did not do what was reasonably sufficient to give the plaintiff notice of the exempting condition. That admission was properly made. I do not pause to enquire whether the exempting condition is void for unreasonableness. All I say is that it is so wide and so destructive of rights that the court should not hold any man bound by it unless it is drawn to his attention in the most explicit way. It is an instance of what I had in mind in *J Spurling Ltd* v *Bradshaw* [1956] 1 WLR 461. In order to give sufficient notice, it would need to be printed in red ink with a red hand pointing to it, or something equally startling.

However, although reasonable notice of it was not given, counsel for the defendants said that this case came within the second question propounded by Mellish LJ, namely that the plaintiff 'knew or believed that the writing contained conditions'. There was no finding to that effect. The burden was on the defendants to prove it, and they did not do so. Certainly there was no evidence that the plaintiff knew of this exempting condition. He is not, therefore, bound by it ... the whole question is whether the exempting condition formed part of the contract. I do not think it did. The plaintiff did not know of the condition, and the defendants did not do what was reasonably sufficient to give him notice of it.'

Comment

Applied in *Interfoto Picture Library Ltd* v *Stiletto Visual Programmes Ltd* [1988] 1 All ER 348 (unreasonable and extortionate clause in a delivery note of no effect since attention had not been drawn to it fairly and reasonably).

2 Consideration

Argy Trading Development Co Ltd v Lapid Developments Ltd [1977] 1 WLR 444 High Court (Croom-Johnson J)

- *Estoppel – fire insurance cover*

Facts
Under the terms of a lease, the tenants were obliged to insure against loss or damage by fire. At the time the lease was granted, the landlords had the premises so covered: they told the tenants and charged them an appropriate proportion of the premium. This arrangement was continued for the following year but, after the landlords had been taken over, this policy was allowed to lapse. The tenants were not informed of the decision and some nine months later the premises were gutted by fire. The tenants sought damages against the landlord.

Held
Their action would be dismissed as there was no consideration for the landlords' alleged agreement to insure the premises. Further, the landlords were not estopped from denying that they were under a duty to insure.

Croom-Johnson J:

'Therefore, if there was no consideration given by the plaintiffs so as to support a contract on which they can sue, what is the effect of the estoppel alleged in the reply? The plaintiffs seek to say that by reason of representations express or implied made ... they acted to their detriment by not taking out their own insurance cover, and therefore the defendants are estopped from alleging there was no consideration. The representations referred to in the reply are first that the defendants would arrange and effect the insurance. That is a representation as to intention and not of an existing fact. Second, that the defendants had arranged to effect the insurance. That is representation of fact and was true at the time it was made. By itself it is not enough. Thereafter the plaintiffs go on to say that there were implied representations that they would continue the insurance or would not cancel the same without notice. Those again are representations of intention as to the future and not of existing fact. Estoppel at law will not be raised by those facts. The plaintiffs go further and rely on the form of equitable estoppel, promissory in effect, which was applied in *Central London Property Trust Ltd* v *High Trees House Ltd*. But there are restrictions on the use of that form of estoppel. In the first place, the representation must be intended to affect the legal relations of the parties. I do not think that that was so in this case. There was no intention to vary the lease. If there had been, then the plaintiffs would run into the difficulty of having to say, as they do ... but have not argued in this court, that there is an oral variation of an instrument under seal. Secondly, the promise may be used only as a shield and not as a sword. In *Combe* v *Combe* Birkett LJ said so in terms, and Asquith LJ stated that the promise could not found an action brought by the promisee where there was no consideration.

In the present case, if there was no contract such as the plaintiffs sue on because it turns out that there are no consideration [sic], then to estop the defendants from raising that in their defence would only be to try by a sidewind to make the promise give rise to the cause of action. This the plaintiffs cannot do.'

Atlas Express Ltd v Kafco (Importers and Distributors) Ltd
[1989] 3 WLR 389

See Chapter 9.

Carlill v Carbolic Smoke Ball Co
[1893] 1 QB 256

See Chapter 1.

Central London Property Trust Ltd v High Trees House Ltd [1947] KB 130 High Court (Denning J)

• *Promise without consideration – estoppel*

Facts
By a lease of 1937, the plaintiffs leased a block of flats to the defendants for 99 years at a rent of £2,500 pa. With the advent of war and many vacancies in the flats, the plaintiffs agreed in 1940 to reduce the rent by 50 per cent. No time limit was set for the reduction. By 1945 the flats were full again. The plaintiff company thereupon wrote to the defendants, asking for the full amount of rent plus arrears. Subsequently, the present action was instituted to test the legal position. The plaintiffs claimed the full rent for the last two quarters of 1945. The defendants pleaded, inter alia, that the agreement of 1940 related to the whole term of the lease; or, alternatively, that by failing to demand rent in excess of £1,250 before September 1945, the plaintiffs had waived their rights in respect of any rent in excess of that amount which had accrued before that date.

Held
The plaintiffs' claim would succeed although, as regards the earlier period, the promise to reduce the rent was binding even though it had been given without consideration.

Denning J:

'I am satisfied that that arrangement was intended simply as a temporary expedient to deal with the exceptional conditions then prevailing, under which the block of flats was only partially let. The arrangement had no reference to events in which the block of flats was wholly let, if they subsequently occurred. ...

If I consider this matter without regard to recent developments in the law there is no doubt that the whole claim must succeed. This is a lease under seal, and at common law, it could not be varied by parol or by writing, but only by deed; but equity has stepped in, and the courts may now give effect to a variation in writing (see *Berry v Berry* [1929] 2 KB 316). That equitable doctrine could hardly apply, however, in this case because this variation might be said to be without consideration.

As to estoppel, this representation with reference to reducing the rent was not a representation of existing fact, which is the essence of common law estoppel; it was a representation in effect as to the future – a representation that the rent would not be enforced at the full rate but only at the reduced rate. At common law, that would not give rise to an estoppel, because, as was said in *Jorden v Money* (1854) 5 HL Cas 185, a representation as to the future must be embodied as a contract or be nothing. So at common law it seems to me there would be no answer to the whole claim.

What, then, is the position in view of developments in the law in recent years? The law has not been standing still even since *Jorden v Money*. There has been a series of decisions over the last fifty years which, although said to be cases of estoppel, are not really such. They are cases of promises which were intended to create legal relations and which, in the knowledge of the person making the promise, were going to be acted on by the party to whom the promise was made, and have in fact been so acted on. In such cases the courts have said these promises must be honoured. There are certain cases to which I particularly refer: *Fenner v Blake* [1900] 1 QB 426, *Re Wickham* (1917) 34 TLR 158, *Re William Porter & Co Ltd* [1937] 2 All ER 361 and *Buttery v Pickard* (1946) 174 TLR 144.

Although said by the learned judges who decided them to be cases of estoppel, all these cases are not estoppel in the strict sense. They are cases of promises which were intended to be binding, which the parties making them knew would be acted on and which the parties to whom they were made did act on. *Jorden* v *Money* can be distinguished because there the promisor made it clear that she did not intend to be legally bound, whereas in the cases to which I refer the promisor did intend to be bound. In each case the court held the promise to be binding on the party making it, even though under the old common law it might be said to be difficult to find any consideration for it. The courts have not gone so far as to give a cause of action in damages for breach of such promises, but they have refused to allow the party making them to act inconsistently with them. It is in that sense, and in that sense only, that such a promise gives rise to an estoppel. The cases are a natural result of the fusion of law and equity; for the cases of *Hughes* v *Metropolitan Ry Co* (1877) 2 App Cas 439, *Birmingham & District Land Co* v *London and North Western Ry Co* (1888) 40 Ch D 268, and *Salisbury* v *Gilmore* [1942] 1 All ER 457, show that a party will not be allowed in equity to go back on such a promise. The time has now come for the validity of such a promise to be recognised. The logical consequence, no doubt, is that a promise to accept a smaller sum in discharge of a larger sum, if acted on, is binding, notwithstanding the absence of consideration, and if the fusion of law and equity leads to that result, so much the better. At this time of day it is not helpful to try to draw a distinction between law and equity. They have been joined together now for over seventy years, and the problems have to be approached in a combined sense. ...

I am satisfied that such a promise is binding in law, and the only question is the scope of the promise in the present case. I am satisfied on the evidence that the promise was that the ground rent should be reduced to £1,250 a year as a temporary expedient, while the block of flats was not fully or substantially fully let owing to the conditions prevailing. That means that this reduction of rent applied up to the end of 1944. But early in 1945 the flats were fully let and the rents received from them (many were not caught by the Rent Restrictions Acts) had been increased more than originally anticipated. At all events the revenue from them must have been very considerable. The conditions prevailing when the reduction was made had completely passed away, as I find, by the early months of 1945. I am satisfied that the promise was understood by all parties only to apply in the conditions prevailing at the time of the flats being partially let, and the promise did not extend any further than that. When the flats became fully let early in 1945 the reduction ceased to apply.

In those circumstances under the law as I hold it, it seems to be that the quarter's rents are fully payable for the quarter ending 29 September 1945, and the quarter ending 25 December 1945, which are the amounts claimed in this action.

If it had been a case of estoppel, it might have been said that the estoppel in any event would end with the ending of the conditions to which the representation applied, or alternatively only on notice. But in either case it is only a way of asking what is the scope of the representation. I prefer to apply the principle that the promise, intended to be binding, intended to be acted on and in fact acted on, is binding so far as its terms properly apply. It is binding as covering the period down to early 1945, and from that time full rent is payable.'

Comment

Distinguished: *Jorden* v *Money* (1854) 5 HL Cas 185. See also *Combe* v *Combe* [1951] 2 KB 215, *Argy Trading Development Co Ltd* v *Lapid Developments Ltd* [1977] 1 WLR 444, *Brikom Investments Ltd* v *Carr* [1979] 2 WLR 737 and *Société Italo-Belge pour le Commerce et l'Industrie SA* v *Palm and Vegetable Oils (Malaysia) Sdn Bhd, The Post Chaser* [1982] 1 All ER 19.

Chappell & Co Ltd v *The Nestlé Co Ltd* [1959] 3 WLR 168 House of Lords (Viscount Simonds, Lords Reid, Tucker, Keith of Avonholm and Somervell of Harrow)

• *Consideration – value*

Facts
The plaintiffs (Chappell & Co Ltd) owned the copyright in a piece of music. The Hardy Co made records of the music, which they sold to the defendants (Nestlé Co Ltd) for 4d each. Nestlé advertised to the public that the records could be obtained from them for 1s 6d each, plus three wrappers from Nestlé's 6d chocolate bars. The wrappers, when received, were thrown away. Section 8(1) of the Copyright Act 1956 permitted a person to make a record of a piece of music for the purpose of its being sold retail if he gave notice to the owner of the copyright and paid him a royalty of six and a quarter per cent of 'the ordinary retail selling price'. The Hardy Co had given notice of their intention to manufacture the records, stating 1s 6d to be the ordinary retail selling price and offering to pay Chappell & Co royalties on this figure. Chappell & Co refused and sought an injunction restraining Nestlé & Co Ltd and the Hardy Co from infringing their copyright.

Held (Viscount Simonds and Lord Keith of Avonholm dissenting)
The wrappers were part of the consideration and the plaintiffs were therefore entitled to succeed.

Lord Reid:

'It seems to me clear that the main intention of the offer was to induce people interested in this kind of music to buy ... chocolate which otherwise would not have been bought ... The requirement that wrappers should be sent was of great importance to the Nestlé Co; there would have been no point in their simply offering records for 1s 6d each. It seems quite unrealistic to divorce the buying of the chocolate from the supplying of the records'.

Lord Somervell:

'I think they (the wrappers) are part of the consideration. They are so described in the offer ... This is not conclusive but, however described, they are, in my view in law, part of the consideration. It is said that when received the wrappers are of no value to Nestlés. This, I would have thought, irrelevant. A contracting party can stipulate for what consideration he chooses. A peppercorn does not cease to be good consideration if it is established that the promisee does not like pepper and will throw away the corn.'

Combe v *Combe* [1951] 2 KB 215 Court of Appeal (Asquith, Denning and Birkett LJJ)

• *Consideration – promise of maintenance*

Facts
A divorced wife obtained a promise from her ex-husband to pay her £100 pa maintenance. The wife did not apply to the Divorce Court for maintenance – but not as a result of any request from her husband to this effect. The husband never made any of the payments and the wife sued for the arrears.

Held
She was not entitled to succeed as there had been no consideration for the husband's promise.

Denning LJ:

'The principle of the *High Trees* case ... does not create new causes of action where none existed before. It only prevents a party from insisting upon his strict legal rights when it would be unjust to allow him to enforce them, having regard to the dealings which have taken place between the parties ... The principle ... is that ... where one party has, by his words or conduct, made to the other a promise or assurance which was intended to affect the legal relations between them and to be acted on accordingly, then once the other party has taken him at his word and acted on it, the one who gave the promise or assurance cannot afterwards be allowed to revert to the previous legal relations as if no such promise or assurance has been made by him, but he must accept their legal relations subject to the qualification which he himself has so introduced, even though it is not supported in point of law by any consideration but only by his word. Seeing that the principle never stands alone as giving a cause of action in itself, it can never do away with the necessity of consideration when that is an essential part of the cause of action. The doctrine of consideration is too firmly fixed to be overthrown by a side-wind. Its ill effects have been largely mitigated of late, but it still remains a cardinal necessity of the formation of a contract, although not of its modification or discharge. I fear that it was my failure to make this clear in *Central London Property Trust Ltd* v *High Trees House Ltd* [1947] KB 130 which misled Byrne J in the present case. He held that the wife could sue on the husband's promise as a separate and independent cause of action by itself, although, as he held, there was no consideration for it. That is not correct. The wife can only enforce the promise if there was consideration for it. That is, therefore, the real question in the case: Was there sufficient consideration to support the promise?

If it were suggested that, in return for the husband's promise, the wife expressly or impliedly promised to forbear from applying to the court for maintenance – that is, a promise in return for a promise – there would clearly be no consideration because the wife's promise would not be binding on her and, therefore, would be worth nothing. Notwithstanding her promise, she could always apply to the divorce court for maintenance – perhaps, only with leave – but nevertheless she could apply. No agreement by her could take away that right: *Hyman* v *Hyman* [1929] AC 601, as interpreted by this court in *Gaisberg* v *Storr* [1950] 1 KB 107. There was, however, clearly no promise by the wife, express or implied, to forbear from applying to the court. All that happened was that she did, in fact, forbear

– that is, she did an act in return for a promise. Is that sufficient consideration? Unilateral promises of this kind have long been enforced so long as the act or forbearance is done on the faith of the promise and at the request of the promisor, express or impliedly. The act done is then in itself sufficient consideration for the promise, even though it arises ex post facto, as Parker J pointed out in *Wigan* v *English and Scottish Law Life Assurance Association* [1909] 1 Ch 298. If the findings of Byrne J are accepted, they are sufficient to bring this principle into play. His finding that the husband's promise was intended to be binding, intended to be acted on, and was, in fact, acted on – although expressed to be a finding on the principle of the *High Trees* case – is equivalent to a finding that there was consideration within this long-settled rule, because it comes to the same thing expressed in different words: see *Oliver* v *Davis* [1949] 2 KB 727. My difficulty, however, is to accept the findings of Byrne J that the promise was "intended to be acted on". I cannot find any evidence of any intention by the husband that the wife should forbear from applying to the court for maintenance, or, in other words, any request by the husband, express or implied, that the wife should forbear. He left her to apply, if she wished to do so. She did not do so, and I am not surprised, because it is very unlikely that the divorce court would have made any order in her favour, since she had a bigger income than her husband. Her forbearance was not intended by him, nor was it done at his request. It was, therefore, no consideration.'

Birkett LJ:

'... we have had the great advantage of hearing Denning LJ deal with *Central London Property Trust Ltd* v *High Trees House Ltd* [1947] KB 130 and *Robertson* v *Minister of Pensions* [1949] 1 KB 227 which formed such a prominent part of the judgment of the court below. I am bound to say that reading them for myself I think the description which was given by counsel for the husband in this court, namely, that the doctrine there enunciated was, so to speak, a doctrine which would enable a person to use it as a shield and not as a sword, is a very vivid way of stating what, I think, is the principle underlying both those cases.'

Comment

See also *Argy Trading Development Co Ltd* v *Lapid Developments Ltd* [1977] 1 WLR 444 and *Syros Shipping Co SA* v *Elaghill Trading Co* [1981] 3 All ER 189. In *Tool Metal Manufacturing Co Ltd* v *Tungsten Electric Co Ltd* [1955] 2 All ER 657, Viscount Simonds said:

'... the gist of the equity lies in the fact that one party has by his conduct led the other to alter his position. I lay stress on this, because I would not have it supposed, particularly in commercial transactions, that mere acts of indulgence are apt to create rights, and I do not wish to lend the authority of this House to the statement of the principle which is to be found in *Combe* v *Combe* ([1951] 1 All ER at p770) and may well be far too widely stated.'

D & C Builders Ltd v *Rees* [1966] 2 WLR 288 Court of Appeal (Lord Denning MR, Danckwerts and Winn LJJ)

• *Debt – acceptance of smaller sum – entitlement to balance*

Facts

The plaintiffs (D & C Builders) were a small firm who did work for the defendant, for which he owed them £482. After the amount had been outstanding for some time, the defendant's wife, acting for the defendant and knowing that the plaintiffs were in financial difficulties, offered them £300 in settlement. She said the plaintiffs could have £300 or nothing and rejected an offer to find the disputed £182 over a further twelve months. The plaintiffs reluctantly agreed, since without the £300 their firm would have gone bankrupt. The plaintiffs then sued for the balance.

Held

The plaintiffs' action was not barred: there had been no true accord and there was no equitable ground for rejecting their claim.

Lord Denning MR:

'... it is a daily occurrence that a merchant or tradesman, who is owed a sum of money, is asked to take less. The debtor says he is in difficulties ... The creditor ... accepts the proffered sum and forgives him the rest of the debt. The question arises: is the settlement binding on the creditor? The answer is that, in point of law, the creditor is not bound by the settlement. He can, the next day, sue the debtor for the balance and get judgment ...

This doctrine of the common law has come under heavy fire ... But a remedy has been found. The harshness of the common law has been relieved. Equity has stretched out a merciful hand to help the debtor. The courts have invoked the broad principle stated by Lord Cairns LC in *Hughes* v *Metropolitan Rail Co* (1877) 2 App Cas 439 ... This principle has been applied to cases where a creditor agrees to accept a lesser sum in discharge of a greater ... In applying this principle, however, he must note the qualification. The creditor is barred from his legal rights only when it would be *inequitable* for him to insist on them. Where there has been a *true accor*d under which the creditor voluntarily agrees to accept a lesser sum in satisfaction and the debtor acts on that accord by paying the lesser sum and the creditor accepts it, then it is inequitable for the creditor afterwards to insist on the balance. But he is not bound unless there has been truly an accord between them.

In the present case, on the facts as found by the judge, it seems to me that there was no true accord. The debtor's wife held the creditor to ransom. The creditor was in need of money to meet his own commitments, and she knew it. When the creditor asked for payment of the £480 due to him, she said to him in effect: "We cannot pay you the £480. But we will pay you £300 if you will accept it in settlement. If you do not accept it on those terms, you will get nothing. £300 is better than nothing." She had no right to say any such thing. She could properly have said: "We canot pay you more than £300. Please accept it on account." But she had no right to insist on his taking it in settlement. When she said: "We will pay you nothing unless you accept £300 in settlement", she was putting undue pressure on the creditor. She was making a threat to break the contract (by paying nothing) and she was doing it so as to compel the creditor to do what he was unwilling to do (to accept £300 in settlement): and she succeeded. He complied with her demand. That was ... a case of intimidation ... In these circumstances there was no true accord so as to found a defence of accord and satisfaction ... There is also no equity in the defendant to warrant any departure from the due course of law. No person can insist on a settlement procured by intimidation.'

Comment
Applied in *Ferguson* v *Davies* [1997] 1 All ER 315. See also *Atlas Express Ltd* v *Kafco (Importers and Distributors) Ltd* [1989] 3 WLR 389.

Ferguson v *Davies* [1997] 1 All ER 315 Court of Appeal (Evans, Henry and Aldous LJJ)

• *Accord and satisfaction – consideration – cheque stated to be in full payment – ability to sue for balance due*

Facts
The parties contracted for the sale and purchase of records, tapes and discs and when the plaintiff delivered his county court particulars of claim there was due to him from the defendant dealer some £1,550: for reasons unknown, the plaintiff limited his claim to £486.50. In his response, the defendant admitted that he owed the plaintiff £150 and he sent him a cheque for that amount 'as a full payment of the county court summons', but he denied that any balance was due. The plaintiff presented the cheque and it was cleared and then, with the court's leave, claimed the full amount owed to him. Although the judge accepted that the plaintiff had not intended to accept the cheque in full settlement, the claim failed on the ground that it had been compromised by the presentation of the cheque, a binding accord and satisfaction. The plaintiff sought and was given leave to appeal.

Held
His appeal would be allowed.

Henry LJ:

'An open admission of money due is something quite different from an offer of a sum in compromise. ...
   In *D & C Builders Ltd* v *Rees* [1965] 3 All ER 837 the court found, in the words of Danckwerts LJ:

"*Foakes* v *Beer* (1884) 9 App Cas 605, applying the decision in *Pinnel's Case* (1602) 5 Co Rep 117a, settled definitely the rule of law that payment of a lesser sum than the amount of a debt due cannot be a satisfaction of the debt, unless there is some benefit to the creditor added so there is an accord and satisfaction." ...

In my judgment, the judge here erred in law in that he did not consider the legal significance of the fact that the defendant had unequivocally admitted liability for the sum paid by cheque, and was not giving the plaintiff any additional benefit on top of that. Therefore, there was in law no consideration for the accord suggested. ... Against that background, I believe that, on the facts of this case, it was wrong in law for the judge to conclude that cashing the cheque sent as a result of a formal and unqualified admission on the pleadings constituted "a clear and unequivocal acceptance that no further sum was due" because of a side letter seeking to impose a term for which there was no consideration once the admission had been made. Had he directed himself properly, he would inevitably have come to the decision that there was no binding accord ...'

Evans LJ:

'I have come reluctantly to the conclusion ... that the question whether there was an "accord" in the present case depends almost entirely on the correct interpretation of the defendant's letters, to the plaintiff and to the court, and of the defence which he submitted ... and which the plaintiff saw at the court offices. The question is whether those documents contained an unequivocal offer by the defendant to pay a further £150 only upon that basis that, if he accepted it, the plaintiff would withdraw the balance of his claim. That has to be distinguished from and contrasted with an admission that £150 was due and the balance of the claim remained in dispute.

In my judgment, the documents cannot be interpreted in the former unequivocal, sense. The defendant's letter to the plaintiff offered the cheque "in full payment", but the whole of the circumstances and all the documents have to be taken into account. The defendant's entries in [the county court] form were to the effect that £150 was admittedly due, and was being paid, leaving the balance in dispute. The plaintiff was entitled to understand the defendant's offer in this sense, and it follows that his acceptance of the cheque did not give rise to an agreement that he would forego the balance of his claim.

I would allow the appeal on this ground alone, and I express no view as to whether, if the accord on which the defendant relies was established, the agreement would fail as a contract for want of consideration as required by law.'

Foakes v Beer (1884) 9 App Cas 605 House of Lords (Earl of Selborne LC, Lords Blackburn, Watson and FitzGerald)

- *Judgment debt – payment of smaller sum – entitlement to interest*

Facts

B had obtained judgment against F for £2,000.

Sixteen months later, F asked for time to pay and B and F agreed in writing that if F paid £500 immediately and the balance by instalments, B would not to take 'any proceedings whatsoever' on the judgment. A judgment debt bears interest from the date of judgment, but the agreement did not mention interest. F finally paid the whole of the outstanding sum and B then claimed interest. B then applied to commence proceedings on the judgment and F pleaded the written agreement as a defence. B argued it was unsupported by consideration.

Held

B was entitled to succeed.

The Earl of Selborne LC:

'... the question remains whether the agreement is capable of being legally enforced. Not being under seal, it cannot be legally enforced against [B] unless she received consideration for it from [F], or unless, though without consideration, it operates by way of accord and satisfaction, so as to extinguish the claim for interest. What is the consideration? On the fact of the agreement none is expressed except a present payment of £500 on account and in part of the larger debt then due and payable by law under the judgment. [F] did not contract to pay the future instalments of £150 each at the times therein mentioned; much less did he give any new security in the shape of negotiable paper, or in any other form. The promise de futuro was only that of [B], that, if the half-yearly payments of £150 each were regularly paid, she would "take no proceedings whatever on the judgment". No doubt, if [F] had been under no antecedent obligation to pay the whole debt, his fulfilment of the condition might have imported some consideration on his part for that promise. But he was under that antecedent obligation; and payment at those deferred dates, by the forbearance and indulgence of the creditor, of the residue of the principal debt and costs could not, in my opinion, be a consideration for the relinquishment of interest and discharge of the judgment unless the payment of the £500 at the time of signing the agreement was such a consideration.

As to accord and satisfaction, in point of fact there could be no complete satisfaction so long as any future instalment remained payable; and I do not see how any new payments on account could operate in law as a satisfaction ad interim conditionally upon other payments being afterwards duly made, unless there was a consideration sufficient to support the agreement while still unexecuted. Nor was anything in fact done by [B] in this case, on the receipt of the last payment, which could be tantamount to an acquittance, if the agreement did not previously bind her. The question, therefore, is nakedly raised by this appeal whether your Lordships are now prepared, not only to overrule as contrary to law the doctrine state by Sir Edward Coke to have been laid down by all the judges of the Common Pleas in *Pinnel's Case* 5 Co Rep 117a in 1602, and repeated in his note to Littleton, s344 (Co Litt 212b), but to treat a prospective agreement, not under seal, for satisfaction of a debt by a series of payments on account to a total amount less than the whole debt, as binding in law, provided those payments are regularly made, the case not being one of a composition with a common debtor agreed to inter se by several creditors. I prefer so to state the question instead of treating it, as it was put at the Bar, as depending on the authority of *Cumber* v *Wane* (1721) 1 Stra 425.

It may well be that distinctions, which in later cases have been held sufficient to exclude the application of that doctrine, existed and were improperly disregarded in *Cumber* v *Wane*, and yet that the doctrine itself may be law, rightly recognised in *Cumber* v *Wane*, and not really contradicted by any later authorities; and this appears to me to be the true state of the case. The doctrine itself, as laid down by Sir Edward Coke, may have been criticised as questionable in principle by some persons whose opinions are entitled to respect, but it has never been judicially overruled. On the contrary, I think it has always, since the 16th century, been accepted as law. If so, I cannot think that your Lordships would do right if

you were now to reverse as erroneous a judgment of the Court of Appeal proceeding upon a doctrine which has been accepted as part of the law of England for 280 years.

The doctrine, as stated in *Pinnel's Case* is:

"that payment of a lesser sum on the day in satisfaction of a greater cannot be any satisfaction for the whole, because it appears to the judges that by no possibility a lesser sum can be a satisfaction to the plaintiff for a greater sum."

As stated in Coke on Littleton, 212b, it is:

"where a condition is for payment of £20, the obligor or feoffor cannot at the time appointed pay a lesser sum in satisfaction of the whole, because it is apparent that a lesser sum of money cannot be a satisfaction of a greater."

He added, what is beyond controversy, that an acquittance under seal, in full satisfaction of the whole, would, under like circumstances, be valid and binding. The distinction between the effect of a deed under seal and that of an agreement by parol, or by writing not under seal, may seem arbitrary, but is established in our law: nor is it really unreasonable or practically inconvenient that the law should require particular solemnities to give to a gratuitous contract the force of a binding obligation. If the question be ... whether consideration is or is not given in a case of this kind by the debtor who pays down part of the debt presently due from him, for a promise by the creditor to relinquish, after certain further payments on account, the residue of the debt, I cannot say that I think consideration is given, in the sense in which I have always understood that word as used in our law. ...

All the authorities subsequent to *Cumber* v *Wane* which were relied upon by [F], such as *Sibree* v *Tripp* (1846) 14 M & W 23, *Curlewis* v *Clark* (1849) 3 Exch 375 and *Goddard* v *O'Brien* (1882) 9 QBD 37, have proceeded upon the distinction that, by giving negotiable paper or otherwise, there had been some new consideration for a new agreement, distinct from mere money payments in or towards discharge of the original liability. I think it unnecessary to go through those cases, or to examine the particular grounds upon which each of them was decided. There are no such facts in the case now before your Lordships. What is called "any benefit, or even any legal possibility of benefit", in Mr Smith's notes to *Cumber* v *Wane* (1 Smith LC, 8th ed, 366) is not, as I conceive, that sort of benefit which a creditor may derive from getting payment of part of the money due to him from a debtor who might otherwise keep him at arm's length, or possibly become insolvent, but is some independent benefit, actual or contingent, of a kind which in law might be a good and valuable consideration for any other sort of agreement not under seal.'

Comment
Followed in *Re Selectmove Ltd* [1995] 2 All ER 531 and *D & C Builders Ltd* v *Rees* [1966] 2 WLR 288; also *Ferguson* v *Davies* [1997] 1 All ER 315.

Pao On v *Lau Yiu Long* [1979] 3 WLR 435 Privy Council (Viscount Dilhorne, Lords Wilberforce, Simon of Glaisdale, Salmon and Scarman)

• *Consideration – duress*

Facts
The plaintiffs owned a private company ('Shing On') and the defendants were majority shareholders in Fu Chip, a public investment company. By a written agreement dated 27 February 1973, the plaintiffs contracted to sell Shing On's shares to Fu Chip, the price being an allotment of Fu Chip shares at a deemed value of $2.50 a share: the plaintiffs undertook that they would not sell 2.5 million of the shares allotted to them before the end of April 1974. By a subsidiary agreement of the same date, the defendants agreed to buy back, on or before 30 April 1974, 2.5 million Fu Chip shares at $2.50 a share. As it was generally expected that the Fu Chip shares would rise in value, the plaintiffs realised that they had made a bad bargain and they told the defendants that they would not complete the main

agreement unless the subsidiary agreement was replaced by an agreement guaranteeing the price of the 2.5 million shares at $2.50 a share. Anxious to complete the main agreement, but knowing that they could claim specific performance of it, the defendants, wishing to avoid litigation, agreed. By 30 April 1974 Fu Chip's share price had fallen to 36 cents: the plaintiffs sought to enforce the guarantee. Before the Board, the questions for decision were: was there consideration for the contract of guarantee? If there was, was the defendant's consent vitiated by duress?

Held
The plaintiffs were entitled to succeed.

Lord Scarman:

'The Board agrees with the submission of counsel for the plaintiffs that the consideration expressly stated in the written guarantee is sufficient in law to support the Laus' promise of indemnity. An act done before the giving of a promise to make a payment or to confer some other benefit can sometimes be consideration for the promise. The act must have been done at the promisor's request, the parties must have understood that the act was to be remunerated either by a payment or the conferment of some other benefit, and payment, or the conferment of a benefit, must have been legally enforceable had it been promised in advance. All three features are present in this case. The promise given to Fu Chip under the main agreement not to sell the shares for a year was at Lau's request. The parties understood at the time of the main agreement that the restriction on selling must be compensated for by the benefit of a guarantee against a drop in price: and such a guarantee would be legally enforceable. The agreed cancellation of the subsidiary agreement left, as the parties knew, the Paos unprotected in a respect in which at the time of the main agreement all were agreed they should be protected.

Counsel's submission for the plaintiffs is based on *Lampleigh* v *Brathwait* (1615) Hob 105 ... The modern statement of the law is in the judgment of Bowen LJ in *Re*

Casey's Patents, Stewart v *Casey* [1892] 1 Ch 104 ...

Counsel for the defendants does not dispute the existence of the rule but challenges its application to the facts of this case. He submits that it is not a necessary inference or implication from the terms of the written guarantee that any benefit or protection was to be given to the Paos for their acceptance of the restriction on selling their shares. Their Lordships agree that the mere existence or recital of a prior request is not sufficient in itself to convert what is prima facie past consideration into sufficient consideration in law to support a promise: as they have indicated, it is only the first of three necessary preconditions. As for the second of those preconditions, whether the act done at the request of the promisor raises an implication of promised remuneration or other return is simply one of the construction of the words of the contract in the circumstances of its making. Once it is recognised, as the Board considers it inevitably must be, that the expressed consideration includes a reference to the Paos' promise not to sell the shares before 30 April 1974, a promise to be performed in the future, though given in the past, it is not possible to treat the Laus' promise of indemnity as independent of the Paos' antecedent promise, given at Lau's request, not to sell. The promise of indemnity was given because at the time of the main agreement the parties intended that Lau should confer on the Paos the benefit of his protection against a falling price. When the subsidiary agreement was cancelled, all were well aware that the Paos were still to have the benefit of his protection as consideration for the restriction on selling. It matters not whether the indemnity thus given be regarded as the best evidence of the benefit intended to be conferred in return for the promise not to sell, or as the positive bargain which fixed the benefit on the faith of which the promise was given, though where, as here, the subject is a written contract, the better analysis is probably that of the "positive bargain". Their Lordships, therefore, accept the submission that the contract itself states a valid consideration for the promise of indemnity ...

There is no doubt, and it was not challenged, that extrinsic evidence is admissible to prove the real consideration where: (a) no consideration, or a nominal consideration, is expressed in the instrument, or (b) the expressed consideration is in general terms or ambiguously stated, or (c) a substantial consideration is stated, but an additional consideration exists. The additional consideration must not, however, be inconsistent with the terms of the written instrument. Extrinsic evidence is also admissible to prove the illegality of the consideration ...

The extrinsic evidence in this case shows that the consideration for the promise of indemnity, while it included the cancellation of the subsidiary agreement, was primarily the promise given by the Paos to the Laus, to perform their contract with Fu Chip, which included the undertaking not to sell 60% of the shares allotted to them before 30 April 1974. Thus the real consideration for the indemnity was the promise to perform, or the performance of, the Paos' pre-existing contractual obligations to Fu Chip. This promise was perfectly consistent with the consideration stated in the guarantee. Indeed, it reinforces it by imposing on the Paos an obligation now owed to the Laus to do what, at Lau's request, they had agreed with Fu Chip to do.

Their Lordships do not doubt that a promise to perform, or the performance of, a pre-existing contractual obligation to a third party can be valid consideration. In *New Zealand Shipping Co Ltd* v *AM Satterthwaite & Co Ltd* [1974] 2 WLR 865 the rule and the reason for the rule were stated ... Unless, therefore, the guarantee was void as having been made for an illegal consideration or voidable on the ground of economic duress, the extrinsic evidence establishes that it was supported by valid consideration.

Counsel for the defendants submits that the consideration is illegal as being against public policy. He submits that to secure a party's promise by a threat of repudiation of a pre-existing contractual obligation owed to another can be, and in the circumstances of this case was, an abuse of a dominant bargaining position and so contrary to public policy. This, he submits, is so even though economic duress cannot be proved.

This submission found favour with the majority in the Court of Appeal. Their Lordships, however, consider it misconceived. Reliance was placed on the old "seaman" cases of *Harris* v *Watson* (1791) Peake 72 and *Stilk* v *Myrick* (1809) 2 Camp 317 ...

Their Lordships' conclusion is that where businessmen are negotiating at arm's length it is unnecessary for the achievement of justice, and unhelpful in the development of the law, to invoke such a rule of public policy. It would also create unacceptable anomaly. It is unnecessary because justice requires that men, who have negotiated at arm's length, be held to their bargains unless it can be shown that their consent was vitiated by fraud, mistake or duress. If a promise is induced by coercion of a man's will, the doctrine of duress suffices to do justice. The party coerced, if he chooses and acts in time, can avoid the contract. If there is no coercion, there can be no reason for avoiding the contract where there is shown to be real consideration which is otherwise legal ... Accordingly, the submission that the additional consideration established by the extrinsic evidence is invalid on the ground of public policy is rejected.

Duress, whatever form it takes, is a coercion of the will so as to vitiate consent. Their Lordships agree with the observation of Kerr J in *The Siboen and The Sibotre* [1976] 1 Lloyd's Rep 293 that in a contractual situation commercial pressure is not enough. There must be present some factor "which could in law be regarded as a coercion of his will so as to vitiate his consent". This conception is in line with what was said in this Board's decision in *Barton* v *Armstrong* [1976] AC 104 by Lord Wilberforce and Lord Simon of Glaisdale ... In determining whether there was a coercion of will such that there was no true consent, it is material to enquire whether the person alleged to have been coerced did or

did not protest; whether, at the time he was allegedly coerced into making the contract, he did or did not have an alternative course open to him such as an adequate legal remedy; whether he was independently advised; and whether after entering the contract he took steps to avoid it. All these matters are, as was recognised in *Maskell* v *Horner* [1915] 3 KB 106, relevant in determining whether he acted voluntarily or not.

In the present case there is unanimity amongst the judges below that there was no coercion of Lau's will. In the Court of Appeal the trial judge's finding ... that Lau considered the matter thoroughly, chose to avoid litigation, and formed the opinion that the risk in giving the guarantee was more apparent than real was upheld. In short, there was commercial pressure, but no coercion. Even if this Board was disposed, which it is not, to take a different view, it would not substitute its opinion for that of the judges below on this question of fact.

It is, therefore, unnecessary for the Board to embark on an enquiry into the question whether English law recognises a category of duress known as "economic duress". But, since the question has been fully argued in this appeal, their Lordships will indicate very briefly the view which they have formed. At common law money paid under economic compulsion could be recovered in an action for money had and received: see *Astley* v *Reynolds* (1731) 2 Stra 915. The compulsion had to be such that the party was deprived of "his freedom of exercising his will". It is doubtful, however, whether at common law any duress other than duress to the person sufficed to render a contract voidable; see Blackstone's Commentaries and *Skeate* v *Beale* (1841) 11 Ad & El 983 ... Recently two English judges have recognised that commercial pressure may constitute duress the pressure of which can render a contract voidable: see Kerr J in *The Siboen and The Sibotre* and Mocatta J in *North Ocean Shipping Co Ltd* v *Hyundai Construction Co Ltd* [1978] 3 All ER 1170. Both stressed that the pressure must be such that the victim's consent to the contract was not a voluntary act on his part. In their

Lordship's view, there is nothing contrary to principle in recognising economic duress as a factor which may render a contract voidable, provided always that the basis of such recognition is that it must amount to a coercion of will, which vitiates consent. It must be shown that the payment made or the contract entered into was not a voluntary act.'

Comment

The Siboen and The Sibotre: see *Occidental World Investment Corp v Skibs A/S Avanti* [1976] 1 Lloyd's Rep 293. See also *Williams* v *Roffey Bros & Nicholls (Contractors) Ltd* [1990] 2 WLR 1153.

Pinnel's Case (1602) 5 Co Rep 117a Court of Common Pleas

• *Payment of part*

Facts

The plaintiff sued for £8 10s and the defendant pleaded that, before the date when the payment was due, he had paid the plaintiff £5 2s 2d which he (the plaintiff) had accepted in full satisfaction of the £8 10s.

Held

The plaintiff was entitled to judgment because of the defendant's 'insufficient pleading'. However, the whole court resolved that the payment and acceptance of parcel [part] before the day in satisfaction of the whole, would be a good satisfaction in regard of circumstance of time; for peradventure parcel of it before the day would be more beneficial to him than the whole at the day, and the value of the satisfaction is not material. So if I am bound in £20 to pay you £10 at Westminster and you request me to pay you £5 at the day at York, and you will accept it in full satisfaction of the whole £10 it is a good satisfaction for the whole for the expense to pay it at York, is sufficient satisfaction. The court also resolved that payment of a lesser sum on the day in satisfaction of a greater, cannot be any satisfaction for the whole, because it appears to the judges that by no possibility a lesser sum can be a satisfaction to the plaintiff for a greater sum; but the gift of a horse, hawk or robe, etc, in satisfaction is good, for it shall be intended that a horse, hawk or robe, etc, might be more beneficial to the plaintiff than the money, in respect of some circumstance, or otherwise the plaintiff would not have accepted of it in satisfaction. But when the whole sum is due, by no intendment the acceptance of parcel can be a satisfaction to the plaintiff.

Comment

This decision was applied, amongst others, in *D& C Builders Ltd* v *Rees* [1966] 2 QB 617 and *Foakes* v *Beer* (1884) 9 App Cas 605. See also *Ferguson* v *Davies* [1997] 1 All ER 315.

Williams v *Roffey Bros & Nicholls (Contractors) Ltd* [1990] 2 WLR 1153 Court of Appeal (Purchas, Glidewell and Russell LJJ)

• *Extra payment – consideration*

Facts

The defendants contracted to refurbish a block of flats and sub-contracted the carpentry work to the plaintiff for £20,000: it was an implied term of the sub-contract that the plaintiff would receive interim payments according to the work completed. After the plaintiff had completed some of the work, and received interim payments of £16,200, he found himself in financial difficulty, partly because his price had been too low. Aware of these things, and facing a penalty if the main contract was not completed on time, the defendants agreed to pay the plaintiff an additional £575 per flat on completion to ensure that the plaintiff continued with the work and completed it on time.

Held

This agreement would be enforced. Although the plaintiff had not been required to undertake any work additional to his original contract, the advantages which the defendants hoped to obtain (avoidance of penalty and the need to engage another sub-contractor) were consideration for the extra payment.

Glidewell LJ:

'... following the view of the majority in *Ward* v *Byham* [1956] 1 WLR 496 and of the whole court in *Williams* v *Williams* [1957] 1 WLR 148 and that of the Privy Council in *Pao On* v *Lau Yiu* [1979] 3 WLR 435 the present state of the law on this subject can be expressed in the following proposition: (i) if A has entered into a contract with B to do work for, or to supply goods or services to, B in return for payment by B and (ii) at some stage before A has completely performed his obligations under the contract B has reason to doubt whether A will, or will be able to, complete his side of the bargain and (iii) B thereupon promises A an additional payment in return for A's promise to perform his contractual obligations on time and (iv) as a result of giving his promise B obtains in practice a benefit, or obviates a disbenefit, and (v) B's promise is not given as a result of economic duress or fraud on the part of A, then (vi) the benefit to B is capable of being consideration for B's promise, so that the promise will be legally binding.

As I have said, counsel for the defendants accepts that in the present case by promising to pay the extra ... the defendants secured benefits. There is no finding, and no suggestion, that in this case the promise was given as a result of fraud or duress.

If it be objected that the propositions above contravene the principle in *Stilk* v *Myrick* (1809) 2 Camp 317, I answer that in my view they do not: they refine and limit the application of that principle, but they leave the principle unscathed, eg where B secures no benefit by his promise. It is not in my view surprising that a principle enunciated in relation to the rigours of seafaring life during the Napoleonic wars should be subjected during the succeeding 180 years to a process of refinement and limitation in its application in the present day.

It is therefore my opinion that on his findings of fact in the present case, the judge was entitled to hold, as he did, that the defendants' promise to pay the extra ... was supported by valuable consideration, and thus constituted an enforceable agreement.

As a subsidiary argument, counsel for the defendants submits that on the facts of the present case the consideration, even if otherwise good, did not "move from the promisee". This submission is based on the principle illustrated in the decision in *Tweddle* v *Atkinson* (1861) 1 B & S 393.

My understanding of the meaning of the requirement that "consideration must move from the promisee" is that such consideration must be provided by the promisee, or arise out of his contractual relationship with the promisor. It is consideration provided by somebody else, not a party to the contract, which does not "move from the promisee". This was the situation in *Tweddle* v *Atkinson*, but it is, of course, not the situation in the present case. Here the benefits to the defendants arose out of their agreement ... with the plaintiff, the promisee. In this respect I would adopt the following passage from *Chitty on Contracts* (25th edn, 1983) para 173, and refer to the authorities there cited:

"The requirement that consideration must move from the promisee is most generally satisfied where some detriment is suffered by him: eg where he parts with money or goods, or renders services, in exchange for the promise. But the requirement may equally well be satisfied where the promisee confers a benefit on the promisor without in fact suffering any detriment." (Chitty's emphasis).

That is the situation in this case.'

Comment

In *Re Selectmove Ltd* [1995] 2 All ER 531 Peter Gibson LJ noted that here no reference had been made to *Foakes* v *Beer* (1884) 9 App Cas 605. In his Lordship's view, if the principle of *Williams* were to be extended to an obligation to make payment, it would in effect leave the principle in *Foakes* v *Beer* without any application.

3   Certainty and Form of Contract

Balfour v Balfour [1919] 2 KB 571
Court of Appeal (Warrington, Duke
and Atkin LJJ)

• *Agreement – no intention that it be
enforceable*

Facts

After their marriage, the parties went to
Ceylon where the husband was director of
immigation. Fifteen years later they came
home on leave. On medical advice, it was
decided that the wife should remain in
England, but she alleged that, as the husband
was about to sail back to Ceylon, he had
entered into an oral contract to make her an
allowance of £30 a month until she rejoined
him in Ceylon. At that time they had not
agreed to live apart, although they subsequently did so when differences arose. The
wife sought to recover money allegedly due
to her under the oral agreement.

Held

Her action would fail as there was no contract
in a legal sense.

Atkin LJ:

'It is quite common, and it is the natural and
inevitable result of the relationship of
husband and wife, that the two spouses
should make agreements between themselves, agreements such as are in dispute in
this action, agreements for allowances by
which the husband agrees that he will pay
to his wife a certain sum of money per week
or per month or per year to cover either her
own expenses or the necessary expenses of
the household and of the children, and in
which the wife promises either expressly or
impliedly to apply the allowance for the
purpose for which it is given. To my mind

those agreements, or many of them, do not
result in contracts at all, and they do not
result in contracts even though there may
be what as between other parties would constitute consideration for the agreement. The
consideration, as we know, may consist
either in some right, interest, profit, or
benefit accruing to one party, or some forbearance, detriment, loss or responsibility
given, suffered, or undertaken by the other.
That is a well-known definition, and it con-
stantly happens, I think, that such arrangements made between husband and wife are
arrangements in which there are mutual
promises, or in which there is consideration
in form within the definition that I have
mentioned. Nevertheless they are not contracts, and they are not contracts because the
parties did not intend that they should be
attended by legal consequences. ...

   The only question in the present case is
whether or not this promise was of such a
class or not. ... I think it is plainly established that the promise here was not
intended by either party to be attended by
legal consequences. I think the onus was
upon the wife, and that the wife has not
established any contract.'

Comment

Distinguished in *Merritt* v *Merritt* [1970] 1
WLR 1211 (agreement between husband and
wife living apart as to future financial arrangements found to have been intended to create
legal relations); applied in *Spellman* v
Spellman [1961] 2 All ER 498 (dealings
between an unhappy couple with regard to a
car found to have been informal and lacking
an intent to create legal relationships) and
Pettitt v *Pettitt* [1970] AC 777. See also *Gould*
v *Gould* [1969] 3 WLR 490 and *Edwards* v
Skyways Ltd [1964] 1 WLR 349.

27

Campbell v *Edwards* [1976] 1 WLR 403 Court of Appeal (Lord Denning MR and Geoffrey Lane LJ)

* *Price – surveyor's valuation*

Facts
Wishing to assign the lease of her flat, in accordance with its terms the tenant first offered to surrender it to her landlord 'at a price fixed by a chartered surveyor to be agreed by the Landlord and the Tenant'. Surveyors were duly appointed and they said that the landlord should pay the tenant £10,000. The landlord asked two other firms to give a valuation: their figures were £3,500 and £1,250. The landlord sought, inter alia, a declaration that he was not bound by the original valuation: the claim was struck out: the landlord appealed.

Held
The appeal would be dismissed as, in the absence of fraud or collusion, the first valuation was binding on the parties by contract.

Lord Denning MR:

'It is simply the law of contract. If two persons agree that the price of property should be fixed by a valuer on whom they agree, and he gives that valuation honestly and in good faith, they are bound by it. Even if he has made a mistake they are still bound by it. The reason is because they have agreed to be bound by it. If there were fraud or collusion, of course, it would be different. Fraud or collusion unravels everything.

It may be that, if a valuer gives a speaking valuation – if he gives his reasons or his calculations – and you can show on the face of them that they are wrong, it might be upset. But this not such a case. [The original valuers] simply gave the figure. Having given it honestly, it is binding on the parties. It is no good for either party to say that it is incorrect. But even if the valuation could be upset for mistake, there is no room for it in this case. The premises have been surrendered to the landlord. He has entered into

occupation of them. Months have passed. There cannot be restitutio in integrum.'

Comment
Distinguished in *Burgess* v *Purchase & Sons (Farms) Ltd* [1983] 2 All ER 4 (speaking valuation (ie one for which reasons given) on its face made on a fundamentally erroneous basis could be impugned).

Edwards v *Skyways Ltd* [1964] 1 WLR 349 High Court (Megaw J)

* *Intention to create legal relations?*

Facts
As it was necessary to make some of their pilots redundant, the defendants agreed that those concerned, including the plaintiff, would be given an ex gratia payment approximating to the defendants' contributions to their pension fund. Due to their financial difficulties, the defendants failed to make such a payment to the plaintiff: when he sued to recover the amount of the promised ex gratia payment, the defendants maintained that the agreement was not binding as there had been no intention to create legal relations and its terms were too vague.

Held
The plaintiff was entitled to succeed.

Megaw J:

'It is clear from such cases as *Rose and Frank Co* v *J R Crompton & Bros Ltd* [1923] 2 KB 261 and *Balfour* v *Balfour* [1919] 2 KB 571 that there are cases in which English law recognises that an agreement, in other respects duly made, does not give rise to legal rights, because the parties have not intended that their legal relations should be affected. Where the subject-matter of the agreement is some domestic of social relationship or transaction, as in *Balfour* v *Balfour*, the very law will often deny legal consequences to the agreement, because of the very nature of the subject-matter. Where the subject-matter of the agreement is not domestic or social, but is related to business affairs, the parties may, by using clear words, show that their intention is to make the transaction binding in honour only, and not in law; and the courts will give effect to the expressed intention. ...

In the present case, the subject-matter of the agreement is business relations, not social or domestic matters. There was a meeting of minds – an intention to agree. There was, admittedly, consideration for the defendant company's promise. I accept the propositions of counsel for the plaintiff that in a case of this nature the onus is on the party who asserts that no legal effect was intended, and the onus is a heavy one ... the defendant company say, first ... that the mere use of the phrase "ex gratia" by itself, as a part of the promise to pay, shows that the parties contemplated that the promise, when accepted, should have no binding force in law. They say, secondly, that even if their first proposition is not correct as a general proposition, nevertheless here there was certain background knowledge, present in the minds of everyone, which gave unambiguous significance to "ex gratia" as excluding legal relationship.

As to the first proposition, the words "ex gratia" do not, in my judgment, carry a necessary, or even a probable, implication that the agreement is to be without legal effect. It is, I think, common experience amongst practitioners of the law that litigation or threatened litigation is frequently compromised on the terms that one party shall make to the other a payment described in express terms as "ex gratia" or "without admission of liability". The two phrases are, I think, synonymous ... No one would imagine that a settlement, so made, is unenforceable at law. The words "ex gratia" or "without admission of liability" are used simply to indicate ... that the party agreeing to pay does not admit any pre-existing liability on his part; but he is certainly not seeking to preclude the legal enforceability of the settlement itself by describing the contemplated payment as "ex gratia". So here, there are obvious reasons why the phrase might have been used by the defendant company

in just such a way. They might have desired to avoid conceding that any such payment was due under the employers' contract of service. They might have wished – perhaps ironically in the event – to show, by using the phrase, their generosity in making a payment beyond what was required by the contract of service. I see nothing in the mere use of the words "ex gratia", unless in the circumstances some very special meaning has to be given to them, to warrant the conclusion that this promise, duly made and accepted, for valid consideration, was not intended by the parties to be enforceable in law.

The defendant company's second proposition seeks to show that in the circumstances here the words "ex gratia" had a special meaning ...

Thus, it is said, the phrase "ex gratia" was used, and was understood by all present to be used, deliberately and advisedly as a formula to achieve that there would be no binding legal obligation on the company to pay, and hence to save the recipient from a tax liability ... The question of tax liability, and the possible influence thereon of the use of the words "ex gratia", may indeed have been present in some degree, and as one element, in the minds of some of the persons ... That, however, is far from sufficient to establish that the parties – both of them – affirmatively intended not to enter into legal relations in respect of the defendant company's promise to pay.

Lastly, the defendant company say that, even if the agreement were otherwise in all respects a binding agreement, it is not enforceable because its terms are too vague. This is founded on the submission that the precise words used ... were "approximating to"; that these precise words are a part of the agreement; that they leave a discretion to the defendant company; that therefore there is no enforceable agreement, and they can refuse to pay anything ... I do not think that English law provides that in such circumstances the plaintiff would be entitled to nothing. At most "approximating to", if that were the contractual term, would on the evidence connote a rounding off of a few pounds downwards to a round figure.'

Comment

Considered in *Kleinwort Benson Ltd* v *Malaysia Mining Corp Bhd* [1989] 1 WLR 379.

Elpis Maritime Co Ltd v *Marti Chartering Co Inc, The Maria D*
[1991] 3 All ER 758 House of Lords (Lords Keith of Kinkel, Brandon of Oakbrook, Ackner, Oliver of Aylmerton and Lowry)

• *Guarantee – Statute of Frauds 1677 – enforcement*

Facts

A charterparty of the appellants' ship was negotiated through brokers and, by telephone, the respondents, the charterers' agents, agreed to guarantee certain of the charterers' liabilities under the charterparty. The written charterparty was in standard form and it expressly incorporated six pages of additional clauses, by one of which (c124) the respondents guaranteed the charterers' liabilities. The front sheet of the charterparty, together with the incorporation of the additional clauses, was signed by the respondents 'for and on behalf of charterers as brokers only': they simply signed the additional pages and the last page and above this latter signature the word 'charterers' was typed. The charterers having failed to pay, the appellants sued the respondents as guarantors. The respondents relied on s4 of the Statute of Frauds.

Held

The appellants' claim would be successful.

Lord Brandon of Oakbrook:

'The present case differs fundamentally from *Young* v *Schuler* (1883) 11 QBD 651 in that it is not in dispute that there was an oral contract by which Marti guaranteed the

liabilities of the charterers in respect of demurraged and balance of freight, such contract having been made in the course of conversations on the telephone between Mr Zafeiriou of Tramp and Mr Atala of Marti before the charterparty was signed. The evidence from Marti further showed that, without Marti's agreement to the giving of the guarantee, it is likely that no charterparty would have come into being.

My Lords, it is standard practice, when two brokers, acting on behalf of their respective principals, negotiate by telephone or telex or both, the terms on which a ship is to be chartered, and terms are fully agreed, for those terms to be embodied in a written charterparty in which they are subsumed. It seems to me to be clear that Tramp and Marti intended to follow this standard practice in the present case, not only in respect of the terms of the main contract between the owner and the charterers, but also in respect of the terms of the collateral contract of guarantee between the owners and Marti. The question is, however, whether, so far as the collateral contract of guarantee between the owners and Marti is concerned, the two brokers achieved the resulted intended. That question arises because Marti have raised what the Court of Appeal regarded, rightly in my view, as an arguable case, that all the signatures affixed by Marti to the pages of the charterparty, including the page containing cl24, were affixed by them solely as agents of the charterers and not also for themselves as a contracting party.

In these circumstances it is necessary, in order to decide whether the owners can enforce the agreement of guarantee against Marti, to consider that question on two alternative assumptions. The first assumption is that Marti affixed their signature to the page of the charterparty containing cl24 as a contracting party. The second and alternative assumption is that every signature affixed by Marti to the charterparty, including the signature on the page containing cl24, was affixed by them solely as agents for the charterers. ...

My Lords, there were cited to your

Lordships in the course of argument a considerable number of cases in which the courts have had to consider and decide what does or does not constitute a sufficient memorandum or note of an agreement of guarantee signed by the party to be charged for the purposes of s4. I do not propose, however, to refer to more than one of those cases, *R Hoyle, Hoyle* v *Hoyle* [1893] 1 Ch 84, in which it seems to me that the basic principle relevant to the present case was shortly and in my view correctly explained by A L Smith LJ. He said (at p100):

> "The statute enacts that no action shall be brought upon a promise of a certain description unless there is a note or memorandum thereof signed by the party to be charged. A letter to a third party has been held enough; an affidavit made in a different matter has been held to suffice; and I should say that an entry in a man's diary, if it were signed by him and the contents were sufficient, would do. The question is not what is the intention of the person signing the memorandum, but is one of fact, viz, is there a note or memorandum of the promise signed by the party to be charged? Here the testator by his will, which he signs, recites the guarantee sued on. The contents of the statement are sufficient, and why is this not a memorandum in writing signed by a party to be charged? I say that it is."...

Applying the statements of principle made in *Re Hoyle* above to the present case, it seems to me to be wholly irrelevant, in relation to the question which I am now considering, with what intention, or in what capacity, Marti signed the page in the charterparty containing cl24, whether as agents for the charterers only or for themselves as well. Clause 24 contained all the terms of the prior oral agreement of guarantee and Marti's signature was affixed to the page containing that clause. On those facts the page of the charterparty concerned contained, in my opinion, a sufficient memorandum or note of the prior oral agreement of guarantee signed by the party to be charged, so as to satisfy the second require-

ment for achieving enforceability prescribed by s4. ...

As will be apparent, the conclusion which I have reached is that it makes no difference to the question of enforceability under s4 whether one makes the first or the second of the two assumptions referred to and discussed above. On either of the two assumptions the result is that there was an agreement of guarantee between the owners and Marti which satisfied the requirements for enforceability prescribed by s4. On the first assumption there was an agreement in writing signed my Marti. On the second assumption there was an oral agreement of which there was a sufficient memorandum or note signed by Marti.

Since the owners were bound to succeed on the question of enforceability either on the one assumption or on the other, Marti had no arguable defence to the owners' claim ...'

Comment

The first requirement for achieveing enforceability prescribed by s4 of the Statute of Frauds in that there should be a written argeement signed by the party to be charged or his agent.

Gould v *Gould* [1969] 3 WLR 490 Court of Appeal (Lord Denning MR, Edmund Davies and Megaw LJJ)

- *Husband's qualified promise*

Facts

On leaving his wife, a husband orally agreed to pay her £15 a week 'as long as I can manage it'. He kept to this agreement for over a year, but then fell behind with the payments and five months later said he could not pay the full amount in future. The wife sued for the arrears.

Held (Lord Denning MR dissenting)

Her claim would fail as a legally binding

agreement had not been within the contemplation of the parties.

Edmund Davies LJ:

'There can be no doubt that husband and wife can enter into a contract which binds them in law … But it is on the spouse asserting that such a contract has been entered into to prove that assertion … In the general run of cases the inclination would be against inferring that spouses intended to create a legal relationship … The evidence establishing such an intention, needs, in my judgment, to be clear and convincing.

It is true that the facts of the present case differ from those of *Balfour* v *Balfour* [1919] 2 KB 571, in that although the original agreement there relied on was entered into on the eve of the husband's leaving the wife to take up his governmental duties in Ceylon, at that time amity reigned between them; whereas here the arrangement sued on was made after the husband had left the wife. While I agree that in the present circumstances the probability that a legally-binding agreement was intended may be greater than in *Balfour* v *Balfour*, nevertheless the best key in my judgment to the parties' intention is the language they employed. The importance of this aspect of the case is not restricted simply to the question whether the agreement is bad for uncertainty, but extends to the initial question whether a legally binding agreement was ever intended within the parties' contemplation. According to the wife, the husband promised to pay her £15 a week "as long as he had it" and "as long as the business was OK". The husband's evidence was substantially to the same effect, namely,

" … I suggested I would give her £15 each week; and she said for how long? and I said as long as I can manage it."

In my judgment those words import such uncertainty as to indicate strongly that legal relations were not contemplated.'

Comment

Distinguished in *Merritt* v *Merritt* [1970] 1

WLR 1211. See also *Balfour* v *Balfour* [1919] 2 KB 571.

Hillas & Co Ltd v *Arcos Ltd* (1932) 147 LT 503 House of Lords (Lords Tomlin, Warrington, Thankerton, Macmillan and Wright)

- *Construction – 'fair specification'*

Facts

The plaintiffs agreed to buy from the defendants '22,000 standards of softwood goods of fair specification over the season 1930' at 5 per cent below the official price.

Held

There was an enforceable contract.

Lord Tomlin:

'If the words "of fair specification" have no meaning which is certain or capable of being made certain, then … there cannot have been a contract with regard to the 22,000 standards … This may be the proper conclusion; but before it is reached it is, I think, necessary to exclude as impossible all reasonable meanings which would give certainty to the words. In my opinion, this cannot be done. The parties undoubtedly attributed to the words in connection with the 22,000 standards some meaning which was precise or capable of being made precise. …

Reading the document … as a whole, and having regard to the admissible evidence as to the course of the trade, I think that upon their true construction the words "of fair specification over the season, 1930", used in connection with the 22,000 standards, mean that the 22,000 standards are to be satisfied in goods distributed over kinds, qualities, and sizes in the fair proportions having regard to the output of the season 1930, and the classifications of that output in respect of kinds, qualities, and sizes. That is something which if the parties fail to agree can be ascertained just as much as the fair value of a property. ... Thus, there is a description of the goods which, if not immediately, yet ultimately, is capable of being rendered certain.'

Comment
Applied in *Foley* v *Classique Coaches Ltd* [1934] 2 KB 1 (implied term that petrol should be supplied at a reasonable price and be of reasonable quality).

Kleinwort Benson Ltd v *Malaysia Mining Corp Bhd* [1989] 1 WLR 379
Court of Appeal (Fox, Ralph Gibson and Nicholls LJJ)

- *Letter of comfort – contractual effect?*

Facts
The plaintiff bank negotiated with the defendants for the making of loan facility of up to £10m available to the defendants' wholly-owned subsidiary MMC Metals Ltd ('Metals'). The plaintiffs having sought from the defendants assurances as to the responsibility of the defendants for the repayment by Metals of any sums lent by the plaintiffs, the defendants provided a comfort letter containing the statement (in para 3): 'It is our policy to ensure that the business of [Metals] is at all times in a position to meet its liabilities to you under the ... arrangements.' Metals went into liquidation owing the whole amount of the facility and the plaintiffs sought payment from the defendants.

Held
Their action would fail as, on the facts, the letter gave rise to no more than a moral responsibility on the defendants' part to meet Metals' debt.

Ralph Gibson LJ:

'The concept of a comfort letter was, as counsel for the defendants acknowledged, not shown to have acquired any particular meaning at the time of the negotiations in this case with reference to the limits of any legal liability to be assumed under its terms by a parent company. ... The court would not, merely because the parties had referred to the document as a comfort letter, refuse to give effect to the meaning of the words used. But in this case it is clear ... that the concept of a comfort letter, to which the parties had resort when the defendants refused to assume joint and several liability or to give a guarantee, was known by both sides at least to extend to or to include a document under which the defendants would give comfort to the plaintiffs by assuming, not a legal liability to ensure repayment of the liabilities of its subsidiary, but a moral responsibility only. ... The comfort letter was drafted in terms which in para 3 do not express any contractual promise and which are consistent with being no more than a representation of fact. If they are treated as no more than a representation of fact, they are in that meaning consistent with the comfort letter containing no more than the assumption of moral responsibility by the defendants in respect of the debts of Metals. There is nothing in the evidence to show that, as a matter of commercial probability or common sense, the parties must have intended para 3 to be a contractual promise, which is not expressly stated, rather than a mere representation of fact which is so stated ...

For this purpose it seems to me that the onus of demonstrating that the affirmation appears on evidence to have been intended as a contractual promise must lie on the party asserting that it does, but I do not rest my conclusion on failure by the plaintiffs to discharge any onus. I think it is clear that the words of para 3 cannot be regarded as intended to contain a contractual promise as to the future policy of the defendants ... Most importantly [the] factual background explains, notwithstanding the commercial importance to the plaintiffs of security against failure by Metals to pay and the plaintiffs' reliance on the comfort letter, why the plaintiffs drafted and agreed to proceed on a comfort letter which, on its plain meaning, provided to the plaintiffs no legally enforceable security for the repayment of the liabilities of Metals. I therefore find it impossible to hold that by the words of para 3 the parties must be held to have intended that the plaintiffs be given that security.'

Pettitt v *Pettitt* [1970] AC 777 House of Lords (Lords Reid, Morris of Borth-y-Gest, Hodson, Upjohn and Diplock)

• *Cottage – beneficial interests*

Facts
A wife paid for a cottage and it stood in her name. The husband carried out internal decorations, built a wardrobe, laid out the garden and constructed a wall. Subsequently they were divorced and the husband maintained that he was entitled to a beneficial interest in the cottage's proceeds of sale.

Held
This was not the case: he had merely done in his leisure time jobs which husbands normally do.

Lord Hodson:

'... disputes between husbands and wives as to the ownership of property ... are difficult to resolve ... if only because of the special relationship between husband and wife. They do not as a rule enter into contracts with one another so long as they are living together on good terms. It would be very odd if they did.

An illustration, perhaps an extreme one, is provided by *Balfour* v *Balfour* [1919] 2 KB 571. There Sargant J held that the parties who were husband and wife had entered into a contract fixing the husband's obligation to maintain his wife during a temporary separation at £30 a month. Apart from the husband and wife relationship the judge's decision could hardly have been questioned, but the Court of Appeal used strong words in support of the proposition that mutual provisions made in the ordinary domestic relationship of the husband and wife do not of necessity give cause for action on a contract. Atkin LJ pointed out that these arrangements are not sued on because the parties in the inception of the arrangement never intended that they should be sued on. *Balfour* v *Balfour* has no direct bearing on the kind of situation which has arisen here but I think it rightly indicates that the court will be slow to infer legal obligations from transactions between husband and wife in the ordinary course of their domestic life.'

Lord Diplock:

'... many of the ordinary domestic arrangements between man and wife do not possess the legal characteristics of a contract. So long as they are executory they do not give rise to any chose in action for neither party intended that non-performance of their mutual promises should be the subject of sanctions in any court (see *Balfour* v *Balfour* [1919] 2 KB 571). But this is relevant to non-performance only. If spouses do perform their mutual promises the fact that they could not have been compelled to do so while the promises were executory cannot deprive the acts done by them of all legal consequences on proprietary rights; for these are within the field of the law of property rather than of the law of contract. It would, in my view, be erroneous to extend the presumption accepted in *Balfour* v *Balfour* that mutual promises between man and wife in relation to their domestic arrangements are prima facie not intended by either to be legally enforceable to a presumption of a common intention of both spouses that *no* legal consequences should flow from acts done by them in performance of mutual promises with respect to the acquisition, improvement or addition to real or personal property – for this would be to intend what is impossible in law.'

Record v Bell [1991] 1 WLR 853
Chancery Division (Judge Paul Baker QC)

• *Sale of land – s2 Law of Property (Miscellaneous Provisions) Act 1989 – sale of chattels – specific performance*

Facts
On 1 June 1990, the day before contracts were exchanged for the sale of a house in Smith Square, the vendor's solicitor wrote to the purchaser's solicitor informing him that he was awaiting original office copy entries from the Land Registry confirming his client's title. The purchaser's solicitor replied stating that the contract was conditional on, inter alia, delivery to the purchaser of the office copy entries and that the letter setting out this condition was to be attached to the contract. This letter was attached to the purchaser's part of the contract, but no letter was attached to the other part. There were also separate contracts for the sale of certain chattels in the house. The office copy entries having been duly delivered, the vendor sought specific performance of all contracts.

Held
He was entitled to succeed. Although the letter did not satisfy the requirements of s2 of the Law of Property (Miscellaneous Provisions) Act 1989 (it was not referred to in the contract and no letter was attached to one part of it), there was a contract collateral to the main contract which was not caught by s2 of the 1989 Act. The vendor's solicitor's letter had been an offer of a warranty as to the state of the title and this offer had been accepted by exchanging contracts. The circumstances were such that the court could and would also grant specific performance of the contracts for the sale of the accompanying chattels, in so far as those contracts had been established.

Judge Paul Baker QC:

'Section 2(1) [of the 1989 Act] requires that a contract for the sale or other disposition "can only be made in writing and only by incorporating all the terms which the parties have expressly agreed in one document." The document in that subsection must be the document which contains the contract for sale. Going to subs (2), "The terms may be incorporated in a document either by being set out in it or by reference to some other document." The former document was a direct reference to the document referred to in subs (1), and the purpose of subs (2) is to expand what is meant in subs (1) by incorporating the terms. There are two ways they could be incorporated. They could be set out at length in the contract for sale, or the contract for sale can refer to some other document in which these terms are to be found. The document referred to need not itself be signed, but it has to be identified in the document which is signed.

A letter of variation or a letter of additional term, not itself a contract for sale, which is signed by both parties may be a variation of the original contract after it has been exchanged as, indeed, we have in this very case relating to the completion date. But it could not, as I see it, be part of the original contract without there being some reference to it contained in the contract for sale. The terms agreed before exchange have to be incorporated. I do not have to deal with the case of physical attachment of a paper containing an additional term without verbal reference to it in the main contract. On the facts before me, there was no reference in the contracts for sale to the supplementary term. It is true that [the purchaser's solicitor's] letter had been physically attached to the purchaser's part of the contract, but there was no similar attachment of the other party's letter to the other part of the contract. Under the new Act the terms have to be expressly incorporated in each of the contracts where there is more than one.

I return to [counsel for the vendor's] point that what happened to a collateral contract, that is an independent contract collateral to the main contract. In such a case it is not caught by s2 unless it is itself a contract for sale. [He] relied on the well-known case of

De Lassalle v *Guildford* [1901] 2 KB 215, a decision of the Court of Appeal ...

This was, in my judgment, an offer of a warranty by [the vendor's solicitor] to [the purchaser's solicitor] as to the state of the title, and it was done to induce him to exchange. That offer was accepted by exchanging contracts. It would be unfortunate if common transactions of this nature should nevertheless cause the contracts to be avoided. It may, of course, lead to a greater use of the concept of collateral warranties than has hitherto been necessary. ...

I must now turn briefly to the chattel contracts. I said that there were three. The first one was in writing and was part of the original deal. The second one was oral for additional chattels to be sold for £46,400, and then there was the one relating to the piano. The first two are not disputed but the third is. The plaintiff seeks specific performance of those contracts in addition to the one relating to the land. It was argued before me that this was not a case for specific performance. It is not the normal remedy for a breach of a contract to sell goods, certainly not goods in isolation. There are certain exceptions to that general proposition. One is if the goods are of unique value. Another exception was called to my attention in a case before Lord Eldon LC, *Nutbrown* v *Thornton* (1804) 10 Ves 159, where there was an entire contract of land and goods. Another exception may occur where the goods are of such a nature that it would damage the land to remove them. It was said, by contrast, that these are removable chattels, that they were not fixtures but movable chattels of one sort or another on the land and that therefore I should not award specific performance. But in my judgment the remedy is not limited to those exceptions. The principle behind the remedy is that damages would not be adequate. Where you have a contract for the sale of a house and chattels in it, with the furnishings in situ, it seems to me that there, in appropriate cases, the court can award specific performance. If the court is going to grant an order for specific performance for the house itself, the jurisdiction is not so restricted that the court cannot extend the decree to the accompanying furnishings. The jurisdiction cannot depend, in my judgment, on whether the land and chattels were all in one contract or in two separate contracts. Therefore I propose to give judgment for specific performance in regard to the contract for the sale of [the house] and for the two chattel contracts, the contemporaneous one and the oral agreement ... As to the piano, there is a dispute of fact as to whether that agreement was entered into, and therefore as regards that part of the transactions I shall give unconditional leave to defend and order that part of the claim to be transferred to the county court.'

Comment

See also *Spiro* v *Glencrown Properties Ltd* [1991] 2 WLR 931.

Spiro v *Glencrown Properties Ltd*
[1991] 2 WLR 931 Chancery Division (Hoffmann J)

• *Option to purchase land – s2 Law of Property (Miscellaneous Provisions) Act 1989*

Facts

By a written agreement, the vendor of land granted an option to purchase land. The option could be exercised the same day and exercised by notice in writing given by the purchaser to the vendor or his solicitor. The option agreement was executed in two exchanged parts, each containing the agreed terms and each signed by the party or his solicitor. The purchaser exercised the option by written notice in the agreed manner, but failed to complete. The question arose as to whether the notice was required to comply with s2 of the Law of Property (Miscellaneous Provisions) Act 1989.

Held

It did not: the vendor was entitled to damages for breach of contract.

Hoffmann J:

'Here the underlying principles are clear enough. The granting of the option imposes no obligation upon the purchaser and an obligation upon the vendor which is contingent upon the exercise of the option. When the option is exercised, vendor and purchaser come under obligations to perform as if they had concluded an ordinary contract of sale. ...

An option is not strictly speaking either an offer or a conditional contract. It does not have *all* the incidents of the standard form of either of these concepts. To that extent it is a relationship sui generis. But there are ways in which it resembles each of them. Each analogy is in the proper context a valid way of characterising the situation created by an option. The question in this case is not whether one analogy is true and and the other false, but which is appropriate to be used in the construction of s2 of the Law of Property (Miscellaneous Provisions) Act 1989. ...

In my judgment there is nothing in the authorities which prevents me from giving s2 the meaning which I consider to have been the clear intention of the legislature. ... And the plain purpose of s2 was ... to prescribe the formalities for recording the consent of the parties. It follows that in my view the grant of the option was the only "contract for the sale or other disposition of an interest in land" within the meaning of the section and the contract duly complied with the statutory requirements.'

Comment

See also *Record* v *Bell* [1991] 1 WLR 853; compare *McCausland* v *Duncan Lawrie Ltd* [1996] 4 All ER 995 (variation of contract).

4 Contents of Contracts

Ali v *Christian Salvesen Food Services Ltd* [1997] 1 All ER 721 Court of Appeal (Waite, Saville and Otton LJJ)

• *Collective employment agreements – annualised pay – implied term?*

Facts

The appellant employers concluded annualisation agreements with two trade unions whereby, for the coming 12 months, their workforce would be paid a standard wage based broadly on an assumed working week of 40 hours. The contracts of employment of individual employees incorporated the collective agreements: no provision was made in either place for the eventuality of an employee ceasing work during the 12-month period. Mr Ali was such an employee: he was made redundant after 22 weeks. He maintained that during those weeks his hours of work had exceeded the 'norm' on which the standard wage was based and that he should be paid extra for that excess. The industrial tribunal dismissed his claim, but the Employment Appeal Tribunal took the view that there should be implied into the individual and collective agreements, as a matter of law, a term that would entitle an employee whose employment was terminated by the employer before the end of the pay year to be paid the standard hourly rate for the hours actually worked by him in excess of 40 hours per week.

Held

The employers' appeal against this decision would be allowed.

Waite LJ:

'[Counsel for Mr Ali's] submission (which prevailed before the Employment Appeal Tribunal) is that this term should be implied on the basis: (a) that it was an obvious inference from the collective and individual agreements, because the parties cannot have intended the obvious injustices which would follow if it were not implied; and/or (b) that, without it, the agreement is incomplete. This was a contract for hourly paid employment. It is a legal incident of such a contract that an employee is to be paid for the hours which he has actually worked, regardless of when his employment is terminated.

The first submission rests on the well-known "officious bystander" test, and the second on the principle approved by the House of Lords in *Liverpool City Council* v *Irwin* [1976] 2 All ER 39. No reliance is placed on the other established heads for term implication – business efficacy, and custom and practice. ...

The importance of an implied term depends, in the final analysis, upon "the intention of the parties as collected from the words of the agreement and the surrounding circumstances" (see *Chitty on Contracts* (27th edn, 1994) vol 1, para 13–003). The collective agreement itself and the individual contracts are wholly silent as to consequences of a premature termination of the employment contract in individual cases before the end of the rostered term. This is not therefore a case where the contractual documents create by their wording an internal context in favour – or for that matter against – the implication of the proposed term. What of the surrounding circumstances?

The circumstances which are in my view crucial to the present case are that this was a collective agreement negotiated across a broad front for a substantial labour force. It represented a carefully negotiated compromise between two potentially conflicting obligations – the desire on the one hand of the employees to have an assured rate of weekly pay spread over a long period to which they would be entitled regardless of hours actually worked; and the desire on the other hand of the employers to avoid the high cost of paying overtime rates for work done at periods of peak demand. It is in the nature of such an agreement that it should be concise and clear – so as to be readily understood by all who are concerned to operate it. One would expect the parties to such an agreement to set their face against any attempt to legislate for every possible contingency. Should there be any topic left uncovered by an agreement of that kind, the natural inference, in my judgment, is not that there has been an omission so obvious as to require judicial correction, but rather that the topic was omitted advisedly from the terms of the agreement on the ground that it was seen as too controversial or too complicated to justify any variation of the main terms of the agreement to take account of it.

When the collective and individual agreements are approached in that light, I find, for my part, that [counsel for the employers'] submissions are wholly persuasive. This was an agreement which, by its very nature, would require it to be applied to many eventualities that it did not, and could not realistically, cover specifically. The omission of any reference at all to the contingency of a premature termination (for any reason) of the contracts of employment before the end of the roster period may at first sight be surprising, but it becomes less so when regard is had to the immensity of the task of legislating for every eventuality resulting from such termination. ... Once it is apparent that the situation for which it is sought to imply a term is only one of the numerous eventualities on which the agreement is silent, it becomes difficult, if not impossible, to devise for any particular eventuality, a term of which it can be predicated with certainty that the negotiating parties would inevitably have been of one mind about it if a decision had been taken

to make specific provision for it in the agreement.

The point is also well made, in my view, that the absence of any reciprocal arrangement for "claw-back" against the prematurely dismissed employee who has worked less than the norm of hours makes it even more difficult to imply the particular term that is claimed here.'

Bentley (Dick) Productions Ltd v Harold Smith (Motors) Ltd [1965] 1 WLR 623 Court of Appeal (Lord Denning MR, Danckwerts and Salmon LJJ)

• *Sale of car – misrepresentation as to mileage*

Facts
The defendants, car dealers, sold a Bentley to the plaintiffs and stated that the car had only done 20,000 miles since being fitted with a replacement engine and gear box. In truth, the mileage was nearer 100,000 and the car repeatedly broke down.

Held
The defendants were in breach of warranty and the plaintiffs were entitled to damages. Although the statement was made innocently, the defendants were in a position, as dealers, to check its accuracy and, having made the statement to induce the plaintiffs to enter into the contract, they would not be allowed to resile from it.

Lord Denning MR:

'The first point is whether this representation, namely that it had done 20,000 only since it had been fitted with a replacement engine and gear box, was an innocent misrepresentation (which does not give rise to damages), or whether it was a warranty. It was said by Holt CJ, and repeated in *Heilbut, Symons & Co v Buckleton* [1913] AC 30 that: "An affirmation at the time of the sale is a warranty, provided it appear on evidence to be so intended". But that word "intended" has given rise to difficulties. I endeavoured to explain, in *Oscar Chess Ltd v Williams* [1957] 1 WLR 370 that the question whether a warranty was intended depends on the conduct of the parties on their words and behaviour, rather than on their thoughts. If an intelligent bystander would reasonably infer that a warranty was intended, that will suffice. What conduct, then? What words and behaviour lead to the inference of a warranty?

Looking at the cases once more, as we have done so often, it seems to me that if a representation is made in the course of dealings for a contract for the very purpose of inducing the other party to act upon it, and actually inducing him to act upon it by entering into the contract, that is prima facie ground for inferring that it was intended as a warranty. It is not necessary to speak of it as being collateral. Suffice it that it was intended to be acted upon and was, in fact, acted upon. But the maker of the representations can rebut this inference if he can show that it really was an innocent misrepresentation, in that he was in fact innocent of fault in making it, and that it would not be reasonable in the circumstances for him to be bound by it ... in the present case it is very different. The inference is not rebutted. Here we have a dealer, Smith, who was in a position to know, or at least to find out, the history of the car. He could get it by writing to the makers. He did not do so. Indeed, it was done later. When the history of this car was examined, his statement turned out to be quite wrong. He ought to have known better. There was no reasonable foundation for it.'

Comment

Applied in *Evans (J) & Son (Portsmouth) Ltd v Andrea Merzario Ltd* [1976] 1 WLR 1078. Distinguished: *Oscar Chess Ltd v Williams* [1957] 1 WLR 370.

Bettini v *Gye* (1876) 1 QBD 183
High Court (Blackburn, Quain and Archibald JJ)

• *Arrival time for rehearsals – condition precedent?*

Facts

The defendant director of the Royal Italian Opera in London engaged the plaintiff tenor for the period 30 March to 13 July 1875: it was a term of the agreement that the plaintiff would 'be in London without fail at least six days before the commencement of this engagement for ... rehearsals'. Because of temporary illness, he said, he did not arrive until 28 March. Was the defendant justified in refusing to proceed with the engagement?

Held

He was not as the stipulation in question was not a condition precedent.

Blackburn J:

'The answer ... depends on whether this part of the contract is a condition precedent to the defendant's liability or only an independent agreement, a breach of which will not justify a repudiation of the contract, but will only be a cause of action for a compensation in damages ... We think the answer ... depends on the true construction of the contract taken as a whole. Parties may think some matter apparently of very little importance essential, and if they sufficiently express an intention to make the literal fulfilment of such a thing a condition precedent, it will be one, or they may think that the performance of some matter apparently of essential importance, and prima facie a condition, is not really vital, and may be compensated for in damages, and if they sufficiently express such an intention, it will not be a condition precedent ...

If the plaintiff's engagements had been only to sing in operas at the theatre it might very well be that previous attendance at rehearsals with the actors in company with whom he was to perform was essential. If the engagement had only been for a few performances, or for a short time, it would afford a strong argument that attendance for the purpose of rehearsals during the six days immediately before the commencement of the engagement was a vital part of the agreement. But we find on looking to the agreement that the plaintiff was to sing in theatres, halls, and drawing rooms, public and private, from Mar. 30 to July 13 1875, and that he was to sing in concerts as well as in operas ... As far as we can see the failure to attend at rehearsals during the six days immediately before Mar. 31, could only affect the theatrical performances, and, perhaps, the singing in duets or concerted pieces during the first week or fortnight of this engagement, which is to sing in theatres, halls, and drawing rooms, and concerts for fifteen weeks. We think, therefore, that it does not go to the root of the matter so as to require us to consider it a condition precedent. The defendant must, therefore, we think, seek redress by a cross claim for damages.'

Comment

This decision should be compared with *Poussard* v *Spiers and Pond* (1876) 1 QBD 410 where a singer's inability (due to illness) to attend final rehearsals and the first four performances was found to amount to a breach of a condition precedent.

Bunge Corpn v *Tradax SA* [1981] 1 WLR 711 House of Lords (Lords Wilberforce, Fraser of Tullybelton, Scarman, Lowry and Roskill)

• *Shipping contract – right to terminate*

Facts

Under a contract for the sale and purchase of soya bean meal, it was agreed that a shipment was to be made in June. The buyers had to provide a vessel and to give at least 15 days'

notice of its probable readiness. In the event, they gave such notice on 17 June and the sellers contended that the late notice was a breach of contract amounting to a repudiation.

Held

The sellers' view would be upheld and they were also entitled to damages.

Lord Wilberforce:

'... the statement of the law in 9 Halsbury's Laws (4th edn) paras 481–482, (including the footnotes to para 482) (generally approved in the House in *United Scientific Holdings Ltd* v *Burnley Borough Council* [1978] AC 904) appears to me to be correct, in particular in asserting (1) that the court will require precise compliance with stipulations as to time wherever the circumstances of the case indicate that this would fulfil the intention of the parties, and (2) that broadly speaking time will be considered of the essence in "mercantile" contracts ...

The relevant clause falls squarely within these principles, and such authority as there is supports its status as a condition (see *Bremer Handelsgesellschaft mbH* v *J H Rayner & Co Ltd* [1978] 2 Lloyd's Rep 73 and cf *Peter Turnbull & Co Pty Ltd* v *Mundas Trading Co (Australasia) Pty Ltd* [1954] 2 Lloyd's Rep 198). In this present context it is clearly essential that both buyer and seller (who may change roles in the next series of contracts, or even in the same chain of contracts) should know precisely what their obligations are, most especially because the ability of the seller to fulfil his obligation may well be totally dependent on punctual performance by the buyer.'

Lord Scarman:

'I wish, however, to make a few observations on the topic of "innominate" terms in our contract law. In *Hong Kong Fir Shipping Co Ltd* v *Kawasaki Kisen Kaisha Ltd* [1962] 2 QB 26 the Court of Appeal rediscovered and reaffirmed that English law recognises contractual terms which, on a true construction of the contract of which they are part, are neither conditions nor warranties but are, to quote Lord Wilberforce's words in *Bremer Handelsgesellschaft mbH v Vanden Avenne-Izegem* [1978] 2 Lloyd's Rep 109, "intermediate". A condition is a term the failure to perform which entitles the other party to treat the contract as at an end. A warranty is a term breach of which sounds in damages but does not terminate, or entitle the other party to terminate, the contract. An innominate or intermediate term is one the effect of non-performance of which the parties expressly or (as is more usual) impliedly agree will depend on the nature and the consequences of breach. In the *Hong Kong Fir* case the term in question provided for the obligation of seaworthiness, breach of which it is well known may be trivial (eg one defective rivet) or very serious (eg a hole in the bottom of the ship). It is inconceivable that parties when including such a term in their contract could have contemplated or intended (unless they expressly say so) that one defective rivet would entitle the charterer to end the contract or that a hole in the bottom of the ship would not. I read the *Hong Kong Fir* case as being concerned as much with the construction of the contract as with the consequences and effect of breach. The first question is always, therefore, whether, on the true construction of a stipulation and the contract of which it is part, it is a condition, an innominate term, or only a warranty. If the stipulation is one which on the true construction of the contract the parties have not made a condition, and breach of which may be attended by trivial, minor or very grave consequences, it is innominate, and the court (or an arbitrator) will, in the event of dispute, have the task of deciding whether the breach that has arisen is such as the parties would have said, had they been asked at the time they made their contract, "It goes without saying that, if that happens, the contract is at an end" ... The seller needed sufficient notice to enable him to choose the loading port; the parties were agreed that the notice to be given him was 15 days; this was a mercantile contract in which the parties required to know where they stood not merely later with hindsight but at once as events occurred. Because it

makes commercial sense to treat the clause in the context and circumstances of this contract as a condition to be performed before the seller takes his steps to comply with bargain, I would hold it to be not an innominate term but a condition.'

Comment
See also *Barber* v *NWS Bank Ltd* [1996] 1 All ER 906.

Hong Kong Fir Shipping Co Ltd v *Kawasaki Kisan Kaisha Ltd* [1962] 2 WLR 474 Court of Appeal (Sellers, Upjohn and Diplock LJJ)

• *Charter – vessel breakdowns – repudiation*

Facts
The defendants chartered the vessel 'Hong Kong Fir' from the plaintiffs for 24 months; the charter party provided 'she being fitted in every way for ordinary cargo service'. It transpired that the engine room staff were incompetent and the vessel spent less than nine weeks of the first seven months of the charter at sea because of breakdowns and consequent repairs required to make her seaworthy. The defendants repudiated the charter party and claimed that the term as to seaworthiness was a condition of the contract, any breach of which entitled them so to do.

Held
The term was neither a condition nor a warranty and in determining whether the defendants could terminate the contract, it was necessary to look at the consequences of the breach to see if they deprived the innocent party of substantially the whole benefit he should have received under the contract. On the facts, this was not the case, because the charter party still had a substantial time to run.

Diplock LJ:

'No doubt there are many simple contractual undertakings, sometimes express but more often, because of their very simplicity ("It goes without saying"), to be implied, of which it can be predicted that every breach of such an undertaking must give rise to an event which will deprive the party not in default of substantialy the whole benefit which it was intended that he should obtain from the contract. And such a stipulation, unless the parties have agreed that breach of it shall not entitle the non-defaulting party to treat the contract as repudiated, is a "condition". So too, there may be other simple contractual undertakings of which it can be predicted that *no* breach can give rise to an event which will deprive the party not in default of substantially the whole benefit which it was intended that he should obtain from the contract; and such a stipulation, unless the parties have agreed that breach of it shall entitle the non-defaulting party to treat the contract as repudiated, is a "warranty".

There are, however, many contractual undertakings, of a more complex character which cannot be categorised as being "conditions" or "warranties" if the late nineteenth-century meaning adopted in the Sale of Goods Act 1893 and uscd by Bowen LJ in *Bentsen* v *Taylor Sons & Co* [1893] 2 QB 274 be given to those terms. Of such undertakings, all that can be predicted is that some breaches will, and others will not, give rise to an event which will deprive the party not in default of substantially the whole benefit which it was intended that he should obtain from the contract; and the legal consequences of a breach of such an undertaking, unless provided for expressly in the contract, depend upon the nature of the event to which the breach gives rise and do not follow automatically from a prior classification of the undertaking as a "condition" or a "warranty". For instance, to take Bramwell B's example in *Jackson* v *Union Marine Insurance Co Ltd* (1874) LR 10 CP 125 itself, breach of an undertaking by a shipowner to sail with all possible dispatch to a named port, does not necessarily relieve the charterer of further performance of his obligation under the charter party, but if the breach is so prolonged that the contemplated

voyage is frustrated, it does have this effect.

In 1874, when the doctrine of frustration was being foaled by "impossibility of performance" out of "condition precedent", it is not surprising that the explanation given by Bramwell B should give full credit to the dam by suggesting that, in addition to the express warranty to sail with all possible dispatch, there was an implied *condition precedent* that the ship should arrive at the named port in time for the voyage contemplated. In *Jackson* v *Union Marine Insurance Co Ltd* there was no breach of the express warranty; but if there had been, to engraft the implied condition upon the express warranty would have been merely a more complicated way of saying that a breach of a shipowner's undertaking to sail with all possible dispatch may, but will not necessarily, give rise to an event which will deprive the charterer of substantially the whole benefit which it was intended that he should obtain from the charter. Now that the doctrine of frustration has matured and flourished for nearly a century, and the old technicalities of pleading "conditions precedent" are more than a century out of date, it does not clarify but, on the contrary, obscures the modern principle of law where such an event *has* occurred as a result of a breach of an express stipulation in a contract, to continue to add the now unnecessary colophon "Therefore it was an implied *condition* of the contract that a particular 'kind of breach' of an express *warranty* should not occur". The common law evolves not merely by breeding new principles but also, when they are fully grown, by burying their progenitors.

As my brethren have already pointed out, the shipowner's undertaking to tender a seaworthy ship has, as a result of numerous decisions as to what can amount to "unseaworthiness", become one of the most complex of contractual undertakings. It embraces obligations with respect to every part of the hull and machinery, stores and equipment, and the crew itself. It can be broken by the presence of trivial defects easily and rapidly remediable, as well as by defects which must inevitably result in a total loss of the vessel.

Consequently, the problem in this case is, in my view, neither solved nor soluble by debating whether the shipowner's express or implied undertaking to tender a seaworthy ship is a "condition" or a "warranty". It is like so many other contractual terms; an undertaking, one breach of which may give rise to an event which relieves the charterer of further performance of his undertakings if he so elects, and another breach of which may not give rise to such an event but entitle him only to monetary compensation in the form of damages. It is, with all deference to Mr Ashton Roskill's skilful argument, by no means surprising that among the many hundreds of previous cases about the shipowner's undertaking to deliver a seaworthy ship, there is none where it was found profitable to discuss in the judgments the question whether that undertaking is a "condition" or a "warranty"; for the true answer, as I have already indicated, is that it is neither, but one of that large class of contractual undertakings, one breach of which may have the same effect as that ascribed to a breach of "condition" under the Sale of Goods Act 1893 and a different breach of which may have only the same effect as that ascribed to a breach of "warranty" under that Act. The cases referred to by Sellers LJ illustrate this and I would only add that in the dictum which he cites from *Kish* v *Taylor* [1912] AC 604 it seems to me, from the sentence which immediately follows it, as from the actual decision in the case, and the whole tenor of Lord Atkinson's speech itself, that the word "will" was intended to be "may".'

Comment

Applied in *Decro-Wall International SA* v *Practitioners in Marketing Ltd* [1971] 1 WLR 361. See also *Barber* v *NSW Bank Ltd* [1996] 1 All ER 906, *Bunge Corpn* v *Tradax SA* [1981] 1 WLR 711 and *The Mihalis Angelos* [1970] 3 WLR 601.

McCausland v *Duncan Lawrie Ltd*
[1996] 4 All ER 995 Court of Appeal (Neill, Morritt LJJ and Tucker J)

• *Contract for sale of land – variation – statutory requirements*

Facts

By a written agreement dated 26 January 1995, land was to be sold and completion was to take place on 26 March 1995. Realising a few days later that 26 March was a Sunday, the vendor's solicitor wrote to the purchasers' solicitors suggesting that completion be re-arranged for 24 March. The purchasers' solicitors replied by letter to the effect that this arrangement was acceptable. In the light of the requirements of s2 of the Law of Property (Miscellaneous Provisions) Act 1989, was this variation effective?

Held

It was not.

Morritt LJ:

'The question here is whether the contract for the sale of the land was varied so as to justify the notice to complete served by the vendor. Thus the vendor has to establish that the contract with the purchaser provided that the sale of the property was to be completed on Friday 24 March. For that purpose he has to demonstrate that there is a document or two documents which were exchanged containing all the terms of that contract and signed by both parties. Obviously he cannot do that for the completion date he relies on is different from that specified in the contract and there is no other document which is signed by both parties. ...

In this case there is no suggestion of ... rescission of the contract altogether which may well be capable of being done otherwise than in writing. Nor in my view can there be any doubt but that the contractual date for completion is a material term if only because it specifies the time from which one or other party is entitled to serve a notice to complete and make time of the essence. ...

The choice lies between permitting a variation, however fundamental, to be made without any formality at all and requiring it to satisfy s2. In my view it is evident that Parliament intended the latter. There would be little point in requiring that the original contract comply with s2 if it might be varied wholly informally. ...

In his speech in *Morris* v *Baron* [1918] AC 1 at 39 per Lord Parmoor recognised ... that equivalent formality is only required for the variation of "a material term". Thus the formalities prescribed by s2 must be observed in order to effect a variation of a term material to the contract for the sale or other disposition of an interest in land but are not required for a variation which is immaterial in that respect. There is no doubt that in this case the term was material in that respect as it advanced the contractual date for completion and therefore the time when either party might make time of the essence by the service of a notice to complete. But it does not follow that s2 must be observed in order to secure the variation of a term which is immaterial. ...

In my judgment, the variation of a term material to a contract for the sale or other disposition of an interest in land must comply with the formalities prescribed by s2 of the 1989 Act if either party is able to enforce such contract as varied.'

Comment
Compare *Spiro* v *Glencrown Properties Ltd* [1991] 2 WLR 931 (option to purchase).

Malik v *Bank of Credit and Commerce International SA* [1997] 3 All ER 1 House of Lords (Lords Goff of Chieveley, Mackay of Clashfern, Mustill, Nicholls of Birkenhead and Steyn)

• *Contract of service – breach of implied term – damages for stigma*

Facts
For the purpose of the present proceedings it was assumed that the defendant bank had been operated in a corrupt and dishonest manner, that the plaintiff former employees were innocent of any involvement, that following the collapse of the bank its corruption and dishonesty had become widely known, that in consequence the plaintiffs were at a handicap on the labour market because they were stigmatised by reason of their previous employment by the bank, and that they had suffered loss in consequence. In making their claim in respect of such assumed loss, the plaintiffs contended that it had been an implied term of their contracts of employment that their employer would not conduct its business in a manner calculated or likely to destroy or seriously damage the relationship of confidence and trust between the employer and its employee.

Held
Should the assumed facts be established, the plaintiffs would be entitled to damages.

Lord Nicholls of Birkenhead:

'... the parties were agreed that the contracts of employment of these two former employees each contained an implied term to the effect that the bank would not, without reasonable and proper cause, conduct itself in a manner likely to destroy or seriously damage the relationship of confidence and trust between employer and employee. Argument proceeded on this footing, and ranged round the type of conduct and other circumstances which could or could not constitute a breach of this implied term. The submissions embraced questions such as the following: whether the trust-destroying conduct must be directed at the employee, either individually or as part of a group; whether an employee must know of the employer's trust-destroying conduct while still employed; and whether the employee's trust must actually be undermined. Furthermore, and at the heart of this case, the submissions raised an important question on the damages recoverable for breach of the implied term, with particular reference to the decisions in *Addis* v *Gramophone Co Ltd* [1909] AC 488 and *Withers* v *General Theatre Corp Ltd* [1933] 2 KB 536.

A DISHONEST AND CORRUPT BUSINESS ...

This was a dishonest business, a corrupt business. It is against this background that the position of an innocent employee has to be considered. In my view, when an innocent employee of the bank learned the true nature of the bank's business, from whatever source, he was entitled to say: "I wish to have nothing more to do with this organisation. I am not prepared to help this business, by working for it. I am leaving at once." This is my intuitive response in the case of all innocent employees of the business, from the most senior to the most junior, from the most long serving to the most recently joined. No one could be expected to have to continue to work with and for such a company against his wish.

This intuitive response is no more than a reflection of what goes without saying in any ordinary contract of employment, namely, that in agreeing to work for an employer the employee, whatever his status, cannot be taken to have agreed to work in furtherance of a dishonest business. This is as much true of a doorkeeper or cleaner as a senior executive or branch manager.

AN IMPLIED OBLIGATION

Two points can be noted here. First, as a matter of legal analysis, the innocent employee's entitlement to leave at once must derive from the bank being in breach of a term of the contract of employment which the employee is entitled to treat as a repudiation by the bank of its contractual obligations. That is the source of his right to step away from the contract forthwith. ...

Second, I do not accept the ... submission that the conduct of which complaint is made must be targeted in some way at the employee or a group of employees. No doubt that will often be the position, perhaps usually so. But there is no reason in principle why this must always be so. The trust and confidence required in the employment relationship can be undermined by an employer, or indeed an employee, in many different ways. I can see no justification for the law giving the employee a remedy if the unjustified trust-destroying conduct occurs in some ways but refusing a remedy if it occurs in others. The conduct must, of course, impinge on the relationship in the sense that, looked at objectively, it is likely to destroy or seriously damage the degree of trust and confidence the employee is reasonably entitled to have in his employer. That requires one to look at all the circumstances.

BREACH

The objective standard just mentioned provides the answer to the liquidators' submission that unless the employee's confidence is actually undermined there is no breach. A breach occurs when the proscribed conduct takes place: here, operating a dishonest and corrupt business. Proof of a subjective loss of confidence in the employer is not an essential element of the breach, although the time when the employee learns of the misconduct and his response to it may affect his remedy.

REMEDIES

(1) Acceptance of breach as repudiation

The next step is to consider the consequences which flow from the bank being in breach of its obligation to its innocent employees by operating a corrupt banking business. The first remedy of an employee has already been noted. The employee may treat the bank's conduct as a repudiatory breach, entitling him to leave. He is not compelled to leave. He may choose to stay. The extent to which staying would be more than an election to remain, and would be a waiver of the breach for all purposes, depends on the circumstances.

I need say no more about waiver in the present case. The assumed facts do not state whether the appellants first learned of the corrupt nature of BCCI after their dismissal ... or whether they acquired this knowledge earlier ... If anything should turn on this, the matter can be investigated further in due course.

In the nature of things, the remedy of

treating the conduct as a repudiatory breach, entitling the employee to leave, can only avail an employee who learns the facts while still employed. If he does not discover the facts while his employment is still continuing, perforce this remedy is not open to him. But this does not mean he has no remedy. In the ordinary course breach of a contractual term entitles the innocent party to damages.

(2) Damages

Can an employee recover damages for breach of the trust and confidence term when he first learns of the breach after he has left the employment? The answer to this question is inextricably bound up with the further question of what damages are recoverable for a breach of this term. In turn, the answer to this further question is inextricably linked with one aspect of the decision in *Addis* v *Gramophone Co Ltd* [1909] AC 488.

At first sight it seems almost a contradiction in terms that an employee can suffer recoverable loss if he first learns of the trust-destroying conduct after the employment contract has already ended for other reasons. But of the many forms which trust-destroying conduct may take, some may have continuing adverse financial effects on an employee even after his employment has ceased. In such a case the fact that the employee only learned of the employer's conduct after the employment had ended ought not, in principle, to be a bar to recovery. If it were other otherwise, an employer who conceals a breach would be better placed than an employer who does not. ...

ADDIS V GRAMOPHONE CO ...
[This] case is generally regarded as having decided, echoing the words of Lord Loreburn LC, that an employee cannot recover damages for the manner in which the wrongful dismissal took place, for injured feelings or for any loss he may sustain from the fact that his having been dismissed of itself makes it more difficult for him to obtain fresh employment ... In particular, *Addis*'s case is generally understood to have decided that any loss suffered by the adverse impact on the employee's chances of obtaining alternative employment is to be excluded from an assessment of damages for wrongful dismissal: see eg *O'Laoire* v *Jackel International Ltd (No 2)* [1991] ICR 718 at 730–731 ...

In my view these observations [of Lord Loreburn LC] cannot be read as precluding the recovery of damages where the manner of dismissal involved a breach of the trust and confidence term and this caused financial loss. *Addis* v *Gramophone Co Ltd* was decided in the days before this implied term was adumbrated. Now that this term exists and is normally implied in every contract of employment, damages for its breach should be assessed in accordance with ordinary contractual principles. This is as much true if the breach occurs before or in connection with dismissal as at any other time.

CONCLUSION
... there are many circumstances in which an employee's reputation may suffer from his having been associated with an unsuccessful business, or an unsuccessful department within a business. In the ordinary way this will not found a claim of the nature made in the present case, even if the business or department was run with gross incompetence. A key feature in the present case is the assumed fact that the business was dishonest or corrupt. Finally, although the implied term that the business will not be conducted dishonestly is a term which avails all employees, proof of consequential handicap in the labour market may well be much more difficult for some classes of employees than others. An employer seeking to employ a messenger, for instance, might be wholly unconcerned by an applicant's former employment in a dishonest business, whereas he might take a different view if he were seeking a senior executive.'

Comment

It should be remembered that this decision was based upon assumed facts and that the crucial implied term had not been acknowledged or recognised when the House of Lords made its decision in *Addis* v *Gramophone Co Ltd* [1909] AC 488.

Maredelanto Compania Naviera SA v *Bergbau-Handel Gmbh, The Mihalis Angelos.*

See *Mihalis Angelos, The.*

Mihalis Angelos, The [1970] 3 WLR 601 Court of Appeal (Lord Denning MR, Edmund Davies and Megaw LJJ)

• *Charter – breach of condition – repudiation*

Facts
On 25 May 1965 the owners of the 'Mihalis Angelos' let the vessel to charterers for the voyage from Haiphong, Vietnam, to Hamburg, the vessel being 'expected ready to load under the charter about 1 July 1965'. At the time the charter was made, she was on her way to Hong Kong to discharge and to be surveyed, and she only completed discharging on 23 July. It was found as a fact that the owners had no reasonable grounds for believing that the vessel would arrive at Haiphong about 1 July.

Held
Law and practice had established that an 'expected ready to load' clause was a condition, any breach of which gave the charterer the right to terminate the contract.

Lord Denning MR:

'The contest resolved itself simply into this: was the "expected ready to load" clause a condition, such that for breach of it the charterers could throw up the charter? Or was it a mere warranty, such as to give rise to damages if it was broken but not a right to cancel, seeing that cancellation was expressly dealt with in the cancelling clause? Sir Frederick Pollock divided the terms of the contract into two categories, conditions and warranties. The difference between them was this: if the promisor broke a *condition* in *any* respect, however slight, it gave the other party a right to be quit of his future obligations and to sue for damages, unless he, by his conduct, waived the condition, in which case he was bound to perform his future obligations but could sue for the damage he suffered. If the promisor broke a *warranty* in *any* respect, however serious, the other party was not quit of his future obligations. He had to perform them. His only remedy was to sue for damages.

This division was adopted by Sir MacKenzie Chalmers when he drafted the Sale of Goods Act and by Parliament when it passed it. It was stated by Fletcher Moulton LJ, in his celebrated dissenting judgment in *Wallis, Son & Wells* v *Pratt & Haynes* [1910] 2 KB 1003, which was adopted in its entirety by the House of Lords [1911] AC 394. It would be a mistake, however, to look on that division as exhaustive. There are many terms of many contracts which cannot be fitted into either category. In such cases, the courts, for nigh on 200 years, have not asked themselves: was the term a condition or a warranty? But rather was the breach such as to go to the root of the contract? If it was, then the other party is entitled, at his election, to treat himself as discharged from any further performance. That is made clear by the judgment of Lord Mansfield in *Boone* v *Eyre* (1779) 1 Hy Bl 273n and by the speech of Lord Blackburn in *Mersey Steel and Iron Co* v *Naylor, Benzon & Co* (1884) 9 App Cas 434 and the notes to *Cutter* v *Powell* (1795) 2 Smith LC 1. *Hong Kong Fir Shipping Co Ltd* v *Kawasaki Kisen Kaisha Ltd* [1962] 2 WLR 474 is a useful reminder of this large category.

Although this large category exists, there is still remaining a considerable body of law by which certain stipulations have been classified as "conditions" so that any failure to perform, however slight, entitles the other to treat himself as discharged. Thus a statement in a charter party on 19 October 1860 that the ship is "now in the port of Amsterdam" was held to be a "condition". On that date she was just outside Amsterdam and could not get in owing to strong gales; but she got in a day or two later when the gales abated. The Court of Exchequer Chamber held that the charterer was entitled to call off the charter; see *Behn* v *Burness* (1863) 3 B & S 751, overruling the Court of Exchequer.

The question in this case is whether the statement by the owner, "expected ready to load under this charter about 1 July 1965" is likewise a "condition". The meaning of such a clause is settled by a decision of this court. It is an assurance by the owner that he honestly expects that the vessel will be ready to load on that date and that his expectation is based on reasonable grounds: see *Samuel Sanday & Co* v *Keighley, Maxted & Co* (1922) 91 LJKB 624. The clause with that meaning has been held in this court to be a "condition", which, if not fulfilled, entitled the other party to treat himself as discharged; see *Finnish Government (Ministry of Food)* v *H V Ford & Co Ltd* (1921) 6 Ll LR 188. Those were sale of goods cases; but I think that the clause should receive the same interpretation in charter party cases. It seems to me that if the owner of a ship, or his agent, states in a charter that she is "expected ready to load about 1 July 1965", he is making a representation as to his own state of mind, ie of what he himself expects; and what is more, he puts it in the contract as a term of it, binding himself to its truth. If he or his agent breaks that term by making the statement without any honest belief in the truth, or without any reasonable grounds for it, he must take the consequences. It is, at lowest, a misrepresentation, which entitles the other party to rescind and, at highest, a breach of contract, which goes to the root of the matter. The charterer who is misled by the statement is entitled, on discovering its falsity, to throw up the charter. It may therefore properly be described as a "condition". I am confirmed in this view by the illustration given by Scrutton LJ himself in all the editions of his work on charter parties:

> "A ship was chartered 'expected to be at X about the 15 December ... shall with all convenient speed sail to X'. The ship was in fact then on such a voyage that she could not complete it and be at X by 15 December. *Submitted*, that the charterer was entitled to throw up the charter."

I do not regard *Associated Portland Cement Manufacturers [1900] Ltd* v *Houlder Brothers & Co Ltd* (1917) 86 LJKB 1495 as any authority to the contrary. The facts are too shortly reported for any guidance to be got from it.

I hold, therefore, that on 17 July 1965 the charterers were entitled to cancel the contract on the ground that the owners had broken the "expected ready to load" clause.'

Megaw LJ:

> 'In my judgment, such a term ought to be regarded as being a condition of the contract, in the old sense of the word "condition": that is, that when it has been broken, the other party can, if he wishes, by intimation to the party in breach, elect to be released from performance of his further obligations under the contract; and he can validly do so without having to establish that, on the facts of the particular case, the breach has produced serious consequences which can be treated as "going to the root of the contract" or as being "fundamental", or whatever other metaphor may be thought appropriate for a frustration case.'

Comment
Applied in *Decro-Wall International SA* v *Practitioners in Marketing Ltd* [1971] 1 WLR 361.

Oscar Chess Ltd v *Williams* [1957] 1 WLR 370 Court of Appeal (Denning, Hodson and Morris LJJ)

• *Age of car – condition or representation?*

Facts
In May 1955, the defendant acquired a new car from the plaintiffs, who were motor car dealers and who took the defendant's Morris in part exchange. The defendant said it was a 1948 model, as per the registration document, and the plaintiffs made him an allowance of

£290. The registration book had been altered by an unknown third party and the car was, in reality, a 1939 model worth £175. The county court judge held that it was a condition of the contract that the car was a 1948 model.

Held (Morris LJ dissenting)

The defendant's statement as to the age of the car was a mere representation, not a term of the contract. He had no special knowledge as to its age and the plaintiffs knew that he was relying on the date in the registration book. Therefore the defendant was not liable.

Denning LJ:

'I entirely agree with the judge that both parties assumed that the Morris was a 1948 model and that this assumption was fundamental to the contract. But this does not prove that the representation was a term of the contract. The assumption was based by both of them on the date given in the registration book as the date of first registration. They both believed it was a 1948 model when it was only a 1939 one. They were both mistaken and their mistake was of fundamental importance.

The effect of such a mistake is this: It does not make the contract a nullity from the beginning, but it does, in some circumstances, enable the contract to be set aside in equity. If the buyer had come promptly, he might have succeeded in getting the whole transaction set aside in equity on the ground of this mistake: see *Solle* v *Butcher* [1949] 2 All ER 1107; but he did not do so and it is too late for him to do it: see *Leaf* v *International Galleries* [1950] 1 All ER 693. His only remedy is in damages and, to recover these, he must prove a warranty.

In saying that he must prove a warranty, I used the word "warranty" in its ordinary English meaning to denote a binding promise. Everyone knows what a man means when he says "I guarantee it" or "I warrant it" or "I give you my word on it". He means that he binds himself to it. That is the meaning it has borne in English Law for 300 years, from the leading case of *Chandelor* v *Lopus* (1603) Cro Jac 4

onwards. During the last fifty years, however, some lawyers have come to use the word "warranty" in another sense. They use it to denote a subsidiary term in contract, as distinct from a vital term, which they call a "condition". In so doing, they depart from the ordinary meaning, not only of the word "warranty" but also of the word "condition". There is no harm in their doing this, so long as they confine this technical use to its proper sphere, namely to distinguish between a vital term, the breach of which gives the right to treat the contract as at an end, and a subsidiary term which does not. But the trouble comes when one person uses the word "warranty" in its ordinary meaning and another uses it in its technical meaning. When Holt CJ in *Crosse* v *Gardner* (1689) Carth 90 (as glossed by Buller J in *Pasley* v *Freeman* (1789) 3 Term Rep 51, 57) and *Medina* v *Stoughton* (1700) 1 Salk 210 made his famous ruling that an affirmation at the time of a sale is a warranty, provided it appears on evidence to be so intended, he used the word "warranty" in its ordinary English meaning of a binding promise: and when Lord Haldane LC and Lord Moulton in 1913 in *Heilbut, Symons & Co* v *Buckleton* [1913] AC 30 adopted his ruling, they used it likewise in its ordinary meaning. These different uses of the word seem to have been the source of confusion in the present case. The judge did not ask himself, "Was the representation (that it was a 1948 Morris) intended to be a warranty?" He asked himself "Was it fundamental to the contract?" He answered it by saying that it was fundamental; and therefore it was a condition and not a warranty. By concentrating on whether it was fundamental, he seems to me to have missed the crucial point in the case, which is whether it was a term of the contract at all. The crucial question is: was it a binding promise or only an innocent misrepresentation? The technical distinction between a "condition" and a "warranty" is quite immaterial in this case, because it is far too late for the buyer to reject the car. He can, at best, only claim damages. The material distinction here is between a statement which is a term of the contract and a statement which is only an innocent misrepresentation. This distinction is best expressed by the ruling of Lord Holt: Was it intended as a warranty or not? Using the word "warranty" there in its ordinary English meaning: because it gives the exact shade of meaning that is required. It is something to which a man must be taken to bind himself.

In applying Lord Holt's test, however, some misunderstanding has arisen by the use of the word "intended". It is sometimes supposed that the tribunal must look into the minds of the parties to see what they themselves intended. That is a mistake. Lord Moulton made it quite clear that "the intention of the parties can only be deduced from the totality of the evidence". The question whether a warranty was intended depends on the conduct of the parties, on their words and behaviour, rather than on their thoughts. If an intelligent bystander would reasonably infer that a warranty was intended, that will suffice. And this, when the facts are not in dispute, is a question of law. That is shown by *Heilbut, Symons & Co* v *Buckleton* itself, where the House of Lords upset the finding by a jury of a warranty.

It is instructive to take some recent instances to show how the courts have approached this question. When the seller states a fact which is or should be within his own knowledge and of which the buyer is ignorant, intending that the buyer should act on it and he does so, it is easy to infer a warranty: see *Couchman* v *Hill* [1947] 1 All ER 103, where the farmer stated that the heifer was served, and *Harling* v *Eddy* [1951] 2 All ER 212, where he stated that there was nothing wrong with her. So also, if he makes a promise about something which is or should be within his own control: see *Birch* v *Paramount Estates Ltd* (1958) 167 EG 396, decided on 2 October 1956, in this court, where the seller stated that the house would be as good as the show house. But if the seller, when he states a fact, makes it clear that he has no knowledge of his own, but has got his information elsewhere and is merely passing it on, it is not so easy to imply a warranty. Such a case was

Routledge v *McKay* [1954] 1 WLR 615, 636, where the seller "stated that it was a 1942 model and pointed to the corroboration found in the book", and it was held that there was no warranty.

Turning now to the present case; much depends on the precise words that were used. If the seller says "I believe it is a 1948 Morris, here is the registration book to prove it", there is clearly no warranty. It is a statement of belief, not a contractual promise. But if the seller says "I guarantee that is a 1948 Morris. This is borne out by the registration book, but you need not rely solely on that. I give you my own guarantee that it is ", there is clearly a warranty. The seller is making himself contractually responsible, even though the registration book is wrong.

In this case, much reliance was placed by the judge on the fact that the buyer looked up *Glass's Guide* and paid £290 on the footing that it was a 1948 model: but that fact seems to me to be neutral. Both sides believed the car to have been made in 1948 and, in that belief, the buyer paid £290. That belief can be just as firmly based on the buyer's own inspection of the log book as on a contractual warranty by the seller.

Once that fact is put on one side, I ask myself: What is the proper inference from the known facts? It must have been obvious to both that the seller had himself no personal knowledge of the year when the car was made. He only became owner after a great number of changes. He must have been relying on the registration book. It is unlikely that such a person would warrant the year of manufacture. The most he could do would be to state his belief and then produce the registration book in verification of it. In these circumstances, the intelligent bystander would, I suggest, say that the seller did not intend to bind himself so as to warrant that it was a 1948 model. If the seller was asked to pledge himself to it, he would at once have said "I cannot do that. I have only the log book to go by, the same as you."

The judge seems to have thought that there was a difference between written contracts and oral contracts. He thought that the reason why the buyer failed in *Heilbut, Symons & Co* v *Buckleton* and *Routledge* v *McKay* was because the sales were afterwards recorded in writing and the written contracts contained no reference to the representation. I agree that that was an important factor in those cases. If an oral representation is afterwards recorded in writing, it is good evidence that it was intended as a warranty. If it is not put into writing, it is evidence against a warranty being intended. But it is by no means decisive. There have been many cases where the courts have found an oral warranty collateral to a written contract, such as *Birch* v *Paramount Estates* (1956) 16 EG 396. But when the purchase is not recorded in writing at all, it must not be supposed that every representation made in the course of the dealing is to be treated as a warranty. The question then is still: Was it intended as a warranty? In the leading case of *Chandelor* v *Lopus* (1603) Cro Jac 4 a man, by word of mouth, sold a precious stone for £100 affirming it to be a bezar stone, whereas it was not. The declaration averred that the seller affirmed it to be a bezar stone, but did not aver that he warranted it to be so. The declaration was held to be ill because "the bare affirmation that it was a bezar stone, without warranting it to be so, is no cause of action". That has been the law from that day to this and it was emphatically reaffirmed by the House of Lords in *Heilbut, Symons & Co* v *Buckleton*.

One final word: It seems to me clear that the motor dealers who bought the car relied on the year stated in the log book. If they had wished to make sure of it, they could have checked it then and there by taking the engine number and chassis number and writing to the makers. They did not do so at the time, but only eight months later. They are experts and, not having made that check at the time, I do not think they should now be allowed to recover against the innocent seller, who produced to them all the evidence he had, namely the registration book. I agree that it is hard on the dealers to have paid more than the car is worth: but it would be equally hard on the seller to make him pay the difference. He would never have

bought the Hillman at all unless he had got the allowance of £290 from the Morris. The best course in all these cases would be to "shunt" the difference down the train of innocent sellers until one reaches the rogue who perpetrated the fraud: but he can rarely be traced or, if he can, he rarely has the money to pay the damages. So one is left to decide between a number of innocent people who is to bear the loss. That can only be done by applying the law about representations and warranties as we know it: and that is what I have tried to do. If the rogue can be traced, he can be sued by whomsoever has suffered the loss: but if he cannot be traced, the loss must lie where it falls. It should not be inflicted on innocent sellers, who sold the car many months, perhaps many years, before and have forgotten all about it and have conducted their affairs on the basis that the transaction was concluded. Such a seller would not be able to recollect, after all this length of time, the exact words he used, such as whether he said "I believe it is a 1948 model", or "I warrant it is a 1948 model". The right course is to let the buyer set aside the transaction if he finds out the mistake quickly and comes promptly, before other interests have irretrievably intervened; otherwise the loss must lie where it falls: and that is, I think, the course prescribed by law. I would allow this appeal accordingly.'

Comment

Applied: *Routledge* v *McKay* [1954] 1 WLR 615. Distinguished in *Bentley (Dick) Productions Ltd* v *Harold Smith (Motors) Ltd* [1965] 1 WLR 623.

Prenn v *Simmonds* [1971] 1 WLR 1381 House of Lords (Lords Reid, Donovan, Wilberforce, Pearson and Diplock)

• *Contract – construction*

Facts

Following detailed negotiations, agreement was reached for the sale and purchase of shares if 'profits' reached a certain level. Did this refer to profits of the group or just of the holding company?

Held

In the light of the aim of the agreement and commercial good sense, the reference to 'profits' was to the consolidated profits of the group.

Lord Wilberforce:

'There were prolonged negotiations between solicitors, with exchanges of draft clauses, ultimately emerging in … the agreement. The reason for not admitting evidence of these exchanges is not a technical one or even mainly one of convenience … It is simply that such evidence is unhelpful. By the nature of things, where negotiations are difficult, the parties' positions, with each passing letter, are changing and until the final agreement, although converging, still divergent. It is only the final document which records a consensus. If the previous documents use different expressions, how does construction of those expressions, itself a doubtful process, help on the construction of the contractual words? If the same expressions are used, nothing is gained by looking back; indeed, something may be lost since the relevant surrounding circumstances may be different. And at this stage there is no consensus of the parties to appeal to. It may be said that previous documents may be looked at to explain the aims of the parties. In a limited sense this is true; the commercial, or business object, of the transaction, objectively ascertained, may be a surrounding fact … And if it can be shown that one interpretation completely frustrates that object, to the extent of rendering the contract futile, that may be a strong argument for an alternative interpretation, if that can reasonably be found. But beyond that it may be difficult to go; it may be a matter of degree, or of judgment, how far one interpretation, or another, gives effect to a common intention; the parties, indeed, may be pursuing that intention with differing emphasis, and hoping to achieve it to an extent which may differ, and in different ways. The words used may, and often do, represent a formula which means different things to each side, yet may be accepted because that is the only way to get "agreement" and in the hope that disputes will not arise. The only course then can be to try to ascertain the "natural" meaning. Far more, and indeed totally, dangerous it is to admit evidence of one party's objective – even if this is known to the other party. However strongly pursued this may be, the other party may only be willing to give it partial recognition, and in a world of give and take, men often have to be satisfied with less than they want. So, again, it would be a matter of speculation how far the common intention was that the particular objective should be realised … In my opinion, then, evidence of negotiations, or of the parties' intentions … ought not to be received, and evidence should be restricted to evidence of the factual background known to the parties at or before the date of the contract, including evidence of the "genesis" and objectively the "aim" of the transaction.'

Comment

See also *Investors Compensation Scheme Ltd* v *West Bromwich Building Society* [1998] 1 All ER 98.

Reardon Smith Line Ltd v *Yngvar Hansen-Tangen* [1976] 1 WLR 989 House of Lords (Viscount Dilhorne, Lords Wilberforce, Simon of Glaisdale, Kilbrandon and Russell of Killowen)

• *Charter – words of identification or contractual description?*

Facts

In order to perform a charter, a steamship company nominated a vessel 'to be built by Osaka Shipbuilding Co Ltd and known as Hull No 354 until named'. Osaka was unable to build the ship in its own yard and so subcontracted the work to Oshima, a newly created company in which it held 50 per cent of the shares. Osaka provided a large part of Oshima's work force and managerial staff. In Osaka's books the ship was numbered 354; in Oshima's 004. Although the vessel when built complied fully with the physical specifications in the charter and was fit for the contemplated service, delivery was refused.

Held

The charterers were not entitled to refuse delivery.

Lord Wilberforce:

'The appellants sought, necessarily, to give to the ... provision in the ... charter contractual effect. They argued that these words formed part of the "description" of the future goods contracted to be provided, that, by analogy with contracts for the sale of goods, any departure from the description entitled the other party to reject, that there were departures in that the vessel was not built by Osaka and was not Hull No 354. I shall attempt to deal with each of these contentions.

In the first place, I am not prepared to accept that authorities as to "description" in sale of goods cases are to be extended, or applied, to such a contract as we have here. Some of these cases either in themselves (*Re Moore & Co and Landauer & Co* [1921] 2 KB 519) or as they have been interpreted (eg *Behn* v *Burness* (1863) 3 B & S 571) I find to be excessively technical and due for fresh examination in this House. Even if a strict and technical view must be taken as regards the description of unascertained future goods (eg commodities) as to which each detail of the description must be assumed to be vital, it may be, and in my opinion is, right to treat other contracts of sale of goods in a similar manner to other contracts generally, so as to ask whether a particular item in a description constitutes a substantial ingredient of the "identity" of the thing sold, and only if it does to treat it as a condition ... It is one thing to say of given words that their purpose is to state

(identify) an essential part of the description of the goods. It is another to say that they provide one party with a specific indication (identification) of the goods so that he can find them and if he wishes subdispose of them. The appellants wish to say of words which "identify" the goods in the second sense, that they describe them in the first. I have already given reasons why I can only read the words in the second sense. The difference is vital. If the words are read in the first sense, then, unless I am right in the legal argument above, each element in them has to be given contractual force. The vessel must, as a matter of contract, and as an essential term, be built by Osaka and must bear their yard number 354; if not, the description is not complied with and the vessel tendered is not that contracted for. If in the second sense, the only question is whether the words provide a means of identifying the vessel. If they fairly do this, they have fulfilled their function ...

So the question becomes simply whether, as a matter of fact, it can fairly be said that – as a means of identification – the vessel was ... "built by Osaka Shipping Co Ltd and known as Hull No 354, until named". To answer this, regard may be had to the actual arrangements for building the vessel and numbering it before named. My Lords, I have no doubt ... that an affirmative answer must be given. I shall not set out the evidence which clearly makes this good. The fact is that the vessel always was Osaka Hull No 354 – though also Oshima No 004 – and equally it can fairly be said to have been "built" by Osaka as the company which planned, organised and directed the building and contractually engaged ... to build it, though also it could be said to have been built by Oshima. For the purpose of the identificatory clause, the words used are quite sufficient to cover the facts. No other vessel could be referred to: the reference fits the vessel in question.

There are other facts not to be overlooked. (1) So long as the charterers could identify the nominated vessel they had not the slightest interest in whatever contracting or subcontracting arrangements were made in the course of the building … (2) In making the arrangements they did for building the vessel, Osaka acted in a perfectly straight-forward and open manner. They cannot be said to be substituting one vessel for another; they have not provided any ground on which the charterers can claim that their bargain has not been fulfilled. The contracts all down the chain were closely and appro-priately knitted into what Osaka did. (3) If the market had risen instead of falling, it would have been quite impossible for Osaka … to refuse to tender the vessel in accor-dance with the charters on the ground that it did not correspond with that contracted for. No more on a falling market is there, in my opinion, any ground on which the char-terers can reject the vessel. In the end I find this a simple and clear case.'

Comment
Applied: *Charrington & Co Ltd* v *Wooder* [1914] AC 21. See also *Staffordshire Area Health Authority* v *South Staffordshire Waterworks Co* [1978] 1 WLR 1387 and *Investors Compensation Scheme Ltd* v *West Bromwich Building Society* [1998] 1 All ER 98.

St Albans City and District Council v *International Computers Ltd*
[1996] 4 All ER 481

See Chapter 14.

5 Misrepresentation

Bissett v *Wilkinson* [1927] AC 177
Privy Council (Viscount Dunedin,
Lords Atkinson, Phillimore, Carson
and Merrivale)

• *Expression of opinion – number of
sheep land would carry*

Facts

A vendor admitted that he had told prospective purchasers of part of his land in New Zealand that the land in question, in his view, 'would carry 2,000 sheep' and that the purchasers, who were not experienced farmers, had bought the land in this belief. The purchasers contended that the land did not have this capacity and, inter alia, they claimed rescission of the agreement on grounds of misrepresentation by the vendor is a material particular.

Held

Their claim would fail.

Lord Merrivale:

'In an action for rescission, as in an action for specific performance of an executory contract, when misrepresentation is the alleged ground of relief of the party who repudiates the contract, it is, of course, essential to ascertain whether that which is relied on is a representation of a specific fact, or a statement of opinion, since an erroneous opinon stated by the party affirming the contract, though it may have been relied on and have induced the contract on the part of the party who seeks rescission, gives no title to relief unless fraud is established.

The application of this rule, however, is not always easy, as is illustrated in a good many reported cases, as well as in this. A representation of fact may be inherent in a statement of opinion and, at any rate, the existence of the opinion in the person stating it is a question of fact. In *Re Metropolitan Coal Consumers' Association, Karberg's Case* [1892] 3 Ch at p11, Lindley LJ in course of testing a representation which might have been, as it was said to be by interested parties, one of opinion or belief, used this inquiry: "Was the statement of expectation a statement of things not really expected?" The Court of Appeal applied this test and rescinded the contract which was in question. In *Smith* v *Land and House Property Corporation* (1884) 28 Ch D 7 there came in question a vendor's description of the tenant of the property sold as "a most desirable tenant" – a statement of his opinion, as was argued on his behalf in an action to enforce the contract of sale. This description was held by the Court of Appeal to be a misrepresentation of fact, which, without proof of fraud, disentitled the vendor to specific performance of the contract of purchase. ... The kind of distinction which is in question is illustrated again in a well-known case, *Smith* v *Chadwick* (1882) 20 Ch D 27. There the words under consideration involved the inquiry in relation to the sale of an industrial concern whether a statement of "the present value of the turnover or output" was of necessity a statement of fact that the produce of the works was of the amount mentioned, or might be and was a statement that the productive power of the works was estimated at so much. The words were held to be capable of the second of these meanings. The decisive inquiries came to be, what meaning was actually conveyed to the party complaining; was he deceived, and, as the action was based on a charge of fraud, was the statement in question made fraudulently?

In the present case, as in those cited, the

56

material facts of the transaction, the knowledge of the parties respectively, and their relative positions, the words of representation used, and the actual condition of the subject-matter spoken of, are relevant to the two inquiries necessary to be made. What was the meaning of the representation? Was it true? ...

As was said by Sim J [the trial judge]:

"In ordinary circumstances, any statement made by an owner who has been occupying his own farm as to its carrying capacity would be regarded as a statement of fact ... This, however, is not such a case. The purchasers knew all about Hogan's block and knew also what sheep the farm was carrying when they inspected it. In these circumstances ... the purchasers were not justified in regarding anything said by the vendor as to the carrying capacity as being anything more than an expression of his opinion on the subject."

In this view of the matter their Lordships concur.

Whether the vendor honestly and in fact held the opinion which he stated remained to be considered. This involved examination of the history and condition of the property. If a reasonable man with the vendor's knowledge could not have come to the conclusion he stated, the description of that conclusion as an opinion would not necessarily protect him against rescission for misrepresentation, but what was actually the capacity in competent hands of the land the purchasers purchased had never been, and never was, practically ascertained ...

It is of dominant importance that Sim J negatived the purchasers' charge of fraud.

After attending to the close and very careful examination of the evidence which was made by learned counsel for each of the parties, their Lordships entirely concur in the view which was expressed by the learned judge who heard the case. The purchasers failed to prove that the farm, if properly managed, was not capable of carrying 2,000 sheep.'

Comment

Distinguished in *Esso Petroleum Co Ltd* v *Mardon* [1976] 2 All ER 5 (pre-contractual forecast, negligently made, as to garage's throughput of petrol held to be a breach of warranty). See also *Brown* v *Raphael* [1958] Ch 636.

Brown v *Raphael* [1958] Ch 636
Court of Appeal (Lord Evershed MR, Romer and Ormerod LJJ)

* *Implied representation – rescission*

Facts

Auction particulars of the reversion in a trust fund stated that the annuitant was 'believed to have no aggregable estate': this belief was held honestly but mistakenly and the eventual purchaser sought, inter alia, rescission of the contract. The name of the vendor's solicitors appeared at the foot of the auction particulars.

Held

The purchaser was entitled to succeed as it was impliedly represented that there were reasonable grounds belief as to a material fact.

Lord Evershed MR:

'In order that the plaintiff may succeed ... it is necessary that three things should be established: (i) he must show that the language relied on imports or contains a representation of some material fact; (ii) he must show that the representation is untrue; and (iii) he must show that, in entering into the contract, he was induced so to do in reliance on it. The learned judge concluded all those three matters in the plaintiff's favour ... in my judgment there is no ground shown for this court to disturb the learned judge's conclusions. ...

The first point is, to my mind, the most significant and perhaps the most difficult: Is there here a representation of a material fact? ...

I am ... entirely of the same opinion as was the learned judge, namely, that this is a case in which there was not merely the representation that the defendant entertained the belief, but also, inescapably, the further representation that he, being competently advised, had reasonable grounds for supporting that belief. The learned judge put the matter thus in his judgment. He first observed that, if the purchaser was not entitled to suppose that the vendor was in possession of facts which enabled him to express an opinion which was based on reasonable grounds, that would, he thought (and I agree with him) make business dealings, certainly in this class of business, almost impossible. He said:

> "It must be remembered that in this case the purchaser going to the auction had no means whatever of finding out anything about the annuitant's means. When the contract was signed, the purchaser did not even know the name of the annuitant. On the other hand, the vendor must be expected to be in possession of facts unavailable to the purchaser and the purchaser is entitled to suppose that he is in possession of facts which enable him to express an opinion which is based on reasonable grounds. As I have already said, if that is not so, business relationships become quite impossible. It may be different where the facts on which the opinion is expressed are equally available to both parties. Then the opinion may be no more than an expression of opinion, but, where the opinion is expressed on facts assumed to be available to the vendor, which certainly are not available to the purchaser, and that opinion is expressed to induce the contract, in my judgment the purchaser is entitled to expect that the opinion is expressed on reasonable grounds."

The learned judge, using that general language in relation to this case, was reflecting the language of Bowen LJ in *Smith* v *Land and House Property Corporation* (1884) 28 Ch D 7. I, therefore, am satisfied that the relevant language in the present case involved the representation that there were reasonable grounds for the belief, and certainly that was a representation of a most material fact.'

Comment
See also *Bissett* v *Wilkinson* [1927] AC 177.

Curtis v *Chemical Cleaning & Dyeing Co Ltd* [1951] 1 KB 805

See Chapter 6.

East v *Maurer* [1991] 2 All ER 733 Court of Appeal (Mustill, Butler-Sloss and Beldam LJJ)

• *Fraudulent misrepresentation – assessment of damages*

Facts
In 1979 the defendant, who owned two successful hair salons, agreed to sell one of them (Exeter Road) to the plaintiffs. In part, the plaintiffs were induced to purchase by a representation from the defendant to the effect that he hoped in future to work abroad and did not intend to work in the other salon, save in emergencies. In fact the defendant, who had built up a considerable reputation in the area, continued to work full-time at the other salon. The result of this was that the plaintiffs saw a steady fall-off in business and never made a profit. They were finally forced to sell it in 1989, for considerably less than they paid. The plaintiffs sued for breach of contract and fraudulent misrepresentation. The court at first instance found that the defendant's representations were false. The defendant appealed as to the award of damages for loss of profits.

Held
The appeal would be allowed.

Beldam LJ:

> 'The learned judge found that the plaintiffs had behaved reasonably throughout; that they could not have sold the business before they actually did. He awarded them damages totalling £33,328; interest on the sums awarded brought the total award to £55,205.
> His award was made up in this way.

Firstly, he took the capital expenditure by taking the cost price of the business, £20,000, and deducting from it the amount realised on the sale, thus arriving at the figure of £12,500. Secondly, he awarded the plaintiffs the fees and expenses incurred by them in buying and selling the business, and in carrying out improvements in an attempt to make it profitable. The figures awarded there amounted in total to £2,390. Next, he awarded trading losses incurred during the three and a quarter years during which the plaintiffs attempted to run the business. Those amounted to £2,438.

The next head of damages he awarded has led the defendants to appeal to this court against the amount of damages. In addition to the sums already mentioned, he awarded the plaintiffs loss of profits during the three and a quarter year period arriving at a figure of £15,000. Finally he awarded the figure of £1,000 as general damages for disappointment and inconvenience to the plaintiffs in their attempt to establish this business. It is against the award of £15,000 for loss of profit that the defendants now appeal. ...

That the measure of damages for the tort of deceit and for breach of contract are different no longer needs support from authority. Damages for deceit are not awarded on the basis that the plaintiff is to be put in as good a position as if the statement had been true; they are to be assessed on a basis which would compensate the plaintiff for all the loss he has suffered, so far as money can do it.

This was confirmed in *Doyle* v *Olby (Ironmongers) Ltd* [1969] 2 All ER 119, to which both the learned judge and this court were referred, in which the facts were similar to those of the present case.

In the course of his judgment Lord Denning MR said ([1969] 2 All ER 119 at 121–122):

"The second question is what is the proper measure of damages for fraud, as distinct from damages for breach of contract. It was discussed during the argument in *Hadley* v *Baxendale* (1854) 9 Exch 341, and finds a place in the notes to Smith's Leading Cases (13th edn, 1929 p563), where it is suggested there is no difference. But in *McConnel* v *Wright* [1903] 1 Ch 546 at 554 Sir Richard Henn Collins MR pointed out the difference. It was an action for fraudulent statements in a prospectus whereby a man was induced to take up shares. He said of the action for fraud: 'It is not an action for breach of contract, and, therefore, no damages in respect of prospective gains which the person contracting was entitled by his contract to expect come in, but it is an action of tort – it is an action for a wrong done whereby the plaintiff was tricked out of certain money in his pocket; and therefore, prima facie, the highest limit of his damages is the whole extent of his loss, and that loss is measured by the money which was in his pocket and is now in the pocket of the company.' But that statement was the subject of comment by Lord Atkin in *Clarke* v *Urquhart* [1930] AC 28 at 67–68. He said 'I find it difficult to suppose that there is any difference in the measure of damages in an action of deceit depending upon the nature of the transaction into which the plaintiff is fraudulently induced to enter. Whether he buys shares or buys sugar, whether he subscribes for shares, or agrees to enter into a partnership, or in any other way alters his position to his detriment, in principle, the measure of damages should be the same, and whether estimated by a jury or judge. I should have thought it would be based on the actual damage directly flowing from the fraudulent inducement. The formula in *McConnel* v *Wright* [1903] 1 Ch 546 may be correct or it may be expressed in too rigid terms.' I think that Sir Richard Henn Collins MR did express himself in too rigid terms. He seems to have overlooked consequential damages. On principle the distinction seems to be this: in contract, the defendant has made a promise and broken it. The object of damages is to put the plaintiff in as good a position, as far as money can do it, as if the promise had been performed. In fraud, the defendant has been guilty of a deliberate wrong by inducing the plaintiff to act to his detriment. The object of damages is to compensate the plaintiff for all the loss he has suffered, so far, again, as money can do it. In contract, the damages are limited to what may reasonably be supposed to have been in the contemplation of the parties. In fraud, they are not so limited. The defendant is bound to make reparation for all the actual damage directly flowing from the fraudulent inducement. The person who has been defrauded is entitled to say: 'I would not have entered into this bargain at all but for your representation. Owing to your fraud, I have not only lost all the money I paid you, but, what is more, I have been put to a large amount of extra expense as well and suffered this or that extra damages.' All such damages can be recovered: and it does not lie in the mouth of the fraudulent person to say that they could not reasonably have been foreseen. For instance, in this very case the plaintiff has not only lost the money which he paid for the business, which he would never have done if there had been no fraud: he put all that money in and lost it; but also he has been put to expense and loss in trying to run a business which has turned out to be a disaster for him. He is entitled to damages for all his loss, subject, of course, to giving credit for any benefit that he has received. There is nothing to be taken off in mitigation: for there is nothing more that he could have done to reduce his loss. He did all that he could reasonably be expected to do."

In the present case it seems to me that the difference can be put in this way. The first defendant did not warrant to the plaintiffs that all the customers with whom he had a professional rapport would remain customers of the salon at Exeter Road. He represented that he would be be continuing to practise as a stylist in the immediate area.

The observations of Lord Denning MR, to which I have referred, are supported by an earlier judgment of Dixon J in *Toteff* v *Antonas* (1952) 87 CLR 647, a decision of the High Court of Australia. ...

[Counsel for the defendants] has pointed out that both in *Doyle* v *Olby* and in *Toteff* v *Antonas* none of the judgments referred to loss of profit as a recoverable head of damage; it may well be that the facts of each of those cases and the period involved before the claims were made may not have made loss of profit a considerable head of damage. But, as to the statements of principle to which I have referred, it seems to me clear that there is no basis upon which one could say that loss of profits incurred whilst waiting for an opportunity to realise to its best advantage a business which has been purchased are irrecoverable. It is conceded that losses made in the course of running the business of a company are recoverable. If in fact the plaintiffs lost the profit which they could reasonably have expected from running a business in the area of a kind similar to the business in this case I can see no reason why those do not fall within the words of Lord Atkin in *Clark* v *Urquhart, Stracey* v *Urquhart* [1930] AC 28 at 68: "... actual damage directly flowing from the fraudulent inducement."

So I consider that on the facts found by the learned judge in the present case, the plaintiffs did establish that they had suffered a loss due to the defendants' misrepresentation which arose from their inability to earn the profits in the business which they hoped to buy in the Bournemouth area.

I would therefore reject the submission ... that loss of profits is not a recoverable head of damage in cases of this kind.

However, I am not satisfied that in arriving at the figure of £15,000 the learned judge approached the quantification of those damages on the correct basis. It seems to me that he was inclined to base his award on an assessment of the profits which the business actually bought by the plaintiffs might have made if the statement made by the first defendant had amounted to a warranty that customers would continue to patronise the salon in Exeter Road; further, that he left out of account a number of significant factors. What he did was to found his award on an evaluation which he made of the profits of the business at Exeter Road made by the first defendant in the year preceding the purchase of the business by the plaintiffs. Basing himself on figures which had been given to him by an accountant, and making an allowance for inflation he arrived at a figure for the profits which might have been made if the first defendant had continued to run the business at Exeter Road during the three and a quarter years. He then made an allowance only for the fact that the second plaintiff's experience in hair styling and hairdressing was not as extensive or as cosmopolitan as that of the first defendant. Thus he based his award on an assessment of what the profits would have been, less a deduction of 25 per cent for the second plaintiff's lack of experience.

It seems to be that he should have begun by considering the kind of profit which the second plaintiff might have made if the representation which induced her to buy the business at Exeter Road had not been made, and that involved considering the kind of profits which *she* might have expected to make in another hairdressing business bought for a similar sum. [Counsel for the plaintiffs] has argued that on the evidence of ... an experienced accountant, the learned judge could have arrived at the same or an equivalent figure on that basis. I do not agree. The learned judge left out of account the fact that the second plaintiff was moving into an entirely different area and one in which she was, comparatively speaking, a stranger, secondly, that she was going to deal with a different clientele and, thirdly, that there were almost certainly in that area of Bournemouth other smart hairdressing salons which represented competition and which, in any event, if the first defendant had, as he had represented, gone to open a salon on the continent, could have attracted the custom of his former clients.

The learned judge ... had two clear starting points: first, that any person investing £20,000 in a business would expect a greater return that if the sum was safely in the bank or in a building society earning interest, and a reasonable figure for that at the rates then prevailing would have been at least £6,000; secondly, that the salary of a hairdresser's assistant in the usual kind of establishment was at this time £40 per week and that the assistant could expect tips in addition. That

would produce a figure of over £2,000, but the proprietor of a salon would clearly expect to earn more, having risked his money in the business. It seems to me that those are valid points from which to start to consider what would be a reasonable sum to award for loss of profits of a business of this kind. As was pointed out by Winn LJ in *Doyle* v *Olby*, this is not a question which can be considered on a mathematical basis. It has to be considered essentially in the round, making what he described as a 'jury assessment' (see [1969] 2 All ER 119 at 124).

Taking all the factors into account, I think that the learned judge's figure was too high; for my part I would have awarded a figure of £10,000 for that head of damage, and to this extent I would allow the appeal.'

Comment

The plaintiffs were husband and wife; the wife, the second plaintiff, ran the business. The second defendant was Maurer's company.

Compare *Royscot Trust Ltd* v *Rogerson* [1991] 3 All ER 294 (damages for innocent misrepresentation).

Economides v *Commercial Union Assurance Co plc* [1997] 3 All ER 636 Court of Appeal (Simon Brown, Peter Gibson LJJ and Sir Iain Glidewell)

• *Insurance policy – valuations – duty of disclosure*

Facts

The appellant covered the contents of his flat for £12,000 by way of a policy issued by the respondent. Two years later his parents came to live with him, bringing with them some jewellery and silverware. His father, a former police divisional commander in Cyprus, suggested that the cover should be increased by £3,000–£4,000 to take account of these items: the plaintiff took this advice. Following the further renewal of the policy and a burglary at the flat, it appeared that the value of the contents had been some £40,000. The respondent sought to avoid liability on grounds of misrepresentation and non-disclosure.

Held

On the facts of the case, liability could not be avoided on either of these grounds.

Simon Brown LJ:

> '*Misrepresentation* ...
>
> In my judgment, if insurers wish to place on their assured an obligation to carry out specific inquiries or otherwise take steps to provide objective justification for their valuations, they must spell out these requirements in the proposal form.
>
> I would hold, therefore, that the sole obligation on the appellant when he represented to the respondent on renewal that he believed the full contents value to be £16,000 was that of honesty. That obligation the judge apparently found him to have satisfied. Certainly, given that the appellant was at the time aged 21, given that the figure for the increase in cover was put forward by his father, and given that the father was a retired senior police officer, inevitably better able than the appellant himself to put a valuation on the additional contents, there would seem to me every reason to accept the appellant's honesty. ...
>
> *Non-disclosure* ...
>
> I have not the least doubt that the sole obligation on an assured in the position of this appellant is one of honesty. Honesty, of course, requires ... that the assured does not wilfully shut his eyes to the truth. But that, sometimes called Nelsonian blindness – the deliberate putting of the telescope to the blind eye – is equivalent to knowledge, a very different thing from imputing knowledge of a fact to someone who is in truth ignorant of it.
>
> The test, accordingly, for non-disclosure was, in my judgment, precisely the same as that for misrepresentation, that of honesty. And by the same token that the appellant was under no obligation to make further inquiries to establish reasonable grounds for

his belief in the accuracy of his valuations, so too he was not required to inquire further into the facts so as to discharge his obligation to disclose all material facts known to him. Indeed, the appellant's case on non-disclosure seems to be a fortiori to his case on misrepresentation. ... In short, the appellant's knowledge in the present case merely of the presence of jewellery and silverware in the flat, to my mind, gave rise to no duty of disclosure beyond that subsumed in an honest estimate of the required increase in cover under the policy.'

Comment

The decisions in *Smith* v *Land and House Property Corp* (1884) 28 Ch D 7 and *Brown* v *Raphael* [1958] 2 All ER 79 were distinguished on their facts. Simon Brown LJ noted that *PCW Syndicates* v *PCW Reinsurers* [1996] 1 All ER 774 had established that certain sections of the Marine Insurance Act 1906 apply equally to non-marine as to marine insurance.

Royscot Trust Ltd v *Rogerson* [1991] 3 All ER 294 Court of Appeal (Balcombe and Ralph Gibson LJJ)

- *Measure of damages – innocent misrepresentation*

Facts

A car dealer agreed to sell a second-hand car on hire purchase to a customer for a cash price of £7,600, of which the customer was to pay a deposit of £1,200. In order to satisfy the finance company's requirement that the deposit be at least 20 per cent of the purchase price, these amounts were stated as £8,000 and £1,600 respectively to the finance company. The finance company paid the dealer £6,400 but, after the customer had paid instalments amounting to £2,774.76, he dishonestly sold the car for £7,200 to a private purchaser who obtained a good title to it. The finance company obtained judgment against the customer and the dealer. In the Court of Appeal, the question was whether the measure of damages for innocent misrepresentation giving rise to an action under s2(1) of the Misrepresentation Act 1967 was the measure of damages in tort or the measure of damages in contract.

Held

It was the measure of damages in tort for fraudulent misrepresentation.

Balcombe LJ:

'Before us neither side sought to uphold the judge's assessment of damages. It assumed a hypothetical sale of the car with a deposit of £1,200 and a balance of £4,800 payable by the finance company to the dealer, and there was no evidence that such a sale would ever have taken place. ...

So I turn to the issue on this appeal which the dealer submits raises a pure point of law: where (a) a motor dealer innocently misrepresents to a finance company the amount of the sale price of, and the deposit paid by the intended purchase of, the car and (b) the finance company is thereby induced to enter into a hire-purchase agreement with the purchaser which it would not have done if it had known the true facts and (c) the purchaser thereafter dishonestly disposes of the car and defaults on the hire-purchase agreement, can the finance company recover all or part of its losses on the hire-purchase agreement from the motor dealer?

The finance company's cause of action against the dealer is based on s2(1) of the Misrepresentation Act 1967. ...

As a result of some dicta by Lord Denning MR in two cases in the Court of Appeal – *Gosling* v *Anderson* [1972] EGD 709 and *Jarvis* v *Swans Tours Ltd* [1973] 1 All ER 71 at 73 – and the decision at first instance in *Watts* v *Spence* [1975] 2 All ER 528, there was some doubt whether the measure of damages for an innocent misrepresentation giving rise to a cause of action under the 1967 Act was the tortious measure, so as to put the representee in the position in which he would have been if he had never entered into the contract, or the contractual

measure, so as to put the representee in the position in which he would have been if the misrepresentation had been true, and thus in some cases give rise to a claim for damages for loss of bargain. Lord Denning MR's remarks in *Gosling* v *Anderson* were concerned with an amendment to a pleading, while his remarks in *Jarvis* v *Swans Tours Ltd* were clearly obiter. *Watts* v *Spence* was disapproved by this court in *Sharneyford Supplies Ltd* v *Edge (Barrington Black Austin & Co (a firm), third party)* [1987] 1 All ER 588 at 598. However, there is now a number of decisions which make it clear that the tortious measure of damages is the true one. Most of the decisions are at first instance ... One at least, *Chesneau* v *Interhome Ltd* (1983) 134 NLJ 341 is a decision of this court. ... In view of the wording of the subsection it is difficult to see how the measure of damages under it could be other than the tortious measure and, despite the initial aberrations referred to above, that is now generally accepted. Indeed counsel before us did not seek to argue the contrary.

The first main issue before us was: accepting that the tortious measure is the right measure, is it the measure where the tort is that of fraudulent misrepresentation, or is it the measure where the tort is negligence at common law? The difference is that in cases of fraud a plaintiff is entitled to any loss which flowed from the defendant's fraud, even if the loss could not have been foreseen: see *Doyle* v *Olby (Ironmongers) Ltd* [1969] 2 All ER 119. In my judgment the wording of the subsection is clear: the person making the innocent misrepresentation shall be "so liable", ie liable to damages as if the representation had been made fraudulently. ... In my judgment, therefore, the finance company is entitled to recover from the dealer all the losses which it suffered as a result of its entering into the agreements with the dealer and the customer, even if those losses were unforeseeable, provided that they were not otherwise too remote.

If the question of foreseeability had been the only issue in this appeal, the judgment so far would have rendered it unnecessary to decide whether, in the circumstances of the present case, the wrongful sale of the car by the customer was reasonably foreseeable by the dealer. Since the judge did not expressly deal with this point in his judgment, it might have been preferable that we should not do so. Nevertheless there is a separate issue of whether the wrongful sale of the car was novus actus interveniens and thus broke the chain of causation, and the reasonable foreseeability of the event in question is a factor to be taken into account on that issue. Accordingly, it is necessary to deal with this matter. [Counsel] for the dealer submitted that, while a motor car dealer might be expected to foresee that a customer who buys a car on hire purchase may default in payment of his instalments, he cannot be expected to foresee that he will wrongfully dispose of the car. He went on to submit that, in the particular circumstances of this case, where the customer was apparently reputable, being a young married man in employment, it was even less likely that the dealer could have foreseen what might happen. There appears to have been no oral evidence directed to this particular point.

In my judgment this is to ignore both the reality of the transaction and general experience. While in legal theory the car remains the property of the finance company until the last hire-purchase instalment is paid, in practice the purchaser is placed in effective control of the car and treats it as his own. Further, there have been so many cases, both civil and criminal, where persons buying a car on hire purchase have wrongfully disposed of the car that we can take judicial notice that this is an all too frequent occurrence. Accordingly I am satisfied that, at the time when the finance company entered into the agreements with the dealer and the customer, it was reasonably foreseeable that the customer might wrongfully sell the car.

[Counsel for the dealer's] next submission was that the customer's wrongful sale of the car was novus actus interveniens. This issue was considered by the judge, although the brief note of his judgment on this point

is corrupt and is not agreed by counsel. It is implicit in his decision to award £1,600 damages to the finance company that the sale was not novus actus interveniens: otherwise on the figures in this case he would have been bound to find that the finance company had suffered no loss. However, the judgment contains no indication of how he came to that conclusion.

In the present case the customer was a free agent and his act in selling the car was unlawful. Nevertheless neither of these facts is conclusive in determining whether the sale of the car was a novus actus sufficient to break the chain of causation … However, if the dealer should reasonably have foreseen the possibility of the wrongful sale of the car, then that is a strong indication that the sale did not break the chain of causation. …

I doubt whether further citation of authority will be helpful: in this field authority is almost too plentiful. For the reasons I have already given, in my judgment the dealer should reasonably have foreseen the possibility that the customer might wrongfully sell the car. In my judgment, therefore, the sale was not novus actus interveniens and did not break the chain of causation.

[Counsel's] final submission was that the normal rule is that the plaintiff's loss must be assessed as at the date of his reliance upon the misrepresentation: since the finance company paid £6,400 to the dealer and in return acquired title to a car which was worth at least that sum, its loss assessed at that date was nil. This submission again falls into the error of treating the transaction according to its technicalities: that the finance company was interested in purchasing the car. That was not the reality: the finance company was interested in receiving the totality of the instalments from the customer. Once the transaction is looked at in this way the authorities on which [counsel] relied to support this submission, being all concerned with misrepresentations leading to the acquisition of chattels, can be seen to be of little assistance. But even in such a case the rule is not a hard and fast one – see the recent case of *Naughton* v *O'Callaghan*

[1990] 3 All ER 191. So I reject this submission also.

Accordingly, I would dismiss the dealer's appeal. I would allow the finance company's cross-appeal, set aside the judgment of 22 February 1990 and direct that in its place judgment be entered for the finance company against the dealer in the sum of £3,625.24 together with interest. The finance company accepts that it will have to give credit for any sums that it may receive from its judgment against the customer.'

Comment
In other words, the finance company's loss was the difference between the £6,400 which it paid to the dealer and the £2,744.76 paid by the customer.

Compare *East* v *Maurer* [1991] 2 All ER 733.

6   Exclusion Clauses

Ailsa Craig Fishing Co Ltd v *Malvern Fishing Co Ltd* [1983] 1 WLR 964 House of Lords (Lords Wilberforce, Elwyn-Jones, Salmon, Fraser of Tullybelton and Lowry)

- *Exception clause – loss of fishing boat – failure to perform contract*

Facts

The appellants' fishing boat sank in Aberdeen harbour and was a complete loss. The judge found that the loss had been caused by negligence and breach of contract on the part of the respondent security company (Securicor), but the respondents sought to rely on the clause that limited their liability to £1,000 or £10,000, according to the circumstances. The appellants contended, inter alia, that the clause could not apply because there had been a total failure by the respondents to perform the contract.

Held

This contention would be rejected.

Lord Fraser of Tullybelton:

'The question whether Securicor's liability has been limited falls to be answered by construing the terms of the contract in accordance with the ordinary principles applicable to contracts of this kind. The argument for limitation depends on certain special conditions attached to the contract prepared on behalf of Securicor and put forward in their interest. There is no doubt that such conditions must be construed strictly against the proferens, in this case Securicor, and that in order to be effective they must be "most clearly and unambiguously expressed": see *W & S Pollock & Co* v *Macrae* 1922 SC (HL) 192 at 199 per Lord Dunedin. *Pollock* v *Macrae* was a decision on an exclusion clause but in so far as it emphasised the need for clarity in clauses to be construed contra proferentem it is in my opinion relevant to the present case also. It has sometimes apparently been regarded as laying down, as a proposition of law, that a condition excluding liability can never have any application where there has been a total breach of contract, but I respectfully agree with the Lord President (Lord Emslie) who said in his opinion in the present case that that was a misunderstanding of *Pollock* v *Macrae*. ...

There are later authorities which lay down very strict principles to be applied when considering the effect of clauses of exclusion or of indemnity: see particularly the Privy Council case of *Canada Steamship Lines Ltd* v *R* [1952] AC 192 at 208, where Lord Morton, delivering the advice of the Board, summarised the principles in terms which have recently been applied by this House in *Smith* v *UMB Chrysler (Scotland) Ltd* 1978 SC (HL) 1. In my opinion these principles are not applicable in their full rigour when considering the effect of conditions merely limiting liability. Such conditions will of course be read contra proferentem and must be clearly expressed, but there is no reason why they should be judged by the specially exacting standards which are applied to exclusion and indemnity clauses. The reason for imposing such standards on these conditions is the inherent improbability that the other party to a contract including such a condition intended to release the proferens from a liability that would otherwise fall on him. But there is no such high degree of improbability that he would agree to a limitation of the liability of the proferens, especially when, as explained in condition 4(i) of the present contract, the potential losses that might be caused by the negligence of the proferens or its servants are so great in proportion to the sums that can reasonably be charged for the services contracted for. It is enough in the present case that the condition must be clear and unambiguous. ...

Having considered these particular criticisms of [the relevant] condition ... the question remains whether in its context it is sufficiently clear and unambiguous to receive effect in limiting the liability of Securicor for its own negligence or that of its employees. In my opinion it is. It applies to any liability "whether under the express or implied terms of this contract, or at common law, or in any other way". Liability at common law is undoubtedly wide enough to cover liability including the negligence of the proferens itself, so that even without relying on the final words "any other way", I am clearly of opinion that the negligence of Securicor is covered.'

Lord Wilberforce:

'Whether a condition limiting liability is effective or not is a question of construction of that condition in the context of the contract as a whole. If it is to exclude liability for negligence, it must be most clearly and unambiguously expressed, and, in such a contract as this, must be construed contra proferentem. I do not think that there is any doubt so far. But I venture to add one further qualification, or at least clarification: one must not strive to create ambiguities by strained construction, as I think the appellants have striven to do. The relevant words must be given, if possible, their natural, plain meaning. Clauses of limitation are not regarded by the courts with the same hostility as clauses of exclusion; this is because they must be related to other contractual terms, in particular to the risks to which the defending party may be exposed, the remuneration which he receives and possibly also the opportunity of the other party to insure.'

Comment
Applied in *Mitchell (George) (Chesterhall)*

Ltd v *Finney Lock Seeds Ltd* [1983] 3 WLR 163 where Lord Bridge of Harwich said:

'*Photo Production Ltd* v *Securicor Transport* [1980] AC 827 gave the final quietus to the doctrine that a "fundamental breach" of contract deprived the party in breach of the benefit of clauses in the contract excluding or limiting his liability. The *Ailsa Craig* case drew an important distinction between exclusion and limitation clauses.'

Chapelton v *Barry Urban District Council* [1940] 1 KB 532

See Chapter 1.

Curtis v *Chemical Cleaning & Dyeing Co Ltd* [1951] 1 KB 805
Court of Appeal (Somervell, Singleton and Denning LJJ)

• *Damage to wedding dress – exclusion clause – misrepresentation as to extent*

Facts
The plaintiff took a white satin wedding dress to the defendants to be cleaned. On being asked to sign a 'receipt' which stated, inter alia, that articles were 'accepted on condition that the company is not liable for any damage howsoever arising', she asked why her signature was required: she was told it was because the defendants did not accept liability for damages to beads and sequins. When the dress was returned to the plaintiff, there was a stain on it: her action for damages was successful and the defendants appealed.

Held
The appeal would be dismissed.

Denning LJ:

'If the party affected signs a written document, knowing it to be a contract which governs the relations between him and the other party, his signature is irrefragable evidence of his assent to the whole contract, including the exempting clauses, unless the signature is shown to be obtained by fraud or misrepresentation: see *L'Estrange* v *Graucob* [1934] 2 KB 394. What is a sufficient misrepresentation for this purpose? ...

In my opinion, any behaviour by words or conduct is sufficient to be a misrepresentation if it is such as to mislead the other party about the existence or extent of the exemption. If it conveys a false impression, that is enough. If the false impression is created knowingly, it is a fraudulent misrepresentation; if it is created unwittingly, it is an innocent misrepresentation ... by failing to draw attention to the width of the exemption clause, the assistant created the false impression that the exemption related to the beads and sequins only, and that it did not extend to the material of which the dress was made. It was done perfectly innocently, but, nevertheless, a false impression was created ... it was a sufficient misrepresentation to disentitle the cleaners from relying on the exemption, except in regard to the beads and sequins ... In my opinion, when a condition, purporting to exempt a person from his common law liabilities, is obtained by an innocent misrepresentation, the party who has made that misrepresentation is disentitled to rely on the exemption. Whether one calls that a rule of law or one of equity does not matter in these days.'

Comment

Denning LJ also said:

'... if nothing was said by the assistant, [the receipt] might reasonably be understood to be, like a boot repairer's receipt, only a voucher for the customer to produce when collecting the goods, and not to contain conditions exempting the cleaners from their common law liability for negligence, in which case it would not protect the cleaners: see *Chapelton* v *Barry Urban District Council* [1940] 1 KB 532. I say this because I do not wish it to be supposed that the cleaners would have been better off if the assistant had simply handed over the document to the customer without asking her to sign it, or if the customer was not so inquir-

ing as the plaintiff, but was an unsuspecting person who signed whatever she was asked without question. In those circumstances the conduct of the cleaners might well be such that it conveyed the impression that the document contained no conditions, or, at any rate, no condition exempting them from their common law liability, in which case they could not rely on it.'

Harris v *Wyre Forest District Council* [1989] 2 WLR 790

See *Smith* v *Eric S Bush* (below).

McCutcheon v *David MacBrayne Ltd* [1964] 1 WLR 125 House of Lords (Lords Reid, Hodson, Guest, Devlin and Pearce)

• *Oral contract – previous transactions – notices excluding liabiliy*

Facts

At the appellant's request, his brother-in-law took his car to the respondents' office in Islay where he was quoted the freight for shipping to the mainland. Brother-in-law paid and was given a receipted invoice which he did not read. On the voyage, the ship sank, as a result of the respondents' negligent navigation, and the car was lost. The appellant claimed damages for negligence and the respondents relied on an exclusion clause exhibited in their office and on the ship: on the invoice was a statement, too, that goods were carried subject to the conditions specified on the respondents' notices. It was the respondents' usual practice to ask consignors to sign a risk note, but due to an oversight brother-in-law was not asked to sign one on this occasion. Both the appellant and brother-in-law had shipped goods through the respondents before: sometimes risk notes had been signed and, although the appellant knew that conditions of some kind existed, neither of them had ever read them. The respondents contended that, by reason of the previous dealings, the conditions were imported into the contract of carriage.

Held

This was not the case.

Lord Reid:

'The respondents contend that, by reason of the knowledge thus gained by the appellant and his agent in these previous transactions, the appellant is bound by their conditions. But this case differs essentially from the ticket cases. There, the carrier in making the contract hands over a document containing or referring to conditions which he intends to be part of the contract. So if the consignor or passenger, when accepting the document, knows or ought as a reasonable man to know that this is the carrier's intention, he can hardly deny that the conditions are part of the contract, or claim, in the absence of special circumstances, to be in a better position than he would be if he had read the document. But here, in making the contract neither party referred to, or indeed had in mind, any additional terms, and the contract was complete and full effective without any additional terms. If it could be said that when making the contract [brother-in-law] knew that the respondents always required a risk note to be signed and knew that the purser was simply forgetting to put it before him for signature, then it might be said that neither he nor his principal could take advantage of the error of the other party of which he was aware. But counsel frankly admitted that he could not put his case as high as that. The only other ground on which it would seem possible to import these conditions is that based on a course of dealing. If two parties have made a series of similar contracts each containing certain conditions, and then they make another without expressly referring to those conditions it may be that those conditions ought to be implied. If the officious bystander had asked them whether they had intended to leave out the conditions this time, both must, as honest men, have said "of course not". But again the facts here will not support that ground. According to [brother-in-law], there had been no consistent course of dealing; sometimes he was asked to sign and sometimes not. And, moreover, he did not know what the conditions were. This time he was offered an oral contract without any reference to conditions, and he accepted the offer in good faith.

The respondents also rely on the appellant's previous knowledge. I doubt whether it is possible to spell out a course of dealing in his case. In all but one of the previous cases he had been acting on behalf of his employer in sending a different kind of goods and he did not know that the respondents always sought to insist on excluding liability for their own negligence. So it cannot be said that, when he asked his agent to make a contract for him, he knew that this or, indeed, any other special term would be included in it. He left his agent a free hand to contract, and I see nothing to prevent him from taking advantage of the contract which his agent in fact made.

"The judicial task is not to discover the actual intentions of each party: it is to decide what each was reasonably entitled to conclude from the attitude of the other." [*Law of Contract* by William M Gloag].

In this case I do not think that either party was reasonably bound or entitled to conclude from the attitude of the other as known to him that these conditions were intended by the other party to be part of this contract. I would therefore allow the appeal ...'

Comment

Distinguished: *Parker* v *South Eastern Railway Co* (1877) 2 CPD 416. Applied in *Hollier* v *Rambler Motors (AMC) Ltd* [1972] 2 WLR 401 (insufficient previous dealing between parties for exemption clause to be included in present oral contract).

Parker v *South Eastern Railway Co*

(1877) 2 CPD 416 Court of Appeal
(Mellish, Baggallay and Bramwell
LJJ)

• *Deposit of bag in station cloakroom –
clause on back of ticket – effect*

Facts

The plaintiff deposited a bag in a cloakroom
of a railway station owned by the defendants.
He was given a ticket which stated on its face,
'See back'. On the back was a clause limiting
the defendants' liability to £10. The plaintiff's
bag, worth £24 10s, was lost.

Held

The plaintiff was bound by the clause, even
though he had not read it; the defendants had
done all that was reasonably necessary to
bring the clause to his attention.

Mellish LJ:

'The question then is, whether the plaintiff
was bound by the conditions contained in
the ticket. In an ordinary case, where an
action is brought on a written agreement
which is signed by the defendant, the agreement is proved by proving his signature and,
in the absence of fraud, it is wholly immaterial that he has not read the agreement and
does not know its contents. The parties may,
however, reduce their agreement into
writing, so that the writing constitutes the
sole evidence of the agreement, without
signing it; but in that case, there must be evidence independently of the agreement itself
to prove that the defendant has assented to
it. In that case also, if it is proved that the
defendant has assented to the writing constituting the agreement between the parties, it
is, in the absence of fraud, immaterial that
the defendant had not read the agreement
and did not know its contents. Now if, in the
course of making a contract, one party delivers to another a paper containing writing and
the party receiving the papers knows that
the papers contain conditions which the
party delivering it intends to constitute the

contract, I have no doubt that the party
receiving the paper does, by receiving and
keeping it, assent to the conditions contained in it, although he does not read them
and does not know what they are. I hold,
therefore, that the case of *Harris* v *Great
Western Railway* (1876) 1 QBD 515 was
rightly decided, because in that case, the
plaintiff admitted, on cross examination,
that she believed there were some conditions on the ticket. On the other hand, the
case of *Henderson* v *Stevenson* (1875) LR
2 Sc & Div 470, is a conclusive authority
that if the person receiving the ticket does
not know that there is any writing upon the
back of the ticket, he is not bound by a condition printed on the back. The facts in the
cases before us differ from those in both
Henderson v *Stevenson* (1875) LR 2 Sc &
Dir 470 and *Harris* v *Great Western
Railway* because, in both the cases which
have been argued before us, though the
plaintiffs admitted that they knew there was
writing on the back of the ticket, they swore
not only that they did not read it, but that
they did not know or believe that the writing
contained conditions, and we are to consider
whether, under those circumstances, we can
lay down, as a matter of law, either that the
plaintiff is bound or that he is not bound by
the conditions contained in the ticket, or
whether his being bound depends on some
question of fact to be determined by the jury
and, if so, whether, in the present case, the
right question was left to the jury.

Now I am of the opinion that we cannot
lay down, as a matter of law, either that the
plaintiff was bound or that he was not bound
by the conditions printed on the ticket, from
the mere fact that he knew there was writing
on the ticket but did not know that the
writing contained conditions. I think there
may be cases in which a paper containing
writing is delivered by one party to another
in the course of a business transaction,
where it would be quite reasonable that the
party receiving it should assume that the
writing contained in it no condition and
should put it in his pocket unread. For
instance, if a person driving through a turnpike gate received a ticket upon paying the

toll, he might reasonably assume that the object of the ticket was that by producing it, he might be free from paying toll at some other turnpike gate and might put it in his pocket unread. On the other hand, if a person who ships goods to be carried on a voyage by sea receives a bill of lading signed by the master, he would plainly be bound by it, although afterwards, in an action against the shipowners for the loss of the goods, he might swear that he had never read the bill of lading and that he did not know that it contained the terms of the contract of carriage and that the shipowner was protected by the exception contained in it. Now the reason why the person receiving the bill of lading would be bound, seems to me to be that in the great majority of cases, persons shipping goods do know that the bill of lading contains the terms of the contract of carriage; and the shipowner, or the master delivering the bill of lading, is entitled to assume that the person shipping goods has that knowledge. It is, however, quite possible to suppose that a person who is neither a man of business nor a lawyer might, on some particular occasion, ship goods without the least knowledge of what a bill of lading was, but in my opinion, such a person must bear the consequences of his own exceptional ignorance, it being plainly impossible that business could be carried on if every person who delivers a bill of lading had to stop to explain what a bill of lading was.

Now the question we have to consider is whether the railway company was entitled to assume that a person depositing luggage and receiving a ticket in such a way that he could see that some writing was printed on it, would understand that the writing contained the conditions of contract; this seems to me, to depend upon whether people in general would, in fact, and naturally, draw that inference. The railway company, as it seems to me, must be entitled to make some assumptions respecting the person who deposits luggage with them: I think they are entitled to assume that he can read and that he understands the English language and that he pays such attention to what he is

about as may be reasonably expected from a person in such a transaction as that of depositing luggage in a cloakroom. The railway company must, however, take mankind as they find them and if what they do is sufficient to inform people in general that the ticket contains conditions, I think that a particular plaintiff ought not to be in a better position than other persons on account of his exceptional ignorance or stupidity or carelessness. But if what the railway company do is not sufficient to convey to the minds of people in general that the ticket contains conditions, then they have received goods on deposit without obtaining the consent of the persons depositing them to the conditions limiting their liability. I am of the opinion, therefore, that the proper direction to leave to the jury in these cases is, that if the person receiving the ticket did not see or know that there was any writing on the ticket, he is not bound by the conditions; that if he knew there was writing and knew or believed that the writing contained conditions, then he is bound by the conditions; that if he knew there was writing on the ticket, but did not know or believe that the writing contained conditions, nevertheless he would be bound if the delivering of the ticket to him was in such a manner that he could see there was writing upon it was, in the opinion of the jury, reasonable notice that the writing contained conditions.

I have, lastly, to consider whether the direction of the learned judge was correct, namely, "Was the plaintiff, under the circumstances, under any obligation in the exercise of reasonable and proper caution, to read, or to make himself aware, of the condition?" I think that this direction was not strictly accurate and was calculated to mislead the jury. The plaintiff was certainly under no obligation to read the ticket, but was entitled to leave it unread if he pleased; and the question does not appear to me to direct the attention of the jury to the real question, namely whether the railway company did what was reasonably sufficient to give the plaintiff notice of the condition.

On the whole, I am of the opinion that there ought to be a new trial.'

Comment
Distinguished in *McCutcheon* v *David MacBrayne Ltd* [1964] 1 WLR 125. Applied in *Burnett* v *Westminster Bank Ltd* [1965] 3 All ER 81 (condition printed on cheque book cover did not bind customer) and *Interfoto Picture Library Ltd* v *Stiletto Visual Programmes Ltd* [1988] 1 All ER 348 (unreasonable and extortionate condition in delivery note had not been fairly and reasonably brought to customer's attention).

St Albans City and District Council v International Computers Ltd
[1996] 4 All ER 481

See Chapter 14.

Smith v Eric S Bush, Harris v Wyre Forest District Council [1989] 2 WLR 790 House of Lords (Lords Keith of Kinkel, Brandon of Oakbrook, Templeman, Griffiths and Jauncey of Tullichettle)

• *Surveyor's report – disclaimer of liability – Unfair Contract Terms Act 1977*

Facts
The cases were heard together: their facts were similar and they involved the same points of law. In *Smith* the plaintiff applied to the Abbey National Building Society to enable her to buy a terraced house in Norwich for £17,500. She paid an inspection fee and signed an application form which stated that a copy of the survey report and mortgage valuation obtained by the society would be given to her. The form also contained a disclaimer to the effect that neither the society nor its surveyor warranted that the report and valuation would be accurate and that the report and valuation would be supplied without any acceptance of responsibility. The society instructed the defendant surveyors: in due course the plaintiff received a copy of their report and it contained a disclaimer in similar terms. On the strength of the report, the plaintiff completed the purchase, but the defendants had failed to notice that chimney breasts had been removed and 18 months later the house flues collapsed, causing substantial damage. The plaintiff sued for negligence and the defendants, inter alia, relied on the disclaimer which the plaintiff admitted she had read.

Held
The plaintiff was entitled to succeed. The defendants had owed her a duty of care, they had been in breach of that duty and in view of the Unfair Contract Terms Act 1977, they could not rely on the disclaimer.

Lord Templeman:

'It was submitted ... that the valuation ... obtained by the Abbey National was essential to enable them to fulfil their statutory duty imposed by the Building Societies Act 1962. But in *Candler* v *Crane Christmas & Co* [1951] 1 All ER 426 the draft accounts were prepared for the company, which was compelled by statute to produce accounts.

In the present appeals ... the contractual duty of a valuer to value a house for the Abbey National did not prevent the valuer coming under a tortious duty to Mrs Smith, who was furnished with a report of the valuer and relied on the report.

In general, I am of the opinion that in the absence of a disclaimer of liability the valuer who values a house for the purpose of a mortgage, knowing that the mortgagee will rely and the mortgagor will probably rely on the valuation, knowing that the purchaser mortgagor has in effect paid for the valuation, is under a duty to exercise reasonable skill and care and that duty is owed to both parties to the mortgage for which the valuation is made. Indeed, in both the appeals now under consideration the existence of such a dual duty is tacitly accepted and acknowledged because notices excluding liability for breach of the duty owed to the purchaser were drafted by the mortgagee and imposed on the purchaser. In these circumstances it is necessary to consider the second question which arises in these appeals, namely whether the disclaimers of liability are notices which fall within the Unfair Contract Terms Act 1977 ...

Section 11(3) of the 1977 Act provides that, in considering whether it is fair and reasonable to allow reliance on a notice which excludes liability in tort, account must be taken of "all the circumstances obtaining when the liability arose or (but for the notice) would have arisen". Section 13(1) of the Act prevents the exclusion of any right or remedy and (to that extent) s2 also prevents the exclusion of liability "by reference to ... notices which exclude ... the relevant obligation or duty". ... In my opinion both these provisions support the view that the 1977 Act requires that all exclusion notices which would in common law provide a defence to an action for negligence must satisfy the requirement of reasonableness.

The answer to the second question involved in these appeals is that the disclaimer of liability made by ... the Abbey National on behalf of the appellant surveyors in *Smith's* case constitute notices which fall within the 1977 Act and must satisfy the requirement of reasonableness.

The third question is whether in relation to each exclusion clause it is, in the words of s11(3) of the 1977 Act:

> "fair and reasonable to allow reliance on it, having regard to all the circumstances obtaining when the liability arose or (but for the notice) would have arisen." ...

Counsel for the surveyors ... urged on behalf of his clients in this appeal, and on behalf of valuers generally, that it is fair and reasonable for a valuer to rely on an exclusion clause, particularly an exclusion clause which is set forth so plainly in building society literature. The principal reasons urged by counsel for the surveyors are as follows. (1) The exclusion clause is clear and understandable and reiterated and is forcefully drawn to the attention of the purchaser. (2) The purchaser's solicitors should reinforce the warning and should urge the purchaser to appreciate that he cannot rely on a mortgage valuation and should obtain and pay for his own survey. (3) If valuers cannot disclaim liability they will be faced by more claims from purchasers, some of which will be unmeritorious but difficult and expensive to resist. (4) A valuer will become more cautious, take more time and produce more gloomy reports, which will make house transactions more difficult. (5) If a duty of care cannot be disclaimed the cost of negligence insurance for valuers and therefore the cost of valuation fees to the public will be increased.

Counsel for the surveyors also submitted that there was no contract between a valuer and a purchaser and that, so far as the purchaser was concerned, the valuation was "gratuitous", and the valuer should not be forced to accept a liability he was unwilling to undertake. My Lords, all these submissions are, in my view, inconsistent with the ambit and thrust of the 1977 Act ...

It is open to Parliament to provide that members of all professions or members of one profession providing services in the normal course of the exercise of their profession for reward shall be entitled to exclude or limit their liability for failure to exercise reasonable skill and care. In the absence of any such provision valuers are not, in my opinion, entitled to rely on a general exclusion of the common law duty of care owed to purchasers of houses by valuers to exercise reasonable skill and care in valuing houses for mortgage purposes.'

Lord Griffiths:

'It must ... be remembered that this is a decision in respect of a dwelling house of modest value in which it is widely recognised by surveyors that purchasers are in fact relying on their care and skill. It will obviously be of general application in broadly similar circumstances. But I expressly reserve my position in respect of valuations of quite different types of property for mortgage purposes, such as industrial property, large blocks of flats or very expensive houses. In such cases it may well be that the general expectation of the behaviour of the purchaser is quite different. With very large sums of money at stake prudence would seem to demand that the purchaser obtain his own structural survey to guide him in his purchase and, in such circumstances with very much larger sums of money at stake, it may be reasonable for the surveyors valuing on behalf of those who are providing the finance either to exclude or limit their liability to the purchaser.'

Comment

Approved: *Yianni* v *Edwin & Sons* [1981] 3 All ER 592 (surveyors instructed by building society owed purchaser of house a duty of care). Applied in *Al Saudi Banque* v *Clark Pixley* [1989] 3 All ER 361 and *Al-Nakib Investments (Jersey) Ltd* v *Longcroft* [1990] 3 All ER 321.

Thornton v *Shoe Lane Parking Ltd* [1971] 2 WLR 585

See Chapter 1.

7   Incapacity

Ashbury Railway Carriage & Iron Co v Riche (1875) LR 7 HL 653 House of Lords (Lord Cairns LC, Lords Chelmsford, Hatherley, O'Hagan and Selborne)

- *Company – contract ultra vires*

Facts
The memorandum of association of the appellant company stated that its objects were 'to make, and sell, or lend on hire, railway carriages and waggons, and all kinds of railway plant, fittings, machinery, and rolling-stock; to carry on the business of mechanical engineers and general contractors; to purchase, lease, work, and sell mines, minerals, land, and buildings; to purchase and sell, as merchants, timber, coal, metals, or other materials, and to buy and sell any such materials on commission or as agents'. The directors of the appellant company agreed to purchase a concession for making a railway in Belgium and afterwards contracted to assign the concession to a company formed in that country.

Held
Such an agreement was ultra vires and void since it was of a nature not included in the memorandum of association and as such could not be ratified even by the whole body of shareholders.

Lord Cairns LC:

> ' ... the question is as to the competency and power of the company to make the contract. Now I am clearly of the opinion that this contract was entirely, as I have said, beyond the objects of the memorandum of the association. If so, it was thereby placed beyond the powers of the company to make the con-

tract. If so, it is not a question whether the contract ever was ratified or was not ratified. It was a contract void at its beginning, it was void because the company could not make the contract.'

Comment
The ultra vires rule was much modified – for external purposes eliminated – by ss35, 35A and 35B of the Companies Act 1985 as substituted by s108(1) of the Companies Act 1989 with effect from 4 February 1991. As to the formalities of company contracts see s36 of the 1985 Act.

A contract which is ultra vires one of the parties to it is devoid of any legal effect and payments made in purported performance thereof are necessarily made for a consideration which has totally failed and are therefore recoverable as money had and received: see, eg, *Guinness Mahon & Co Ltd v Kensingon and Chelsea Royal London Borough Council* [1998] 2 All ER 272.

Doyle v White City Stadium Ltd [1935] 1 KB 110 Court of Appeal (Lord Hanworth MR, Romer and Slesser LJJ)

- *Minor – boxing contract*

Facts
An infant professional boxer made a contract to fight for £3,000, win, lose or draw. Under the terms of the contract, the fight was subject to the rules of the British Boxing Board of Control. The rules contained a provision that a boxer who was disqualified forfeited his prize money. The infant was disqualified for hitting below the belt and sued for his £3,000.

Held

The rules were, on the whole, for the infant's benefit (they encouraged clean fighting) and, accordingly, he was bound by them. His claim for the £3,000 must fail.

Slessor LJ:

'But in substance, two arguments have been used in this case to support the view that ... the plaintiff is entitled himself to have it paid over to him by the promoters. The first of those arguments rests upon the fact that he is an infant. It is said that any contract or alleged contract he has entered into under these rules is not binding on him on account of his infancy. If that contention is right, it is an answer to the defendant's claim to keep the money ... It is an argument which ... does not find favour with me. It depends really on two separate considerations – first whether this agreement is of the order of agreement under which an infant can properly bind himself and, secondly, if it does come within that order, whether this particular agreement can be stated to be so for the benefit of the infant as to be binding on him.

I would like to associate myself with what has been said by Kay LJ in *Clements* v *London and North Western Railway Co* [1894] 2 QB 482 to the effect that it is doubtful whether there is a general principle, that if an agreement be for the benefit of the infant it shall bind him ... I am not prepared here to say that there is any general principle that all agreements for the benefit of an infant will necessarily bind him ... In all those circumstances, I think that without laying down any general principles and looking at the facts of this case ... the learned judge was right when he said that he could find in *Clements* v *London and North Western Railway Co* ample authority for saying that this contract was so associated with the Class of contract of service which an infant may make so as to be binding on him, that it was binding upon him.

There remains the question, was it for his benefit? ... there are many dicta to the effect that where a contract imposes a penalty or a forfeiture that is not good as against the infant. But I, on the other hand, have been impressed with the consideration which has been pointed out in several cases that an infant cannot make a contract of service without having in it some incidents which may not, in themselves, be directly beneficial to him, but may be beneficial to the master. In *Wood* v *Fenwick* (1842) 10 M & W 195, the headnote says:

"A contract of hiring and services for wages, is a contract beneficial to and binding upon an infant, though it contain clauses for referring disputes to arbitration and for the imposition of forfeitures in case of neglect of duty, to be deducted from the wages."

In contracts of apprenticeship, which are admittedly contracts binding upon an infant, the right of the master to proceed, not only financially but, in the old days, corporeally against the infant, have not made the contract of apprenticeship invalid as against the infant. Therefore I agree that this contract is for the benefit of the infant and is one binding on him.'

Comment

Applied in *Chaplin* v *Leslie Frewin (Publishers) Ltd* [1965] 3 All ER 764 (publishing contract would be binding on an infant if it were for his benefit).

Edwards v *Carter* [1893] AC 360
House of Lords (Lord Herschell LC, Lords Watson, Halsbury, Macnaghten, Morris and Shand)

- *Minor – covenant in marriage settlement*

Facts

An infant covenanted, by a marriage settlement dated 16 October 1883, to settle after-acquired property. The infant attained majority in November 1883 and, in 1887, became entitled under the will of his father to a large sum of money which, in accordance with the marriage settlement, he should have settled on trustees. In July 1888 he repudiated the marriage settlement. The trustees of the settlement commenced proceedings to enforce the covenant.

Held

The infant was bound by it.

Lord Herschell LC:

'It is not disputed that this contract executed and entered into by [the infant] was not absolutely void, but was voidable only – that is to say, that after he came of age it was binding as if he had been of age at the time when he executed it, subject only to this, that the law enabled him to avoid his obligations provided he did so within a reasonable time. I did not understand the learned counsel for the appellants to dispute the proposition that the repudiation in order that the obligations may be got rid of must be within a reasonable time after the minor ceases to be a minor. The controversy has been as to what elements may be taken into account in determining whether more than a reasonable time has elapsed. In the present case, as I have shown your Lordships, there was no repudiation at all during the life time of the father. ...

The first question is whether the infant was entitled to wait until an actual sum of money came to him to which this covenant could apply before he made the repudiation. I think that is a proposition which it is absolutely impossible to regard seriously – that this covenant being binding unless he repudiates it within a reasonable time he is entitled to wait and see how in respect of any particular sum of money the covenant will operate, and when he has made up his mind whether with regard to that sum of money it will be beneficial to him or not, he can then, and not till then, be said to have his proper opportunity of making the determination.

Then it is said that in considering whether a reasonable time has elapsed you must take into account the fact that he did not know what were the terms of the settlement and that it contained this particular covenant. He

knew that he had executed a deed – he must be taken to have known that that deed though binding upon him could be repudiated when he came of age, and it seems to me that in measuring a reasonable time whether in point of fact he had or had not acquainted himself with the nature of the obligations which he had undertaken is wholly immaterial – the time must be measured in precisely the same way whether he had so made himself acquainted or not. I do not say that he was under any obligation to make himself acquainted with the nature of the deed, which, having executed it as an infant, he might or might not at his pleasure repudiate when he came of age – all I say is this, that he cannot maintain that the reasonable time when measured must be a longer time because he has chosen not to make himself acquainted with the nature of the deed which he has executed.

Having put aside those two contentions the only question comes to be, has a reasonable time been exceeded? The learned judges in the court below expressed their opinion that the period which elapsed, a period between four and five years, was more than a reasonable time. It is not all necessary for your Lordships to lay down what would have been a reasonable time in this case – it is enough to say that, in my opinion, it is impossible to hold that the learned judges in the court below in saying that more than a reasonable time had elapsed have in any way erred.'

Leslie (R) Ltd v *Sheill* [1914] 3 KB 607 Court of Appeal (Lord Sumner, Kennedy LJ and A T Lawrence J)

- *Minor – fraudulent misrepresentation – recovery of loans*

Facts

The plaintiffs, registered moneylenders, were induced to make two loans of £200 each by the fraudulent misrepresentations of the defendant that he was of full age. The plaintiffs sued to recover the £400.

Held

Their action could not succeed.

Lord Sumner:

'In 1914 in *Stocks* v *Wilson* [1913] 2 KB 235 an infant who had obtained furniture from the plaintiff by falsely stating that he was of age and had sold part of it for £30, was personally adjudged by Lush J to pay this £30 as part of the relief granted to the plaintiff. ... I think it is plain that Lush J conceived himself to be merely applying the equitable principle of restitution. The form of the claim was that, by way of equitable relief, the infant should be ordered to pay the reasonable value of the goods which he could not restore because he had sold them. The argument was that equity would not allow him to keep the goods and not pay for them, that if he kept the property he must discharge the burden, and that he could not better his position by having put it out of his power to give up the property. Lush J expressly said that it was a jurisdiction to compel the infant to make satisfaction, and the remedy was not on the contract. He said ([1913] 2 KB at pp242, 243):

"What the court of equity has done in cases of this kind is to prevent the infant from retaining the benefit of what he has obtained by reason of his fraud. It has done no more than this, and this is a very different thing from making him liable to pay damages or compensation for the loss of the other party's bargain. If the infant has obtained property by fraud he can be compelled to restore it."

But now comes the proposition which applies to the present case, and it is open to challenge, "if he has obtained money he can be compelled to refund it". The learned judge thought that the fundamental principle in *Re King* (1858) 3 De G & J 63 was a liability to account for the money obtained by the fraudulent representation, and that in the case before him there must be a similar liability to account for the proceeds of the sale of the goods obtained by this fraud. If this be the ratio decidendi, though I have difficulty in seeing what liability to account there can

be, and certainly none is named in *Re King*, the decision is distinguishable from the present case and is independent of the above dictum, and I need express no opinion about it. In the present case there is clearly no accounting. There is no fidicuary relation. The money was paid over in order to be used as the defendant's own, and he has so used and, I suppose, spent it. There is no question of tracing it, no possibility of restoring the very thing got by the fraud, nothing but a compulsion through a personal judgment to pay an equivalent sum out of his present or future resources, in a word nothing but a judgment in debt to repay the loan. I think this would be nothing but enforcing a void contract. So far as I can find the Court of Chancery never would have enforced any liability under circumstances like the present any more than a court of law would have done ...'

Comment

Applied in *Fawcett* v *Smethurst* (1914) 84 LJKB 473 (contract containing an onerous term as to the hire of a car not a contract for a necessary).

For the court's power to order restitution in the case of contracts entered into after 9 June 1987, see s3 Minors' Contracts Act 1987.

Nash v *Inman* [1908] 2 KB 1 Court of Appeal (Sir Herbert Cozens-Hardy MR, Fletcher Moulton and Buckley LJJ)

• *Minor – fancy waistcoats*

Facts

A tailor commenced proceedings to recover £122 19s 6d for clothes, including eleven fancy waistcoats, supplied to an infant Cambridge undergraduate.

Held

The action would fail.

Fletcher Moulton LJ:

'An infant, like a lunatic, is incapable of

making a contract of purchase in the strict sense of the words; but if a man satisfies the needs of the infant or lunatic by supplying to him necessaries, the law will imply an obligation to repay him for the services so rendered and will enforce that obligation ... That the articles were necessaries had to be alleged and proved by the plaintiff as part of his case and the sum he recovered was based on a quantum meruit. If he claimed anything beyond this he failed and it did not help him that he could prove that the prices were agreed prices. All this is ... confirmed by the provision of section 2 of the Sale of Goods Act 1893 – an Act which was intended to codify the existing law. That section expressly provides that the consequence of necessaries sold and delivered to an infant is that he must pay a reasonable price therefor ...

The elaborate argument of counsel for the plaintiff founded on the authorities of the past, going back nearly a hundred years, does not appear to me to touch the plain and obvious principle that the plaintiff has got to show that he has supplied "necessaries", that is to say, first, that the goods supplied by him are suitable to the condition in life of the infant; and, secondly, that they are suitable to his actual requirements at the time of the sale and delivery – or, in other words, that the infant has not then got a supply from other sources. ...

The defendant's father proved the infancy, and then proved that he knew perfectly well, as he had examined into the matter, that the defendant had an adequate supply of clothes, and he stated what they were. That evidence was not contradicted by any other evidence, nor was there any cross-examination tending to shake the credit of the witness ... On that uncontradicted evidence, the judge came to the conclusion – to use the language of the court in *Ryder* v *Wombwell* (1868) LR 3 Exch 90 – that there was no evidence on which the jury might properly find that the goods in question were necessary to the actual requirements of the infant at the time of sale and delivery, and, therefore, in accordance with the duty of the judge in all cases of trial by jury he withdrew the case from the jury, and directed judgment to be entered for the defendant. In my opinion, he was justified in so doing ...'

Comment

See now s3 of the Sale of Goods Act 1979 and note that that section applies also 'to a person who by reason of mental incapacity or drunkenness is incompetent to contract'.

8 Mistake

Amalgamated Investment and Property Co Ltd v John Walker & Sons Ltd [1977] 1 WLR 164 Court of Appeal (Buckley and Lawton LJJ and Sir John Pennycuick)

• *Contract – mistake – frustration*

Facts
Having ceased to use a purpose-built bonded warehouse and bottling factory for those purposes, the defendants advertised the premises for sale as suitable for occupation or redevelopment. The plaintiffs agreed, subject to contract, to buy the property for £1,710,000. In their enquiries before contract the plaintiffs asked whether the property was designated as a building of special architectural or historic interest: on 14 August the defendants replied in the negative although, unknown to the parties, an official of the Department of the Environment had included the building in a list of buildings which it was proposed should be so designated. Contracts were exchanged on 25 September and the following day the department wrote to the defendants to inform them that the designation was about to be given legal effect, a step which was taken the next day. The plaintiffs sought rescission of the contract on the ground of common mistake or a declaration that it was void or voidable. At the trial, the judge found that the property's value without redevelopment potential was probably £1.5m less than the contract price.

Held
The plaintiffs could not succeed since, inter alia, the mistake had not existed at the date of the contract.

Buckley LJ:

'For the application of the doctrine of mutual mistake as a ground for setting the contract aside, it is of course necessary to show that the mistake existed at the date of the contract; and so counsel for the plaintiffs relies in that respect not on the signing of the list by the officer who alone was authorised to sign it on behalf of the Secretary of State, but on the decision of [the official] to include the property in the list. That decision, although in fact it led to the signature of the list in the form in which it was eventually signed, was merely an administrative step in the carrying out of the operations of the branch of the Ministry ... It seems to me that it is no more justifiable to point to that date as being the crucial date than it is to point to other earlier dates or later dates. The crucial date, in my judgment, is the date when the list was signed. It was then that the building became a listed building, and it was only then that the expectations of the parties (who no doubt both expected that this property would be capable of being developed, subject always of course to obtaining planning permission, without it being necessary to obtain listed building permission) were disappointed ... In my judgment, there was no mutual mistake as to the circumstances surrounding the contract at the time when the contract was entered into. The only mistake that there was was one which related to the expectation of the parties. They expected that the building would be subject only to ordinary town planning consent procedures, and that expectation has been disappointed. But at the date when the contract was entered into I cannot see that there is any ground for saying that the parties were then subject to some mutual mistake of fact relating to the circumstances surrounding the contract ...

I now turn to the alternative argument which has been presented to us in support of this appeal, which is on frustration. Counsel for the plaintiffs has relied on what was said in the speeches in the House of Lords in *Davis Contractors Ltd* v *Fareham Urban District Council* [1956] 3 WLR 37, and it may perhaps be useful if I refer to what was said by Lord Radcliffe:

> "So, perhaps, it would be simpler to say at the outset that frustration occurs whenever the law recognises that, without default of either party, a contractual obligation has become incapable of being performed because the circumstances in which performance is called for would render it a thing radically different from that which was undertaken by the contract."

... Then, a little later on, after referring to *Denny, Mott and Dickson Ltd* v *James B Fraser & Co Ltd* [1944] AC 265, Lord Radcliffe said:

> "It is for that reason that special importance is necessarily attached to the occurrence of any unexpected event that, as it were, changes the fact of things. But, even so, it is not hardship or inconvenience or material loss itself which calls the principle of frustration into play. There must be as well such a change in the significance of the obligation that the thing undertaken would, if performed, be a different thing from that contracted for."

Now, the obligation undertaken to be performed in this case by the defendants was to sell this property for the contract price, and of course, to show a good title and so forth. The defendants did not warrant in any way that planning permission could be obtained for the development of the property. No doubt both parties considered that the property was property which could advantageously be developed and was property for which planning permission would probably be satisfactorily obtained. But

there was no stipulation in the contract relating to anything of that kind; nor as I say, was there any warranty on the part of the defendants. I am prepared to assume for the purposes of this judgment that the law relating to frustration of contract is capable of being applied in the case of a contract for sale of land ... But, making that assumption I have reached the conclusion that there are not here the necessary factual bases for holding that this contract has been frustrated. It seems to me that the risk of property being listed as property of architectural or historical interest is a risk which inheres in all ownership of buildings. In many cases it may be an extremely remote risk. In many cases it may be a marginal risk. In some cases it may be a substantial risk. But it is a risk, I think, which attaches to all buildings and it is a risk that every owner and every purchaser of property must recognise that he is subject to. The purchasers in the present case bought knowing that they would have to obtain planning permission in order to develop the property. The effect of listing ... makes the obtaining of planning permission, it may be, more difficult, and it may also make it a longer and more complicated process. But still, in essence, the position is that the would-be developer has to obtain the appropriate planning permissions, one form of permission being the "listed building permission" ... It is a risk which I think the purchaser must carry, and any loss that may result from the maturing of that risk is a loss which must lie where it falls. Moreover, the plaintiffs have not yet established that they will be unable to obtain all the necessary planning permissions, including "listed building permission". So it has not yet, I think, been established that the listing of this building has had the drastic effect which the figures ... suggest that it may have had. It may well turn out to be the case that "listed building permission" will be obtainable here and the purchasers will be able to carry into effect the development which they desire.'

Associated Japanese Bank (International) Ltd v *Credit du Nord SA* [1989] 1 WLR 255 High Court (Steyn J)

• *Guarantee – mistake as to subject matter*

Facts

Under a sale and leaseback transaction the plaintiffs (AJB) purchased four machines from a Mr Bennett and then leased them back to him. As a condition of the transaction, the defendants (CDN) guaranteed Bennett's obligations and at all material times both parties believed that the machines existed and were in Bennett's possession. After Bennett defaulted in payments under the lease it was discovered that the machines did not exist and that Bennett had perpetrated a fraud. When the plaintiffs sued on the guarantee, the defendants contended that it was subject to an express or implied condition precedent that the machines in fact existed and therefore that the guarantee was void ab initio for common mistake.

Held

The plaintiffs' claim would be dismissed.

Steyn J:

'It might be useful if I now summarised what appears to me to be a satisfactory way of approaching this subject. Logically, before one can turn to the rules as to mistake, whether at common law or in equity, one must first determine whether the contract itself, by express or implied condition precedent or otherwise, provides who bears the risk of the relevant mistake. It is at this hurdle that many pleas of mistake will either fail or prove to have been unnecessary. Only if the contract is silent on the point is there scope for invoking mistake. That brings me to the relationship between common law mistake and mistake in equity. Where common law mistake has been pleaded, the court must first consider this plea. If the contract is held to be void, no question of mistake in equity arises. But, if the contract is held to be valid, a plea of mistake in equity may still have to be considered: see *Grist* v *Bailey* [1966] 2 All ER 875 ... Turning now to the approach to common law mistake, it seems to me that the following propositions are valid although not necessarily all entitled to be dignified as propositions of law.

The first imperative must be that the law ought to uphold rather than destroy apparent contracts. Second, the common law rules as to a mistake regarding the quality of the subject matter, like the common law rules regarding commercial frustration, are designed to cope with the impact of unexpected and wholly exceptional circumstances on apparent contracts. Third, such a mistake in order to attract legal consequences must substantially be shared by both parties, and must relate to facts as they existed at the time the contract was made. Fourth, and this is the point established by *Bell* v *Lever Bros Ltd* [1932] AC 161, the mistake must render the subject matter of the contract essentially and radically different from the subject matter which the parties believed to exist ... Fifth, there is a requirement which was not specifically discussed in *Bell* v *Lever Bros Ltd*. What happens if the party who is seeking to rely on the mistake had no reasonable grounds for his belief? An extreme example is that of the man who makes a contract with minimal knowledge of the facts to which the mistake relates but is content that it is a good speculative risk. In my judgment a party cannot be allowed to rely on a common mistake where the mistake consists of a belief which is entertained by him without any reasonable grounds for such relief: cf *McRae* v *Commonwealth Disposals Commission* (1951) 84 CLR 377 at 408. That is not because principles such as estoppel or negligence require it, but simply because policy and good sense dictate that the positive rules regarding common mistake should be so qualified ... a recognition of this qualification is consistent with the approach in equity where fault on the part of the party adversely affected by the mistake will generally preclude the granting of equitable relief: see *Solle* v *Butcher* [1949] 2 All ER 1107 at 1120.

Applying the law to the facts

It is clear, of course, that in this case both parties, the creditor and the guarantor, acted on the assumption that the lease related to existing machines. If they had been informed that the machines might not exist, neither AJB nor CDN would for one moment have contemplated entering into the transaction. That, by itself, I accept, is not enough to sustain the plea of common law mistake. I am also satisfied that CDN had reasonable grounds for believing that the machines existed. That belief was based on CDN's discussions with Mr Bennett, information supplied by ... a respectable firm of lease brokers, and the confidence created by the fact that AJB were the lessors.

The real question is whether the subject matter *of the guarantee* (as opposed to the sale and lease) was essentially different from what it was reasonably believed to be. The real security of the guarantor was the machines. The existence of the machines, being profit-earning chattels, made it more likely that the debtor would be able to service the debt. More importantly, if the debtor defaulted and the creditor repossessed the machines, the creditor had to give credit for 97.5 per cent of the value of the machines. If the creditor sued the guarantor first, and the guarantor paid, the guarantor was entitled to be subrogated to the creditor's rights in respect of recovery against the debtor ... No doubt the guarantor relied to some extent on the creditworthiness of Mr Bennett. But I find that the prime security to which the guarantor looked was the existence of the four machines as described to both parties. For both parties the guarantee of obligations under a lease with non-existent machines was essentially different from a guarantee of a lease with four machines which both parties at the time of the contract believed to exist. The guarantee is an accessory contract. The non-existence of the subject matter of the principal contract is therefore of fundamental impor-

tance. Indeed the analogy of the classic res extincta cases, so much discussed in the authorities, is fairly close. In my judgment, the stringent test of common law mistake is satisfied; the guarantee is void ab initio ...

Equitable mistake

Having concluded that the guarantee is void ab initio at common law, it is strictly unnecessary to examine the question of equitable mistake. Equity will give relief against common mistake in cases where the common law will not, and it provides more flexible remedies, including the power to set aside the contract on terms. It is not necessary to repeat my findings of fact save to record again the fundamental nature of the common mistake, and that CDN was not at fault in any way. If I had not decided in favour of CDN on construction and common law mistake, I would have held that the guarantee must be set aside on equitable principles.'

Citibank NA v *Brown Shipley & Co Ltd* [1991] 2 All ER 690 Queen's Bench Division (Waller J)

- *Mistaken identity induced by fraud – passing of title*

Facts

In three separate transactions a person claiming to be a signatory of a company's account at one bank (the issuing bank – Citibank NA or Midland Bank plc) telephoned another bank (the receiving bank – Brown Shipley) with a request to buy substantial amounts of foreign currency, payment to be made by a bankers' draft issued by the issuing bank. The caller then telephoned the issuing bank, instructing them to prepare this bankers' draft to be drawn on the company's account. This the issuing bank did and handed the draft over to someone they thought was from the company, in exchange for a letter that purported to confirm the telephoned instructions, with forged signatures. The draft was then presented to the receiving bank, who after checking that the draft was genuinely issued by the issuing bank and had been issued in the ordinary course of business, paid the cash to the fraudster. In due course the receiving bank presented the draft to and were paid by the issuing bank. When the fraud was finally discovered the issuing bank brought an action against the receiving bank to recover the value of the draft on the ground of conversion.

Held

The claim would be dismissed.

Waller J:

'Once again there is in issue which of the innocent parties should bear the loss from a fraud. ...

The cornerstone of [counsel for Citibank and Midland's] submissions is *Cundy* v *Lindsay* (1878) 3 App Case 459. He submits that if Brown Shipley were to obtain title to the banker's drafts, they can only do so through the fraudsters. He submits that the fraudsters had no title because on the principle of *Cundy* v *Lindsay* there was no contract between them and Citibank, or them and Midland, under which even a voidable title was transmitted.

Apart from authority which I must refer to in a moment and which [counsel] suggested supported his approach, it seemed to me that there were fallacies in [his] approach.

First the *Cundy* v *Lindsay* principle only reaches the result of no title at least in a bilateral contract situation where the findings of fact are: (i) A thinks he had agreed with C because he believes B, with whom he is negotiating, is C; (ii) B is aware that A did not intend to make an agreement with him; and (iii) A has established that the identity of C was a matter of crucial importance.

Where A issues a document promising to pay B under which he fully intends to promise to pay B, and which is only to take effect on its delivery to B, but which he gives to C thinking he is D, and which he expects (as happens) will be delivered to B, the question arises as to which contract it is alleged the *Cundy* v *Lindsay* principle

should render void. The "title" of B does not seem to me to be derived through C or D at all. C or D would seem to me to be a little more than a conduit pipe carrying what at that stage is an inchoate instrument: the instrument only becomes a valid instrument on delivery to B (see s21(1) of the Bills of Exchange Act 1882). Delivery to be effective must be made either by or under the authority of party drawing (see s21(2)), but a valid and unconditional delivery is presumed until the contrary is proved (s21(3)). It would seem to me that only if it could be established that delivery was without authority would there be no quite separate contract on which B could rely as against A. That contract, ie the one between A and B, may be voidable, but once B has had the instrument delivered to him with the authority of A, it seems to me that a contract comes into existence between A and B (as A intended) under which, as between those two, B has a good title. So far as authority is concerned, it will usually be very difficult for A to establish that it was of crucial importance to him who actually physically transported the draft to B. In this case, for example, delivery might have been done by post; it might have been done by one or other of the banks' messengers; it might have been done by some other messenger. It so happened that in this case that it was done by someone thought to be the customer or his messenger, but that was not of crucial importance. That being so, the authority, as it seems to me, albeit induced by fraud, would not be void; the authority would be actual, even if voidable.

I must now turn to the authorities to see what effect they have on the thoughts expressed above.

(1) I have been referred to the cases relating to mistake in the *Cundy* v *Lindsay* sense, eg *Lake* v *Simmons* [1927] AC 487, *Phillips* v *Brooks Ltd* [1919] 2 KB 243, *Ingram* v *Little* [1961] 1 QB 31 and *Lewis* v *Averay* [1972] 1 QB 198.

I do not think at the end of the day the last three cases assist very much, save to emphasise (1) that each case rests on its own facts, (2) that in the bilateral contract context for no title to pass it must be established that there is no contract under which such a title can pass and (3) the no contract situation, as opposed to a voidable contract, only arises if it is fundamental to the contract that one party to the contract should be who he says he is. That is easier to establish where contracts are made entirely by documents and is less easy to establish in an inter praesentes position.

I should perhaps however say a little more about *Lake* v *Simmons* because in that case careful consideration was being given as to whether a mere bailment was void. The rogue in that case induced the shop to part with possession of articles one the basis that she was the wife of a certain person and wanted to show them to that person, who was said to be her husband. As a fact, the person named was not her husband, and it was never intended by the lady that that person should have the goods. The issue was whether she was "entrusted" with the goods, since if she had been, liability under an insurance policy would have been excluded. The House of Lords held that she was not entrusted with the article within the meaning of an exceptions clause because there was no real consent to her having them. Viscount Haldane said:

> "No doubt she got possession physically, but there was no mutual assent to any contract which would give her even the qualified proprietary right to hold it as a bailee proper. The appellant thought that he was dealing with the wife of Van der Borgh, and it was on that footing alone that he parted with the goods."

The distinction as I see it between that case and the present is (i) there was a fundamental mistake, both about the identity of the bailee rogue *and* the person to whom the article was in fact to be delivered, and (ii) it was important fundamentally who the actual physical bailee was: the article would never have been entrusted simply to the postman or to a messenger.

(2) I was also referred to some cases concerned with claims made for money paid under a mistake of fact. Neither Citibank nor

Midland had made a claim for money paid under a mistake of fact ... but I think it is right to say something ...

First, the type of mistake necessary to give rise to a right to recover under the restitutionary remedy of money paid under a mistake of fact need not necessarily be of the same fundamental character that makes a contract totally void. Thus to point to a case where the plaintiff has succeeded on a restitutionary remedy, would not establish that the plaintiff would also have established a mistake fundamental enough to avoid any contract altogether.

Second, albeit [counsel for Citibank and Midland] suggested that *R E Jones Ltd* v *Waring & Gillow Ltd* [1926] AC 670 was a case in his favour since it showed, as he submitted, that he could in fact have succeeded in a claim for money paid under a mistake of fact, I doubt whether on analysis it does so show.

The facts of that case were that a rogue, B, had bought certain furniture worth some £13,500 from W & G under hire purchase. B's cheque for the deposit of £5,000 was dishonoured. W & G repossessed the furniture. B, by an elaborate and expanding story, persuaded Jones that B represented 'International Motors', who wanted to appoint Jones as agents and that W & G were the financiers and thus that Jones should pay to W & G £5,000. Jones drew two cheques, which they handed to B and were then persuaded by W & G to exchange those for one cheque for £5,000 which they sent directly to W & G, who then released the furniture to B. On discovery of the fraud, W & G again took possession of the furniture. This last fact, as it seems to me, is not unimportant.

As I read the speeches in that case, (i) all their Lordships found that there was a mistake which would entitle Jones to recover from W & G under the restitutionary remedy of money paid under a mistake of fact, but of relevance to the instant case the rogue B in that case was described as "commissioned ... to carry" the first cheques to W & G (per Viscount Cave LC, concurred in by Lord Atkinson) and "the means of transit" or no difference from "a boy messenger" (per Lord Sumner) ... I think it would have been a matter of surprise if it had been suggested that W & G did not get title to the two cheques on delivery of B, albeit possibly a voidable title. Of course, in *Jones* v *Waring & Gillow* the two cheques were ultimately exchanged for one cheque sent directly to W & G. [Counsel] submitted that the position on title might be different as between cheques delivered by the rogues and cheques sent direct. That would seem to me to be illogical, and to emphasise that on analysis the rogues were in no different position than a mere messenger.

(ii) In relation to change of position [counsel] suggested that the House of Lords were holding there was no such defence, save in a case where an agent is sued but has handed on to his principal. I must accept that that may have been what Lord Sumner and Lord Carson had in mind as the limitation of the defence ... but there is no such suggestion in the other party to the majority decision, Lord Shaw, who does not mention this defence at all, and it is contrary in my view to what Viscount Cave LC and Lord Atkinson were saying. Furthermore, it is certainly not the interpretation put upon the decision by Robert Goff J in *Barclays Bank Ltd* v *W J Simms Son & Cooke (Southern) Ltd* [1980] QB 677. In that case, having reviewed the authorities and analysed in particular *Jones* v *Waring & Gillow*, he sets out the simple principles which he says can be deduced from the "formidable line of authority". Those principles are as follows:

"1. If a person pays money to another under a mistake of fact which causes him to make the payment, he is prima facie entitled to recover it as money paid under a mistake of fact. 2. His claim may however fail if: (a) the payer intends that the payee shall have the money at all events, whether the fact be true or false, or is deemed in law so to intend; (b) the payment is made for good consideration, in particular if the money is paid to discharge, and does discharge, a debt owed to the payee (or a principal on whose

behalf he is authorised to receive the payment) by the payer or by a third party by whom he is authorised to discharge the debt; (c) the payee has changed his position in good faith, or is deemed in law to have done so."

It is obvious to (c) that I particularly draw attention.

It is perhaps important to stress that on the facts of *Jones* v *Waring & Gillow*, the recipient W & G had originally supplied furniture on a cheque that was dishonoured and, more importantly, had repossessed the furniture since discovery of the fraud, leading the counsel for W & G having to give the undertaking. Viscount Cave LC's holding of a change of position incorporated that undertaking ... but it was a case where there was clearly a difficulty as to whether there had in fact been sufficient change in position to provide a defence to money paid under a mistake.

So far as Citibank and Midland are concerned, it seems to me that they would prima facie have been entitled to recover their money as money paid under a mistake of fact, but would have been met by the defence of Brown Shipley having changed their position in good faith. It is possibly for this reason that the claim was never made on that basis.

Returning now to the facts of the instant case, it seems to me that the key lies in whether there was any authority to deliver the banker's drafts to Brown Shipley. The presumption is in favour of there being authority. The *Cundy* v *Lindsay* principle could be applied so as to negative that authority (as per *Lake* v *Simmons*), but only if the precise identity of the bailee and possibly also the identity of the person to whom the banker's draft was to be delivered were mistaken *and* proved to be of fundamental importance. Neither Midland nor Citibank were under any mistake or misapprehension as to whom the draft was to be delivered. Furthermore, the bailee who physically carried the draft was a messenger whose precise identity was unimportant. Even if it could be suggested that it is going too far to say his precise identity was unimportant, it seems to me that neither Citibank nor Midland have established to the degree required that it was fundamental to them that the bailee was a particular person about whom they were mistaken, as opposed to a person whose attributes did not include authority from their customer as they believed. Once there was authority, title to the banker's drafts was, as I see it, transmitted directly from Citibank or Midland to Brown Shipley, on the drafts becoming valid instruments as a result of delivery through whomever the messenger was.

My conclusion ... accordingly is that Brown Shipley did not convert the drafts by presenting them for payment.'

Gallie v *Lee*

See *Saunders v Anglia Building Society* (below).

Hadley v Baxendale (1854) 9 Ex 341

See Chapter 14.

Lewis v *Averay* [1971] 3 WLR 603 Court of Appeal (Lord Denning MR, Phillimore and Megaw LJJ)

• *Contract – deception and mistaken belief as to identity*

Facts

The plaintiff, having advertised his car for sale in a local newspaper, was visited on 8 May 1969 by a rogue who offered to buy it. The rogue claimed to be a well known actor and talked of the film business. When the plaintiff was reluctant to allow him to take the car away before the cheque had been cleared, he was shown an official pass for Pinewood film studios, with the name Richard A Green (the actor's name) and a photograph of the rogue and he consequently allowed the car to be driven away by the rogue. The car was then sold to the defendant and, in the meantime, the rogue's cheque to the plaintiff bounced.

The defendant, finding the plaintiff's name in the car log-book, contacted him to see if he had a workshop manual. The plaintiff sued the defendant in conversion.

Held

The action could not succeed since the plaintiff had not avoided the contract before the rogue parted with the property in the car.

Lord Denning MR:

'The real question in the case is whether on 8 May 1969 there was a contract of sale under which the property in the car passed from Mr Lewis to the rogue. If there was such a contract, then even though it was voidable for fraud, nevertheless Mr Averay would get a good title to the car. But if there was no contract of sale by Mr Lewis to the rogue – either because there was, on the face of it, no agreement between the parties, or because any apparent agreement was a nullity and void ab initio for mistake, then no property would pass from Mr Lewis to the rogue. Mr Averay would not get a good title because the rogue had no property to pass to him.

There is no doubt that Mr Lewis was mistaken as to the identity of the person who handed him the cheque. He thought that he was Richard Greene, a film actor of standing and worth; whereas, in fact he was a rogue whose identity is quite unknown. It was under the influence of that mistake that Mr Lewis let the rogue have the car. He would not have dreamed of letting him have it otherwise.

What is the effect of this mistake? There are two cases in our books which cannot, in my mind, be reconciled the one with the other. One of them is *Phillips* v *Brooks Ltd* [1919] 2 KB 243, where a jeweller had a ring for sale. The other is *Ingram* v *Little* [1960] 3 WLR 505, where two ladies had a car for sale. In each case the story is very similar to the present. A plausible rogue comes along. The rogue says he likes the ring, or the car, as the case may be. He asks the price. The sellers name it. The rogue says he is prepared to buy it at that price. He pulls out a cheque book. He writes, or prepares to write, a cheque for the price. The seller hesitates. He has never met this man before. He does not want to hand over the ring or the car not knowing whether the cheque will be met. The rogue notices the seller's hesitation. He is quick with his next move. He says to the jeweller, in *Phillips* v *Brooks Ltd*: "I am Sir George Bullough of 11 St James's Square"; or the ladies in *Ingram* v *Little*: "I am P G M Hutchinson of Standstead House, Standstead Road, Caterham"; or to Mr Lewis in the present case: "I am Richard Greene, the film actor of the Robin Hood series". Each seller checks up the information. The jeweller looks up the directory and finds there is a Sir George Bullough at 11 St James' Square. The ladies check up too. They look at the telephone directory and find there is a "P G M Hutchinson of Standstead House, Standstead Road, Caterham". Mr Lewis checks up too. He examines the official pass of the Pinewood Studios and finds that it is a pass for "Richard A Green" to the Pinewood Studios with this man's photograph on it. In each case the seller finds that this is sufficient confirmation of the man's identity. So he accepts the cheque signed by the rogue and lets him have the ring in the one case and the car and log book in the other two cases. The rogue goes off and sells the goods to a third person, who buys them in entire good faith and pays the price to the rogue. The rogue disappears. The original seller presents the cheque. It is dishonoured. Who is entitled to the goods? The original seller or the ultimate buyer? The courts have given different answers. In *Phillips* v *Brooks Ltd* the ultimate buyer was held to be entitled to the ring. In *Ingram* v *Little* the original seller was held to be entitled to the car. ...

It seems to me that the material facts in each case are quite indistinguishable the one from the other. In each case there was, to all outward appearance, a contract: but there was a mistake by the seller as to the identity of the buyer. This mistake was fundamental. In each case it led to the handing over of the goods. Without it, the seller would not have parted with them.

This case therefore, raises the question:

What is the effect of a mistake by one party as to the identity of the other? It has sometimes been said that if a party makes a mistake as to the identity of the person with whom he is contracting, there is no contract, or if there is a contract, it is a nullity and void so that no property can pass under it. ...

For instance, in *Ingram* v *Little*, the majority of the court suggested that the difference between *Phillips* v *Brooks* and *Ingram* v *Little* was that in *Phillips* v *Brooks* the contract of sale was concluded (so as to pass the property to the rogue) before the rogue made the fraudulent misrepresentation, whereas in *Ingram* v *Little* the rogue made the fraudulent misrepresentation before the contract was concluded. My own view is that in each case the property in the goods did not pass until the seller let the rogue have the goods.

Again it has been suggested that a mistake as to the identity of a person is one thing: and a mistake as to his attributes is another. A mistake as to identity, it is said, avoids a contract; whereas a mistake as to attributes does not. But this is a distinction without a difference. A man's very name is one of his attributes. It is also a key to his identity. ... I do not ... accept the theory that a mistake as to identity renders a contract void.

I think the true principle is that which underlies the decision of this court in *King's Norton Metal Co Ltd* v *Eldridge, Merrett & Co Ltd* (1897) 14 TLR 98 and of Horridge J in *Phillips* v *Brooks Ltd*, which has stood for these last 50 years. It is this: when two parties have come to a contract – or rather what appears, on the face of it, to be a contract – the fact that one party is mistaken as to the identity of the other does not mean that there is no contract or that the contract is a nullity and void from the beginning. It only means that the contract is voidable, that is, liable to be set aside at the instance of the mistaken person, so long as he does so before third parties have in good faith acquired rights under it.

Applied to the cases such as the present, this principle is in full accord with the presumption stated by Pearce LJ and also Devlin LJ in *Ingram* v *Little*. When a dealing is had between a seller like Mr Lewis and a person who is actually there present before him, then the presumption in law is that there is a contract, even though there is a fraudulent impersonation by the buyer representing himself as a different man than he is. There is a contract made with the very person there, who is present in person. It is liable no doubt to be avoided for fraud, but it is still a good contract under which title will pass unless and until it is avoided. …

In this case, Mr Lewis made a contract of sale with the very man, the rogue, who came to the flat. I say that he "made a contract" because in this regard we do not look into his intentions or into his mind to know what he was thinking, or into the mind of the rogue. We look to the outward appearances. On the face of the dealing, Mr Lewis made a contract under which he sold the car to the rogue, delivered the car and the log book to him and took a cheque in return. … It was, of course, induced by fraud. The rogue made false representations as to his identity. But it was still a contract, though voidable for fraud. It was a contract under which this property passed to the rogue and, in due course, passed from the rogue to Mr Averay, before the contract was voided.

Although I very much regret that either of these good and reliable gentlemen should suffer, in my judgment, it is Mr Lewis who should do so.'

Comment
Followed: *Phillips* v *Brooks Ltd* [1919] 2 KB 243. Distinguished and doubted: *Ingram* v *Little* [1960] 3 WLR 505.

Saunders v *Anglia Building Society*
[1970] 3 WLR 1078 House of Lords (Viscount Dilhorne, Lords Reid, Hodson, Wilberforce and Pearson)

* *Mistake – plea of non est factum*

Facts
The plaintiff, executrix of Mrs Gallie, a widow aged 84, ran a boarding house in Essex with the assistance of her nephew. Her nephew had possession of the deeds of the house and she was quite content that he should use them to raise money if he so wished, so long as she could stay in the house for the rest of her life. Lee, a friend of the nephew, was a man heavily in debt. Lee had a document of sale drawn up in respect of the house and took it to Mrs Gallie for her to sign. The nephew acted as witness. When she asked what the document was, she was told by Lee that it was a deed of gift in favour of the nephew. Lee paid Mrs Gallie nothing, but raised a loan for himself on the strength of the document. When he defaulted on one of the mortgages, the building society sought to recover possession and the plaintiff raised the defence of non est factum.

Held
The building society would succeed.

Lord Reid:

'The existing law seems to me to be in a state of some confusion. I do not think that it is possible to reconcile all the decisions, let alone all the reasons given for them. In view of some general observations made in the Court of Appeal I think that it is desirable to try to extract from the authorities the principles on which most of them are based. When we are trying to do that my experience has been that there are dangers in there being only one speech in this House. Then statements in it have often tended to be treated as definitions and it is not the function of a court or of this House to frame definitions; some latitude should be left for future developments. The true ratio of a decision generally appears more clearly from a comparison of two or more statements in different words which are intended to supplement each other.

The plea of non est factum obviously applies when the person sought to be held liable did not in fact sign the document. But at least since the sixteenth century it has also been held to apply in certain cases so as to enable a person who in fact signed a document to say that it is not his deed. Obviously any such extension must be kept within narrow limits if it is not to shake the confidence of those who habitually and rightly rely on signatures when there is no obvious reason to doubt their validity. Originally this extension appears to have been made in favour of those who were unable to read owing to blindness or illiteracy and who therefore had to trust someone to tell them what they were signing. I think that it must also apply in favour of those who are permanently or temporarily unable through no fault of their own to have without explanation any real understanding of the purport of a particular document, whether that be from defective education, illness or innate incapacity.

But that does not excuse them from taking such precautions as they reasonably can. The matter generally arises where an innocent third party has relied on a signed document in ignorance of the circumstances in which it was signed, and where he will suffer loss if the maker of the document is allowed to have it declared a nullity. So there must be a heavy burden of proof on the person who seeks to invoke this remedy. He must prove all the circumstances necessary to justify its being granted to him, and that necessarily involves his proving that he took all reasonable precautions in the circumstances. I do not say that the remedy can never be available to a man of full capacity. But that could only be in very exceptional circumstances; certainly not where his reason for not scrutinising the document before signing it was that he was too busy or too lazy. In general I do not think that he can be heard to say that he signed in reliance on someone he trusted. But, particularly when he was led to believe that the document which he signed was not one which affected his legal rights, there may be cases where this plea can properly be applied in favour of a man of full capacity.

The plea cannot be available to anyone who was content to sign without taking the trouble to try to find out at least the general effect of the document. Many people do frequently sign documents put before them for

signature by their solicitor or other trusted advisers without making any enquiry as to their purpose or effect. But the essence of the plea non est factum is that the person signing believed that the document he signed had one character or one effect whereas in fact its character or effect was quite different. He could not have such a belief unless he had taken steps or been given information which gave him some grounds for his belief. The amount of information he must have and the sufficiency of the particularity of his belief must depend on the circumstances of each case. Further the plea cannot be available to a person whose mistake was really a mistake as to the legal effect of the document, whether that was is own mistake or that of his adviser. That has always been the law and in this branch of the law at least I see no reason for any change.

We find in many of the authorities statements that a man's deed is not his deed if his mind does not go with his pen. But that is far too wide. It would cover cases where the man had taken no precautions at all, and there was no ground for his belief that he was signing something different from that which in fact he signed. I think that it is the wrong approach to start from that wide statement and then whittle it down by excluding cases where the remedy will not be granted. It is for the person who seeks the remedy to show that he should have it.

Finally, there is the question to what extent or in what way must there be a difference between that which in fact he signed and that which he believed he was signing. In an endeavour to keep the plea within bounds there have been many attempts to lay down a dividing line. But any dividing line suggested has been difficult to apply in practice and has sometimes led to unreasonable results. In particular I do not think that the modern division between the character and the contents of a document is at all satisfactory. Some of the older authorities suggest a more flexible test so that one can take all factors into consideration. There was a period when here as elsewhere in the law hard and fast dividing lines were sought, but I think that experience has shown that often they do not produce certainty but do produce unreasonable results.

I think that in the older authorities difference in practical result was more important than difference in legal character. If a man thinks that he is signing a document which will cost him £10 and the actual document would cost him £1,000 it could not be right to deny him this remedy simply because the legal character of the two was the same. It is true that we must then deal with questions of degree but that is a familiar task for the courts and I would not expect it to give rise to a flood of litigation.

There must I think be a radical difference between what he signed and what he thought he was signing – or one could use the words "fundamental" or "serious" or "very substantial". But what amounts to a radical difference will depend on all the circumstances. If he thinks he is giving property to A whereas the document gives it to B the difference may often be of vital importance, but in the circumstances of the present case I do not think that it is. I think that it must be left to the courts to determine in each case in light of all the facts whether there was or was not a sufficiently great difference. The plea non est factum is in sense illogical when applied to a case where the man in fact signed the deed. But it is none the worse for that if applied in a reasonable way.'

Comment
Approved: *Foster* v *Mackinnon* (1869) LR 4 CP 704. Overruled: *Carlisle and Cumberland Banking Co* v *Bragg* [1911] 1 KB 489. Disapproved: *Howatson* v *Webb* [1907] 1 Ch 537. Applied in *Avon Finance Co Ltd* v *Bridger* [1985] 2 All ER 281 (non est factum has limited application and can be relied on only if defendant has exercised reasonable care in connection with transaction). See also *Norwich and Peterborough Building Society* v *Steed (No 2)* [1993] 1 All ER 330 (heavy burden of proof on person who seeks to rely on non est factum).

9 Duress and Undue Influence

Allcard v Skinner (1887) 36 Ch D 145 Court of Appeal (Cotton, Lindley and Bowen LJJ)

- *Undue influence – gift to sisterhood – delay in seeking recovery*

Facts

In 1867 an unmarried woman aged 27 sought a clergyman as a confessor. The following year she became an associate of the sisterhood of which he was spiritual director and in 1871 she was admitted a full member, taking vows of poverty, chastity and obedience. Without independent advice, she made gifts of money and stock to the mother superior on behalf of the sisterhood. She left the sisterhood in 1879 and in 1884 claimed the return of the stock. Proceedings to recover the stock were commenced in 1885.

Held

Although the plaintiff's gifts were voidable, (Cotton LJ dissenting) she was disentitled to recover because of her conduct and the delay.

Lindley LJ:

'The principle must be examined. What, then, is the principle? Is it that it is right and expedient to save persons from the consequences of their own folly? Or is it that it is right and expedient to save them from being victimised by other people?

In my opinion, the doctrine of undue influence is founded upon the second of these two principles. Courts of equity have never set aside gifts on the ground of the folly, imprudence, or want of foresight on the part of donors. The courts have always repudiated any such jurisdiction. ...

I believe that in this case there was in fact no unfair or undue influence brought to bear upon the plaintiff other than such as inevitably resulted from the training she had received, the promise she had made, the vows she had taken, and the rules to which she had submitted herself. But her gifts were in fact made under a pressure which, while it lasted, the plaintiff could not resist, and were not, in my opinion, past recall when the pressure was removed. When the plaintiff emancipated herself from the spell by which she was bound she was entitled to invoke the aid of the court in order to obtain the restitution from the defendant of so much of the plaintiff's property as had not been spent in accordance with the wishes of the plaintiff but remained in the hands of the defendant. The plaintiff now demands no more.

I proceed to consider the second point which arises in this case, viz, whether it is too late for the plaintiff to invoke the assistance of the court. More than six years had elapsed between the time when the plaintiff left the sisterhood and the commencement of the present action. The action is not one of those to which the Statute of Limitations in terms applies, nor is that statute pleaded. But this action very closely resembles an action for money had and received, laches and acquiescence are relied upon as a defence, and the question is whether this defence ought to prevail. In my opinion, it ought ...

It is not, however, necessary to decide whether this delay alone would be a sufficient defence to the action. The case by no means rests on mere lapse of time. There is far more than inactivity and delay on the part of the plaintiff. There is conduct amounting to confirmation of her gift. Gifts liable to be set aside by the court on the ground of undue influence have always been treated as voidable, and not void ... such gifts are voidable on equitable grounds only. A gift intended when made to be absolute and irrevocable, but liable to be set aside by a court of justice, not on the ground of change of mind on the part of the donor, but on grounds of public policy based upon the fact that the donor was not sufficiently free relatively to the donee – such a gift is very different from a loan which the borrower knows he is under an obligation to repay, and is also different from a gift expressly made revocable, and never intended to be absolute and unconditional. A gift made in terms absolute and unconditional naturally leads the donee to regard it as his own, and the longer he is left under this impression the more difficult it is justly to deprive him of what he has naturally so regarded.

So long as the relation between the donor and the donee which invalidates the gifts lasts, so long is it necessary to hold that lapse of time affords no sufficient ground for refusing relief to the donor. But this necessity ceases when the relation itself comes to an end; and if the donor desires to have his gift declared invalid and set aside, he ought, in my opinion, to seek relief within a reasonable time after the removal of the influence under which the gift was made. If he does not, the inference is strong, and if the lapse of time is long the inference becomes inevitable and conclusive – that the donor is content not to call the gift in question or, in other words, that he elects not to avoid it, or, what is the same thing in effect, that he ratifies and confirms it ... In this particular case the plaintiff considered, when she left the sisterhood, what course she should take, and she determined to do nothing, but to leave matters as they were. She insisted on having back her will, but she never asked for her money until the end of five years or so after she left the sisterhood. In this state of things I can only come to the conclusion that she deliberately chose not to attempt to avoid her gifts but to acquiesce in them, or, if the expression be preferred, to ratify or confirm them. I regard this as a question of fact, and upon the evidence I can come to no other conclusion than that which I have mentioned.

Moreover, by demanding her will and not her money, she made her resolution known to the defendant.'

Comment
Distinguished in *Re Brocklehurst, Hall* v *Roberts* [1978] 1 All ER 767 (on the facts, relationship not one of confidence and trust). See also *National Westminister Bank plc* v *Morgan* [1985] 2 WLR 588 and *Bank of Credit and Commerce International SA* v *Aboody* [1989] 2 WLR 759.

Atlas Express Ltd v *Kafco (Importers and Distributors) Ltd* [1989] 3 WLR 389 High Court (Tucker J)

• *Duress – commercial pressure*

Facts
The plaintiffs, a national road carrier, contracted with the defendants, a small company, to deliver cartons of the defendants' basketware to branches of Woolworth throughout the United Kingdom. Before entering into the contract, the plaintiffs' manager had inspected the cartons and estimated that each load would contain a minimum of 400 and possibly as many as 600 cartons: on that basis he agreed a charge of £1.10 per carton. In fact, the first load contained only 200 cartons, so the manager said they would not take any more unless the defendants agreed to pay a minimum of £440 per load. As they were heavily dependent on their Woolworth contract and could not at that time find an alternative carrier, the defendants agreed to the new terms but later refused to pay at the new rate.

Held
The defendants were not bound by the new terms: economic duress had vitiated the new agreement and, in any case, there was no consideration for it.

Tucker J:

'The issue which I have to determine is

whether the defendants are bound by the [new] agreement signed on their behalf ... The defendants contend that they are not bound, for two reasons: first, because the agreement was signed under duress; second, because there was no consideration for it.

The first question raises an interesting point of law, ie whether economic duress is a concept known to English law.

Economic duress must be distinguished from commercial pressure, which on any view is not sufficient to vitiate consent. The borderline between the two may in some cases be indistinct. But ... authors ... appear to recognise that in appropriate cases economic duress may afford a defence, and in my judgment it does. It is clear to me that in a number of English cases judges have acknowledged the existence of this concept.

Thus, in *D & C Builders Ltd* v *Rees* [1965] 3 All ER 837 at 841 Lord Denning MR said: "No person can insist on a settlement procured by intimidation." And in *Occidental Worldwide Investment Corp* v *Skibs A/S Avanti, The Siboen and the Sibotre* [1976] 1 Lloyd's Rep 293 at 336 Kerr J appeared to accept that economic duress could operate in appropriate circumstances. A similar conclusion was reached by Mocatta J in *North Ocean Shipping Co Ltd* v *Hyundai Construction Co Ltd, The Atlantic Baron* [1978] 3 All ER 1170 at 1182.

In particular, there are passages in the judgment of Lord Scarman in *Pao On* v *Lau Yiu* [1979] 3 All ER 65 at 78-79 which clearly indicate recognition of the concept ...

A further case, which was not cited to me was *B & S Contracts and Design Ltd* v *Victor Green Publications Ltd* [1984] ICR 419 at 423, where Eveleigh LJ referred to the speech of Lord Diplock in another uncited case, *Universe Tankships Inc of Monrovia* v *International Transport Workers' Federation* [1982] 2 All ER 67 at 75-76:

> "The rationale is that his apparent consent was induced by pressure exercised on him by that other party which the law does not regard as legitimate, with the consequence that the consent is treated in law as revocable unless approbated either

expressly or by implication after the illegitimate pressure has ceased to operate on his mind."

In commenting on this Eveleigh LJ said of the word "legitimate" ([1984] ICR 419 at 423):

> "For the purpose of this case it is sufficient to say that if the claimant has been influenced against his will to pay money under the threat of unlawful damage to his economic interest he will be entitled to claim that money back ..."

Reverting to the case before me, I find that the defendants' apparent consent to the agreement was induced by pressure which was illegitimate and I find that it was not approbated. In my judgment that pressure can properly be described as economic duress, which is a concept recognised by English law, and which in the circumstances of the present case vitiates the defendants' apparent consent to the agreement.

In any event, I find that there was no consideration for the new agreement. The plaintiffs were already obliged to deliver the defendants' goods at the rates agreed under the terms of the original agreement. There was no consideration for the increased minimum charge of £440 per trailer.'

Bank of Credit and Commerce International SA v *Aboody* [1989] 2 WLR 759 Court of Appeal (Slade, Balcombe and Woolf LJJ)

* *Undue influence – husband and wife*

Facts

A husband and wife owned a family company (Eratex Ltd) and the company's liabilities to its bank were secured, inter alia, by charges of the wife's house. The bank sought to enforce the securities and the wife pleaded actual undue influence by the husband. Although the judge found that such influence had been established, he refused to set aside the charges as it had not been proved that they were manifestly disadvantageous to the wife. The wife appealed.

Held

The appeal would be dismissed as the judge's conclusion that there had been no manifest disadvantage was correct and, further, it was probable that the wife would have entered into the charges even in the absence of undue influence.

Slade LJ:

'We now turn to consider the point of law which constitutes the first ground of appeal, namely that a party who proves that a transaction was induced by the actual exercise of undue influence is entitled to have it set aside without also proving that the transaction was manifestly disadvantageous to him or her.

Ever since the judgments of this court in *Allcard* v *Skinner* (1887) 36 Ch D 145 a clear distinction has been drawn between (1) those cases in which the court will uphold a plea of undue influence only if it is satisfied that such influence has been affirmatively proved on the evidence (commonly referred to as cases of "actual undue influence" and, in argument before us, as "class 1" cases); (2) those cases (commonly referred to as cases of "presumed undue influence," and, in argument before us, as "class 2" cases) in which the relationship between the parties will lead the court to presume that undue influence has been exerted unless evidence is adduced proving the contrary, eg by showing that the complaining party has had independent advice.

There are well established categories of relationship, such as a religious superior and inferior and doctor and patient where the relationship as such will give rise to the presumption (frequently referred to in argument before us as "class 2A" cases). The relationship of husband and wife does not as such give rise to the presumption: see *National Westminster Bank plc* v *Morgan* [1985] AC 686, 703B, and *Bank of Montreal* v *Stuart* [1911] AC 120. Nor does the normal relationship of banker and customer as such give rise to it. Nevertheless, on particular facts (frequently referred to in argument as "class 2B" cases) relationships

not falling within the class 2A category may be shown to have become such as to justify the court in applying the same presumption.

"the presumption of undue influence, like other presumptions, is a tool of the lawyer's trade whose function it is to enable him to arrive at a just result by bridging a gap in the evidence at a point where, in the nature of the case, evidence is difficult or impossible to come by:" see *In re The Estate of Brocklehurst, decd* [1978] Ch 14, 43, per Bridge LJ.

In the majority of reported cases on undue influence successful plaintiffs appear to have succeeded in reliance on the presumption. If on the facts both pleas are open to him, a plaintiff in such a case may well be advised to rely on actual and presumed undue influence cumulatively or in the alternative.

In the present case, however, no doubt after carefully considered advice, no attempt has been made to plead or submit that Mrs Aboody is entitled to the benefit of any presumption. Her case throughout has been pleaded and argued on the footing that it is a class 1 case, so that the onus falls on her to establish undue influence – an onus which, subject to the question of manifest disadvantage, the judge considered that she had discharged …

… we must reject the first ground of appeal. In our judgment, and in the light of *National Westminster Bank plc* v *Morgan* [1985] AC 686, even a party who affirmatively proves that a transaction was induced by the exercise of undue influence is not entitled to have it set aside in reliance on the doctrine of undue influence without proving that the transaction was manifestly disadvantageous to him or her.

Since Mrs Aboody's claim in the present case is based exclusively on undue influence, it thus becomes necessary to consider whether, contrary to the judge's view, she has shown that all or any of the six transactions were manifestly disadvantageous to her … Eratex Ltd was the family business and the sole or principal means of support of Mr and Mrs Aboody. Eratex Ltd might still have collapsed with or without the facilities covered by the six transactions. But at least these facilities gave it some hope of survival. The judge found that ... it had "more than an equal chance of surviving," and that, [later], it had "at least a reasonably good chance of surviving." If it had survived, the potential benefits to Mrs Aboody would have been substantial.

In the end, we can see no sufficient grounds for disagreeing with his conclusion that on balance a manifest disadvantage has not been shown by Mrs Aboody in respect of any of the six transactions ...

... in our judgment ... the jurisdiction exercised by the court in such cases is not essentially of a punitive nature; its purpose is to do justice to the complainant in suitable circumstances giving him or her relief from a disadvantageous transaction. We think that, at least in ordinary circumstances, it would not be appropriate for the court to exercise this jurisdiction in a case where the evidence establishes that on balance of probabilities the complainant would have entered into the transaction in any event. In the present case there is the additional factor that the transactions under attack are relied on not by Mr Aboody himself but by the bank, which was not personally responsible for exerting the undue influence. Even if Mrs Aboody had succeeded on all the other issues in this case, we are therefore disposed to think that it would not have been right to grant her equitable relief as against the bank, our decision being based not merely on narrow considerations of causation.'

Comment
See also *Barclays Bank plc* v *O'Brien* [1993] 3 WLR 786 (classification of undue influence) and *Barclays Bank plc* v *Thomson* [1997] 4 All ER 816.

Barclays Bank plc v *O'Brien* [1993] 3 WLR 786 House of Lords (Lords Templeman, Lowry, Browne-Wilkinson, Slynn of Hadley and Woolf)

• *Misrepresentation by husband – bank's constructive knowledge*

Facts
Husband and wife made a joint application for overdraft facilities for a company in which the husband had an interest. The overdraft was secured on their home. The husband misrepresented the situation to the wife saying the facility was short-term and for a fixed low sum. The wife appealed on the basis that she had not read any of the documents and was unaware of the extent of the overdraft because of her husband's misrepresentation.

Held
A wife who stood surety for her husband's debt and who had been induced by undue influence, misrepresentation or similar wrong had a right to have the transaction set aside if the third party (in this case the bank) had actual or constructive knowledge. Unless reasonable steps had been taken to ascertain (a) whether the transaction was of financial advantage to the wife, and (b) if there were reasons to suspect that the husband had committed a legal or equitable wrong which had induced the wife into the transaction, there would be, at the least, constructive knowledge. The bank, having failed to take any such steps to verify the situation, had constructive knowledge of the husband's wrongful misrepresentation. The wife was entitled to have the charge set aside.

Lord Browne-Wilkinson:

'A person who has been induced to enter into a transaction by the undue influence of another (the wrongdoer) is entitled to set that transaction aside as against the wrongdoer. Such undue influence is either actual or presumed. In *Bank of Credit and*

Commerce International SA v *Aboody* [1989] 2 WLR 759 the Court of Appeal helpfully adopted the following classification.

Class 1: actual undue influence. In these cases it is necessary for the claimant to prove affirmatively that the wrongdoer exerted undue influence on the complainant to enter into the particular transaction which is impugned.

Class 2: presumed undue influence. In these cases the complainant only has to show, in the first instance, that there was a relationship of trust and confidence between the complainant and the wrongdoer of such a nature that it is fair to presume that the wrongdoer abused that relationship in procuring the complainant to enter into the impugned transaction. In class 2 cases therefore there is no need to produce evidence that actual undue influence was exerted in relation to the particular transaction impugned: once a confidential relationship has been proved, the burden then shifts to the wrongdoer to prove that the complainant entered into the impugned transaction freely, for example by showing that the complainant had independent advice. Such a confidential relationship can be established in two ways, viz:

Class 2A. Certain relationships (for example solicitor and client, medical advisor and patient) as a matter of law raise the presumption that undue influence has been exercised.

Class 2B. Even if there is no relationship falling within class 2A, if the complainant proves the de facto existence of a relationship under which the complainant generally reposed trust and confidence in the wrongdoer, the existence of such relationship raises the presumption of undue influence. In a class 2B case therefore, in the absence of evidence disproving undue influence, the complainant will succeed in setting aside the impugned transaction merely by proof that the complainant reposed trust and confidence in the wrongdoer without having to prove that the wrongdoer exerted actual undue influence or otherwise abused such trust and confidence in relation to the particular transaction impugned. ...

Although there is no class 2A presumption of undue influence as between husband and wife, it should be emphasised that in any particular case a wife may well be able to demonstrate that de facto she did leave decisions on financial affairs to her husband thereby bringing herself within class 2B, ie that the relationship between husband and wife in the particular case was such that the wife reposed confidence and trust in her husband in relation to their financial affairs and therefore undue influence is to be presumed. Thus, in those cases which still occur where the wife relies in all financial matters on her husband and simply does what he suggests, a presumption of undue influence within class 2B can be established solely from the proof of such trust and confidence without proof of actual undue influence.

... in my judgment a creditor is put on inquiry when a wife offers to stand surety for her husband's debts by the combination of two factors: (a) the transaction is on its face not to the financial advantage of the wife; and (b) there is a substantial risk in transactions of that kind that, in procuring the wife to act as surety, the husband has committed a legal or equitable wrong that entitles the wife to set aside the transaction.

It follows that, unless the creditor who is put on inquiry takes reasonable steps to satisfy himself that the wife's agreement to stand surety has been property obtained, the creditor will have constructive notice of the wife's rights.

What, then are the reasonable steps which the creditor should take to ensure that it does not have constructive notice of the wife's rights, if any? Normally the reasonable steps necessary to avoid being fixed with constructive notice consist of making inquiry of the person who may have the earlier right (ie the wife) to see if whether such right is asserted. It is plainly impossible to require of banks and other financial institutions that they should inquire of one spouse whether he or she has been unduly influenced or misled by the other. But, in my judgment, the creditor, in order to avoid being fixed with constructive notice, can reasonably be expected to take steps to bring home to the wife the risk she is running by standing as surety and to advise her to take independent advice. As to past transactions, it will depend on the facts of each case whether the steps taken by the creditor satisfy this test. However for the future, in my judgment, a creditor will have satisfied these requirements if it insists that the wife attend a private meeting (in the absence of the husband) with a representative of the creditor at which she is told of the extent of her liability as surety, warned of the risk she is running and urged to take independent legal advice. If these steps are taken in my judgment the creditor will have taken such reasonable steps as are necessary to preclude a subsequent claim that it had constructive notice of the wife's rights.'

Comment
For the raising of a '*Barclays Bank* v *O'Brien* defence' to a claim under a legal charge, see *Barclays Bank plc* v *Thomson* [1997] 4 All ER 816.

Barclays Bank plc v *Thomson*
[1997] 4 All ER 816 Court of Appeal (Simon Brown, Waite and Morritt LJJ)

• *Undue influence – husband and wife – solicitor's assurance that wife properly advised*

Facts
A husband and wife had a joint account with the plaintiff bank. Prior to obtaining a legal charge over the wife's family home ('the property') in order to secure borrowing on that account, the bank wrote to solicitors (who acted for the husband's business and were then transferring the property from trustees to the wife) and asked them to register the charge and explain to her its full content and effect. By letter the solicitors assured the bank that

they had given such an explanation. The husband and wife having failed to repay the amount borrowed, the bank sought and obtained an order for possession of the property. The wife applied to have the order set aside and, for the purpose of those proceedings, it was assumed that the loan transaction was to her manifest disadvantage and that she had been subject to undue influence by her husband. The crucial question was whether the bank was fixed with constructive notice of this undue influence.

Held
The bank was not so fixed and it had been entitled to the order for possession.

Simon Brown LJ:

'The starting point ... must be the trilogy of recent Court of Appeal decisions which clearly establish a bank's entitlement to rely upon a solicitor's certificate that proper advice has been given to the signatory of a relevant instrument even though that solicitor acts principally for the very person against whose undue influence the signatory must be guarded: *Massey* v *Midland Bank plc* [1995] 1 All ER 929, *Banco Exterior Internacional* v *Mann* [1995] 1 All ER 936 and *Bank of Baroda* v *Rayarel* [1995] 2 FLR 376. ...

I pass next to two further Court of Appeal cases in which the solicitor advising the signatory was acting also for the lender, at any rate with regard to certain aspects of the transaction: *Midland Bank plc* v *Serter* [1995] 1 FLR 1034 and *Halifax Mortgage Services Ltd (formerly BNP Mortgages Ltd)* v *Stepsky* [1996] 2 All ER 277. ... The final decision to which reference must be made – it is, indeed, the decision most strongly relied upon by the [wife] – is *Bank of Credit and Commerce International SA* v *Aboody* [1992] 4 All ER 955, in which the very full judgment of the Court of Appeal was given by Slade LJ. ... It is time to state my conclusions. I can do so really quite shortly. I see no distinction in principle between *Aboody*'s case and the present case. ... I can see no good reason whatever why a bank, perhaps conscientiously instructing solicitors to give independent advice to a signatory who might otherwise go unadvised, should thereby be disabled from relying on the solicitors' certificate that such advice has been properly given. The contrary argument founded on the agency principle is wholly artificial and to my mind now discredited. [Counsel for the wife's] suggestion that lenders may choose to instruct solicitors whom they know will advise the signatory incompetently I reject utterly. ... In short, I find nothing in the present case to distinguish it from all five of the recent Court of Appeal cases to which I have referred. The bank was equally entitled to rely on [the solicitors'] assurance here as were the lenders in all those cases to rely on the various certificates and declarations there.'

Comment

The wife raised – unsuccessfully – 'the *Barclays Bank* v *O'Brien* defence' and the proceedings fell within class 2(B) in the undue influence classification. See *Barclays Bank plc* v *O'Brien* [1993] 3 WLR 786, but compare *Royal Bank of Scotland plc* v *Etridge* [1997] 3 All ER 628.

Barton v *Armstrong* [1975] 2 WLR 1050 Privy Council (Lords Wilberforce, Simon of Glaisdale, Cross of Chelsea, Kilbrandon and Sir Garfield Barwick)

* *Duress – reason for contracting*

Facts

Armstrong and Barton had struggled for control of a public company and Barton had executed a deed (and certain ancillary deeds) in the course of various negotiations. Barton alleged that these deeds had been executed by him under duress exerted by Armstrong and were therefore void. It was found as a fact that Armstrong had uttered threats to kill Barton, but the Court of Appeal of the Supreme Court of New South Wales found that Barton had not discharged the onus of showing that, but for the threats, he would not have executed the deeds.

Held (Lords Wilberforce and Simon of Glaisdale dissenting)

The deeds were void as Armstrong had failed to establish that his threats had contributed nothing to Barton's decision to sign them.

Lord Cross of Chelsea:

'Their Lordships turn now to consider the question of law ... It is hardly surprising that there is no direct authority on the point, for if A threatens B with death if he does not execute some document and B, who takes A's threats seriously, executes the document it can be only in the most unusual circumstances that there can be any doubt whether the threats operated to induce him to execute the document. But this is a most unusual case and the findings of fact made below do undoubtedly raise the question whether it was necessary for Barton in order to obtain relief to establish that he would not have executed the deed in question but for the threats ...

Had Armstrong made a fraudulent misrepresentation to Barton for the purpose of inducing him to execute the [deeds] the answer to the problem which has arisen would have been clear. If it were established that Barton did not allow the representation to affect his judgment then he could not make it a ground for relief even though the representation was designed and known by Barton to be designed to affect his judgment. If on the other hand Barton relief on the misrepresentation Armstrong could not have defeated his claim to relief by showing that there were other more weighty causes which contributed to his decision to execute the deed, for in this field the court does not allow an examination into the relative importance of contributory causes. "Once make out that there has been anything like deception, and no contract resting in any degree on that foundation can stand" (per Lord Cranworth LJ in *Reynell* v *Sprye* (1852) 1 De GM & G 660 ... Their

Lordships think that the same rule should apply in cases of duress and that if Armstrong's threats were "a" reason for Barton's executing the deed he is entitled to relief even though he might well have entered into the contract if Armstrong had uttered no threats to induce him to do so. ...

It remains to apply the law to the facts. ... If Barton had to establish that he would not have made the agreement but for Armstrong's threats then their Lordships would not dissent from the view that he had not made out his case. But no such onus lay on him. On the contrary it was for Armstrong to establish, if he could, that the threats which he was making and the unlawful pressure which he was exerting for the purpose of inducing Barton to sign the agreement and which Barton knew were being made and exerted for this purpose in fact contributed nothing to Barton's decision to sign. ... It is true that on the facts as their Lordships assume them to have been, Armstrong's threats may have been unnecessary; but it would be unrealistic to hold that they played no part in making Barton decide to execute the documents. The proper inference to be drawn from the facts found is, their Lordships think, that though it may be that Barton would have executed the documents even if Armstrong had made no threats and exerted no unlawful pressure to induce him to do so the threats and unlawful pressure in fact contributed to his decision to sign the documents ... It may be, of course, that Barton's fear of Armstrong had evaporated before he issued his writ in this action but Armstrong – understandably enough – expressly disclaimed reliance on the defence of delay on Barton's part in repudiating the deed.

In the result therefore the appeal should be allowed and a declaration made that the deeds in question were executed by Barton under duress and are void so far as concerns him.'

Comment
See also *Pao On* v *Lau Yiu Long* [1979] 3 WLR 435.

CTN Cash and Carry Ltd v Gallaher Ltd [1994] 4 All ER 714 Court of Appeal (Sir Donald Nicholls VC, Farquharson and Steyn LJJ)

• *Duress – economic duress – 'lawful act duress'*

Facts
The defendants, sole distributors of certain popular brands, supplied cigarettes for sale in the plaintiffs' six warehouses. They were not contractually bound to sell them any cigarettes: separate contracts were made from time to time. The defendants granted the plaintiffs credit facilities, but these could be withdrawn at any time. The manager of one of the plaintiffs' warehouses placed an order; by mistake they were delivered to the wrong one. The defendants agreed to collect the cigarettes and deliver them to the right one: before they could do so, the goods were stolen. Although property in the stolen cigarettes had not passed to the plaintiffs, the defendants invoiced them for them. The defendants thought (mistakenly but in good faith) that the cigarettes were, at the time of the robbery, at the plaintiffs' risk. The plaintiffs rejected the invoice but, after the defendants had made it clear that they would not in future be granted credit facilities, they paid it, believing it to be the lesser of the two evils. The plaintiffs now claimed repayment on the ground that the money had been paid under duress.

Held
Their action would fail since the defendants' conduct had not amounted to duress.

Steyn LJ:

'I also readily accept that the fact that the defendants have used lawful means does not by itself remove the case from the scope of the doctrine of economic duress. ... there are a number of cases where English courts have accepted that a threat may be illegitimate when coupled with a demand for payment even if the threat is one of lawful action (see *Thorne* v *Motor Trade Association* [1937] 3 All ER 157 at 160–161, *Mutual Finance Ltd* v *John Wetton & Sons Ltd* [1937] 2 All ER 657 and *Universe Tankships Inc of Monrovia* v *International Transport Workers' Federation* [1982] 2 All ER 67 at 75, 89). On the other hand, Goff and Jones *Law of Restitution* (3rd edn, 1986) p240 observed that English courts have wisely not accepted any general principle that a threat not to contract with another, except on certain terms, may amount to duress.

We are being asked to extend the categories of duress of which the law will take cognisance. That is not necessarily objectionable, but it seems to me that an extension capable of covering the present case, involving "law act duress" in a commercial context in pursuit of a bona fide claim, would be a radical one with far-reaching implications. It would introduce a substantial and undesirable element of uncertainty in the commercial bargaining process. Moreover, it will often enable bona fide settled accounts to be reopened when parties to commercial dealings fall out. The aim of our commercial law ought to be to encourage fair dealing between parties. But it is a mistake for the law to set its sights too highly when the critical inquiry is not whether the conduct is lawful but whether it is morally or socially unacceptable. That is the inquiry in which we are engaged. In my view there are policy considerations which militate against ruling that the defendants obtained payment of the disputed invoice by duress.

Outside the field of protected relationships, and in a purely commercial context, it might be a relatively rare case in which "lawful act duress" can be established. And it might be particularly difficult to establish duress if the defendant bona fide considered that his demand was valid. In this complex and changing branch of the law I deliberately refrain from saying "never". But as the law stands, I am satisfied that the defendants' conduct in this case did not amount to duress.

It is an unattractive result, inasmuch as the defendants are allowed to retain a sum which at the trial they become aware was not in truth due to them. But in my view the law compels the result.'

Comment

Since at a late stage of the trial the defendants had accepted that the risk in the goods had not in law passed to the plaintiffs and therefore that they had not been entitled to be paid for them, Sir Donald Nicholls V-C suggested tentatively that the defendants could be said to have been unjustly enriched and that a new claim for restitution could possibly succeed.

National Westminster Bank plc v *Morgan* [1985] 2 WLR 588 House of Lords (Lords Scarman, Keith of Kinkel, Roskill, Bridge of Harwich and Brandon of Oakbrook)

- *Undue influence – banker and customer*

Facts

Mrs Morgan and her husband owned a house. It was mortgaged to the building society, who threatened to seek possession for unpaid debts. The defendant bank offered to 'refinance' the couple and to relieve the pressure put on them by the society. This was to be done by way of a loan, secured by a further mortgage, this time in favour of the bank. Mr Morgan readily agreed, but when the bank manager visited Mrs Morgan to obtain her signature to the mortgage deed, she wanted reassurance that the loan to be made would not be used by her husband for the purpose of his business, but would go to pay off the society. The manager reassured her and she signed the deed. The loan was not repaid and the bank, in turn, sued for possession of the house. Mrs Morgan argued that the bank manager exercised undue influence over her and that a special relationship existed between her and the bank which required it to ensure that she receive independent legal advice before entering into a further mortgage.

Held

The bank was entitled to possession.

Lord Scarman:

'The principle justifying the court in setting aside a transaction for undue influence can now be seen to have been established by Lindley LJ in *Allcard* v *Skinner* (1887) 36 Ch D 145. It is not a vague "public policy" but specifically the victimisation of one party by the other. ...

The wrongfulness of the transaction must, therefore, be shown: it must be one in which an unfair advantage has been taken of another. The doctrine is not limited to transactions of gift. A commercial relationship can become a relationship in which one party assumes a role of dominating influence over the other. In *Poosathurai* v *Kannappa Chettiar* (1919) LR 47 Ind App 1 the Board recognised that a sale at an undervalue could be a transaction which a court could set aside as unconscionable if it was shown or could be presumed to have been procured by the exercise of undue influence. Similarly, a relationship of banker and customer may become one in which the banker acquires a dominating influence. If he does and a manifestly disadvantageous transaction is proved, there would then be room for the court to presume that it resulted from the exercise of undue influence.

This brings me to *Lloyds Bank Ltd* v *Bundy* [1975] QB 326. It was, as one would expect, conceded by counsel for the wife that the relationship between banker and customer it not one which ordinarily gives rise to a presumption of undue influence; and that in the ordinary course of banking business a banker can explain the nature of the proposed transaction without laying himself open to a charge of undue influence. This proposition has never been in doubt, though some, it would appear, have thought that the Court of Appeal held otherwise in *Lloyds Bank Ltd* v *Bundy*. If any such view has gained currency, let it be destroyed now once and for all time ... The question which the House does have to answer is: did the court in *Lloyds Bank Ltd* v *Bundy* accurately state the law?

Lord Denning MR believed that the doctrine of undue influence could be subsumed under a general principle that English courts will grant relief where there has been "inequality of bargaining power" (see [1975] QB 326 at 339). He deliberately avoided reference to the will of one party being dominated or overcome by another. The majority of the court did not follow him; they based their decision on the orthodox view of the doctrine as expounded in *Allcard* v *Skinner*. This opinion of Lord Denning MR, therefore, was not the ground of the court's decision, which has to be found in the view of the majority ...

The doctrine of undue influence has been sufficiently developed not to need the support of a principle which by its formulation in the language of the law of contract is not appropriate to cover transactions of gift where there is no bargain. The fact of an unequal bargain will, of course, be a relevant feature in some cases of undue influence. But it can never become an appropriate basis of principle of an equitable doctrine which is concerned with transactions "not to be reasonably accounted for on the ground of friendship, relationship, charity, or other ordinary motives on which ordinary men act ..." (see *Allcard* v *Skinner* 36 Ch D 145 at 185 per Lindley LJ). And even in the field of contract I question whether there is any need in the modern law to erect a general principle of relief against inequality of bargaining power. Parliament has undertaken the task (and it is essentially a legislative task) of enacting such restrictions on freedom of contract as are in its judgment necessary to relieve against the mischief: for example, the hire-purchase and consumer protection legislation ... I doubt whether the courts should assume the burden of formulating further restrictions. ...

... the relationships which may develop a dominating influence of one over another are infinitely various. There is no substitute in this branch of the law for a "meticulous examination of the facts".

A meticulous examination of the facts of the present case reveals that [the bank] never "crossed the line". Nor was the transaction unfair to the wife. The bank was, therefore, under no duty to ensure that she had independent advice. It was an ordinary banking transaction whereby the wife sought to save her home; and she obtained an honest and truthful explanation of the bank's intention which, notwithstanding the terms of the mortgage deed which in the circumstances the trial judge was right to dismiss as "essentially theoretical", was correct; for no one has suggested that ... the bank sought to make the wife liable, or to make her home the security, for any debt of her husband other than the loan and interest necessary to save the house from being taken away from them in discharge of their indebtedness to the building society.

For these reasons, I would allow the appeal. In doing so, I would wish to give a warning. There is no precisely defined law setting limits to the equitable jurisdiction of a court to relieve against undue influence. This is the world of doctrine, not of neat and tidy rules. The courts of equity have developed a body of learning enabling relief to be granted where the law has to treat the transaction as unimpeachable unless it can be held to have been procured by undue influence. It is the unimpeachability at law of a disadvantageous transaction which is the starting point from which the court advances to consider whether the transaction is the product merely of one's own folly or of the undue influence exercised by another. A court in the exercise of this equitable jurisdiction is a court of conscience. Definition is a poor instrument when used to determine whether a transaction is or is not unconscionable: this is a question which depends on the particular facts of the case.'

Comment

Followed in *Cornish* v *Midland Bank plc* [1985] 3 All ER 513 and *O'Sullivan* v *Management Agency and Music Ltd* [1985] 3 All ER 351. See also *Midland Bank plc* v *Shephard* [1988] 3 All ER 17 and *Bank of Credit and Commerce International SA* v *Aboody* [1989] 2 WLR 759.

Pao On v *Lau Yiu Long* [1979] 3 WLR 435

See Chapter 2.

Royal Bank of Scotland plc v *Etridge* [1997] 3 All ER 628 Court of Appeal (Hobhouse and Mummery LJJ)

• *Undue influence – husband and wife – bank's constructive notice – solicitor bank's agent*

Facts

The plaintiff was banker of a husband and his various businesses and it asked him to provide additional security by way of a mortgage on his wife's house. The wife duly executed a legal charge in the form of a mortgage in the presence of a solicitor who had been instructed by the bank to act on its behalf for the purpose of giving the wife appropriate information and advice. By way of a certificate stamped on the charge, the solicitor confirmed that he had explained its contents and effect to her, but the wife now denied that this had been the case.

Held

Should the wife's view be established, the bank would be fixed with constructive notice of any undue influence.

Hobhouse LJ:

'Returning to the question whether the situation had changed from the time of the previous directions, first, it had changed in favour of the plaintiff in that there had been two Court of Appeal decisions (which have since been reported) applying *Barclays Bank plc* v *O'Brien* [1993] 4 All ER 417 and which interpreted the effect of that case in the context with which we are concerned in the present case. Those authorities are

Massey v *Midland Bank plc* [1995] 1 All ER 929 and *Banco Exterior Internacional* v *Mann* [1995] 1 All ER 936. ...

On the facts which appeared to exist at the time of the original directions in the present action in 1993, it was simply a case which was indistinguishable from the *Banco Exterior* case. There was a certificate signed by a solicitor which the bank were entitled to take at face value and which, therefore, allowed them to say that they were not affected by any undue influence that may have been practised on the wife.

However, that was not the only change in circumstances. The plaintiffs had disclosed ... the fact that they had themselves instructed the solicitor, to act as their solicitor. ... They were therefore constituting him their own solicitor for the purposes of giving the appropriate information or advice to the wife. ...

In *Massey*'s case ... the bank ... called the wife into the office and told her face to face that she should get independent advice. In the *Banco Exterior* case they did not do that, but they communicated with the wife and told her in writing that she should obtain independent advice. They produced a form for completion by the independent advisor which was completed and returned to the bank. They were entitled to conclude from that that she had received independent advice.

In the present case, the bank adopted a different course. They did not have the wife in, nor did they leave it entirely to the wife to take independent advice. They appointed their own agent to follow the course described by Lord Browne-Wilkinson [in *O'Brien*'s case]. They appointed the solicitor to act as their own agent in this regard. Therefore, since they delegated their task to their own solicitor, they are responsible for this discharge of that duty. If he did not discharge it then they must accept that situation since they are in the same position as their agent. The only evidence is, at present, from the wife who says that he did not.

That is the legal position as it appears to me. I will say no more about the merits. It may be that at a trial when the facts of this particular case are evaluated it will be seen that they are not as I have summarised. But there is clearly an arguable point which can be raised by the wife that the person who it appears the bank are saying was their own agent did not do what was required to satisfy the test referred to by Lord Browne-Wilkinson, nor does the case come into the category of the *Banco Exterior* decision. Those are matters which will have to be evaluated at a trial.'

Comment

Barclays Bank plc v *Thomson* [1997] 4 All ER 816 was decided before these proceedings but reference was not made here to that decision. However, in *Thomson*, Morritt LJ was sure that the solicitors concerned were not acting as the bank's solicitor when advising the wife, even though they did so at the bank's request.

Universe Tankships Inc of Monrovia v International Transport Workers' Federation, The Universe Sentinel [1982] 2 WLR 803 House of Lords (Lords Diplock, Cross of Chelsea, Russell of Killowen, Scarman and Brandon of Oakbrook)

- *Ship 'blacked' – economic duress?*

Facts

A ship was 'blacked' until union demands as to pay and conditions were satisfied. In order to have the blacking lifted, the ship owners, inter alia, made a contribution to the union's welfare fund.

Held (Lords Scarman and Brandon dissenting)

This contribution was recoverable by the owners as money had and received for their use.

Lord Diplock:

'It is ... in my view crucial to the decision of the instant appeal to identify the rationale of this development of the common law. It is not that the party seeking to avoid the contract which he has entered into with another party, or to recover money that he has paid to another party in response to a demand, did not know the nature or the precise terms of the contract at the time when he entered into it or did not understand the purpose for which the payment was demanded. The rationale is that his apparent consent was induced by pressure exercised on him by that other party which the law does not regard as legitimate, with the consequence that the consent is treated in law as revocable unless approbated either expressly or by implication after the illegitimate pressure has ceased to operate on his mind. It is a rationale similar to that which underlies the avoidability of contracts entered into and the recovery of money exacted under colour of office, or under undue influence or in consequence of threats of physical duress.

Commercial pressure, in some degree, exists wherever one party to a commercial transaction is in a stronger bargaining position than the other party. It is not, however, in my view, necessary, nor would it be appropriate in the instant appeal, to enter into the general question of the kinds of circumstances, if any, in which commercial pressure, even though it amounts to a coercion of the will of a party in the weaker bargaining position, may be treated as legitimate and, accordingly, as not giving rise to any legal right of redress. In the instant appeal the economic duress complained of was exercised in the field of industrial relations to which very special considerations apply …

The use of economic duress to induce another person to part with property or money is not a tort per se; the form that the duress takes may, or may not, be tortious. The remedy to which economic duress gives rise is not an action for damages but an action for restitution of property or money exacted under such duress and the avoidance of any contract that had been induced by it; but where the particular form taken by the economic duress used is itself a tort, the restitutional remedy for money had and received by the defendant to the plaintiff's use is one which the plaintiff is entitled to pursue as an alternative remedy to an action for damages in tort.'

Comment
See also *CTN Cash and Carry Ltd* v *Gallaher Ltd* [1994] 4 All ER 714.

10 Privity of Contract

Beswick v Beswick [1967] 3 WLR 932 House of Lords (Lords Reid, Hodson, Guest, Pearce and Upjohn)

- *Contract – enforcement by stranger to it*

Facts

Peter Beswick was a coal merchant. In 1962 he contracted with John Beswick, his nephew, to sell the business in consideration: (1) that for the rest of Peter's life, John would pay him £6.10s per week; (2) that if Peter's wife survived him, John would pay her £5 a week. Peter's wife was not a party to the contract. John took over the business and paid the agreed sum to Peter until he died in November 1963. He made one payment of £5 to Peter's widow and then ceased payments. The widow commenced proceedings, claiming arrears and specific performance and brought the action both as administratrix of the deceased husband's estate and in her personal capacity.

Held

The widow was entitled, as administratrix, to an order for specific performance, but the effect of ss56(1) and 205(1)(xx) of the Law of Property Act 1925 was not to confer upon a third party any right to sue upon a contract.

Lord Hodson:

'The surviving issues in this case are two: first, whether the Court of Appeal were justified in making an order for specific performance by directing that the appellant do pay to the respondent, during the remainder of her life, an annuity, in accordance with the agreement; second, whether or not the common law rule that a contract such as this one, which purports to confer a benefit on a stranger to the contract, cannot be enforced by the stranger, has been to all intents and purposes (with few exceptions) destroyed by the operation of s56(1) of the Law of Property Act 1925. I will deal with this section first. It provides:

"A person may take an immediate or other interest in land or other property, or the benefit of any condition, right of entry, covenant or agreement over or respecting land or other property, although he may not be named as a party to the conveyance or other instrument."

The definition s205 provides:

"(1) In this Act, unless the context otherwise requires, the following expressions have the meanings hereby assigned to them respectively, that is to say ... (xx) Property includes any thing in action and any interest in real or personal property."

...

One cannot deny that the view of Lord Denning MR, expressed so forcibly, not for the first time in his judgment in this case, reinforced by the opinion of Danckwerts LJ in this case, is of great weight, notwithstanding that it runs counter to the opinion of all the other judges who have been faced by the task of interpreting this remarkable section ...

Apart from the definition section (s205) I doubt whether many would have been disposed to the view that the general law, which declares who can sue on a contract, had received the mortal blow which s56 is said to have inflicted on it ... But for the saving words "unless the context otherwise requires", I should have felt grave difficulty in resisting the argument that Parliament, even if it acted per incuriam, had somehow allowed to be slipped into consolidating legislation, which had nothing to do with the general law of contract, an extraordinary provision which had such a drastic effect ...

I am unable to believe that such an enormous change in the law has been made by s56 as to establish that an agreement by A with B to pay money to C gives C a right to sue on the contract.

Like my noble and learned friend, Lord Reid ... I am of the opinion that s56 ... does not have the revolutionary effect claimed for it, appearing as it does in a consolidation Act. I think, as he does, that the context does otherwise require a limited meaning to be given to the word "property" in the section.

Although, therefore, the appellant would succeed if the respondent relied only on s56 of the Act of 1925, I see no answer to the respondent's claim for specific performance and no possible objection to the order made by the Court of Appeal on the facts of this case.'

Comment

See also *Amsprop Trading Ltd* v *Harris Distribution Ltd* [1997] 2 All ER 990 (s56 only allows a person to sue on a covenant, where not named as a party to it, if the covenant purports to be made with him).

Jackson v *Horizon Holidays Ltd*
[1975] 3 WLR 1468 Court of Appeal (Lord Denning MR, Orr and James LJJ)

• *Contract for benefit of third parties – ability to sue and recover damages*

Facts

The plaintiff entered into a contract for a holiday for himself, his wife and two children. The holiday failed to comply with the description given by the defendants and the plaintiff sued, claiming damages.

Held

The plaintiff was entitled to damages not only for himself, but also for his wife and children.

Lord Denning MR:

'We have had an interesting discussion as to the legal position when one person makes a contract for the benefit of a party. In this case, it was a husband making a contract for the benefit of himself, his wife and children ...

It would ... be a mistake to say that ... there was a trust. The transaction bears no resemblance to a trust. There was no trust fund and no trust property. No, the real truth is that ... the father ... was making a contract himself for the benefit of the whole party. In short, a contract by one for the benefit of third persons.

What is the position when such a contract is broken? At present, the law says that the only one who can sue is the one who made the contract. None of the rest of the party can sue, even though the contract was made for their benefit. But when that one does sue, what damages can he recover? Is he limited to his own loss? Or can he recover for the others? ... He can, of course, recover his own damages. But can he not recover for the others? I think he can. The case comes within the principle stated by Lush LJ in *Lloyds* v *Harper* (1880) 16 Ch D 290:

"I consider it to be an established rule of law that where a contract is made with A for the benefit of B, A can sue on the contract for the benefit of B and recover all that B could have recovered if the contract had been made with B himself."

It has been suggested that Lush LJ was thinking of a contract in which A was trustee for B. But I do not think so. He was a common lawyer speaking of the common law. His words were quoted with considerable approval by Lord Pearce in *Beswick* v *Beswick* [1967] 3 WLR 932. I have myself often quoted them. I think they should be accepted as correct, at any rate so long as the law forbids the third person themselves to sue for damages. It is the only way a just result can be achieved.'

Comment

In *Woodar Investment Development Ltd* v

Wimpey Construction UK Ltd [1980] 1 WLR 277 Lord Wilberforce said:

> 'The majority of the Court of Appeal followed ... its previous decision in *Jackson* v *Horizon Holidays Ltd*. I am not prepared to dissent from the actual decision in that case. It may be supported either as a broad decision on the measure of damages (per James LJ) or possibly as an example of a type of contract, examples of which are persons contracting for family holidays, ordering meals in restaurants for a party, hiring a taxi for a group, calling for special treatment. As I suggested in *New Zealand Shipping Co Ltd* v *A M Satterthwaite & Co Ltd* [1974] 1 All ER 1015, there are many situations of daily life which do not fit neatly into conceptual analysis, but which require some flexibility in the law of contract. *Jackson*'s case may well be one. I cannot agree agree with the basis on which Lord Denning MR put his decision in that case. The extract on which he relied from the judgment of Lush LJ in *Lloyd's* v *Harper* was part of a passage in which Lush LJ was stating as an "established rule of law" that an agent (sc an insurance broker) may sue on a contract made by him on behalf of the principal (sc the assured) if the contract gives him such a right, and is no authority for the proposition required in *Jackson*'s case ...'

Scruttons Ltd v *Midland Silicones Ltd* [1962] 2 WLR 186 House of Lords (Viscount Simonds, Lords Reid, Keith of Avonholm, Denning and Morris of Borth-y-Gest)

• *Bill of lading – clause limiting liability – position of stevedores*

Facts

The plaintiffs bought a drum of chemicals, which was shipped by consignors in New York on a vessel owned by the United States Line. The bill of lading contained a clause limiting the liability of the shipowners. The defendants were stevedores who had contracted with the US Lines to act for them in London. Under the contract between the defendants and the US Lines, the defendants were to have the benefit of the clause in the bill of lading (the defendants were not parties to the bill of lading). The plaintiffs were not aware of the existence of the contract between the defendants and the US Lines. As a result of the defendants' negligence, the drum was damaged. The plaintiffs sued the defendants in negligence and the defendants pleaded the clause limiting liability in the bill of lading.

Held (Lord Denning dissenting)

The defendants were not protected by the clause since they were not parties to the contract in which it was contained.

Viscount Simonds:

> 'The question is whether the appellants ... who admittedly, by their negligence, caused damage to certain cargo consigned to the respondents under a bill of lading, can take advantage of a provision for limitation of liability contained in that document. In judgments, with which I entirely agree and to which but for the importance of the case, I should think it necessary to add nothing, the learned judge [Diplock J] and the Court of Appeal have unanimously answered the question in the negative ... Then, to avert the consequences which would appear to follow from the fact that the stevedores were not a party to the contract conferring immunity on the carriers, it was argued that the carriers contracted as agents for the stevedores. They did not expressly do so; if, then, there was an agency, it was the case of an agent acting for an undisclosed principal. I am met at once by the difficulty that there is no ground whatever for saying that the carriers were contracting as agents for this firm of stevedores or any other stevedores whom they might employ. ...
>
> Next, it was argued that there was an implied contract between the cargo owners, the respondents and the stevedores, that the latter should have the benefit of the immunity clause in the bill of lading. This argument presents, if possible, greater difficul-

ties … In the present case, the cargo owners had a contract with the carrier which provided amongst other things for the unloading of their cargo. They knew nothing of the relations between the carrier and the stevedores. It was no business of theirs. They were concerned only to have the job done which the carriers had contracted to do. There is no conceivable reason why an implication should be made that they had entered into any contractual relation with the stevedores.

But, my Lords, all these contentions were but a prelude to one which, had your Lordships accepted it, would have been the foundation of a dramatic decision of this House. It was argued, if I understood the argument, that if A contracts with B to do something for the benefit of C, then C, though not a party to the contract, can sue A to enforce it. This is independent of whether C is A's undisclosed principal or a beneficiary under a trust of which A is trustee. It is sufficient that C is an "interested person". My Lords, if this is the law of England, then, subject always to the question of consideration, no doubt, if the carrier purports to contract for the benefit of the stevedore, the latter can enforce the contract. Whether that premise is satisfied in this case is another matter …

Learned counsel for the respondents met it, as they had successfully done in the courts below, by asserting a principle which is, I suppose, as well established as any in our law, a "fundamental" principle, as Viscount Haldane LC called it in *Dunlop Pneumatic Tyre Co Ltd* v *Selfridge & Co Ltd* [1915] AC 847, an "elementary" principle, as it has been called times without number, that only a person who is a party to a contract can sue on it … If the principle of jus quaesitum tertio is to be introduced into our law, it must be done by Parliament after a due consideration of its merits and demerits. I should not be prepared to give it my support without a greater knowledge than I at present possess of its operation in other systems of law.

I come, finally, to the case which is said to require us to decide in favour of the appellants … *Elder, Dempster & Co* v *Paterson Zochonis & Co* [1924] AC 522 … When, therefore, it is urged that the *Elder, Dempster* case decided that, even if there is no general exception to what I have called the fundamental rule that a person not a party to a contract cannot sue to enforce it, there is at least a special exception in the case of a contract for carriage of goods by sea, an exception which is to be available to every person, servant or agent of the contracting party or independent contractor, then I demand that that particular exception should be plainly deductible from the speeches that were delivered … The question then is whether there is to be extracted from *Elder, Dempster* a decision that there is in a contract for carriage of goods by sea a particular exception to the fundamental rule in favour of all persons including stevedores and presumably other independent contractors. This question must clearly, in my opinion, be answered in the negative …'

Lord Reid:

'Although I may regret it, I find it impossible to deny the existence of the general rule that a stranger to a contract cannot, in a question with either of the contracting parties, take advantage of provisions of the contract, even where it is clear from the contract that some provision in it was intended to benefit him. That rule appears to have been crystallised a century ago in *Tweddle* v *Atkinson* (1861) 1 B & S 393 and finally established in this house in *Dunlop* v *Selfridge*. There are, it is true, certain well established exceptions to that rule – though I am not sure that they are really exceptions and do not arise from other principles. But none of these in any way touches the present case.

The actual words used by Viscount Haldane LC in the *Dunlop* case were made the basis of an argument that, although a stranger to a contract may not be able to sue for any benefit under it, he can rely on the contract as a defence if one of the parties to it sues him in breach of his contractual obligation – that he can use the contract as a shield, though not as a sword. I can find no

justification for that. If the other contracting party can prevent the breach of contract
well and good, but if he cannot I do not see
how the stranger can. As was said in
Tweddle v *Atkinson*, the stranger cannot
"take advantage" from the contract ...

So this case depends on the proper interpretation of the *Elder, Dempster* case. What
was there decided is clear enough. The ship
was under time charter; the bill of lading
made by the shippers and the charterers provided for exemption from liability in the
event which happened and this exemption
was held to enure to the benefit of the
shipowners who were not parties to the bill
of lading, but whose servant, the master,
caused damage to the shippers' goods by his
negligence. The decision is binding on us,
but I agree that the decision by itself will
not avail the present appellants because the
facts of this case are very different from
those in the *Elder, Dempster* case.

It can hardly be denied that the ratio decidendi of the *Elder, Dempster* decision is
very obscure ... I do not think that it is my
duty to pursue the unrewarding task of
seeking to extract a ratio decidendi from
what was said in this House in *Elder,
Dempster*. Nor is it my duty to seek to ratio-
nalise the decision by determining in any
other way just how far the scope of the decision should extend. I must treat the decision
as an anomalous and unexplained exception
to the general principle that a stranger
cannot rely for his protection on provisions
in a contract to which he is not a party. The
decision of this House is authoritative in
cases of which the circumstances are not
reasonably distinguishable from those
which gave rise to the decision. The circumstances in the present case are clearly distinguishable in several respects. Therefore I
must decide this case on the established
principles of the law of England apart from
that decision and, on that basis, I have no
doubt that this appeal must be dismissed.'

Comment
In *The Mahkutai* [1996] 3 All ER 502, Lord
Goff of Chieveley reviewed the cases con-

cerning claims by stevedores to the benefit of
exceptions and limitations in bills of lading
and claims by shipowners to the protection of
such terms in charterers' bills. At first there
appeared to have been a readiness on the part
of judges to recognise such claims, especially
in *Elder, Dempster*, but opinion had hardened
against them in the middle of the century as
the pendulum swung back in the direction of
orthodoxy in *Scruttons Ltd* v *Midland
Silicones Ltd*. In more recent years it had
swung back again to recognition of their commercial desirability, notably in the two leading
cases concerned with claims by stevedores to
the protection of a Himalaya clause – *The
Eurymedon* [1975] AC 154 and *The New York
Star* [1981] 1 WLR 138. Himalaya clauses
were named after the ship involved in *Adler* v
Dickson [1955] 1 QB 158. See also *Southern
Water Authority* v *Carey* [1985] 2 All ER
1077.

Southern Water Authority v Carey
[1985] 2 All ER 1077 High Court
(His Honour Judge David Smout QC)

• *Liability limitation clause – protects
sub-contractor?*

Facts
The main contract (in a standard form) for the
construction of a sewage works limited liability for loss arising from any defects. Were
sub-contractors entitled to the benefits of this
clause?

Held
As a matter of contract they were not because,
inter alia, they were strangers to the contract.

His Honour Judge David Smout QC:

'Counsel for the ... defendants puts his
argument in a number of ways. He points
out that cl 30(vi) [of the constuction con-
tract] refers to the contractor contracting as
trustee for the sub-contractor. But I can give
no meaning to that phrase, for the conception of a trust attaching to a benefit under

an exclusion clause extends far beyond conventional limits. Nor am I attracted to the argument that because the contract was under seal it can therefore be enforced by reason of s56 of the Law of Property Act 1925 at the suit of one who is not a party to it. I conclude, on the authority of *Beswick* v *Beswick* [1967] 2 All ER 1197, that I would not be justified in holding that the old common law rule in *Tweddle* v *Atkinson* (1861) 1 B & S 393 has been abrogated by s56 outside the field of real property ...

It is, however, the agency element in *New Zealand Shipping Co* v *A M Satterthwaite & Co Ltd* [1975] AC 154 that is much to the point. Lord Wilberforce in that case, speaking of the House of Lord's decision in *Scruttons Ltd* v *Midland Silicones Ltd* [1962] 2 WLR 186, commented:

> "There is no need to question or even to qualify that case insofar as it affirms the general proposition that a contract between two parties cannot be sued on by a third person even though the contract is expressed to be for his benefit ... But *Midland Silicones* left open the case where one of the parties contracts as agent for the third person: in particular Lord Reid's speech spelt out, in four propositions, the prerequisites for the validity of such an agency contract. There is of course nothing unique to this case in the conception of agency contracts: well-known and common instances exist in the field of hire-purchase, of bankers' commercial credits and other transactions."

He went on to cite a passage from Lord Reid's judgment in *Scruttons Ltd* v *Midland Silicones Ltd* which has been referred to many times in argument in this case, and in which Lord Reid said:

> "I can see a possibility of success of the agency argument if (first) the bill of lading makes it clear that the stevedore is intended to be protected by the provisions in it which limit liability, (secondly) the bill of lading makes it clear that the carrier, in addition to contracting for these

provisions on his own behalf, is also contracting as agent for the stevedore that these provisions should apply to the stevedore, (thirdly) the carrier has authority from the stevedore to do that, or perhaps later ratification by the stevedore would suffice, and (fourthly) that any difficulties about consideration moving from the stevedore were overcome." ...

Let us then consider the four propositions in the context of the instant case. First, does the main contract make it clear that the sub-contractors are intended to be protected by the provisions in it which limit liability? To my mind the answer must be Yes. Second, does it make it clear that the main contractor in addition to contracting for these provisions on his own behalf is also contracting as agent for the sub-contractors that the provisions should also apply to the sub-contractors? Again, I answer Yes: cl 30(vi) so states. The fourth proposition as to consideration poses no difficulty, for this is a contract under seal. It is the third proposition that is debatable in the instant case: had the main contractor authority from the sub-contractor, at the time of making the contract, and, if not, was there any later ratification that would suffice? Unlike *Satterthwaite's* case, there is no evidence here on which I could conclude that the main contractors had prior authority. What as to ratification? Counsel for the plaintiffs contends that there can be no ratification unless the principal was capable of being ascertained at the time when the act was done, ie when the deed was signed. Herein lies the defendants' difficulty... I do not regard myself in the circumstances of this case entitled to extend the law beyond the limits as at present defined.'

Tweddle v *Atkinson* (1861) 1 B & S 393 Court of Queen's Bench (Wightman, Crompton and Blackburn JJ)

• *Contract – action by stranger to the consideration*

Facts

On 15 July 1855, an agreement was made in the following terms:

'Memorandum of an agreement made this day, between William Guy ... of the one part, and John Tweddle ... of the other part. Whereas, it is mutually agreed that the said William Guy shall and will pay the sum of £200 to William Tweddle, his son-in-law ... and the said John Tweddle, father to the aforesaid William Tweddle, shall and will pay the sum of £100 to the said William Tweddle, each and severally the said sums on or before the 21st day of August 1855. And, it is hereby further agreed by the aforesaid William Guy and the said John Tweddle, that the said William Tweddle has full power to sue the said parties in any court of law or equity for the aforesaid sums hereby promised and specified.'

The plaintiff was the son of John Tweddle and, before the making of the agreement, had married the daughter of William Guy. Before the marriage, William Guy, in consideration of the proposed marriage, had promised a marriage portion (which had not been performed at the time of the making of the agreement). By 21 August 1855, the plaintiff had not been paid the £200 by William Guy, who had subsequently died, or by Guy's executor. The plaintiff sued Guy's executor for the £200.

Held

The plaintiff's action would be dismissed.

Wightman J:

'No doubt there are some old decisions which appear to support the proposition that a stranger to the consideration for the contract, who stands in the relation of child to one of the contracting parties, and for whose benefit the contract is made, may sue upon it. ... But there is no modern case of the kind, and, on the contrary, it is now well established that at law no stranger to the consideration can take advantage of the contract though made for his benefit. If it were otherwise a child might sue his own father in such a case as this. It is admitted that if the relationship of parent and child did not exist, the plaintiff would have no right to sue. Here there is no consideration moving from the plaintiff, for the marriage was before the contract sued on, and according to the modern cases the plaintiff cannot use.'

Crompton J:

'The old cases are inapplicable to the modern action of assumpsit. At the time of those cases the law was not settled as it now is, that natural love and affection are not sufficient to support a contract, and that a stranger to the consideration of a contract cannot sue upon it. The modern cases have in effect overruled the old decisions, and it is now clear law that the consideration must move from the party entitled to sue upon the contract. ...'

Comment

In *Drive Yourself Hire Co (London) Ltd* v *Strutt* [1953] 2 All ER 1475, Denning LJ suggested that s56(1) of the Law of Property Act 1925 had done away with the rule in 'the unfortunate case' of *Tweddle* v *Atkinson*, leaving the courts free, in cases concerning property (real or personal), to go back to the old common law, whereby a third party could sue on a contract made expressly for his benefit. However, in *Beswick* v *Beswick* [1967] 3 WLR 932 Lord Upjohn said that he was convinced that, when passing the 1925 Act, Parliament had never intended to alter the fundamental rule laid down in *Tweddle* v *Atkinson*, but in *Woodar Investment Development Ltd* v *Wimpey Construction (UK) Ltd* [1980] 1 WLR 277 Lord Scarman said that the rule was 'unjust'.

11 Illegality

Alexander v Rayson [1936] 1 KB 169 Court of Appeal (Greer, Romer and Scott LJJ)

• *Illegality – reduction of rateable value – unlawful purpose*

Facts
A lease of a flat made provision for a rent of £450 pa and the rendering of certain services to the tenant: a separate agreement provided for the rendering of substantially the same services on payment by the tenant of £750 pa. The landlord, it was alleged, adopted this dual approach with a view to defrauding the rating authority by leading them to believe that his only income in respect of the flat was £450 pa. The landlord sued for rent under the lease and payment under the agreement.

Held
His action could not succeed, unless he could disprove the charge of fraud.

Romer LJ:

'... if the [landlord] has, by his conduct, placed himself in the same position in law as though he had let the flat with the intention of its being used for an illegal purpose, he has no one but himself to thank for any loss that he may suffer in consequence.

That brings us to the real crux of this case. Has the [landlord] placed himself in that position? Now in the cases to which we have referred there was an intention to use the subject-matter of the agreement for an unlawful purpose. In the present case, on the other hand, the [landlord's] intention was merely to make use of the lease and agreement – that is, the documents themselves – for an unlawful purpose. Does that make any difference? In our opinion, it does not. It seems to us ... that the principles applicable to the two cases are identical ... For these reasons we are of opinion that the [landlord] is not entitled to seek the assistance of a court of justice in enforcing either the lease or the agreement ... the documents themselves were dangerous in the sense that they could be and were intended to be used for a fraudulent purpose, without alteration, and the splitting of the transaction into the two documents was an overt step in carrying out the fraud. We cannot think that the respondent is entitled to bring these documents into a court of justice and ask the court to assist him in carrying them into effect.'

Comment
Within this decision in *Tinsley* v *Milligan* [1993] 3 All ER 65 the House of Lords found support for the proposition that a completely executed transfer of property or of an interest in property made in pursuance of an unlawful agreement is valid and the court will assist the transferee in the protection of his interest provided that he does not require to found on the unlawful agreement. In that case, although an initial agreement had been unlawful (to facilitate fraudulent claims to housing benefit by one of the parties to it), that party succeeded in her claim because, in establishing it, she had not needed to rely on the illegal arrangement.

Dunbar v Plant [1997] 4 All ER 289 Court of Appeal (Hirst, Phillips and Mummery LJJ)

• *Suicide pact – entitlement of survivor – Forfeiture Act 1982*

Facts

Believing that Miss Plant faced prosecution and possibly imprisonment for an alleged offence, she and her fiancé (Mr Dunbar) decided to commit suicide. At the third attempt, he succeeded, she failed. The court was asked to decide, inter alia, whether Miss Plant was entitled to the proceeds of an insurance policy taken out on Mr Dunbar's life and written for the benefit of Miss Plant.

Held

She was. Although the forfeiture rule applied, in all the circumstances and in the exercise of the court's discretion, full relief (Mummery LJ dissenting) would be given against its effect.

Phillips LJ:

'I agree that Miss Plant committed the criminal offence of aiding and abetting the suicide of Mr Dunbar, contrary to s2(1) of the Suicide Act 1961. The more difficult questions are whether the commission by Miss Plant of that offence brought into operation the forfeiture rule and, if it did, whether the manner in which the judge exercised the discretion granted by the Forfeiture Act 1982 is open to attack.

The forfeiture rule
The Forfeiture rule is defined by s1(1) of the 1982 Act as meaning –

"the rule of public policy which in certain circumstances precludes a person who has unlawfully killed another from acquiring a benefit in consequence of the killing."

The rule as so formulated is an example of a wider principle that a person cannot benefit from his own criminal act. ...

There is a difference between obtaining rights and enforcing them, and there is scope for debate as to the extent to which the forfeiture rule differs from the similar principle that a litigant cannot base a cause of action on his own wrong. The two principles are frequently confused. ...

What is important is that neither principle is absolute. It is not every criminal offence which will bring the principle into play. The issue raised on this appeal is whether aiding and abetting the suicide of another necessarily brings the forfeiture rule into operation. That question can be considered in the context of the rule as formulated in the Forfeiture Act, ie in the context of crimes which consist of unlawfully killing another.

Unlawful killing ...
When the forfeiture rule was first applied by the courts any unlawful killing consisted of one or other of two crimes – murder or manslaughter, and the ambit of the crime of murder was much wider than it is today. The forfeiture rule was always applied in a case of murder and, in *Beresford* v *Royal Insurance Co Ltd* [1938] 2 All ER 602 it was applied in a case of suicide ...

In *Re Hall's Estate, Hall* v *Knight* [1914] P 1 the question appears to have been raised for the first time of whether the forfeiture rule applied to a person convicted of manslaughter. The Court of Appeal had no doubt that it did. ...

A desire on the part of the courts to avoid the rigour of the forfeiture rule was first manifest in *Tinline* v *White Cross Insurance Association Ltd* [1921] 3 KB 327. The issue in that case was whether a plaintiff, who had been convicted of manslaughter by reckless driving, was debarred by public policy from obtaining an indemnity under his insurance policy in respect of his civil liability. Bailhache J held that he was not ...

It is time to pause to take stock. Thus far, apart from the motor cases, there has been no instance of the court failing to apply the forfeiture rule to a case of unlawful killing. So far as the rule is concerned, it is hard to see any logical basis for not applying it to all cases of manslaughter. Lord Denning MR himself remarked in *Gray* v *Barr* ([1971] 2 All ER 949 at 956): "... in manslaughter of every kind there must be a guilty mind. Without it, the accused must be acquitted ..."

In the crime of manslaughter, the actus reus is causing the death of another. That actus reus is rendered criminal if it occurs in one of the various circumstances that are prescribed by law. Anyone guilty of manslaughter has, ex hypothesi, caused the death of another by criminal conduct. It is in such circumstances that the rule against forfeiture applies.

However, the harshness of applying the forfeiture rule inflexibly to all classes of manslaughter in all circumstances is such that I do not consider that, absent the statutory intervention which occurred, the rule could have survived invaried to the present day. ...

The pressure for judicial intervention of the type contemplated was removed by the Forfeiture Act. The manner of operation of the provisions of the Act and, in particular, of s2(5), was considered by Vinelott J in *Re K (decd)* [1985] 1 All ER 403. In that case a wife had used a loaded shotgun to deter a brutal husband from violence. The gun had accidentally gone off and killed him. The issue was whether she could recover under his will. Vinelott J, following the approach in *Gray* v *Barr*, held that the rule against forfeiture applied, but that, in the circumstances of the case, he would modify the effect of the rule so as to relieve her of its consequences altogether. ... The Court of Appeal ([1985] 2 All ER 833 upheld his decision ...

Aiding and abetting suicide

Thus far, I have been considering the application of the forfeiture rule in cases of manslaughter. My reasoning leads, however, to the conclusion that the rule applies equally to the offence of aiding and abetting suicide contrary to s2(1) of the Suicide Act. This conclusion seems to have been shared by those who drafted the Forfeiture Act. Section 1(2) of the Act provides:

> "References in this Act to a person who has unlawfully killed another include a reference to a person who has unlawfully aided, abetted, counselled or procured the death of that other person ..."

As the Act does not apply to the crime of murder, these words can only have been intended to apply to the crime of aiding, abetting, counselling or procuring the suicide of another, contrary to the 1961 Act. ...

Suicide pacts

If, as I believe, the forfeiture rule applies to offences under the Suicide Act and the application of the rule is not dependent upon the degree of culpability attaching to the crime, it must follow that the rule applies to aiding and abetting the suicide of another in pursuance of a suicide pact. Such an offence is likely, however, to fall into the categoryo f those in respect of which the public interest does not require the imposition of a penal sanction. ... In such circumstances the appropriate approach under the Forfeiture Act is likely to be to give total relief against forfeiture. Of course, this will not always be the case. One can think of instances of suicide pacts where one would not acquit the instigator of serious culpability.

Discretion under the Forfeiture Act ...

The first, and paramount consideration, must be whether the culpability attending the beneficiary's criminal conduct was such as to justify the application of the forfeiture rule at all. ...

Had Miss Plant's decision to take her own life been an understandable reaction to the pending consequences of her theft, a case could well have been made out for saying that this gave to her participation in the suicide pact a culpability that should properly be reflected by the application, at least to a degree, of the forfeiture rule. I do not, however, see this case in that light. The desperation that led Miss Plant to decide to kill herself, and which led to the suicide pact, was an irrational and tragic reaction to her predicament. I do not consider that the nature of Miss Plant's conduct alters what I have indicated should be the normal approach when dealing with a suicide pact – that there should be full relief against forfeiture.'

Comment

This is the first case in which the Court of Appeal was called upon to consider the effect of the forfeiture rule and the impact of the Forfeiture Act 1982 on the right of a survivor of a suicide pact to acquire benefits in consequence of the death of the other party to the pact.

Fitch v *Dewes* [1921] 2 AC 158
House of Lords (Lord Birkenhead LC, Viscount Cave, Lords Sumner, Parmoor and Carson)

- *Restraint of trade – solicitor's managing clerk – reasonableness*

Facts
The plaintiff, a solicitor practising at Tamworth, employed the defendant as a managing clerk and the contract provided that the defendant would:

'... not directly or indirectly become engaged or manage or be concerned in the office, profession or business of a solicitor within a radius of 7 miles of the Town Hall of Tamworth'

after the expiration of his term of service.

Held
Although unlimited in point of time, the clause would be enforced.

Lord Birkenhead LC:

'The controversy is the old one between freedom of contract and certain considerations of public policy, which have received much attention at the hands of the courts in the last few years. It is sufficient for me to say at this point that the contract was entered into between two solicitors: that at its date the appellant had reached the age of twenty-seven years; that he had been for some thirteen years employed in a solicitor's office; and it is reasonable to infer from the promotion which he had received and from the evident appreciation which his employer had formed of his services, that he was a young man alert and very competent both to understand and to safeguard his own interests. The agreement then into which he entered, and in respect of which he has accepted for a lengthy period the consideration which was to move from the covenan-

tee towards himself, will naturally stand unless he satisfies your Lordships that it is bad as being in restraint of trade.

What then is said by the appellant under that head? He does not complain of the restriction of space, and indeed it would have been very difficult for him to do so. The clause only restricts him from being directly or indirectly engaged in the office profession or business of a solicitor within a radius of seven miles of the Town Hall of Tamworth. We need not therefore trouble ourselves with any question of the restriction in respect of space but may confine ourselves to the complaint which is made that the agreement cannot stand, because the restriction in respect of time is unlimited and is against the public interest. But it is to be noticed here, as has been said in more than one of the earlier cases, that guidance may be derived in dealing with a restriction relating to time from an examination of the restriction which is made in respect of space. And the converse remark is of course equally true. For instance, if the restriction in respect of space is extremely limited, it is evident that a very considerable restriction in respect of time may be more acceptable than would otherwise have been the case.

The courts have been generous in elucidating these matters by the enunciation of general principles in the course of the last few years, and I am extremely anxious not to carry this process further today; therefore I say plainly and, I hope, simply, that it has for long now been accepted that such an agreement as this, if it is impeached, is to be measured by reference to two considerations. First, is it against the public interest? And, second, does that which has been stipulated for exceed what is required for the protection of the convenantee? It might perhaps be more properly stated, as it has sometimes been with the highest authority stated, does it exceed what is necessary for the protection of both the parties? But the impeachment which is in fact made in this case demands the consideration of the earlier question only, does the restriction which is attacked exceed that which was reasonably necessary for the protection of the convenantee? ...

It is not contended that there is anything which is open to attack ... except that part of the clause which for all time excludes the appellant from carrying on practice within seven miles of Tamworth. Are we then to say that such a restriction so unlimited goes farther than is permitted in relation to the standard which I have restated? I am of opinion that it does not go too far. One of your Lordships asked counsel ... in the course of his argument what period in his judgment would be a reasonable period, and counsel replied that he thought that ten years might be a reasonable period. Why? Why is it to be said than ten years is a reasonable period? I can quite easily understand that at the end of a period of ten years the appellant in this case, who by this very clause is not prevented from maintaining and even developing his business acquaintance with the clients of the firm so long as he does not practise within a range of seven miles, might have retained all these circumstances of special, and as I think of illegitimate, advantage for the purpose of competing with the business of the respondent, and then might come forward and do that very thing against which in my judgment the covenantee is abundantly entitled to be protected. Therefore I should dismiss a period of ten years and I should even say of twenty or thirty years that it was quite impossible to be dogmatic upon the period proper to each individual case. Some men live very long lives, and it might easily be that in a case in which two men were both tenacious of life the very same danger which applies at this moment in this case would present itself, in a more striking and formidable shape, at the end of twenty years or at the end of an even longer period. I have no doubt that it is for this reason that the courts long since determined that they would lay down no hard and fast rule either in relation to time or in relation to space, but that they would treat the question alike of time and of space as one of the elements by the light of which they would measure the reasonableness of the restriction taken as a whole.

I am therefore, for the reasons I have stated, of opinion that the attack which has been made upon this restriction fails. I find that it is not opposed to the public interest and that it does not exceed what is reasonably required in the circumstances of this case for the protection of this covenantee.'

Comment
Applied in *Scorer* v *Seymour-Johns* [1966] 3 All ER 347 (estate agent's negotiator and clerk not for three years after termination of his employment to carry out similar work within radius of five miles a reasonable – and enforceable – restriction). Distinguished in *Strange (S W) Ltd* v *Mann* [1965] 1 All ER 1069 (restriction for three years and twelve miles on a bookmaker's manager inappropriate – and unenforceable – since, inter alia, his position was not such as would lead to his obtaining the goodwill of customers by rendering particular personal service to them).

Pearce v *Brooks* (1866) LR 1 Ex 213
Court of Exchequer (Pollock CB, Martin, Pigott and Bramwell BB)

• *Immoral purpose – contract enforceable?*

Facts
The defendant, a prostitute, hired a brougham (one-horse closed carriage) from the plaintiffs. When the plaintiffs sued for money due under the agreement, the jury found that the brougham was used by the defendant as part of her display to attract men and that the plaintiffs had known that it was to be used for that purpose. Judgment having been given for the defendant, the plaintiffs appealed.

Held
The appeal would be dismissed.

Pollock CB:

'I take the rule to be that any person who contributes to the performance of an illegal act, knowing that the subject-matter is to be so applied, cannot recover the price of such subject-matter, and that the old notion, if any such ever existed, which I do not wish to affirm, that the price must be intended to be paid out of the profits of the illegality, has ceased to be part of the law, if ever it was so. I do not think that for this purpose we should make any distinction between an illegal and an immoral act. The rule now is, ex turpi causa non oritur actio, and whether such turpitude be an immorality or an illegality, the effect is the same; no cause of action can arise out of one or the other ... If, therefore, this article was furnished for the purpose of a display favourable to the defendant's immoral vocation, it seems to me no cause of action can arise.'

Comment

In *Archbolds (Freightage) Ltd* v *S Spanglett Ltd* [1961] 2 WLR 170 Pearce LJ cited this case as an example of the exercise of the court's general power, based on public policy, to refuse its aid to guilty parties in respect of contracts which, though apparently lawful, are intended to be performed illegally or for an illegal purpose.

Rock Refrigeration Ltd v *Jones*
[1997] 1 All ER 1 Court of Appeal (Simon Brown, Morritt and Phillips LJJ)

• *Restraint of trade – covenant to take effect on termination of employment 'howsoever occasioned' – enforceability*

Facts

The plaintiff's former managing director set up a company in competition with the plaintiff and the plaintiff's former industrial sales director (Mr Jones) moved to that other company as sales director. Mr Jones' contract of employment with the plaintiff provided that on its termination 'howsoever occasioned' he would not for a period of twelve months, in effect, do business with persons with whom the plaintiff had done business in the previous

twelve months. While it was accepted that the plaintiff had legitimate interests for protection by way of restrictive covenants of this general nature, the court was required to decide whether such covenants were necessarily unreasonable and therefore unenforceable simply because it was expressly provided that they would take effect upon the termination of the employment 'howsoever occasioned'.

Held

Covenants containing such an expression are not necessarily unreasonable and unenforceable, even though on their face they would apply in the event of a repudiatory breach by the employer.

Simon Brown LJ:

'The law applicable to covenants and restraint of trade simply has no relevance to the present situation. Of course covenants which purport to subject ex-employees to greater restrictions than their erstwhile employers can justify are unenforceable, and elementary it is too hard that the legitimacy of such covenants falls to be determined as at the date they are entered into and not by reference to the circumstances in which the employment eventually terminates. But in my judgment the most basic premise upon which the whole restraint of trade doctrine is founded is that, but for the doctrine's application, the covenant in question would otherwise operate to restrain the employee unduly. In other words the doctrine applies only where there exists an otherwise enforceable covenant. It renders unenforceable what otherwise would be enforceable.

The whole point about the *General Billposting Co Ltd* v *Atkinson* [1909] AC 118 principle is that, in cases of repudiatory breach by the employer, the employee is on that account released from his obligations under the contract and restrictive covenants, otherwise valid against him, accordingly cannot be enforced. Once that principle was decided, its future application necessarily postulated that such restrictive covenants upon their true construction would otherwise be enforceable against employees. ... With the best will in the world ... no expensive litigation is necessary to inform an employee that his employer's repudiatory breach of conduct will absolve him from restrictive trade covenants.'

Phillips J:

'Before us [counsel for Mr Jones] did not seek to contend that a restrictive covenant, however drafted, could survive the termination of the employment consequent upon the employer's repudiation. He conceded that a covenant which purported to have this effect agreed to something which was impossible in law. His argument was that it was mischievous for an employer to incorporate within a contract of employment a covenant which purported to bind in circumstances where this was a legal impossibility, and that this mischief alone justified declaring such a covenant void.

In my judgment, once [he] rejected the premise underlying the relevant parts of the three recent judgments upon which he relied, he cut away any support that they could afford to his case. If a covenant, otherwise reasonable, purports to remain binding in circumstances where the law will inevitably strike it down, I can see no justification for holding that it is, on that account, in unlawful restraint of trade.'

Comment

The three recent judgments to which Phillips LJ referred were given in *Briggs* v *Oates* [1991] 1 All ER 407, *Living Designs (Home Improvements) Ltd* v *Davidson* [1994] IRLR 69 and *D* v *M* [1996] IRLR 192. The last two accepted the obiter view of Scott J in the first to the effect that he would hold void a clause which would otherwise, on its true construction, impose restraints after the wrongful termination of the contract of employment. This view has now been set aside.

Sutton v *Sutton* [1984] 2 WLR 146

See Chapter 15.

12 Frustration

Amalgamated Investment and Property Co Ltd v John Walker & Sons Ltd [1977] 1 WLR 164

See Chapter 8.

Krell v Henry [1903] 2 KB 740 Court of Appeal (Vaughan Williams, Romer and Stirling LJJ)

• *Frustration – cancellation of procession*

Facts

In 1902, the defendant hired from the plaintiff a flat in Pall Mall for two days for the purpose of viewing the coronation processions. The King became ill and the processions did not take place The plaintiff sued for the agreed hire charge.

Held

The contract was a licence to use the rooms for a particular purpose and, as the foundation of the licence had been destroyed, the contract was discharged.

Vaughan Williams LJ (referring to the principle in *Taylor* v *Caldwell* (1863) 3 B & S 826):

' ... English Law applies the principle not only to cases where the performance of the contract becomes impossible by the cessation of existence of the thing which is the subject matter of the contract, but also to cases where the event which renders the contract incapable of performance is the cessation or non-existence of an express condition or state of things, going to the root of the contract and essential to its performance. It is said, on the one side, that the specified thing, state of things, or condition, the continued existence of which is neces-sary for the fulfilment of the contract, so that the parties entering into the contract must have contemplated the continued existence of that thing, condition or state of things as the foundation of what was to be done under the contract, is limited to things which are either the subject matter of the contract, or a condition or state of things, present or anticipated, which is expressly mentioned in the contract. But, on the other side, it is said that the condition or state of things need not be expressly specified, but that it is suffi-cient if that condition or state of things clearly appears by extrinsic evidence to have been assumed by the parties to be the foundation or basis of the contract and the event which causes the impossibility is of such a character that it cannot reasonably be supposed to have been in contemplation of the contracting parties when the contract was made ... I do not think that the principle ... is limited to cases in which the event causing the impossibility of performance is the destruction or non-existence of some thing which is the subject matter of the contract, or of some condition or state of things expressly specified as a condition of it. I think that you first have to ascertain, not necessarily from the terms of the contract, but, if necessary, from necessary inference drawn from surrounding circumstances recognised by both contracting parties, what is the substance of the contract, and then to ask the question whether that substantial contract needs for its foundation the assumption of the existence of a particular state of things. ...

Each case must be judged by its own circumstances. In each case one must ask oneself, first, what, having regard to all the circumstances, was the foundation of the contract? Secondly: was the performance of the contract prevented? And thirdly: was the

event which prevented the performance of
the contract of such a character that it cannot
reasonably be said to have been in the contemplation of the parties at the date of the
contract? If all these questions are answered
in the affirmative (as I think they should be
in this case) I think both parties are discharged from further performance of the
contract.'

National Carriers Ltd v Panalpina (Northern) Ltd [1981] 2 WLR 45 House of Lords (Lord Hailsham of St Marylebone LC, Lords Wilberforce, Simon of Glaisdale, Russell of Killowen and Roskill)

• *Frustration – executed lease – closure
of access*

Facts
In 1974 the appellants leased from the respondent for ten years a warehouse. In 1979 the
local authority closed the street giving the
only access to the warehouse because of the
dangerous condition of a listed building opposite. Permission to demolish the building was
given in 1980 and it seemed demolition would
be completed and the street reopened in 1981.
On closure of the street the appellants had
stopped paying rent and the respondents sued
for arrears.

Held
The respondents should succeed. Although in
exceedingly rare circumstances the doctrine of
frustration could apply to an executed lease,
the lease had not been frustrated by the
closure.

Lord Wilberforce:

'It is said that to admit the possibility of
frustration of leases will lead to increased
litigation. Be it so, if that is the route to
justice. But, even if the principle is admitted, hopeless claims can always be stopped
at an early stage, if the facts manifestly
cannot support a case of frustration. The

present may be an example. In my opinion,
therefore, though such cases may be rare,
the doctrine of frustration is capable of
application to leases of land. It must be so
applied with proper regard to the fact that a
lease, ie a grant of a legal estate, is involved.
The court must consider whether any term is
to be implied which would determine the
lease in the event which has happened
and/or ascertain the foundation of the agreement and decide whether this still exists in
the light of the terms of the lease, the surrounding circumstances and any special
rules which apply to leases or to the particular lease in question. If the "frustrating
event" occurs, during the currency of the
lease it will be appropriate to consider the
Law Reform (Frustrated Contracts) Act
1943.

I now come to the second question, which
is whether on the facts of the case the appellants should be given leave to defend the
action: can they establish that there is a
triable issue? I have already summarised the
terms of the lease. At first sight, it would
appear to my mind that the case might be
one for possible frustration. But examination of the facts leads to a negative conclusion …

So the position is that the parties to the
lease contemplated, when Kingston Street
was first closed, that the closure would
probably last for a year or a little longer. In
fact it seems likely to have lasted for just
over eighteen months. Assuming that the
street is reopened in January 1981, the lease
will have three more years to run.

My Lords, no doubt, even with this
limited interruption the appellants' business
will have been severely dislocated. They
will have had to move goods from the warehouse before the closure and to acquire
alternative accommodation. After reopening
the reverse process must take place. But this
does not approach the gravity of a frustrating event. Out of ten years they will have
lost under two years of use; there will be
nearly three years left after the interruption
has ceased. This is a case, similar to others,
where the likely continuance of the term
after the interruption makes it impossible

for the lessee to contend that the lease has been brought to an end. The obligation to pay rent under the lease is unconditional, with a sole exception for the case of fire, as to which the lease provides for a suspension of the obligation. No provision is made for suspension in any other case; the obligation remains. I am of opinion therefore that the lessees have no defence to the action for rent.'

Comment
This case established the principle that an executed lease was capable of being frustrated, even though the circumstances in which this happened would 'hardly ever' (per Lord Hailsham of St Marylebone LC) arise.

Shepherd (F C) & Co Ltd v *Jerrom*
[1986] 3 WLR 801 Court of Appeal (Lawton, Mustill and Balcombe LJJ)

• *Frustration – apprenticeship – employee's imprisonment*

Facts
In September 1979 the applicant entered into a four year contract of apprenticeship with the employers. In June 1981 the applicant was convicted of conspiracy to commit assault and affray and was sentenced to an indeterminate period (between six months and two years) of Borstal training. The applicant he was released after 39 weeks, but his employers refused to take him back and he complained to an industrial tribunal that he had been unfairly dismissed. The tribunal upheld his complaint, rejecting the employers' contention that the apprenticeship had been frustrated by the imprisonment. The Employment Appeal Tribunal affirmed this decision. The employers appealed.

Held
The appeal would be allowed.

Lawton LJ:

'... The first question is whether what hap-

pened was capable in law of frustrating the contract; the second is whether it did frustrate it: this is a question of fact: (see *Pioneer Shipping Ltd* v *BTP Tioxide Ltd* [1982] AC 724 at 752 per Lord Roskill) ...

As to the first of these questions, there was an event, namely, the sentence of Borstal training, which was not foreseen or provided for by the parties at the time of contracting. It was a question of fact ... whether it rendered the performance of the contract radically different from what the parties had contemplated when they entered into it. What has to be decided is whether the outside event and its consequences in relation to the performance of the contract occurred without either the fault or default of either party to it ... There was no fault or default on the part of the employers. They were alleging that because of the unforeseen outside event the contract had been frustrated. If it had been, there had been no dismissal. ... The oddity of this case is that the apprentice, for his own purposes, is seeking to allege that he was in default so as to keep in being a contract which the employers would otherwise have been able to say had been terminated by operation of law ... It seems to me that the apprentice is seeking to rely upon his own default, if in law it should be regarded as such, to establish his right to claim for unfair dismissal.

This is the opposite of what happened in two of the leading cases dealing with the consequences of default in relation to the frustration of contracts, namely *Maritime National Fish Ltd* v *Ocean Trawlers Ltd* [1935] AC 524 and *Mertens* v *Home Freeholds Co* [1921] 2 KB 526. In each of these cases the plaintiff had sought to enforce the contract and the defendants had pleaded frustration because of change of circumstances. It was adjudged in both cases that these pleas failed because the defendants' own acts had caused or contributed to what had made performance impossible. The frustration which the two defendants had sought to rely on were self-induced and in consequence in law there had been no frustrations. In the *Maritime National Fish Ltd* case the act had been an election; in the

Mertens case, reprehensible conduct which could fairly be described as a default. As Lord Brandon commented in *Paal Wilson & Co A/S v Partenreederei Hannah Bluementhal* [1983] 1 AC 843 at 909: "... the courts have never defined with precision the meaning of the expression 'default' in this context." This case does call for this court to decide whether the apprentice's conduct resulting in a sentence of borstal training was a default which prevented the contract from being frustrated.

The classic formulation of the concept 'self-induced frustration' is to be found in the speech of Lord Summer in *Bank Line Ltd v Arthur Capel & Co* [1919] AC 435 at 452 when he said:

> "I think it is now well settled that the principle of frustration of an adventure assumes that the frustration arises without blame or fault on either side. Reliance cannot be placed on a self-induced frustration; indeed, such conduct might give the other party the option to treat the contract as repudiated."

In *Joseph Constantine Steamship Line Ltd v Imperial Smelting Corp Ltd, The Kingswood* [1942] AC 154 the House of Lords had to adjudge whether in a claim by charterers against shipowners for damages for failure to load a cargo when the shipowners pleaded that the contract had been frustrated by an explosion, for which no cause was ascertained, they had to prove that it had not been caused by their act or default. Their Lordships adjudged that they did not have to do so. ...

The apprentice's criminal conduct was deliberate but it did not by itself have any consequences upon the performance of his contract. What affected performance was his sentence of Borstal training which was the act of the judge and which he would have avoided if he could have done so. It cannot be said, I think, that the concept of "self-induced frustration" can be applied to this case ...

In *Hare v Murphy Bros Ltd* [1974] ICR 331; affd [1974] 3 All ER 940 the National Industrial Relations Court had adjudged that the employee's criminal conduct which had resulted in his being sentenced to 12 months' imprisonment amounted to a breach of his contract of employment of so serious a nature that it constituted a unilateral repudiation of that contract at the date when he was convicted and sentenced ... The [court] had said that the sentence was not an event frustrating the contract of employment because it had been brought about by employee's own conduct ... I was a member of the [Court of Appeal]. I agreed that the appeal should be dismissed on what I called the "common sense of the situation" which was not an example of sound legal reasoning. Since it is not clear upon what grounds the court as such decided *Hare*'s case I do not regard it as a binding authority. In my opinion the court can reconsider the problem of the effect of a custodial sentence on a contract of employment. In my judgment such a sentence is capable in law of frustrating the contract.

The next question is whether on the facts of this case the sentence of Borstal training did frustrate the contract. In my judgment it did.'

Taylor v Caldwell (1863) 3 B & S 826 Court of Queen's Bench (Blackburn J)

• *Frustration – destruction of hall*

Facts

C agreed to hire to T a hall for the purpose of holding a concert therein. Before the day of the concert, the hall was destroyed in a fire. T cancelled the concert and C claimed the letting fee.

Held

The contract of hire was frustrated and C was not liable to pay the rent.

Blackburn J:

> 'There seems no doubt that where there is a positive contract to do a thing, not in itself unlawful, the contractor must perform it or

pay damages for not doing it, although in consequence of unforeseen accidents, the performance of his contract has become unexpectedly burdensome or even impossible ... But this rule is only applicable where the contract is positive and absolute and not subject to any condition either express or implied: and there are authorities which, as we think, establish the principle that where, from the nature of the contract, it appears that the parties must, from the beginning, have known that it could not be fulfilled unless, when the time for the fulfilment of the contract arrived, some particular specified thing continued to exist, so that when entering into the contract, they must have contemplated such continuing existence as the foundation of what was to be done; there, in the absence of any express or implied warranty that the thing shall exist, the contract is not to be construed as a positive contract but as subject to an implied condition that the parties shall be excused in case before breach, performance becomes impossible from the perishing of the thing without default of the contractor.

There seems little doubt that this implication tends to further the great object of making legal construction such as to fulfil the intention of those who entered into the contract ... The principle seems to us to be that in contracts in which the performance depends on the continued existence of a given person or thing, a condition is implied that the impossibility of performance ensuing from the perishing of the person or thing, shall excuse the performance.

In none of these cases is the promise in words other than positive, nor is there any express stipulation that the destruction of the person or thing shall excuse the performance; but that excuse is by law implied, because from the nature of the contract, it is apparent that the parties contracted on the basis of the continued existence of the particular person or chattel. In the present case, looking at the whole contract, we find that the parties contracted on the basis of the continued existence of the music hall at the time when the concerts were to be given, that being essential to their performance.'

Comment

It is generally accepted that the doctrine of frustration has its roots in this decision. While Blackburn J found that the true nature of the decision was one of licensor and licensee rather than landlord and tenant, he added 'nothing depends on this'. See also *National Carriers Ltd* v *Panalpina (Northern) Ltd* [1981] 2 WLR 45.

Distinguished in *Herne Bay Steam Boat Company* v *Hutton* [1903] 2 KB 683 (ship hired to review naval review: review postponed: postponement did not discharge contract since happening of review not its foundation: cf *Krell* v *Henry* [1903] 2 KB 740).

Tsakiroglou & Co Ltd v *Noblee and Thorl GmbH* [1961] 2 WLR 633

House of Lords (Viscount Simonds, Lords Reid, Radcliffe, Hodson and Guest)

• *Frustration – closure of Suez Canal – alternative route*

Facts

In October 1956 the appellants agreed to sell to the respondents groundnuts for shipment from Port Sudan to Hamburg during November/December 1956. On 7 October 1956, the appellants booked cargo space in a vessel scheduled to call at Port Sudan at the relevant time. Both parties contemplated that shipment would be made via th Suez Canal. On 2 November 1956, the Suez Canal was closed as a result of the invasion of Egypt by Israel. The appellants refused to ship the goods via the Cape of Good Hope and, when sued, pleaded frustration.

Held

The contract had not been frustrated.

Lord Reid:

'The appellants' first argument was that it was an implied term of the contract that shipment should be via Suez. It is found in the Case that both parties contemplated that shipment would be by that route, but I find nothing in the contract or in the Case to indicate that they intended to make this a term of the contract, or that any such term should be implied; they left the matter to the ordinary rules of law. Admittedly, the ordinary rule is that a shipper must ship by the usual and customary route, or, if there is no such route, then by a practicable and reasonable route. But the appellants' next contention was that this means the usual and customary route at the date of the contract, while the respondents maintain that the rule refers to the time of performance. There appears to be no decided case about this and, perhaps, that is not surprising because the point cannot often arise. ... Regarding the question as an open one, I would ask which is the more reasonable interpretation of the rule.

If the appellants are right, the question whether the contract is ended does not depend on the extent to which the parties or their rights and obligations are affected by the substitution of the new route for the old. If the new route made necessary by the closing of the old is substantially different, the contract would be at an end, however slight the effect of the change might be on the parties. That appears to me to be quite unreasonable; in effect, it means writing the old route into the contract, although the parties have chosen not to say anything about the matter. On the other hand, if the rule is to ascertain the route at the time of performance, then the question whether the seller is still bound to ship the goods by the new route does depend on the circumstances as they affect him and the buyer; whether or not they are such as to infer frustration of the contract. That appears to me much more just and reasonable and, in my opinion, that should be held to be the proper interpretation of the rule.

I turn, then, to consider the position after the canal was closed, and to compare the rights and obligations of the parties thereafter, if the contract sill bound them, with what their rights and obligations would have been if the canal had remained open. As regards the sellers, the appellants, the only difference ... to which I find ... was that they would have had to pay £15 per ton freight instead of £7 10s. They had no concern with the nature of the voyage. Counsel for the appellants rightly did not argue that this increase in the freight payable by the appellants was sufficient to frustrate the contract, and I need not, therefore, consider what the result might be if the increase had reached an astronomical figure. The route by the Cape was certainly practicable. There could be ... no objection to it by the buyers, and the only objection to it from the point of view of the sellers was that it cost them more. And it was not excluded by the contract. Where, then, is there any basis for frustration? It appears to me that the only possible way of reaching a conclusion that this contract was frustrated would be to concentrate on the altered nature of the voyage. I have no means of judging whether, looking at the matter from the point of view of a ship whose route from Port Sudan was altered via Suez to via the Cape, the difference would be so radical as to involve frustration, and I express no opinion about that. As I understand the argument, it was based on the assumption that the voyage was the manner of performing the sellers' obligations and that, therefore, its nature was material. I do not think so. What the sellers had to do was simply to find a ship proceeding by what was a practicable and now a reasonable route – if, perhaps, not yet a usual route – to pay the freight and obtain a proper bill of lading, and to furnish the necessary documents to the buyer. That was their manner of performing their obligations, and, for the reasons which I have given, I think that such changes in these matters as were made necessary fell far short of justifying a finding of frustration. ... the ultimate question is whether the new method of performance is fundamentally different, and that is a question of law.'

13 Discharge of the Contract

Afovos Shipping Co SA v *Pagnan, The Afovos* [1983] 1 WLR 195
House of Lords (Lord Hailsham of St Marylebone LC, Lords Diplock, Keith of Kinkel, Roskill and Brightman)

* *Repudiation – anticipatory breach*

Facts
Under the terms of a two-year three months (more or less at the charterers' option) charterparty, hire was payable semi-monthly in advance. The charterers paid the hire punctually until, due to an error by both parties' banks, one payment was late. The owners claimed that they were entitled to withdraw the vessel, inter alia, under the doctrine of anticipatory breach.

Held
They were not so entitled.

Lord Diplock:

'... The first part of the clause [5] imposes on the respondents as charterers a primary obligation to pay the "said hire" (which by cl 4 had been fixed at a monthly rate and pro rata for any part of a month) punctually and regularly in advance by semi-monthly instalments in the manner specified, which would involve the payment of a minimum of 42 and a maximum of 54 instalments, during the period of the charter. Failure to comply with this primary obligation by delay in payment of one instalment is incapable in law of amounting to a "fundamental breach" of contract by the charterers in the sense to which I suggested in *Photo Production Ltd* v *Securicor Transport Ltd* [1980] AC 827 this expression, if used as a

term of legal art, ought to be confined. The reason is that such delay in payment of one half-monthly instalment would not have the effect of depriving the owners of substantially the whole benefit which it was the intention of the parties that the owners should obtain from the unexpired period of the time charter extending over a period of between 21 and 27 months.

The second part of cl 5, however, starting with the word "otherwise" goes on to provide expressly what the rights of the owners are to be in the event of any such breach by the charterers of their primary obligation to make punctual payment of an instalment. The owners are to be at liberty to withdraw the vessel from the service of the charterers; in other words they are entitled to treat the breach when it occurs as a breach of condition and so giving them the right to elect to treat it as putting an end to all their own primary obligations under the charterparty then remaining unperformed. But although failure by the charterers in punctual payment of any instalment, however brief the delay involved may be, is made a breach of condition it is not also thereby converted into a fundamental breach; and it is to fundamental breaches alone that the doctrine of anticipatory breach is applicable.

The general rule is that a primary obligation is converted into a secondary obligation (whether a "general secondary obligation" or an "anticipatory secondary obligation" in the nomenclature of the analysis used in my speech in *Photo Production Ltd* v *Securicor Transport Ltd*) when and only when the breach of the primary obligation actually occurs. Up until then the primary obligations of both parties which have not yet been performed remain intact. The exception is where one party has manifested to the other party his intention no longer to

126

perform the contract and the result of the non-performance would be to deprive the other party of substantially the whole benefit which it was the intention of the parties that that other party should obtain from the primary obligations of both parties remaining to be performed. In such a case, to which the term "repudiation" is applicable, the party not in default need not wait until the actual breach: he may elect to treat the secondary obligations of the other party as arising forthwith.

The doctrine of anticipatory breach is but a species of the genus repudiation and applies only to fundamental breach. If one party to a contract states expressly or by implication to the other party in advance that he will not be able to perform a particular primary obligation on his part under the contract when the time for performance arrives, the question whether the other party may elect to treat the statement as a repudiation depends on whether the threatened non-performance would have the effect of depriving that other party of substantially the whole benefit which it was the intention of the parties that he should obtain from the primary obligations of the parties under the contract then remaining unperformed. If it would not have that effect there is no repudiation, and the other party cannot elect to put an end to such primary obligations remaining to be performed. The non-performance threatened must itself satisfy the criteria of a fundamental breach.

Similarly, where a party to a contract, whether by failure to take timeous action or by any other default, has put it out of his power to perform a particular primary obligation, the right of the other party to elect to treat this as a repudiation of the contract by conduct depends on whether the resulting non-performance would amount to a fundamental breach. Clearly, in the instant case delay in payment of one semi-monthly instalment of hire would not.'

Bolton v *Mahadeva* [1972] 2 All ER 1322 Court of Appeal (Sachs, Buckley and Cairns LJJ)

• *Lump sum contract – no substantial performance*

Facts
The plaintiff agreed to instal central heating and do other work in the defendant's house. The contract price for the central heating was a lump sum of £560. On completion, the defendant complained that the work was defective and refused to pay. The trial judge found that there were serious defects, the cost of remedying which was £174.50, and gave judgment for the balance, ie £431.50. The defendant appealed.

Held
The appeal would be allowed since, on the facts, the contract had not been substantially performed.

Cairns LJ:

'The main question in the case is whether the defects in workmanship ... were of such a character and amount that the plaintiff could not be said to have substantially performed his contract. That is, in my view, clearly the legal principle which has to be applied to cases of this kind.

The rule which was laid down many years ago in *Cutter* v *Powell* (1795) 6 Term Rep 320 in relation to lump sum contracts was that, unless the contracting party had performed the whole of his contract, he was not entitled to recover anything. That strong rule must now be read in the light of certain more recent cases to which I shall briefly refer. The first of those cases is *H Dakin & Co Ltd* v *Lee* [1916] 1 KB 566, a decision of the Court of Appeal, in which it was held that, where the amount of work which had not been carried out under a lump sum contract was very minor in relation to the contract as a whole, the contractor was entitled to be paid the lump sum, subject to such deduction as might be proper in respect of the uncompleted work. The basis [of the decision] is to be found in a passage of the judgment of Lord Cozens-Hardy MR. I do not think it is necessary to read it in full, but I read this short passage:

"But to say that a builder cannot recover from a building owner merely because some item of the work has been done negligently or inefficiently or improperly is a proposition which I should not listen to unless compelled by a decision of the House of Lords. Take a contract for a lump sum to decorate a house; the contract provides that there shall be three coats of oil paint, but in one of the rooms only two coats of paint are put on. Can anybody say that under these circumstances the building owner could go and occupy the house and take the benefit of all the decorations which had been done in the other rooms without paying a penny for all the work done by the builder, just because only two coats of paint had been put on in one room where there ought to have been three?" ...

Perhaps the most helpful case is the most recent one of *Hoenig* v *Isaacs* [1952] 2 All ER 176. That was a case where the plaintiff was an interior decorator and designer of furniture who had entered into a contract to decorate and furnish the defendant's flat for a sum of £750; and, as appears from the statement of facts, the Official Referee who tried the case at first instance found that the door of a wardrobe required replacing, that a bookshelf which was too short would have to be remade, which would require alterations being made to a bookcase, and that the cost of remedying the defects was £55 12s 2d. That is on a £750 contract. The ground on which the Court of Appeal in that case held that the plaintiff was entitled to succeed, notwithstanding that there was not complete performance of the contract, was that there was substantial performance of the contract and that the defects in the work which there existed were not sufficient to amount to a substantial degree of non-performance.

In considering whether there was substantial performance I am of opinion that it is relevant to take into account both the nature of the defects and the proportion between the cost of rectifying them and the contract price. It would be wrong to say that the contractor is only entitled to payment if the defects are so trifling as to be covered by the de minimus rule. ...

Now, certainly it appears to me that the nature and amount of the defects in this case were far different from those which the court had to consider in *H Dakin & Co Ltd* v *Lee* and *Hoenig* v *Isaacs*. For my part, I find it impossible to say that the judge was right in reaching the conclusion that in those circumstances the contract had been substantially performed. The contract was a contract to instal a central heating system. If a central heating system when installed is such that it does not heat the house adequately and is such, further, that fumes are given out, so as to make living rooms uncomfortable, and if the putting right of those defects is not something which can be done by some slight amendment of the system, then I think that the contract is not substantially performed.'

British and Commonwealth Holdings plc v Quadrex Holdings Inc [1989] 3 WLR 723 Court of Appeal (Sir Nicolas Browne-Wilkinson VC, Woolf and Staughton LJJ)

• *Time 'of the essence'?*

Facts
The plaintiff and defendant companies, both wishing to acquire control of a third company, entered into a written agreement whereby the defendant would withdraw its bid, leaving the way clear for the plaintiff to acquire the company, and the plaintiff would then sell the company's wholesale broking division to the defendant. The defendant had trouble finding the purchase money for the broking division and on 25 January 1985 the plaintiff served on it a notice fixing 28 February as the final

date to complete the contract. The defendant failed to complete and the plaintiff started proceedings claiming damages for the defendant's repudiation of the contract. The defendant denied time was of the essence and further claimed that the plaintiff company was itself in breach and the cause of the delay. At first instance the plaintiff successfully obtained summary judgment.

Held
In such circumstances, if a completion date had been stated in the agreement time would have been of the essence. Further, if the plaintiff had not itself been in breach of contract, it could have given notice to complete within a reasonable time and the time specified here had been reasonable. However, as it was arguable that the plaintiff had been in breach of contract the defendant would be given leave to defend.

Sir Nicolas Browne-Wilkinson VC:

'The phrase "time is of the essence of the contract" is capable of causing confusion since the question in each case is whether time is of the essence of the particular contractual term which has been breached ...

In equity, time is not normally of the essence of a contractual term. The rules of equity now prevail over the old common law rule: see the Law of Property Act 1925 s41. However, in three types of cases time is of the essence in equity: first, where the contract expressly so stipulates; second, where the circumstances of the case or the subject matter of the contract indicate that the time for completion is of the essence; third, where a valid notice to complete has been given. In the present case there was no express stipulation that time was of the essence. The subject matter of the sale (shares in unquoted private companies trading in a very volatile sector) is such that if a date for completion had been specified, in my judgment time would undoubtedly have been of the essence of completion ... For the reasons I have given, time could not be of the essence of completion on a date which was neither specified nor capable of

exact determination by the parties. The only question is whether time was made of the essence by the service of a valid notice to complete.

In the ordinary case, three requirements have to be satisfied if time for completion is to be made of the essence by the service of a notice, viz (1) the giver of the notice (the innocent party) has to be ready, willing and able to complete, (2) the other party (the guilty party) has to have been guilty of unreasonable delay before a notice to complete can be served and (3) the notice when served must limit a reasonable period within which completion is to take place.'

Comment
Followed in *Behzadi* v *Shaftesbury Hotels Ltd* [1991] 2 All ER 477 (in a sale of property, where one party fails to complete by the stipulated date the other may serve notice making time of the essence but time given must be reasonable).

Cutter v Powell (1795) 6 Term Rep 320 Court of King's Bench (Lord Kenyon CJ, Ashhurst, Grose and Lawrence JJ)

• *Incomplete performance – death of a seaman during voyage*

Facts
The defendant, master of the Governor Parry, contracted to pay a seaman 30 guineas 'provided that he proceeds, continues, and does his duty as second mate in the said ship from hence [Kingston, Jamaica] to the port of Liverpool'. The seaman died in the course of the voyage and his administratrix sued for work and labour done.

Held
Her action could not succeed.

Ashhurst J:

'This is a written contract, and it speaks for itself. As it is entire and, as the defendant's promise depends on a condition precedent to be performed by the other party, the condition must be performed before the other party is entitled to receive anything under it. It has been argued, however, that the plaintiff may now recover on a quantum meruit, but she has no right to desert the agreement for whatever there is an express contract the parties must be guided by it, and one party cannot relinquish or abide by it as it may suit his advantage. Here the intestate was by the terms of his contract to perform a given duty before he could call on the defendant to pay him anything; it was a condition precedent, without performing which the defendant is not liable. That seems to me to conclude the question. The intestate did not perform the contract on his part; he was not indeed to blame for not doing it; but still as this was a condition precedent, and as he did not perform it, his representative is not entitled to recover.'

Comment
See also *Bolton* v *Mahadeva* [1972] 2 All ER 1322.

Decro-Wall International SA v *Practitioners in Marketing Ltd*
[1971] 1 WLR 361 Court of Appeal (Salmon, Sachs and Buckley LJJ)

• *Repudiation – breach of term as to time of payment*

Facts
The plaintiff French company contracted with the defendants as sole concessionaires for the sale of their goods in the United Kingdom: the defendants undertook to pay within 90 days. However, although the plaintiffs never doubted that payment would be made, the defendants were consistently late payers; this cost the defendants about £20 each time (interest on bank loans), a loss which could have been, but was not, debited to the defendants. The plaintiffs contended that the defendants had repudiated the agreement.

Held
This was not the case.

Salmon LJ:

'The first question to be decided on this appeal is whether the defendants, by failing punctually to pay ... repudiated the agreement ... I have come to the conclusion that the learned judge was plainly right in holding that there had been no repudiation by the defendants. Clearly the defendants were in breach of the ... agreement by failing to pay the bills punctually. A breach of contract may be of such a nature as to amount to repudiation and give the innocent party the right (if he desires to exercise it) to be relieved from any further performance of the contract or the breach may entitle the innocent party only to damages. How is the legal consequence of a breach to be ascertained? Primarily from the terms of the contract itself. The contract may state expressly or by necessary implication that the breach of one of its terms will go to the root of the contract and accordingly amount to repudiation. Where it does not do so, the courts must look at the practical results of the breach in order to decide whether or not it does go to the root of the contract: see *Mersey Steel and Iron Co Ltd* v *Naylor, Benzon & Co* (1884) 9 App Cas 434 ... *Hong Kong Fir Shipping Co Ltd* v *Kawasaki Kisen Kaisha Ltd* [1962] 1 All ER 474 ... and *The Mihalis Angelos* [1970] 3 All ER 125 ... The same test may be and indeed often has been stated in different language, ie is the term which has been breached of the essence of the contract? Section 10(1) of the Sale of Goods Act 1893 provides:

"Unless a different intention appears from the terms of the contract, stipulations as to time of payment are not deemed to be of the essence of a contract of sale ..."

The present contract is of course not a simple contract of sale but, in my view, the same principle is to be applied to it. I am confident that the terms of the present contract relating to time of payment of the bills cannot properly be regarded as of the essence of the contract, or, to put it the other way, there is nothing expressed in or to be implied from the contract to suggest that a failure punctually to pay the bills goes to the root of the contract and thereby amounts to a repudiation.

Counsel for the plaintiffs relied on *Withers* v *Reynolds* (1831) 2 B & Ad 882 in support of his skilful argument that the failure to pay the bills on time amounted to a repudiation of the contract. In *Withers* v *Reynolds* there was an instalment contract of sale which called for cash on delivery of each instalment. The time came when the buyer refused to pay cash but insisted on credit for each instalment until the next was delivered. The court held that the seller was not obliged to go on with the contract on the terms which the buyer sought to dictate. This decision is explicable on the basis that the stipulation as to time of payment was intended by the parties to be of the essence of the contract, alternatively that the buyer was seeking to alter the nature of the transaction by turning a cash into a credit transaction. Accordingly, I do not consider that this decision is inimical to the view which I have already expressed.

I now turn to the point to whether the practical consequences of the defendants' late payments in breach of contract were of such a character as to make the breaches go to the root of the contract. The fact that over the years the plaintiffs agreed to 120 and then 180 day bills being substituted for 90 day bills and even then extended payment on a number of occasions does not suggest that they regarded late payment as being of vital importance to them. Nor was it; the plaintiffs obtained a loan from their bank of the full amount of each bill immediately it was accepted by the defendants. So far as the plaintiffs were concerned it is clear from the facts stated earlier in this judgment that the only effect of the late payments was that the plaintiffs may have incurred liability to their bank for a comparatively insignificant sum by way of extra interest which in any event they could have recovered from the defendants. The case would have been quite different if the defendants' breaches had been such as reasonably to shatter the plain-

tiffs' confidence in the defendants' ability to pay for the goods with which the plaintiffs supplied them. I think that, in such circumstances, the consequences of the breach could properly have been regarded as most serious, indeed fundamental, and going to the root of the contract so that the plaintiffs would have been entitled to refuse to continue doing business with the defendants. As already indicated, however, ... in ... evidence ... the plaintiffs never doubted that, if they went on supplying the defendants with goods, the defendants would meet the bills. They would, however, in all probability, meet them some days late, as they had done throughout the whole course of the dealings between the parties. For these reasons I agree with the learned judge that the defendants' breaches did not amount to a repudiation of the contract; they were not fundamental breaches going to the root of the contract. They certainly gave the plaintiffs no right to treat the contract as at an end.'

Fercometal SARL v *Mediterranean Shipping Co SA, The Simona* [1988] 3 WLR 200 House of Lords (Lords Bridge of Harwich, Templeman, Ackner, Oliver of Aylmerton and Jauncey of Tullichettle)

* *Wrongful repudiation – effect*

Facts

In June 1982 a charterparty provided for the carriage of steel coils from Durban to Bilbao: the charterers were entitled to cancel if the vessel was not ready to load on or before 9 July. On 2 July the shipowners requested an extension as they wished to load other cargo first; if they did this, the charterers' cargo could not be loaded until 13 July. The charterers forthwith cancelled the contract: the owners did not accept this repudiation and on 5 July notified the charterers that the vessel would start loading on 8 July. The vessel arrived in Durban on that day and the owners gave notice of readiness although they were not in fact ready to load. The charterers rejected the notice and began loading on another vessel which they had engaged after the owners' request for an extension. The owners claimed for deadfreight.

Held

Their claim could not succeed.

Lord Ackner:

'When one party wrongly refuses to perform obligations, this will not automatically bring the contract to an end. The innocent party has an option. He may either accept the wrongful repudiation as determining the contract and sue for damages or he may ignore or reject the attempt to determine the contract and affirm its continued existence ...

When A wrongfully repudiates his contractual obligations in anticipation of the time for their performance, he presents the innocent party, B, with two choices. He may either affirm the contract by treating it as still in force or he may treat it as finally and conclusively discharged. There is no third choice, as a sort of via media, to affirm the contract and yet be absolved from tendering further performance unless and until A gives reasonable notice that he is once again able and willing to perform. Such a choice would negate the contract being kept alive for the benefit of *both* parties and would deny the party who unsuccessfully sought to rescind the right to take advantage of any supervening circumstance which would justify him in declining to complete.

Towards the conclusion of his able address, counsel for the owners sought to raise what was essentially a new point ... He submitted that the charterers' conduct had induced or caused the owners to abstain from having the ship ready prior to the cancellation date. Of course, it is always open to A, who has refused to accept B's repudiation of the contract, and thereby kept the contract alive, to contend that, in relation to a particular right or obligation under the contract, B is estopped from contending that he, B, is entitled to exercise that right or that

he, A, has remained bound by that obligation. If B represents to A that he no longer intends to exercise that right or requires that obligation to be fulfilled by A and A acts on that representation, then clearly B cannot be heard thereafter to say that he is entitled to exercise that right or that A is in breach of contract by not fulfilling that obligation. If, in relation to this option to cancel, the owners had been able to establish that the charterers had represented that they no longer required the vessel to arrive on time because they had already fixed [another ship] and, in reliance on that representation, the owners had given notice of readiness only after the cancellation date, then the charterers would have been estopped from contending they were entitled to cancel the charterparty. There is, however, no finding of any such representation, let alone that the owners were induced thereby not to make the vessel ready to load by 9 July. On the contrary, the owners on 5 July on two occasions asserted that the vessel would start loading on 8 July and on 8 July purported to tender notice of readiness. Indeed, on the following day they instructed their London solicitors to confirm that the vessel was then open in Durban for the charterers' cargo. There is a total lack of any material to show that the owners, because of the charterers' repudiatory conduct, viewed the cancellation clause as other than fully operative and therefore capable of being triggered by the vessel not being ready on time. The non-readiness of the vessel by the cancelling date was in no way induced by the charterers' conduct. It was the result of the owners' decision to load other cargo first.

In short, in affirming the continued existence of the contract, the owners could only avoid the operation of the cancellation clause by tendering the vessel ready to load on time (which they failed to do), or by establishing (which they could not) that their failure was the result of the charterers' conduct in representing that they had given up their option, which representation the owners had acted on by not presenting the vessel on time.'

Comment

See also *Vitol SA v Norelf Ltd, The Santa Clara* [1996] 3 All ER 193.

Ferguson v Davies [1997] 1 All ER 315

See Chapter 2.

Frost v Knight (1872) LR 7 Ex 111 Court of Exchequer Chamber (Sir Alexander Cockburn CJ, Byles, Keating and Lush JJ)

• *Contract – refusal, before contingency, to perform*

Facts

The defendant promised the plaintiff that he would marry her on the death of his father. Before father died, he changed his mind and the plaintiff sued for breach of promise.

Held

She was entitled to do so.

Sir Alexander Cockburn CJ:

'Considering this to be now settled law ... we should have had no difficulty in applying the principle of the decision in *Hochster v De la Tour* (1853) 2 El & Bl 678 to the present case, were it not for the difference which undoubtedly exists between that case and the present, namely, that whereas there the performance of the contract was to take place at a fixed time, here no time is fixed, but the performance is made to depend on a contingency, namely, the death of the defendant's father during the life of both the contracting parties. It is true that in every case of a personal obligation to be fulfilled at a future time, there is involved the possible contingency of the death of the party binding himself before the time of performance arises; but here we have a further contingency, depending on the life of a third person, during which neither party can claim performance of the promise. This being so,

we thought it right to take time to consider whether an action would lie before the death of the defendant's father had placed the plaintiff in a position to claim the fulfilment of the defendant's promise. After full consideration, we are of opinion that, notwithstanding the distinguishing circumstances to which I have referred, this case falls within the principle of *Hochster v De la Tour* and that consequently the present action is well brought.

The considerations on which the decision in *Hochster v De la Tour* is founded are that by the announcement of the contracting party of his intention not to fulfil it, the contract is broken; and that it is to the common benefit of both parties that the contract shall be taken to be broken as to all its incidents, including non-performance at the appointed time, and that an action may be at once brought, and the damages consequent on non-performance be assessed at the earliest moment, as thereby many of the injurious effects of such non-performance may possibly be averted or mitigated.'

Comment

Although actions for breach of promise of marriage have been abolished (see s1(1) of the Law Reform (Miscellaneous Provisions) Act 1970) the principles of this decision still apply to other situations, see eg *Maredelanto Compania Naviera SA v Bergbau-Handel Gmbh, The Mihalis Angelos* [1970] 1 All ER 673.

General Billposting Co Ltd v Atkinson [1909] AC 118 House of Lords (Lord Loreburn LC, Earl of Halsbury, Lords Robertson and Collins)

• *Contract of service – wrongful termination – release from covenant*

Facts

The respondent was employed as the company's manager. His contract of service provided that the engagement should be subject to 12 months' notice by either side and also contained a covenant in restraint of trade. The appellants wrongfully dismissed the respondent without notice.

Held

The wrongful dismissal constituted a repudiation of the contract by the appellants and the respondent was not bound by the clause which restricted his right to engage in similar work.

Lord Collins:

'I think that this case may be, and in fact has been, decided on broader lines than those laid down in the notes to *Pordage v Cole* (1669) 1 Wms Saund 319, as to mutual and independent covenants. I think that the true test applicable to the facts of this case is that which was laid down by Lord Coleridge CJ in *Freeth v Burr* (1874) LR 9 CP 208, and approved in *Mersey Steel and Iron Co v Naylor, Benzon & Co* (1884) 9 App Cas 434:

"That the true question is whether the acts and conduct of the party evince an intention no longer to be bound by the contract."

I think that the Court of Appeal had ample ground for drawing this inference from the conduct of the employers here in dismissing the defendant in deliberate disregard of the terms of the contract, and that the latter was thereupon justified in rescinding the contract and treating himself as absolved from the further performance of it on his part.'

Comment

Applied in *Rock Refrigeration Ltd v Jones* [1997] 1 All ER 1.

Planché v Colburn (1831) 8 Bing 14

See Chapter 16.

Reardon Smith Line Ltd v Yngvar Hansen-Tangen [1976] 1 WLR 989

See Chapter 4.

Sumpter v Hedges [1898] 1 QB 673 Court of Appeal (A L Smith, Chitty and Collins LJJ)

• *Contract abandoned – payment for work done – possibility of new contract*

Facts

The plaintiff builder contracted to erect certain buildings for the defendant for £565. He did part of the work (to the value of about £333) and received payment of part of the price; he then said he had no money and could not go on. The defendant finished the work, using some of the plaintiff's materials left on site. When the plaintiff sued for work done and materials provided, the judge found that the plaintiff had abandoned the contract, allowed his claim for materials used, but gave him nothing for work done. The plaintiff appealed.

Held

The appeal would be dismissed.

Collins LJ:

'I think the case is really concluded by the finding of the learned judge to the effect that the plaintiff had abandoned the contract. If the plaintiff had merely broken his contract in some way so as not to give the defendant the right to treat him as having abandoned the contract, and the defendant had then proceeded to finish the work himself, the plaintiff might perhaps have been entitled to sue on a quantum meruit on the ground that the defendant had taken the benefit of the work done. But that is not the present case. There are cases in which, though the plaintiff has abandoned the performance of a contract, it is possible for him to raise the inference of a new contract to pay for the work done on a quantum meruit from the defendant's having taken the benefit of that work but, in order that that may be done, the circumstances must be such as to give an option to the defendant to take or not to take the benefit of the work done. It is only where the circumstances are such as to give that option that there is any evidence on which to ground the inference of a new contract. Where, as in the case of work done on land, the circumstances are such as to give the defendant no option whether he will take the benefit of the work or not, then one must look to other facts than the mere taking the benefit of the work in order to ground the inference of a new contract. In this case I see no other facts on which such an inference can be founded. The mere fact that a defendant is in possession of what he cannot help keeping, or even has done work upon it, affords no ground for such an inference. He is not bound to keep unfinished a building which in an incomplete state would be a nuisance on his land. I am therefore of opinion that the plaintiff was not entitled to recover for the work which he had done.'

Comment

This case is noteworthy not least because Collins LJ raises the possibility of inferring a new contract to pay for work done on a quantum meruit. Compare *Bolton* v *Mahadeva* [1972] 2 All ER 1322 and cases referred to therein. See also *Planché* v *Colburn* (1831) 8 Bing 14.

Union Eagle Ltd v *Golden Achievement Ltd* [1997] 2 All ER 215

See Chapter 15.

Vitol SA v *Norelf Ltd, The Santa Clara* [1996] 3 All ER 193 House of Lords (Lord Mackay of Clashfern LC, Lords Griffiths, Nolan, Steyn and Hoffmann)

• *Anticipatory breach – whether mere inaction is capable of constituting acceptance of anticipatory breach.*

Facts

The parties entered into a contract for the sale of a cargo of propane for delivery 1–7 March. Loading was not completed until 9 March. The day before (8 March) Vitol sent Norelf a telex, repudiating the contract on the ground that delivery was overdue. On 11 March, Norelf informed Vitol by telex that loading had been completed by 9 March. There was no further contact between the parties for five months. On 15 March, Vitol resold the cargo. On 9 August Norelf claimed the difference between the contract price at which Vitol had agreed to buy and the resale price. The dispute was referred to arbitration and the arbitrator made an award in favour of Norelf. Vitol appealed.

Held

As a matter of law, mere failure to perform a contractual obligation could constitute acceptance of an anticipatory repudiation. Here, the arbitrator's finding of an election by Norelf to treat the contract as at an end had been as to an issue of fact within his (the arbitrator's) exclusive jurisdiction.

Lord Steyn:

'The starting point of the inquiry is that the buyers, who seek to challenge the [arbitrator's] award, must identify a "question of law arising out of an award" within the meaning of s1(2) of the [Arbitration Act] 1979. If the buyers fail to do so, their challenge to the award must fail. It does not follow that because a line of inquiry proceeds from a legal proposition a question of law in the relevant sense is necessarily involved. ... I do accept that the question posed by Phillips J and by the Court of Appeal is a question of law within the meaning of s1(2) of the 1979 Act. That question, it will be recalled, is whether an aggrieved party can ever accept a repudiation of a contract merely by failing to perform. ...

My Lords, the question of law before the House does not call for yet another general re-examination of the principles governing an anticipatory breach of a contract and the acceptance of the breach by an aggrieved party. For present purposes I would accept as established law the following propositions: (1) Where a party has repudiated a contract the aggrieved party has an election to accept the repudiation or to affirm the contract: *Fercometal SARL* v *Mediterranean Shipping Co SA, The Simona* [1988] 2 All ER 742. (2) An act of acceptance of a repudiation requires no particular form: a communication does not have to be couched in the language of acceptance. It is sufficient that the communication or conduct clearly and unequivocally conveys to the repudiating party that that aggrieved party is treating the contract as at an end. (3) It is rightly conceded by counsel for the buyers that the aggrieved party need not personally, or by an agent, notify the repudiating party of his election to treat the contract as at an end. It is sufficient that the fact of the election comes to the repudiating party's attention, for example notification by an unauthorised broker or other intermediary may be sufficient: *Wood Factory Pty Ltd* v *Kiritos Pty Ltd* [1985] 2 NSWLR 105 at 146 per McHugh J, *Majik Markets Pty Ltd* v *S & M Motor Repairs Pty Ltd (No 1)* (1987) 10 NSWLR 49 at 54 per Young J and Carter and Harland *Contract Law in Australia* (3rd edn, 1996) pp689–691, para 1970.

The arbitrator did not put forward any heterodox general theory of the law of repudiation. On the contrary, he expressly stated that unless the repudiation was accepted by the sellers and the acceptance was communicated to the buyers the election was of no effect. It is plain that the arbitrator directed himself correctly in accordance with the governing general principle. The criticism of the arbitrator's reasoning centres on his conclusion that "the failure of [the sellers] to take any further step to perform the contract which was apparent to [the buyers] constituted sufficient communication of acceptance". By that statement the arbitrator was simply recording a finding that the buyers knew that the sellers were treating the contract as at an end. That interpretation is reinforced by the paragraph in his award read

as a whole. The only question is whether the relevant holding of the arbitrator was wrong in law.

It is now possible to turn directly to the first issue posed, namely whether non-performance of an obligation is ever as a matter of law capable of constituting an act of acceptance. ... One cannot generalise on the point. It all depends on the particular contractual relationship and the particular circumstances of the case. But ... I am satisfied that a failure to perform may sometimes signify to a repudiating party an election by the aggrieved party to treat the contract as at an end. Postulate the case where an employer at the end of a day tells a contractor that he, the employer, is repudiating the contract and that the contractor need not return the next day. The contractor does not return the next day or at all. It seems to me that the contractor's failure to return may, in the absence of any other explanation, convey a decision to treat the contract as at an end. ...

Taking the present case as illustrative, it is important to bear in mind that the tender of a bill of lading is the pre-condition to payment of the price. Why should an arbitrator not be able to infer that when, in the days and weeks following loading and the sailing of the vessel, the seller failed to tender a bill of lading to the buyer, he clearly conveyed to a trader that he was treating the contract as at an end? ... Sometimes in the practical world of businessmen an omission to act may be as pregnant with meaning as a positive declaration. While the analogy of offer and acceptance is imperfect, it is not without significance that while the general principle is that there can be no acceptance of an offer by silence, our law does in exceptional cases recognise acceptance of an offer by silence. Thus in *Rust* v *Abbey Life Insurance Co Ltd* [1979] 2 Lloyd's Rep 334 the Court of Appeal held that a failure by a proposed insured to reject a proffered insurance policy for seven months justified on its own an inference of acceptance. See also Treitel *The Law of Contract* (9th edn, 1995) pp30–32. Similarly, in the different field of repudiation, a failure to perform may sometimes by given a colour by special circumstances and may only be explicable to a reasonable person in the position of the repudiating party as an election to accept the repudiation.

My Lords, I would answer the question posed by this case in the same way as Phillips J did. In truth the arbitrator inferred an election, and communication of it, from the tenor of the rejection telex and the failure inter alia to tender the bill of lading. That was an issue of fact within the exclusive jurisdiction of the arbitrator.

White and Carter (Councils) Ltd v *McGregor* [1962] 2 WLR 17 House of Lords (Lords Reid, Morton of Henryton, Tucker, Keith of Avonholm and Hodson)

• *Contract – election not to accept repudiation*

Facts

The respondent's sales manager, acting within his authority, entered into a contract with the appellants for the fixing to litter bins of plates advertising the respondent's business. On the same day upon hearing of the contract, the respondent wrote to the appellants to cancel the agreement, but the appellants refused to accept this cancellation. The contract was for a period of 156 weeks and, under the terms of the contract, if any instalment was unpaid for four weeks, the whole of the amount due for the 156 weeks, or the remainder of that period, became due and payable. The respondent did not pay the first instalment within the time allowed and the appellants sought to recover the whole price.

Held (Lords Morton of Henryton and Keith of Avonholm dissenting)
They were entitled to succeed.

Lord Reid:

'The general rule cannot be in doubt. ... If one party to a contract repudiates it in the sense of making it clear to the other party that he refused or will refuse to carry out his part of the contract, the other party, the innocent party, has an option. He may accept that repudiation and sue for damages for breach of contract, whether or not the time for performance has come; or he may, if he chooses, disregard or refuse to accept it and then the contract remains in full effect. ...

I need not refer to the numerous authorities. They are not disputed by the respondent, but he points out that in all of them, the party who refused to accept the repudiation had no active duties under the contract. The innocent party's option is generally said to be to *wait* until the date of performance and then to claim damages estimated as at that date. There is no case in which it is said that he may, in the face of the repudiation, go on and incur useless expenses in performing the contract and then claim the contract price. The option, it is argued, is merely as to the date at which damages are to be assessed.

Developing this argument, the respondent points out that in most cases the innocent party cannot complete the contract himself without the other party doing, allowing or accepting something and that it is purely fortuitous that the appellants can do so in this case. In most cases, by refusing co-operation, the party in breach can compel the innocent party to restrict his claim to damages. Then it was said that even where the innocent party can complete the contract without such co-operation, it is against the public interest that he should be allowed to do so. An example was developed in argument. A company might engage an expert to go abroad and prepare an elaborate report and then repudiate the contract before anything was done. To allow such an expert to waste thousands of pounds in preparing the report cannot be right if a much smaller sum of damages would give him full compensation for his loss. It would merely enable the expert to extort a settlement giving him far more than reasonable compensation. ...

The other ground would be that there is some general equitable principle or element of public policy which requires this limitation of the contractual rights of the innocent party. It may well be that if it can be shown that a person has no legitimate interest, financial or otherwise, in performing the contract rather than claiming damages, he ought not to be allowed to saddle the other party with an additional burden with no benefit to himself. If a party has no interest to enforce a stipulation, he cannot in general enforce it: so it might be said that if a party has no interest to insist on a particular remedy, he ought not to be allowed to insist on it. And just as party is not allowed to enforce a penalty, so he ought not to be allowed to penalise the other party by taking one course when another is equally advantageous to him. If I may revert to the example which I gave of a company engaging an expert to prepare an elaborate report and then repudiating before anything was done, it might be that the company could show that the expert had no substantial or legitimate interest in carrying out the work rather than accepting damages: I would think that the de minimis principle would apply in determining whether his interest was substantial and that he might have a legitimate interest other than an immediate financial interest. But if the expert had no such interest, then that might be regarded as a proper case for the exercise of the general equitable jurisdiction of the court. But that is not this case. Here, the respondent did not set out to prove that the appellants had no legitimate interest in completing the contract and claiming the contract price rather than claiming damages; there is nothing in the findings of fact to support such a case and it seems improbable that any such case could have been proved. It is, in my judgment, impossible to say that the appellants should be deprived of their right to claim the contract price merely because the benefit to them, as against claiming damages and re-letting their advertising space, might be small in comparison with the loss to the respondent: that is the most that could be said in favour of the respondent. Parliament has on many occasions relieved parties from certain kinds of improvident or oppressive contracts, but common law can only do that in very limited circumstances. Accordingly, I am unable to avoid the conclusion that this appeal must be allowed and the case remitted so that decree can be pronounced as craved in the initial writ.'

Lord Hodson (Lord Tucker concurring):

'It may be unfortunate that the appellants have saddled themselves with an unwanted contract, causing an apparent waste of time and money. No doubt this aspect impressed the Court of Session, but there is no equity that can assist the respondent. It is trite that equity will not rewrite an improvident contract where there is no disability on either side. There is no duty laid upon a party to a subsisting contract to vary it at the behest of the other party so as to deprive himself of the benefit given to him by the contract. To hold otherwise would be to introduce a novel equitable doctrine that a party was not to be held to his contract unless the court in the given instance thought it reasonable to do so. In this case it would make an action for debt a claim for a discretionary remedy. This would introduce an uncertainty into the field of contract which appears to be unsupported by authority ... save for the one case [*Langford & Co Ltd* v *Dutch* 1952 SC 15] upon which the Court of Session founded its opinion and which must, in my judgment, be taken to have been wrongly decided.'

Comment

In *Decro-Wall International SA* v *Practitioners in Marketing Ltd* [1971] 1 WLR 361 Salmon LJ said:

'Counsel for the plaintiffs ... sought to rely on a passage in the speech of Lord Reid in *White & Carter (Councils) Ltd* v *McGregor* in support of the proposition that a contract breaker may in some circumstances by his breach unilaterally bring the contract to an end in law. I do not think that Lord Reid said anything of the kind. Indeed, in that case the majority decision, in which he concurred, was to the contrary.'

14 Remedies for Breach of Contract – Damages

Addis v *Gramophone Co Ltd* [1909] AC 488 House of Lords (Lord Loreburn LC, Lords James of Hereford, Atkinson, Collins, Gorell and Shaw)

- *Wrongful dismissal – measure of damages*

Facts

The plaintiff was employed by the defendants as manager of their business in Calcutta, at a weekly salary, plus commission on the trade done. He could be dismissed on six months' notice. In October 1905, the defendants gave him six months' notice but, at the same time, appointed another to act as his successor and took steps to prevent the plaintiff from acting any longer as manager. The plaintiff claimed damages for breach of contract. At first instance, the jury found for the plaintiff and awarded him, inter alia, £600 for wrongful dismissal and a further £340 in respect of excess commission, over and above what was earned by the plaintiff's successor in the six months between October 1905 and April 1906. The Court of Appeal held, by a majority, that there was no cause of action and entered judgment for the defendants.

Held (Lord Collins dissenting)

The plaintiff's appeal would be allowed.

Lord Atkinson:

'The rights of the plaintiff are, in my opinion, clear. He had been illegally dismissed from his employment. He could have been legally dismissed by the six months' notice which he in fact received, but the defendants did not wait for the expiry of that period. The damages the plaintiff sustained by this illegal dismissal were (1) the wages for the period of six months during which his formal notice would have been current; (2) the profits or commission which would, in all reasonable probability, have been earned by him during the six months had he continued in the employment; and possibly (3) damages in respect of the time which might reasonably elapse before he could find other employment. He has been awarded a sum possibly of some hundreds of pounds, not in respect of any of these heads of damage, but in respect of the harsh and humiliating way in which he was dismissed, including presumably the pain he experienced by reason, as is alleged, of the imputation upon him conveyed by the manner of his dismissal. This is the only circumstance which makes the case of general importance, and this is the only point with which I think it necessary to deal.

I have been unable to find any case decided in this country in which any countenance is given to the notion that a dismissed employee can recover, in the shape of exemplary damages for illegal dismissal, in effect, damages for defamation – for it amounts to that – except *Maw* v *Jones* (1890) 25 QBD 107 ... I have always understood that damages for breach of contract were in the nature of compensation, not punishment, and that the general rule of law applicable in such cases was in effect that stated by Cockburn CJ in *Engell* v *Fitch* (1868) LR 3 QB 314, 330 in these words:

"By the law as a general rule, a vendor who from whatever cause fails to perform his contract is bound ... to place the purchaser, so far as money will do it, in the position in which he would have been if the contract had been performed ..."

In *Sikes* v *Wild* (1861) 1 B & S 587, 594, Lord Blackburn said:

"I do not know how misconduct can alter the rule of law by which damages for breach of contract are to be assessed. It may render the contract voidable on the ground of fraud, or give a cause of action for deceit, but surely it cannot alter the effect of the contract itself."

... in actions of tort, motive, if it may be taken into account to aggregate damages, as undoubtedly it may be, may also be taken into account to mitigate them, as may also the conduct of the plaintiff himself who seeks redress. Is this rule to be applied to actions of breach of contract? There are few breaches of contract more frequent than those which arise where men omit or refuse to repay what they have borrowed. Is the creditor or vendor who sues for one of such breaches to have the sum he recovers lessened if he should be shown to be harsh, grasping or pitiless, or even insulting in enforcing his demand, or lessened because the debtor has struggled to pay, has failed because of misfortune, and has been suave, gracious and apologetic in his refusal? On the other hand, is that sum to be increased if it should be shown the debtor could have paid readily without any embarrassment, but refused with expressions of contempt and contumely from a malicious desire to injure his creditor? ... In my opinion, exemplary damages ought not to be, and are not according to any true principle of law, recoverable in such an action as the present, and the sums awarded to the plaintiff should, therefore, be decreased by the amount at which they have been estimated, and credit for that item should be allowed on his account.'

Comment
Distinguished in *Dunk* v *George Waller & Son Ltd* [1970] 2 WLR 1241. See also *Bliss* v *South East Thames Regional Health Authority* [1985] IRLR 308, *O'Laoire* v *Jackel International Ltd* [1991] IRLR 170, *Malik* v

Bank of Credit and Commerce International SA [1997] 3 All ER 1 and *Kpohraror* v *Woolwich Building Society* [1996] 4 All ER 119.

Alder v *Moore* [1961] 2 WLR 426
Court of Appeal (Sellers and Devlin LJJ and Slade J)

• *Contract of insurance – provision for penalty?*

Facts
A professional footballer, while playing for West Ham, suffered an injury which was believed to be permanent. Under an insurance policy he was paid £500 and, in accordance with the policy, he gave an undertaking that he would pay a 'penalty' of £500 if he played again. Twelve months after the injury he began to play again – for Cambridge United – and the insurers sued to recover the £500.

Held (Devlin LJ dissenting)
They were entitled to succeed.

Sellers LJ:

'The defendant's argument here has the advantage that underwriters have chosen to call the payment that they wish to recover a "penalty". Why they did so I cannot understand, but whilst they run a risk of being taken at their word, the law looks at the substance of the matter and not at the words used, whether "penalty" or "liquidation damages". I would regard it, as the learned judge did, as a repayment of a sum in circumstances which are entirely equitable. It is in no way an imposition of a fine or penal payment and if it has to be made to fall under one head or the other it is to be regarded as a payment by way of damages for breach of an undertaking which is not unfair or unconscionable and therefore not a penalty.

I have not thought it necessary to go through the cases. The law on this subject has from time to time been extensively reviewed. It was the subject of an elaborate exposition by Sir George Jessel MR in *Wallis* v *Smith* (1882) 21 Ch D 243 and somewhat more recently it was considered in the House of Lords in *Dunlop Pneumatic Tyre Co Ltd* v *New Garage & Motor Co Ltd* [1915] AC 79.'

Charter v Sullivan [1957] 2 WLR 528

See Chapter 18.

Clydebank Engineering and Shipbuilding Co v Castaneda [1905] AC 6 House of Lords (Earl of Halsbury LC, Lords Davey and Robertson)

• *Breach of contract – liquidated damages*

Facts

The appellants contracted to build four torpedo-boat destroyers for the Spanish government within specified periods and the contract stipulated a 'penalty for later delivery … at the rate of £500 per week'. The purchasers paid for the vessels and claimed for late delivery.

Held

The claim would succeed as the contract had provided for liquidated damages.

Earl of Halsbury LC:

'This is a case in which one party to an agreement has admittedly been guilty of a breach of that agreement. The action was brought by the Spanish government simply for the purpose of enforcing payment of a sum of money which, by agreement between the parties, was fixed as that which the appellants should pay in the events which have happened. Two objections have been made to the enforcement of that payment. The first objection is one which appears on the face of the instrument itself, namely, that it was a penalty, and, therefore, not recoverable without ascertaining the

measure of damage resulting from the breach of contract. It was frankly admitted that not much reliance could be placed on the mere use of the words "penalty" on one side, or "damage" on the other. It is clear that neither is conclusive as to the rights of the parties …

Then comes the question whether, under the agreement, the damages are recoverable as an agreed sum, or whether it is simply a penalty to be held over in terrorem, or whether it is a penalty so extravagant that no court ought to enforce it. It is impossible to lay down any abstract rule as to what might or might not be extravagant without reference to the principal facts and circumstances of the particular case. A great deal must depend on the nature of the transaction. On the other hand, it is an established principle in both countries to agree that the damages should be so much in the event of breach of agreement. The very reason why the parties agreed to such a stipulation was that, sometimes, the nature of the damage was such that proof would be extremely difficult, complex and expensive. If I wanted an example of what might be done in this way I need only refer to the argument of counsel as to the measure of damage sustained by Spain through the witholding of these vessels. Suppose there had been no agreement in the contract as to damages, and the Spanish government had to prove damages in the ordinary way, imagine the kind of cross-examination of every person connected with the Spanish administration. It is very obvious that what was intended by inserting these damages in the contract was to avoid a minute, difficult and complex system of examination which would be necessary if they had attempted to prove damage in the ordinary way …

If your Lordships look at the nature of the transaction, it is hopeless to contend that the penalty was intended merely to be in terrorem. Both parties recognised that the question was one in which time was the main element of the contract. I have come to the conclusion that the judgment of the court below was perfectly right. There is no ground for the contention that the sum in the contract was not the damages agreed on between the parties for very good and excellent reasons at the time at which the contract was entered into.'

Comment
See also *Dunlop Pneumatic Tyre Co Ltd* v *New Garage and Motor Co Ltd* [1915] AC 79.

Dunlop Pneumatic Tyre Co Ltd v *New Garage and Motor Co Ltd*
[1915] AC 79 House of Lords (Lords Dunedin, Atkinson, Parker and Parmoor)

• *Liquidated damages or penalty? – question for court*

Facts
The appellants manufactured motor tyres and they agreed to supply the respondent retailers on condition that they would not sell at prices below those mentioned in the appellants' price list: if they did, they would pay the appellants £5 for each and every tyre so sold 'as and by way of liquidated damages, and not as a penalty'.

Held
The stipulation was for liquidated damages and the respondants were liable to pay the appellants £5 for each breach of the agreement as to prices.

Lord Dunedin:

'We had the benefit of a full and satisfactory argument, and a citation of the very numerous cases which have been decided on this branch of the law. The matter has been handled, and at a recent date, in the courts of highest resort. I particularly refer to *Clydebank Engineering Co* v *Castaneda* [1905] AC 6, in your Lordships' House, and *Public Works Comr* v *Hills* [1906] AC 368 … in the Privy Council. In … these cases many of the previous authorities were considered. In view of that fact, and of the number of the authorities available, I do not

think it advisable to attempt any detailed review of the various cases, but I shall content myself with stating succinctly the various propositions which I think are deducible from the decisions which rank as authoritative:

(i) Though the parties to a contract who use the words penalty or liquidated damages may prima facie by supposed to mean what they say, yet the expression used is not conclusive. The court must find out whether the payment stipulated is in truth a penalty or liquidated damages. This doctrine may be said to be found passim in nearly every case. (ii) The essence of a penalty is a payment of money stipulated as in terrorem of the offending party; the essence of liquidated damages is a genuine covenanted pre-estimate of damage: *Clydebank Engineering Company* v *Castaneda*. (iii) The question whether a sum stipulated is penalty or liquidated damages is a question of construction to be decided upon the terms and inherent circumstances of each particular contract, judged of as the time of making of the contract, not as at the time of the breach: *Public Works Comr* v *Hills* … (iv) To assist this task of construction various tests have been suggested, which, if applicable to the case under consideration, may prove helpful or even conclusive. Such are (a) It will be held to be a penalty if the sum stipulated for is extravagant and unconscionable in amount in comparison with the greatest loss which could conceivably be proved to have followed from the breach – illustration given by Lord Halsbury L C in the *Clydebank* case. (b) It will be held to be a penalty if the breach consists only in not paying a sum of money, and the sum stipulated is a sum greater than the sum which ought to have been paid: *Kemble* v *Farren* (1829) 6 Bing 141. This, though one of the most ancient instances, is truly a corollary to the last test. Whether it had its historical origin in the doctrine of the common law that, when A promised to pay B a sum of money on a certain day and did not do so, B could only recover the sum with, in certain cases, interest, but could never recover further damages for non-timeous payment, or whether it was a survival of the time when equity reformed unconscionable bargains merely because they were unconscionable – a subject which much exercised Jessel MR, in *Wallis* v *Smith* (1882) 21 Ch D 243 – probably more interesting than material. (c) There is a presumption (but no more) that it is a penalty when

> "a single lump sum is made payable by way of compensation, on the occurrence of one or more or all of several events, some of which may occasion serious and others but trifling damages"

per Lord Watson in *Lord Elphinstone* v *Monkland Iron and Coal Co* (1886) App Cas 332 at p 342. On the other hand: (d) It is no obstacle to the sum stipulated being a genuine pre-estimate of damage that the consequences of the breach are such as to make precise pre-estimation almost an impossibility. On the contrary, that is just the situation when it is probable that pre-estimated damage was the true bargain between the parties: *Clydebank* case per Lord Halsbury …

Turning now to the facts of the case, it is evident that the damage apprehended by the appellants owing to the breaking of the agreement was an indirect and not a direct damage. So long as they got their price from the respondents for each article sold, it could not matter to them directly what the respondents did with it. Indirectly it did. Accordingly, the agreement is headed "Price Maintenance Agreement," and the way in which the appellants would be damaged if prices were cut was clearly explained in evidence, and no successful attempt was made to controvert that evidence. But though damages as a whole from such a practice would be certain, yet damages from any one sale would be impossible to forecast. It is just, therefore, one of those cases where it seems quite reasonable for parties to contract that they should estimate the damage at a certain figure, and provided that the figure is not extravagant there would seem no reason to suspect that it is not truly a bargain to assess damages, but rather a penalty to be held in terrorem.'

Comment

See also *Alder* v *Moore* [1961] 2 WLR 426 and *Bridge* v *Campbell Discount Co Ltd* [1962] 2 WLR 439.

Gibbons v *Westminster Bank Ltd*
[1939] 2 KB 882 High Court
(Lawrence J)

* *Dishonour of cheque – damages*

Facts

Money paid in by the plaintiff to the defendant bank was, by mistake, credited to the wrong account: in consequence, a cheque drawn by the plaintiff in favour of her landlords was dishonoured. The plaintiff had not pleaded special or actual damage: was she entitled to nominal damages only?

Held

She was – in this case £2.

Lawrence J:

> 'The authorities … all lay down that a trader is entitled to recover substantial damages without pleading and proving actual damage for the dishonour of his cheque, but it has never been held that that exception to the general rule as to the measure of damages for breach of contract extends to anyone who is not a trader … In my opinion, I ought to treat this matter as covered by these authorities, and I must hold that the corollary of the proposition which is laid down by these cases is the law – namely, that a person who is not a trader is not entitled to recover substantial damages unless the damages are alleged and proved as special damages. I am therefore of opinion that the plaintiff, whom I hold not to be a trader, is entitled to recover only nominal damages …'

Comment

See also *Kpohrorar* v *Woolwich Building Society* [1996] 4 All ER 119.

Hadley v Baxendale (1854) 9 Ex 341
Court of Exchequer (Parke, Alderson, Platt and Martin BB)

• *Breach of contract – measure of damages*

Facts
The plaintiffs were millers and mealmen in Gloucester. The crankshaft of the steam engine which worked their mill was fractureed and they ordered another from a firm in Greenwich who asked that the old shaft should be sent to them for use as a pattern. The plaintiffs gave the shaft to the defendants, who were common carriers, and the defendants promised to deliver the shaft on the following day. In fact they took a week to deliver it and because their mill was out of action for longer than would otherwise have been the case the plaintiffs claimed damages for loss of profit.

Held
This claim could not succeed since the loss of profit could not reasonably be considered a sequence of the breach of contract which could have been fairly and reasonably contemplated by both parties when they entered into the contract of carriage.

Alderson B:

'We think the proper rule in such a case as the present is this. Where two parties have made a contract which one of them has broken the damages which the other party ought to receive in respect of such a breach of contract should be such as may fairly and reasonably be considered either arising naturally, ie according to the usual course of things, from such a breach of contract itself, or such as may reasonably be supposed to have been in the contemplation of both parties at the time they made the contract as the probable result of the breach of it. If the special circumstances under which the contract was actually made were communicated by the plaintiffs to the defendants, and thus known to both parties, the damages resulting from the breach of such a contract which they would reasonably contemplate would be the amount of injury which would ordinarily follow from a breach of contract under the special circumstances so known and communicated. But, on the other hand, if these special circumstances were wholly unknown to the party breaking the contract, he, at the most, could only be supposed to have had in his contemplation the amount of injury which would arise generally, and in the great multitude of cases not affected by any special circumstances, from such a breach of contract. For, had the special circumstances been known, the parties might have specially provided for the breach of contract by special terms as to the damages in that case; and of this advantage it would be very unjust to deprive them.

The above principles are those by which we think the jury ought to be guided in estimating the damages arising out of any breach of contract. It is said that other cases, such as breaches of contract in the non-payment of money, or in the not making a good title to land, are to be treated as exceptions from this, and as governed by a conventional rule. But as, in such cases, both parties must be supposed to be cognisant of that well-known rule, these cases may, we think, be more properly classed under the rule above enunciated as to cases under known special circumstances, because there both parties may reasonably be presumed to contemplate the estimation of the amount of damages according to the conventional rule. In the present case, if we are to apply the principles above laid down, we find that the only circumstances here communicated by the plaintiffs to the defendants at the time the contract was made were that the article to be carried was the broken shaft of a mill and that the plaintiffs were the millers of that mill. But how do these circumstances show reasonably that the profits of the mill must be stopped by an unreasonable delay in the delivery of the broken shaft by the carrier to the third person? Suppose the plaintiffs had another shaft in their possession, put up or putting up at the time, and that they only wished to send back the broken shaft to the engineer who made it; it is clear that this would be quite consistent with the above circumstances, and yet the unreasonable delay in the delivery would have no effect upon the intermediate profits of the mill. Or, again, suppose that at the time of the delivery to the carrier, the machinery of the mill had been in other respects defective, then, also, the same results would follow. Here it is true that the shaft was actually sent back to serve as a model for a new one, that the want of a new one was the only cause of the stoppage of the mill and that the loss of profits really arose from not sending down the new shaft in proper time, and that this arose from the delay in delivering the broken one to serve as a model. But it is obvious that, in the great multitude of cases of millers sending off broken shafts to third persons by a carrier under ordinary circumstances, such consequences would not, in all probability, have occurred, and these special circumstances were here never communicated by the plaintiffs to the defendants.

It follows, therefore, that the loss of profits here cannot reasonably be considered such a consequence of the breach of contract as could have been fairly and reasonably contemplated by both the parties when they made this contract. For such loss would neither have flowed naturally from the breach of this contract in the great multitude of such cases occurring under ordinary circumstances, nor were the special circumstances, which, perhaps, would have made it a reasonable and natural consequence of such breach of contract, communicated to or known by the defendants. The judge ought, therefore, to have told the jury that, upon the facts then before them, they ought not to take the loss of profits into consideration at all in estimating the damage.'

Comment
Applied in *Wroth* v *Tyler* [1973] 2 WLR 405. Distinguished in *Victoria Laundry (Windsor) Ltd* v *Newman Industries Ltd* [1949] 2 KB 528. See also *Koufos* v *C Czarnikow Ltd* [1967] 3 WLR 1491, *Pilkington* v *Wood* [1953] Ch 770, *Parsons (H) (Livestock) Ltd* v

Uttley Ingham & Co Ltd [1977] 3 WLR 990 and *Kpohraror* v *Woolwich Building Society* [1996] 4 All ER 119.

Investors Compensation Scheme Ltd v West Bromwich Building Society [1998] 1 All ER 98
See Chapter 19.

Jackson v Horizon Holidays Ltd [1975] 3 WLR 1468
See Chapter 10.

Kophraror v Woolwich Building Society [1996] 4 All ER 119 Court of Appeal (Evans, Waite LJJ and Sir John May)

• *Dishonour of cheque – account used for business purposes – measure of damages*

Facts
When converting his savings account with the defendants to a current account, the plaintiff, a Nigerian, had described himself as a self-employed 'exporter/importer' as well as a part-time employee of two businesses. He had stated that his income was below £5,000 pa. A cheque for £4,550 in favour of Phils (Wholesalers) Ltd drawn on his account was mistakenly dishonoured. The cheque was by way of payment for goods which the plaintiff required for shipment to Nigeria. The defendants admitted liability for the wrongful dishonour of the cheque and the plaintiff was awarded general damages of £5,550, with interest. The plaintiff appealed from Master Tennant's decision, contending that he was also entitled to recover special damages for loss of profit on the transaction and on ten further shipments which would have followed from it. The defendants cross-appealed against the award on the ground that the plaintiff was only entitled to nominal damages.

Held

The master's decisions would not be disturbed.

Evans LJ:

'Both parties accept that the claim is governed by the general law, that is to say the plaintiff may recover general damages under the first head of the rule in *Hadley* v *Baxendale* (1854) 9 Exch 341 and special damages under the second head of the rule when the necessary facts are proved. This is not the only sense in which the terms "general" and "special" damages are used nor the only context in which a distinction is made between them. One such distinction is that special damages must be expressly claimed and pleaded, whereas general damages need not ...

The claim for general damages rests upon the first part of the rule in *Hadley* v *Baxendale,* namely, they are claimed as damages "arising naturally (which means in the normal course of things)" from the defendant's breach (see *Monarch Steamship Co Ltd* v *Karlshamns (AB) Oljefabriker* [1949] 1 All ER 1 at 12 per Lord Wright). It is not disputed that a claim does arise for loss of credit or business reputation, but the defendants say that the amount should be nominal unless special facts are proved which were made known to them when the contract was made; in other words, that this should be properly regarded under the second, not the first part of the *Hadley* v *Baxendale* rule. They rely upon a number of reported cases where nominal damages only were awarded: by a jury in *Evans* v *London and Provincial Bank* (1917) 3 LDAB 152, by Lawrence J in *Gibbons* v *Westminster Bank Ltd* [1939] 3 All ER 577 and by this court in *Rae* v *Yorkshire Bank plc* [1988] BTLC 35, where a claim for substantial damages for "inconvenience and humiliation" was dismissed.

However, the plaintiff relies upon the line of authority which holds that actual damage need not be alleged or proved by "a trader", which he claims that he was. The defendants say that they were unaware of this, and that the rule does not apply, for that reason alone.

As will appear below, the issue in my view is whether a person who is not "a trader" for the purposes of the common law rule – and it is not at all clear what the limits of that category are – can recover substantial rather than nominal damages for loss of business reputation when his cheque is wrongly dishonoured by the bank. A subsidiary question is how much the measure of damages is affected by the extent of the bank's knowledge of its customer and of the purposes for which he uses his account.

I will start with the authorities which establish that a "trader" is entitled to recover substantial, rather than nominal, damages for loss of business reputation without proof of actual damage. This was recognised and applied, although in a different context, by the House of Lords in *Wilson* v *United Counties Bank Ltd* [1920] AC 102 ... The rule so stated made it necessary to consider in every case whether or not the plaintiff was a trader. ...

It is abundantly clear, in my judgment, that history has changed the social factors which moulded the rule in the nineteenth century. It is not only a tradesman of whom it can be said that the refusal to meet his cheque is "so obviously injurious to [his] credit" that he should "recover, without allegation of special damage, reasonable compensation for the injury done to his credit" (see [1920] AC 102 at 112 per Lord Birkenhead LC). The credit rating of individuals is as important for their personal transactions, including mortgages and hire-purchase as well as banking facilities, as it is for those who are engaged in trade, and it is notorious that central registers are now kept. I would have no hesitation in holding that what is in effect a presumption of some damage arises in every case, in so far as this is a presumption of fact.

So the question becomes, whether the authorities compel the conclusion as a matter of law that the presumption cannot extend beyond the category of trader. In my judgment, they do not. The most directly relevant are *Gibbons* v *Westminster Bank Ltd* [1939] 3 All ER 577 and *Rae* v *Yorkshire Bank plc* [1988] BTLC 35. In the former case, Lawrence J regarded the presumption in favour of a trader as one of four exceptions to the general rule that the plaintiff in a claim for damages for breach of contract cannot recover substantial damages in the absence of proof that some actual damage has been suffered, and he felt unable to extend the exception to non-traders. ...

In *Rae* v *Yorkshire Bank plc* the plaintiff's claim was for damages for "inconvenience and humiliation" ... Parker LJ, with whom O'Connor LJ agreed, cited *Bliss* v *South East Thames Regional Health Authority* [1987] ICR 700, where Dillon LJ held that the general rule laid down in *Addis* v *Gramophone Co Ltd* [1909] AC 488 is that –

> "where damages fall to be assessed for breach of contract rather than in tort it is not permissible to award general damages for frustration, mental distress, injured feelings or annoyance occasioned by the breach." ...

Dillon LJ also noted a further exception to the general rule which is now permitted "where the contract which has been broken was itself a contract to provide peace of mind or freedom from distress" ... Parker LJ continued ... "That authority, and *Gibbons*, are two of many which in my view make Mr Rae's an appeal which must inevitably fail." Clearly, the judgment in *Rae* v *Yorkshire Bank plc* was based primarily in the application of the law as stated by Dillon LJ to the facts of that case, where the claim was for "inconvenience and humiliation" (only). That is a different kind of damage from loss of reputation or credit, unless "humiliation" is intended to include such injury in the eyes of third parties, but that point was not taken in *Rae's* case because the kinds of damage referred to by Dillon LJ all refer to the injured feelings of the plaintiff himself.

The trial judge in *Rae* had referred to *Gibbons* and said ... "It is clear that Mr Rae was not a trader and that in those circumstances, damages are purely nominal". Apart from the passing reference to *Gibbons* in the passage already quoted, the "trader" rule, or exception, was not considered in the judgments in the Court of Appeal.

In these circumstances, neither *Rae* nor *Gibbons* itself is binding authority which precludes this court from considering whether a bank's customer who is not a trader is precluded from recovering substantial damages for injury to his reputation or credit, unless special damage is alleged and proved. The trader exception itself recognises, as does the general rule regarding the recovery of damages for tort, that this is a kind of injury recognised by law. ...

Moreover, if the exception is a presumption of fact then it is open to the court, in my judgment, to hold that changing social circumstances should cause the presumption to be reviewed and if necessary expanded in order to take those changes into account.

For these reasons, I would reject the defendant's allegation by way of cross-appeal that the master was wrong to award more than a nominal sum by way of general damages. I should, however, also refer to their contention that the master was wrong to do so when the defendants denied that they had knowledge of the fact that he was a trader. In none of the reported cases where a trader has succeeded in recovering substantial damages has the bank's knowledge been an issue. ... But it is unnecessary to express a concluded view, because the evidence is that the plaintiff described himself in the application form as a part-time self-employed "exporter/importer" although clearly on a modest scale. This evidence is not and cannot be disputed and it is sufficient in my judgment to fix the defendants with knowledge that that was the self-styled description of the plaintiff for the purposes of the contract between them with regard to the current account. To this extent, it was a question of "status" and the defendants knew what that status was. ...

Special damages

I come therefore to the plaintiff's main ground of appeal. He asserts, in the "particulars of special damage" already quoted, that he is entitled to recover damages for his loss of profit on the transaction in question and on ten further shipments which, he says, would have followed from it if the first shipment had not been delayed. He claims, moreover, that his losses in respect of the goods which were delayed included a very large sum ... which he was compelled to pay to his Nigerian customer both by reason of his legal liabilities, as he asserts, owed to that customer and because considerable pressures, both commercial and social, were brought to bear upon him and his father and family by that customer in Nigeria. So, [counsel] submits on his behalf, these were all heads of damage which could reasonably be contemplated by the defendants when the banking contract was made, not because they had any knowledge of the circumstances of the particular transaction or of any intended transaction, but because they knew, as the plaintiff asserts, that he was an "exporter/importer" and that he intended to use the account for his business activities. To these might be added the fact which is undisputed that the defendants knew that the plaintiff is Nigerian and so, it might be submitted, were also aware that exports of goods might be delivered there.

The master dealt with this part of the claim on the assumption that the plaintiff was correct as to the extent of the defendants' knowledge. He held that nevertheless these damages could not be recovered, either under the first limb of *Hadley* v *Baxendale* ("this was such an extraordinary outcome it could not possibly be regarded as a natural consequence of a banker's breach of contract") or under the second limb, because even on the basis of the defendants' assumed knowledge "this claim ... raises a narrative of events which though not unimaginable is certainly not foreseeable in the ordinary course". ...

For my part I cannot regard this as a claim falling within the second limb of *Hadley* v *Baxendale*. It is not a case where the defendant is said to have had knowledge of "special circumstances" so that this part of the rule applies. Rather, the question is, in my judgment, whether, given the plaintiff's general description of himself and of the

purposes for which he intended to use the account, it can be said that damages arising from the loss or late performance of his contract to sell and deliver the goods to Nigeria can reasonably be supposed to have been in the contemplation of both parties when the contract was made, or as the "not unlikely consequence" of the defendant's breach, if it should occur (*The Heron II* [1967] 3 All ER 686). This is the first rather than the second limb of the rule, although as I shall say below I am doubtful whether it assists to make a rigid distinction of this sort.

In my judgment, and in agreement with the master, these damages were too remote to be claimed under this head. Even if the defendants were told that the account was to be used for the plaintiff's business, even trading activities, there was nothing to indicate that a cheque, even one drawn in favour of a goods wholesaler, was required for the purposes of international trade and in circumstances where even one day's delay in payment would or might cause the loss of a transaction or a substantial trading loss for the plaintiff. What might perhaps be contemplated was that, if such a situation did arise, then the plaintiff would give the defendants special notice of the need for immediate clearance so that, if they were willing to do so, a special arrangement could be made.

There is also the pragmatic reason given by the master, which is that there is no reported case where a bank's customer has recovered damages such as these for the wrongful dishonour of a cheque, where no special circumstances were alleged to exist.

Generally ...
The contentions for both parties were presented as if in a straitjacket imposed by the strict application of the rule in *Hadley* v *Baxendale* so as to require the separate consideration of each of the two limbs. ... I would prefer to hold that the starting point for any application of *Hadley* v *Baxendale* is the extent of the shared knowledge of both parties when the contract was made (see generally *Chitty on Contracts* (27th edn, 1994) vol 1, para 26–023, including the pos-

sibility that knowledge of the defendant alone is enough). When that is established, it may often be the case that the first and the second parts of the rule overlap. or at least that it is unnecessary to draw a clear line of demarcation between them. This seems to be to be consistent with the commonsense approach suggested by Scarman LJ in *H Parsons (Livestock) Ltd* v *Uttley Ingham & Co Ltd* [1978] 1 All ER 525 at 541, and to be applicable here.'

Malik v Bank of Credit and Commerce International SA
[1997] 3 All ER 1

See Chapter 4.

Payzu Ltd v Saunders [1919] 2 KB 581 Court of Appeal (Bankes and Scrutton LJJ and Eve J)

• *Breach of contract – duty to mitigate loss*

Facts
The defendant, having agreed to sell the plaintiffs 200 pieces of silk, delivered the final consignment for which the plaintiffs failed to pay punctually. In view of this, the defendant said that she would only deliver further supplies if the plaintiffs paid on delivery. This the plaintiffs would not accept, so they sued for breach of contract, claiming the differences between the contract price and the current market price.

Held
Although the defendant was liable, the plaintiffs' failure to pay promptly for the first consignment not amounting to a repudiation of the contract, the plaintiffs should have mitigated their loss by accepting her cash-on-delivery terms and they were entitled to recover only the amount which they would have lost had they done so.

Scrutton LJ:

'Whether it be more correct to say that a

plaintiff must minimise his damages, or to say that he can recover no more than he would have suffered if he had acted reasonably, because any further damages do not reasonably follow from the defendant's breach, the result is the same. The plaintiff must take "all reasonable steps to mitigate the loss consequent on the breach" and this principle "debars him from claiming any part of the damage which is due to his neglect to take such steps": *British Westinghouse Electric and Manufacturing Co* v *Underground Electric Railways Co of London Ltd* [1912] AC 673 per Lord Haldane LC. Counsel for the plaintiffs has contended that in considering what steps should be taken to mitigate the damage all contractual relations with the party in default must be excluded. That is contrary to my experience. In certain cases of personal service it may be unreasonable to expect a plaintiff to consider an offer from the other party who has grossly injured him; but in commercial contracts is is generally reasonable to accept an offer from the party in default. However, it is always a question of fact. About the law there is no difficulty.'

Comment
Distinguished in *Strutt* v *Whitnell* [1975] 2 All ER 510 (purchaser not obliged to return defective property and forego right to substantial damages).

St Albans City and District Council v International Computers Ltd
[1996] 4 All ER 481 Court of Appeal (Nourse, Hirst LJJ and Sir Iain Glidewell)

• *Breach of contract – measure of damages – total loss – unfair term – sale of goods – implied term*

Facts
Faulty software supplied by the defendant to the plaintiffs caused the population of the plaintiffs' area to be overstated by 2,966. As

a result, the plaintiffs' community charge receipts for 1990–91 were £484,000 less than would have been the case had they known the true population and they had to pay an extra £685,000 net to Hertfordshire County Council by way of precept. The £484,000 was recouped by the plaintiffs from their charge-payers by way of increased community charge in 1991–92. The plaintiffs claimed payment of both sums by way of damages for breach of contract. A clause in the contract limited the defendant's liability to £100,000.

Held

The plaintiffs were entitled to £685,000, with interest, and interest on £484,000 for 1990–91.

Nourse LJ:

'Authority apart, I would approach the matter in this way. If the software had not been faulty, the plaintiffs would not have had to pay out the £685,000. Having paid it out, they were unable to recover it from the county council or any other third party. They could only recover it, they were bound to recover it, from their chargepayers. Viewing the plaintiffs as having, for this purpose, the like capacity as a trustee for the chargepayers, I am in no doubt that they can recover the £685,000 from the defendant. Otherwise the chargepayers would be out of pocket.

The £484,000 stands on a different footing. Although [counsel for the plaintiffs] argued to the contrary, I think that we can only work on the inference that if the software had not been faulty, the plaintiffs would have collected the £484,000 by way of an additional charge in 1990–91. Having not collected it, they were unable to recover it from any third party. They could only recover it, they were bound to recover it, from their chargepayers in 1991–92. In this instance, however, the chargepayers were under an obligation to pay in 1991–92 precisely what they ought to have paid, but did not pay in 1990–91. Viewing the plaintiffs in the like capacity as before, I am in no doubt that they cannot recover the £484,000 from the defendant. The effect of the recov-

ery would be to relieve the chargepayers of an obligation to which they were always subject or, if you prefer, to give them a bonus to which they were not entitled. They have not been out of pocket. The plaintiffs, on the other hand, are entitled to recover interest on the £484,000 for the year 1990–91. …

I believe that the key observation in the authorities is to be found in the speech of Lord Reid in *Parry* v *Cleaver* [1969] 1 All ER 555 at 559:

"Surely the distinction between receipts which must be brought into account and those which must not must depend not on their source but on their intrinsic nature."

That observation was quoted by Glidewell LJJ in *Palatine Graphic Arts Co Ltd* v *Liverpool City Council* [1986] 1 All ER 366 at 371 and applied by this court in that case. Here, since the 1990–91 shortfall was an unintended subtraction from the 1990–91 charge which had to be made good by an equivalent addition to the 1991–92 charge, the two are intrinsically the same. As [counsel for the defendant] well put it, the addition to the 1991–92 charge was not the result of benevolence or an accidental circumstance, but the very sum which, but for the defendant's breach of contract, would have been received from the chargepayers in 1990–91 and which the plaintiffs were required to obtain from them in 1991–92. Accordingly, the test propounded by the authorities leads to the same conclusion as that to which I would have come without them.

I come finally to the Unfair Contract Terms Act 1977. As I have said, the judge found that the contract incorporated the defendant's general conditions of contract for the supply of equipment, programmes and services. It has not been suggested that those conditions were not written standard terms of business for the purposes of the 1977 Act. The material provision was contained in cl9(c) whose effect, if it stands, would be to limit the damages recoverable by the plaintiffs to £100,000. …

[The trial judge] dealt with this question

as one of fact, finding that the defendant's general conditions remained effectively untouched in the negotiations and that the plaintiffs accordingly dealt on the defendant's written standard terms for the purposes of s3(1) ... I respectfully agree with him. The consequence of that finding is that the defendant cannot rely on cl9(c) except in so far as it satisfies the requirement of reasonableness. The judge carefully considered that question and held that cl9(c) did not pass the test. ... I am certainly not satisfied that his decision proceeded upon some erroneous principle or was plainly and obviously wrong. Indeed, I believe that I would have given the same answer myself.'

While the Court of Appeal was satisfied that the defendant's liability flowed from an express contractual obligation, on behalf of the court Sir Iain Glidewell also examined the question of a relevant implied term as follows:

'... was the contract between the parties subject to any implied term as to quality or fitness for purpose, and if so, what was the nature of that term? Consideration of this question during argument led to discussion of a more general question, namely: "Is software goods?" ... In order to answer the question ... it is necessary to distinguish between the program and the disk carrying the program.

In both the Sale of Goods Act 1979, s61, and the Supply of Goods and Services Act 1982, s18, the definition of goods includes "all personal chattels other than things in action and money". Clearly, a disk is within this definition. Equally clearly, a program, of itself, is not.

If a disk carrying a program is transferred, by way of sale or hire, and the program is in some way defective, so that it will not instruct or enable the computer to achieve the intended purpose, is this a defect in the disk? Put more precisely, would the seller or hirer of the disk be in breach of the terms as to quality and fitness for purpose implied by s14 of the 1979 Act and s9 of the 1982 Act? ...

There is no English authority on this question, and indeed we have been referred to none from any common law jurisdiction. ...

Suppose I buy an instruction manual on the maintenance and repair of a particular make of car. The instructions are wrong in an important respect. Anybody who follows them is likely to cause serious damage to the engine of his car. In my view, the instructions are an integral part of the manual. The manual, including the instructions, whether in a book or a video cassette, would in my opinion be "goods" within the meaning of the 1979 Act, and the defective instructions would result in a breach of the implied terms in s14.

If this is correct, I can see no logical reason why it should not also be correct in relation to a computer disk onto which a program designed and intended to instruct or enable a computer to achieve particular functions has been encoded. If the disk is sold or hired by the computer manufacturer, but the program is defective, in my opinion there would be prima facie be a breach of the terms as to quality and fitness for purpose implied by the 1979 Act or the 1982 Act.

However, in the present case, it is clear that the defective program ... was not sold, and it seems probable that it was not hired. The evidence is that, in relation to many of the program releases, an employee of ICL went to St Albans' premises where the computer was installed taking with him a disk on which the new program was encoded, and himself performed the exercise of transferring the program into the computer.

As I have already said, the program itself is not "goods" within the statutory definition. Thus a transfer of the program in the way I have described does not, in my view, constitute a transfer of goods. It follows that in such circumstances there is no statutory implication of terms as to quality or fitness for purpose.

Would the contract then contain no such implied term? The answer must be sought in the common law. The terms implied by the 1979 Act and the 1982 Act were originally evolved by the courts of common law and have since by analogy been implied by the courts into other types of contract. Should such a term be implied in a contract of the kind I am now considering, for the transfer of a computer program into the computer without any transfer of a disk or any other tangible thing on which the program is encoded?

The basis upon which a court is justified in implying a term into a contract in which it has not been expressed is strict. Lord Pearson summarised it in his speech in *Trollope & Colls Ltd* v *North West Metropolitan Regional Hospital Board* [1973] 2 All ER 260 at 268:

> "An unexpressed term can be implied if and only if the court finds that the parties must have intended that term to form part of their contract: it is not enough for the court to find that such a term would have been adopted by the parties as reasonable men if it had been suggested to them: it must have been a term that went without saying, a term which, although tacit, formed part of the contract which the parties made for themselves."

In my judgment, a contract for the transfer into a computer of a program intended by both parties to instruct or enable the computer to achieve specified functions is one to which Lord Pearson's words apply. In the absence of any express term as to quality or fitness for purpose, or of any term to the contrary, such a contract is subject to an implied term that the program will be reasonably fit for, ie reasonably capable of achieving the intended purpose.

In the present case if, contrary to my view, the matter were not covered by express terms of the contract, I would hold that the contract was subject to an implied term that [the program] was reasonably fit for, that is, reasonably capable of achieving the purpose specified in ... St Alban's invitation to tender, and that as a result of the defect ... were in breach of that implied term.'

Thompson (W L) Ltd v *R Robinson (Gunmakers) Ltd* [1955] 2 WLR 185

See Chapter 18.

Watts v *Morrow* [1991] 1 WLR 1421
Court of Appeal (Brown, Ralph Gibson and Bingham LJJ)

• *Measure of damages – surveyor's report negligent – damages for distress and inconvenience*

Facts
Relying on the defendant surveyor's survey to the effect that the property's overall condition was sound, the plaintiffs bought Nutford Farm House for £177,500. After taking possession the plaintiffs discovered substantial defects in need of urgent attention and they had the necessary work carried out at a cost of £33,961. They sought to recover the cost of these repairs from the defendant and it was common ground that, in its true condition, the value of the house at the date of purchase had been £162,500. The judge awarded the plaintiffs the cost of the repairs and £8,000 for distress and inconvenience. The defendant appealed.

Held
Applying the principle of restitution, the plaintiffs were entitled to the amount required to put them in the position in which they would have been if the defendant had carried out the contract of survey properly, ie £15,000, the amount they were caused to pay more than the property's value in its true condition. Further, the plaintiffs were not entitled to damages for mental stress not caused by physical discomfort or inconvenience resulting from the breach and damages under this head would therefore be reduced to £1,500 for physical discomfort.

Ralph Gibson LJ:

> 'The task of the court is to award to the plaintiffs that sum of money which will, so far as possible, put the plaintiff into as good a position as if the contract for the survey had been properly fulfilled: see Denning LJ in *Philips* v *Ward* [1956] 1 WLR 471 at 473. It is important to note that the contract in

this case, as in *Philips* v *Ward*, was the usual contract for the survey of a house for occupation with no special terms beyond the undertaking of the surveyor to use proper care and skill in reporting upon the condition of the house.

The decision in *Philips* v *Ward* was based upon that principle: in particular, if the contract had been properly performed the plaintiff either would not have bought, in which case he would have avoided any loss, or, after negotiation, he would have paid the reduced price. In the absence of evidence to show that any other or additional recoverable benefit would have been obtained as a result of proper performance, the price will be taken to have been reduced to the market price of the house in its true condition because it cannot be assumed that the vendor would have taken less.

The cost of doing repairs to put right defects negligently not reported may be relevant to the proof of the market price of the house in its true condition: see *Steward* v *Rapley* [1989] 1 EGLR 159; and the cost of doing repairs and the diminution in value may be shown to be the same. If, however, the cost of repairs would exceed the diminution in value, then the ruling in *Philips* v *Ward*, where it is applicable, prohibits recovery of the excess because it would give to the plaintiff more than his loss. It would put the plaintiff in the position of recovering damages for breach of a warranty that the condition of the house was correctly described by the surveyor and, in the ordinary case, as here, no such warranty has been given.

It is clear, and it was not argued to the contrary, that the ruling in *Philips* v *Ward*, where it is applicable, prohibits recovery of the excess because it would give to the plaintiff more than his loss. It would put the plaintiff in the position of recovering damages for breach of a warranty and that the condition of the house was correctly described by the surveyor and, in the ordinary case, as here, no such warranty has been given.

It is clear, and it was not argued to the contrary, that the ruling in *Philips* v *Ward*

may be applicable to the case where the buyer has, after purchase, extricated himself from the transaction by selling the property. In the absence of any point on mitigation, the buyer will recover the diminution in value together with costs and expenses thrown away in moving in and out of resale: see Romer LJ in *Philips* v *Ward* [1956] 1 WLR 471 at 478. ...

General damages: the award for "distress and inconvenience" ...

[Counsel for the defendant's] submission is, I think, correct. In *Bailey* v *Bullock* [1950] 2 All ER 1167 Barry J, in a case of solicitor's negligence, held that damages for inconvenience and discomfort could be recovered for the solicitor's failure to get possession of premises for his client but not damages for annoyance and mental distress. So holding he relied upon the judgment of Scott LJ in *Groom* v *Crocker* [1938] 2 All ER 394 at 415, where *Addis* v *Gramophone Co Ltd* [1909] AC 488 was held to be a conclusive authority against general damages for injury to reputation or feelings. Barry J contrasted that decision with that of *Hobbs* v *London and South Western Rly Co* (1875) LR 10 QB 111, where damages for physical inconvenience were upheld for breach of a contract of carriage.

In *Jarvis* v *Swans Tours Ltd* [1973] 1 All ER 71 it was held that the old authorities excluding damages for disappointment of mind were out of date and that damages for mental distress can be recovered in contract in a proper case. One such proper case was held there to be breach of a contract for a holiday or of a contract to provide entertainment and enjoyment. Breach of a contract of carriage, where vexation may be caused, was distinguished from a breach of contract for a holiday where the provision of pleasure is promised. ...

It is clear, I think, that the judge was regarding the contract between these plaintiffs and the defendant as a contract in which the subject matter was to provide "peace of mind or freedom from distress" within the meaning of Dillon LJ's phrase in *Bliss* v *South East Thames Regional Health Authority* [1987] ICR 700 at 718 cited by

Purchas LJ in *Hayes* v *James and Charles Dodd* [1990] 2 All ER 815 at 826. That, with respect, seems to me to be an impossible view of the ordinary surveyor's contract. No doubt house buyers hope to enjoy peace of mind and freedom from distress as a consequence of the proper performance by a surveyor of his contractual obligation to provide a careful report, but there was no express promise for the provision of peace of mind or freedom from distress and no such implied promise was alleged. In my view, in the case of the ordinary surveyor's contract, damages are only recoverable for distress caused by physical consequences of the breach of contract. Since the judge did not attempt to assess the award on that basis this court must reconsider the award and determine what it should be.

For my part, I accept that the award was excessive even if the judge had directed himself correctly.'

Comment

Applied in *Gardner* v *Marsh and Parsons* [1997] 3 All ER 871 (where a surveyor negligently surveys a property which the plaintiff subsequently purchases the proper measure of damages is the difference between the market value of the property without the defects and its value with the defects at the date of purchase).

White and Carter (Councils) Ltd v *McGregor* [1962] 2 WLR 17

See Chapter 13.

15 Remedies for Breach of Contract – Equitable Remedies

Beswick v Beswick [1967] 3 WLR 932

See Chapter 10.

Co-operative Insurance Society v Argyll Stores (Holdings) Ltd [1997] 3 All ER 297 House of Lords (Lords Browne-Wilkinson, Slynn of Hadley, Hoffmann, Hope of Craighead and Clyde)

• *Specific performance – covenant to use premises as supermarket and keep open during business hours*

Facts

The defendant tenant decided to close its Safeway supermarket in the plaintiff landlord's shopping centre because the supermarket was losing money. Such closure was in breach of a covenant in the lease which required the premises to be kept open for retail trade during the usual hours of business. The defendant admitted the breach and consented to an order for damages to be assessed. However, the Court of Appeal reversed the trial judge and ordered that the covenant be specifically performed: it made a final injunction ordering the defendant to trade on the premises during the remainder of the term (ie until August 2014), or until an earlier subletting or assignment.

Held

The defendant's appeal would be allowed and the trial judge's order restored.

Lord Hoffmann:

'A degree of specific performance is of course a discretionary remedy and the question for your Lordships is whether the Court of Appeal was entitled to set aside the exercise of the judge's discretion. There are well-established principles which govern the exercise of the discretion but these, like all equitable principles, are flexible and adaptable to achieve the ends of equity. ...

There is no dispute about the existence of the settled practice to which the judge referred. It is sufficient for this purpose to refer to *Braddon Towers Ltd* v *International Stores Ltd* (1979) [1987] 1 EGLR 209 at 213, where Slade J said:

> "Whether or not this may be described as a rule of law, I do not doubt that for many years practitioners have advised their clients that it is the settled and invariable practice of this court never to grant mandatory injunctions requiring persons to carry on business."

But the practice has never, so far as I know, been examined by this House ...

Specific performance is traditionally regarded in English law as an exceptional remedy, as opposed to the common law damages to which a successful plaintiff is entitled as of right. There may have been some element of later rationalisation of an untidier history, but by the nineteenth century it was orthodox doctrine that the power to decree specific performance was part of the discretionary jurisdiction of the Court of Chancery to do justice in cases in which the remedies available at common law were inadequate. This is the basis of the general principle that specific performance will not be ordered when damages are an adequate remedy. ... The principles on which English judges exercise the discretion to grant specific performance are reasonably well settled and depend on a number of considerations, mostly of a practical nature, which are of very general application. ...

The practice of not ordering a defendant to carry on a business is not entirely dependent upon damages being an adequate remedy. ...

From a wider perspective, it cannot be in the public interest for the courts to require someone to carry on business at a loss if there is any plausible alternative by which the other party can be given compensation. It is not only a waste of resources but yokes the parties together in a continuing hostile relationship. The order for specific performance prolongs the battle. If the defendant is ordered to run a business, its conduct becomes the subject of a flow of complaints, solicitors' letters and affidavits. This is wasteful for both parties and the legal system. An award of damages, on the other hand, brings the litigation to an end. The defendant pays damages, the forensic link between them is severed, they go their separate ways and the wounds of conflict can heal.

The cumulative effect of these various reasons, none of which would necessarily be sufficient on its own, seems to me to show that the settled practice is based on sound sense. Of course the grant or refusal of specific performance remains a matter for the judge's discretion. There are no binding rules, but this does not mean that there cannot be settled principles, founded on practical considerations of the kind which I have discussed, which do not have to be re-examined in every case, but which the courts will apply in all but exceptional circumstances.'

Comment

Included amongst Lord Hoffmann's 'various reasons' for upholding the settled practice were:

- specific performance would require constant supervision by the court, possibly

involving an indefinite series of rulings, and enforcement would be by the heavy-handed quasi-criminal procedure of punishment for contempt of court (cf *C H Giles & Co Ltd* v *Morris* [1972] 1 All ER 960);

- it would be difficult to draw up an order with sufficient precision to enable it to be specifically performed (cf *Wolverhampton Corp* v *Emmons* [1901] 1 KB 515 and *Morris* v *Redland Bricks Ltd* [1969] 2 All ER 576);

- the loss suffered by the defendant in having to run the business could be far greater than the plaintiff would suffer through the contract being broken.

Decro-Wall International SA v *Practitioners in Marketing Ltd* [1971] 1 WLR 361

See Chapter 13.

Hill v *C A Parsons & Co Ltd* [1971] 3 WLR 995 Court of Appeal (Lord Denning MR, Sachs and Stamp LJJ)

- *Wrongful dismissal – injunction*

Facts

The plaintiff, a chartered engineer aged 63, had been employed by the defendants for 35 years. He was due to retire at 65 and his pension depended on the average salary during the last three years' service. Following a strike, the defendants said that persons of the plaintiff's grade had to join a certain union; he refused and the defendants purported to dismiss him. In his action for wrongful dismissal, he sought an interim injunction.

Held (Stamp LJ dissenting)

The injunction would be granted.

Lord Denning MR:

'In these circumstance, it is of the utmost importance to Mr Hill ... that the notice ... should not be held to terminate [his] employment. Damages would not be at all an adequate remedy. If ever there was a case where an injunction should be granted against the employers, this is the case. It is quite plain that the employers have done wrong. I know that the employers have been under pressure from a powerful trade union. That may explain their conduct, but it does not excuse it. They have purported to terminate Mr Hill's employment by a notice which is too short by far. They seek to take advantage of their own wrong by asserting that his services were terminated by their own "say so" at the date selected by them – to the grave prejudice of Mr Hill. They cannot be allowed to break the law in this way. It is, to my mind, a clear case for an injunction.

The judge said that he felt constrained by the law to refuse an injunction. But that is too narrow a view of the principles of law. He has overlooked the fundamental principle that, whenever a man has a right, the law should give a remedy. The Latin maxim is ubi jus ibi remedium. This principle enables us to step over the trip-wires of previous cases and to bring the law into accord with the needs of today. I would allow the appeal, accordingly and grant an injunction restraining the company from treating the notice … as having determined Mr Hill's employment.'

Sachs LJ:

'This is … a case where an employee may justifiably consider that there are chances of his employer being persuaded to change his mind – precisely one of the grounds (as indicated in *Decro-Wall International SA* v *Practitioners in Marketing Ltd* [1971] 1 WLR 361 …) why he might elect not to accept a wrongful repudiation of his contract and should not in law be deemed in every case to have accepted it.'

Investors Compensation Scheme Ltd v *West Bromwich Building Society* [1988] 1 All ER 98

See Chapter 19.

Lumley v *Wagner* (1852) 1 De GM & G 604 Lord Chancellor's Court (Lord St Leonards LC)

• *Injunction – contract for personal services*

Facts
The defendant cantatrice bound herself to sing for three months at the plaintiff's London theatre (Her Majesty's) and 'not to use her talents' at any other place during that time.

Held
An injunction could be granted to restrain her from appearing at another theatre.

Lord St Leonards LC:

'It was objected that the operation of the injunction in the present case was mischievous, excluding the defendant Johanna Wagner from performing at any other theatre while this court had no power to compel her to perform at Her Majesty's Theatre. It is true that I have not the means of compelling her to sing, but she has no cause of complaint if I compel her to abstain from the commission of an act which she has bound herself not to do, and thus possibly cause her to fulfil her engagement. The jurisdiction which I now exercise is wholly within the power of the court, and, being of opinion that it is a proper case for interfering, I shall leave nothing unsatisfied by the judgment I pronounce. The effect, too, of the injunction, in restraining Johanna Wagner from singing elsewhere may, in the event of an action being brought against her by the plaintiff, prevent any such amount of vindictive damages being given against her as a jury might probably be inclined to give if she had carried her talents and exercised them at the rival theatre. The injunction may also, as I have said, tend to the fulfilment of her engagement, though, in continuing the injunction, I disclaim doing indirectly what I cannot do directly.'

Comment

See also *Warner Brothers Pictures Inc* v *Nelson* [1937] I KB 209 (actress contracted to appear in plaintiffs' films, injunction granted to restrain her from appearing in another company's films) and *Page One Records Ltd* v *Britton* [1968] 1 WLR 157 (injunction refused to restrain The Troggs engaging another manager). See also *Warren* v *Mendy* [1989] 3 All ER 103.

Patel v *Ali* [1984] 2 WLR 960 High Court (Goulding J)

• *Specific performance – hardship*

Facts

The defendants contracted to sell their house to the plaintiffs: at that time (July 1979) the defendant wife, a Pakistani who spoke little English, had one child and she (the wife) was in good health. Due to the husband's bankruptcy, the wife could not have completed the sale before July 1980: by that time it had been discovered that she was suffering from bone cancer and she had a leg amputated. On 11 August the plaintiffs issued a writ seeking specific performance. At the end of that month the wife gave birth to her second child and in August 1983 she had her third. The following month the court made an order for specific performance and the wife appealed, contending that she would suffer hardship, in being deprived of daily assistance from friends and relations, if she had to move to another area.

Held

The order would be discharged. In view of unforeseeable changes the order would cause the wife hardship amounting to injustice and after the long delay (for which neither party was to blame) it would be just to leave the plaintiffs to their remedy in damages.

Goulding J:

'Another limitation suggested by counsel for the plaintiffs was that, in the reported cases, as he said, hardship successfully relied on has always related to the subject matter of the contract and has not been just a personal hardship of the defendant. Certainly, mere pecuniary difficulties, whether of purchaser or of vendor, afford no excuse from performance of a contract. In a wider sense than that, I do not think the suggested universal proposition can be sustained ...

The important and true principle, in my view, is that only in extraordinary and persuasive circumstances can hardship supply an excuse for resisting performance of a contract for the sale of immovable property. A person of full capacity who sells or buys a house takes the risk of hardship to himself and his dependants, whether arising from existing facts or unexpectedly supervening in the interval before completion. This is where, to my mind, great importance attaches to the immense delay in the present case, not attributable to the defendant's conduct. Even after issue of the writ, she could not complete, if she had wanted to, without the concurrence of the absent Mr Ahmed. Thus, in a sense, she can say she is being asked to do what she never bargained for, namely to complete the sale after more than four years, after all the unforeseeable changes that such a period entails. I think that in this way she can fairly assert that specific performance would inflict on her "a hardship amounting to injustice" to use the phrase employed by James LJ, in a different but comparable context, in *Tamplin* v *James* (1880) 15 Ch D 215 at 221. Equitable relief may, in my view, be refused because of an unforeseen change of circumstances not amounting to legal frustration, just as it may on the ground of mistake insufficient to avoid a contract at law.

In the end, I am satisfied that it is within the court's discretion to accede to the defendant's prayer if satisfied that it is just to do so. And, on the whole, looking at the position of both sides after the long unpredictable delay for which neither seeks to make the other responsible, I am of opinion that it *is* just to leave the plaintiffs to their remedy in damages if that can indeed be effective.'

Comment

It should be noted that there was evidence that sympathetic persons were willing to put up the money to enable damages to be paid. See also s50 of the Supreme Court Act 1981.

Posner v *Scott-Lewis* [1986] 3 WLR 531 High Court (Mervyn Davies J)

• *Specific performance – personal services*

Facts

Under the terms of the leases of the plaintiff tenants at Danes Court, the defendant landlord was obliged to employ a resident porter to keep the communal area clean, to be responsible for the boilers and to collect rubbish from the flats. The resident porter left, but continued to do the work on a non-resident, part-time basis. If the defendant was thereby in breach of the covenant, could the covenant be specifically enforced?

Held

The defendant was in breach and the court could and would make an order for specific performance.

Mervyn Davies J:

'Drawing attention to ... differences between [*Ryan* v *Mutual Tontine Westminster Chambers Association* [1893] 1 Ch 116] and the present case, counsel for the plaintiffs submitted that *Ryan's* case should be distinguished. In short, he said that since the resident porter's functions at Danes Court were already obligations of the lessor to the lessees, there were no duties on the part of the porter towards the tenants that the tenants were seeking to enforce. All that was required was the appointment of a resident porter, whereas in *Ryan's* case the plaintiff was in effect seeking to enforce performance of duties said to be owed by the porter to the plaintiff. I do not accept or reject counsel for the plaintiffs able argument. I suspect that it is difficult to distinguish *Ryan's* case. However that may be,

Ryan's case has been remarked on in many later authorities.

In *C H Giles & Co Ltd* v *Morris* [1972] 1 WLR 307 at 318-319 Megarry J, after referring to *Ryan's* case said:

"One day, perhaps, the courts will look again at the so-called rule that contracts for personal services or involving the continuous performance of services will not be specifically enforced. Such a rule is plainly not absolute and without exception, nor do I think it can be based on any narrow consideration such as difficulties of constant superintendence by the court. Mandatory injunctions are by no means unknown, and there is normally no question of the court having to send its officers to supervise the performance of the order of the court. Prohibitory injunctions are common, and again there is no direct supervision by the court. Performance of each type of injunction is normally secured by the realisation of the person enjoined that he is liable to be punished for contempt if evidence of his disobedience to the order is put before the court; and if the injunction is prohibitory, actual committal will usually, so long as it continues, make disobedience impossible. If instead the order is for specific performance of a contract for personal services, a similar machinery of enforcement could be employed, again without there being any question of supervision by any officer of the court. The reasons why the court is reluctant to decree specific performance of a contract for personal services (and I would regard it as a strong reluctance rather than a rule) are, I think, more complex and more firmly bottomed on human nature ... The present case, of course is a fortiori, since the contract of which specific performance has been decreed requires not the performance of personal services or any continuous series of acts, but merely procuring the execution of an agreement which contains a provision for such services or acts."

Those observations do not of themselves enable me to disregard *Ryan's* case. But then one comes to *Shiloh Spinners Ltd* v *Harding* [1973] 2 WLR 28. Lord Wilberforce seems to say that "the impossibility for the courts to supervise the doing of work" may be rejected as a reason against granting relief (see [1973] AC 691 at 724). Finally there is *Tito v Waddell (No 2), Tito v A-G* [1977] 2 WLR 496 ...

In the light of those authorities it is, I think, open to me to consider the making of an order for specific performance in this case, particularly since the order contemplated is in the fortiori class referred to by Megarry J in the last sentence of the extract from the *Giles'* case ([1972] 1 WLR 307 at 318) quoted above. Damages here could hardly regarded as an adequate remedy.

Whether or not an order for specific performance should be made seems to me to depend on the following considerations: (a) is there a sufficient definition of what has to be done in order to comply with the order of the court; (b) will enforcing compliance involve superintendence by the court to an unacceptable degree; and (c) what are the respective prejudices or hardships that will be suffered by the parties if the order is made or not made?

As to (a) one may in this case sufficiently define what has to be done by the defendants by ordering the defendants, within say two months to employ a porter to be resident at Danes Court for the purpose of carrying out the ... duties. It is to be borne in mind that there is still a vacant flat available for a resident porter. As to (b), I do not see that such an order will occasion any protracted superintendence by the court. If the defendants without good cause fail to comply with the order in due time, then the plaintiffs can take appropriate enforcement proceedings against the defendants. As to (c), I see no hardship or prejudice resulting to the defendants from the order. They will simply be performing what they have promised to do and what has been carried out by the lessors over the past 20 years. On the other hand I see considerable inconvenience, if not exactly hardship, for the plaintiffs if, having bargained for a resident porter and paid a premium and having enjoyed his presence for 20 years, they are to be expected for the future to be content with a porter who simply walks up and down the stairs for two hours only during the day doing his cleaning and refuse collection. It follows that there should be an order for specific performance.'

Price v *Strange* [1977] 3 WLR 943 Court of Appeal (Buckley, Scarman and Goff LJJ)

Specific performance – mutual availability of remedy – crucial date

Facts

In 1966 the defendant sublet her flat to the plaintiff: the sub-tenancy expired in 1971 but he held over, continuing to pay rent. In February 1974 the defendant orally agreed to grant the plaintiff an underlease at an increased rent, the plaintiff agreeing (also orally) to execute certain repairs to the interior and exterior. He paid, and the defendant accepted, rent at the increased rate and completed the interior repairs, but before he could execute the exterior repairs the defendant repudiated the agreement and had the work carried out at her own expense. Nevertheless, she continued to accept rent for a further five months. The plaintiff sought specific performance, but the judge dismissed the action on the ground that the parties were not mutual at the date of the contract since the plaintiff's obligation to execute repairs could not be specifically enforced.

Held

A decree of specific performance would be granted.

Goff LJ:

'Surely the defence of want of mutuality should be governed by the state of affairs as seen at the hearing, since one is dealing not with a question affecting the initial validity of the contract, but with whether or not the discretionary remedy of specific performance should be granted ...

In my judgment ... the true principle is

that one judges the defence of want of mutuality on the facts and circumstances as they exist at the hearing, albeit in the light of the whole conduct of the parties in relation to the subject-matter, and in the absence of any other disqualifying circumstances, the court will grant specific performance if it can be done without injustice or unfairness to the defendant ...

If, therefore, the plaintiff had been allowed to finish the work and had done so, I am clearly of opinion that it would have been right to order specific performance, but we have to consider what is the proper order, having regard to the fact that he was allowed to do an appreciable part and then not allowed to finish. Even so, in my judgment the result is still the same for the following reasons.

First, the defendant by standing by and allowing the plaintiff to spend time and money in carrying out an appreciable part of the work, created an equity against herself ...

Secondly, the work has in fact been finished. The court will not be deterred from granting specific performance in a proper case, even though there remain obligations still to be performed by the plaintiff, if the defendant can be properly protected: see ... also *C H Giles & Co Ltd* v *Morris* [1972] 1 WLR 307, where Megarry J said:

> " ... the court may refuse to let the disadvantages and difficulties of specifically enforcing the obligation to perform personal services outweigh the suitability of the rest of the contract for specific performance, and the desirability of the contract as a whole being enforced. After all, pacta sunt servanda."

Still more readily should it act where the work has been done so that the defendant is not at risk of being ordered to grant the underlease and having no remedy except in damages for subsequent non-performance of the plaintiff's agreement to put the premises in repair.

Thirdly the defendant can be fully recompensed by a proper financial adjustment for the work she has had carried out.

I am fully satisfied that the law is as I have stated it to be, but even if I were wrong and the defence of mutuality ought to be considered according to the position at the date of the contract, still it is conceded, and in my judgment unquestionably correctly, that such a defence may be waived *Halkett* v *Earl of Dudley* [1907] 1 Ch 390 is alone sufficient authority for that proposition. Then on the facts of this case the defence clearly was waived. Not only did the defendant permit the plaintiff to start on the work which would of itself be sufficient in my view, but she also accepted the increased rent payable under the contemplated underlease and went on doing so after her purported repudiation.

For these reasons I would allow this appeal and order specific performance but on terms that the plaintiff do pay to the defendant proper compensation for the work done by her. As a matter of strict right that must take the form of an enquiry what amount it would have cost the plaintiff to complete the works himself, with an order that he do pay or allow the defendant the amount certified with a set-off against any costs payable by the defendant, the costs of the enquiry being reserved. The plaintiff has however offered, subject to any question whether the expense incurred by the defendant was unnecessary or extravagant, to compensate her more handsomely by paying or allowing the actual cost to her, and it may well be possible, and certainly in the best interests of the parties, for them to agree a figure and so obviate proceeding with the enquiry, which could well involve them in further considerable litigation and expense.'

Comment

Applied in *Lyus* v *Prowsa Developments Ltd* [1982] 2 All ER 953 (lack of mutuality did not prevent constructive trust arising) and *Sutton* v *Sutton* [1984] 2 WLR 146.

Record v *Bell* [1991] 1 WLR 853

See Chapter 3.

Sky Petroleum Ltd v VIP Petroleum Ltd [1974] 1 WLR 576 High Court (Goulding J)

• *Contract for supply of petrol – specific performance – when may be ordered*

Facts

In 1970 the plaintiffs agreed that they would, for a minimum period of ten years, buy all the petrol needed for their filling stations from the defendants. Three years later the defendants purported to terminate the contract and the plaintiffs sought an interlocutory injunction to restrain the defendants from withholding supplies. At the time, the plaintiffs had little prospect of obtaining petrol from another supplier.

Held

The injunction would be granted.

Goulding J:

'Now I come to the most serious hurdle in the way of the plaintiff company which is the well-known doctrine that the court refuses specific performance of a contract to sell and purchase chattels not specific or ascertained. That is a well-established and salutary rule and I am entirely unconvinced by counsel for the plaintiff company when he tells me that an injunction in the form sought by him would not be specific enforcement at all. The matter is one of substance and not of form and it is, in my judgment, quite plain that I am for the time being specifically enforcing the contract if I grant an injunction. However the ratio behind the rule is, as I believe, that under the ordinary contract for the sale of non-specific goods, damages are a sufficient remedy. That, to my mind, is lacking in the circumstances of the present case. The evidence suggests, and indeed it is common knowledge, that the petroleum market is in an unusual state in which a would-be buyer cannot go out into the market and contract with another, seller, possibly at some sacrifice as to price. Here, the defendant company appears for practical

purposes to be the plaintiff company's sole means of keeping its business going, and I am prepared so far to depart from the general rule as to try to preserve the position under the contract until a later date. I therefore propose to grant an injunction.'

Comment

Compare s52 of the Sale of Goods Act 1979 (contracts to deliver specific or ascertained goods).

Sutton v Sutton [1984] 2 WLR 146 High Court (John Mowbray QC)

• *Specific performance – agreement to transfer property on divorce*

Facts

Seven years after their marriage, the parties bought the matrimonial home, the husband alone being responsible for the mortgage and, although the wife contributed to the purchase, the house was conveyed into the husband's name. Some years later they separated and the husband sought a divorce. They orally agreed that the wife would consent to a divorce, take over the mortgage and not apply for maintenance; the husband would let her keep her savings and transfer the house to her. After decree absolute, the husband refused to transfer the house, although the wife had paid off the mortgage. She sought specific performance and the husband contended that the agreement was not legally enforceable.

Held

The wife could not succeed as the agreement, which had not be made subject to the court's approval, purported to oust the court's jurisdiction.

John Mowbray QC:

'*Part performance*
In my view, Mrs Sutton's consenting to the divorce as agreed was an act of part performance. It is true that she was quite content to be divorced and that in the abstract con-

senting to a divorce does not indicate any contract, let alone a contract about land. But here the term about the house was in the petition which must have been posted to her when her formal consent was sought under the postal procedure which was followed. That means that her consent to the petition was itself, in the circumstances, tied to the contract about the house. *Steadman* v *Steadman* [1974] 3 WLR 56 is authority for that ...

Mutuality
Counsel for Mr Sutton argued that there was no mutuality, so specific performance should not be granted. He pointed out that Mrs Sutton's promise not to ask for maintenance was not enforceable. That is common ground. I shall come to the reasons later. Mrs Sutton herself said, in cross-examination, that her offer not to ask for maintenance was a big thing to offer. I find that it was an important part of the bargain. If this point had been taken early enough it might well have afforded a defence, but Mrs Sutton's consent to the divorce was at any rate an appreciable part of the agreement. Mr Sutton stood by and let her perform that part of her bargain irretrievably, and that raised an equity which prevents him from asserting this defence: see *Price* v *Strange* [1977] 3 WLR 943 ... For similar reasons, it is no defence to specific performance that Mr Sutton could not have compelled Mrs Sutton to consent to the divorce. Now she has consented and the divorce has been granted, that point comes too late.

Ousting the jurisdiction
The agreement between Mr and Mrs Sutton was that she would consent to the divorce, take over the mortgage and not ask for maintenance, and he would let her keep her savings and car and make over the house to her. They obviously intended by that agreement to dispose of the whole financial consequences of the divorce. There is a plain implication that he was not to transfer any other property to her and that she was not to make any payment or transfer to him. The agreement was not made subject to the court's approval. If it is enforceable as a contract, it leaves nothing for the court to do under ss23 and 24 of the Matrimonial Causes Act 1973 which empower the court to order maintenance and make property adjustments ...

The agreement between Mr and Mrs Sutton purported to dispose of the whole financial consequences of the divorce, both maintenance and property questions. If it was enforceable as a contract there was nothing left for the court to do under ss23 or 24 of the 1973 Act because the agreement prejudged and foreclosed all financial questions.

The House of Lords decided in *Hyman* v *Hyman* [1929] AC 601 that a wife could not validly contract with her husband not to apply for maintenance on a divorce and that a contract of that kind did not prevent her from applying. Lord Hailsham LC stated the principle like this:

" ... I am prepared to hold that the parties cannot validly make an agreement either (1) not to invoke the jurisdiction of the Court, or (2) to control the powers of the Court when its jurisdiction is invoked."

That is the rule of public policy which survived the disappearance of the rule against collusion. In my judgment, it applies to the contract here and prevents the financial settlement it contained, including Mr Sutton's promise to transfer the bungalow, from being enforced as a contract.'

Comment
The finding of a sufficient act of past performance overcame the absence of a memorandum or note of the agreement, as was then required by s40 of the Law of Property Act 1925. See now s2 of the Law of Property (Miscellaneous Provisions) Act 1989.

Union Eagle Ltd v *Golden Achievement Ltd* [1997] 2 All ER 215 Privy Council (Lords Goff of Chieveley, Griffiths, Mustill, Hoffmann and Hope of Craighead)

• *Sale of flat – time of essence – equitable relief available?*

Facts

The appellant purchaser contracted to buy a flat on Hong Kong Island from the respondent vendor and paid a deposit as the contract required. Completion was to take place before 5pm on 30 September 1991 and the contract made it clear that time was to be of the essence. The appellant tendered payment of the purchase price at 5.10 pm on 30 September but the respondent declared that the contract had been rescinded and the deposit forfeited. Did the court have the equitable power to decree, and should it have decreed, specific performance of the contract?

Held

The appellant was not entitled to specific performance.

Lord Hoffmann:

'The boundaries of the equitable jurisdiction to relieve against contractual penalties and forfeitures are in some places imprecise. But their Lordships do not think that it is necessary in this case to draw them more exactly because they agree ... that the facts lie well beyond the reach of the doctrine. The notion that the court's jurisdiction to grant relief is "unlimited and unfettered" (per Lord Simon of Glaisdale in *Shiloh Spinners Ltd* v *Harding* [1973] 1 All ER 90 at 104 was rejected as a "beguiling heresy" by the House of Lords in *Scandinavian Trading Tanker Co AB* v *Flota Petrolera Ecuatoriana, The Scaptrade* [1983] 2 All ER 763 at 766. It is worth pausing to notice why it continues to beguile and why it is a heresy. It has the obvious merit of allowing the court to impose what it considers to be a fair solution in the individual case. The principle that

equity will restrain the enforcement of legal rights when it would be unconscionable to insist upon them has an attractive breadth. But the reasons why the courts have rejected such generalisations are founded not merely upon authority (see Lord Radcliffe in *Campbell Discount Co Ltd* v *Bridge* [1962] 1 All ER 385 at 397 but also upon practical considerations of business. These are, in summary, that in many forms of transaction it is of great importance that if something happens for which the contract has made express provision, the parties should know with certainty that the terms of the contract will be enforced. The existence of an undefined discretion to refuse to enforce the contract on the ground that this would be "unconscionable" is sufficient to create uncertainty. Even if it is most unlikely that a discretion to grant relief will be exercised, its mere existence enables litigation to be employed as a negotiating tactic. The realities of commercial life are that this may cause injustice which cannot be fully compensated by the ultimate decision in the case. ...

Of course the same need for certainty is not present in all transactions and the difficult cases have involved attempts to define the jurisdiction in a way which will enable justice to be done in appropriate cases without destabilising normal commercial relationships.

Their Lordships do not think that it is possible ... to draw a broad distinction between "commercial" cases such as *The Scaptrade* and transactions concerning land, which are the traditional subject matter of equitable rules. Land can also be an article of commerce and a flat in Hong Kong is probably as good an example as one could find. ...

When a vendor exercises his right to rescind, he terminates the contract. The purchaser's loss of the right to specific performance may be said to amount to a forfeiture of the equitable interest which the contract gave him in the land. But this forfeiture is different in its nature from, for example, the vendor's right to retain a deposit or part payments of the purchase price. So far as these retentions exceed a genuine pre-estimate of damage or a reasonable deposit they will constitute a penalty which can be said to be essentially to provide security for payment of the full price. No objectionable uncertainty is created by the existence of a restitutionary form of relief against forfeiture, which gives the court a discretion to order repayment of all or part of the retained money. But the right to rescind a contract, though it involves termination of the purchaser's equitable interest, stands upon a rather different footing. Its purpose is, upon breach of an essential term , to restore to the vendor his freedom to deal with his land as he pleases. In a rising market, such a right may be valuable but volatile. Their Lordships think that in such circumstances a vendor should be able to know with reasonable certainty whether he may resell the land or not.

If is for this reason that, for the past eighty years, the courts in England, although ready to grant restitutionary relief against penalties, have been unwilling to grant relief by way of specific performance against breach of an essential condition as to time. ...

Their Lordships do not think it necessary to consider ... Australian developments further because they provide no help for the purchaser in this case. There is no question of any penalty, or of the vendor being unjustly enriched by improvements made at the purchaser's expense, or of the vendor's conduct having contributed to the breach, or of the transaction being in substance a mortgage. It remains for consideration on some future occasion as to whether the way to deal with the problems which have arisen in such cases is by relaxing the principle in *Steedman* v *Drinkle* [1916] 1 AC 275, as the Australian courts have done, or by developments of the law of restitution and estoppel. The present case seems to their Lordships to be one to which the full force of the general rule applies. The fact is that the purchaser was late. Any suggestion that relief can be obtained on the ground that he was only slightly late is bound to lead to arguments over how late is too late, which can be resolved only by litigation. For five years the vendor has not known whether he is entitled to resell the flat or not. It has been sterilised by a caution pending a final decision in this case. In his dissenting judgment [in the Court of Appeal of Hong Kong], Godfrey J A said that the case "cries out for the intervention of equity". Their Lordships think that, on the contrary, it shows the need for a firm restatement of the principle that in cases of rescission of an ordinary contract of sale of land for failure to comply with an essential condition as to time, equity will not intervene.'

Comment
The 'Australian developments' to which Lord Hoffmann referred are to be found in *Legione* v *Hateley* (1983) 152 CLR 406 and *Stern* v *McArthur* (1988) 165 CLR 489.

Warren v *Mendy* [1989] 3 All ER 103 Court of Appeal (Purchas, Nourse and Stuart-Smith LJJ)

• *Contract of service – injunctions against third party*

Facts
The plaintiff contracted to manage exclusively a professional boxer (Nigel Benn) for three years. Within a few months the boxer agreed that the defendant should be his 'agent'. The plaintiff sought, inter alia, an injunction to restrain the defendant from inducing the boxer to breach his contract with him.

Held
The injunction would not be granted as it would have the effect of compelling the boxer to perform his positive obligations under the contract, if he was to maintain his skill as a boxer, when he had lost confidence in the plaintiff's ability to act as his manager.

Nourse LJ:

'It is well settled that an injunction to restrain a breach of contract for personal services ought not to be granted where its effect will be to decree performance of the contract. Speaking generally, there is no comparable objection to the grant of an injunction restraining the performance of particular services for a third party, because, by not prohibiting the performance of other services, it does not bind the servant to his contract. But a difficulty can arise, usually in the entertainment or sporting worlds, where the services are inseparable from the exercise of some special skill or talent, whose continued display is essential to the psychological and material, and sometimes to the physical, well-being of the servant. The difficulty does not reside in any beguilement of the court into looking more tenderly on such who breach their contracts, glamorous though they often are. It is that the human necessity of maintaining the skill or talent may practically bind the servant to the contract, compelling him to perform it.

The best known of the authorities on this subject are *Lumley* v *Wagner* (1852) 1 De GM & G 604 (impresario and opera singer) and *Warner Bros Pictures Inc* v *Nelson* [1936] 3 All ER 160 (film producer and actress), where injunctions were granted, and *Page One Records Ltd* v *Britton* [1967] 3 All ER 822 (manager and pop group), where an injunction was refused. Here we have the case of manager and boxer. It is in one respect unusual, in that the manager has brought the action not against the boxer but against a third party who seeks to replace him, at all events in some respects. The manager claims that the third party has induced a breach of his contract with the boxer. He seeks an injunction only against the third party. ...

This consideraton of the authorities has led us to believe that the following general principles are applicable to the grant or refusal of an injunction to enforce performance of the servant's negative obligations in a contract for personal services inseparable from the exercise of some special skill or talent. (We use the expressions "master" and "servant" for ease of reference and not out of any regard for the reality of the relationship in many of these cases.) In such a case the court ought not to enforce the performance of the negative obligations if their enforcement will effectively compel the servant to perform his positive obligations under the contract. Compulsion is a question to be decided on the facts of each case, with a realistic regard for the probable reaction of an injunction on the psychological and material, and sometimes the physical, need of the servant to maintain the skill or talent. The longer the term for which an injunction is sought, the more readily will compulsion be inferred. Compulsion may be inferred where the injunction is sought not against the servant but against a third party, if either the third party is the only other available master or if it is likely that the master will seek relief against anyone who attempts to replace him. An injunction will less readily be granted where there are obligations of mutual trust and confidence, more especially where the servant's trust in the master may have been betrayed or his confidence in him has genuinely gone.

In stating the principles as we have, we are not to be taken as intending to pay anything less than a full and proper regard to the sanctity of contract. No judge would wish to detract from his duty to enforce the performance of contracts to the very limit which established principles allow him to go. Nowhere is that duty better indicated than in the words of Lord St Leonards LC in *Lumley* v *Wagner* (1852) 1 De GM & G 604 at 619. To that end the judge will scrutinise most carefully, even sceptically, any claim by the servant that he is under the human necessity of maintaining the skill or talent and thus will be compelled to perform the contract, or that his trust in the master has been betrayed or that his confidence in him has genuinely gone. But, if, having done that, the judge is satisfied that the grant of an injunction will effectively compel performance of the contract, he ought to refuse it. ...

With these considerations in mind we return to the judgment of Pill J [at first instance] ... The question which he asked himself is now shown to have been correct. He said that in reaching his conclusion he bore in mind that the trade of a professional boxer was a very specialist one, requiring dedication, extensive training and expertise and that his professional life was comparatively short. He readily accepted that a high degree of mutual trust and confidence was required between boxer and manager. There were duties of a personal and fiduciary nature to be performed by the manager. Later, he completely rejected the suggestion that the covenant was not compulsive because Benn could get work, for example as a security guard. ... the judge had the correct principles in mind when considering whether an injunction should be granted against the defendant as opposed to Nigel Benn. On the case as a whole, he did not take into account anything which he ought not to have taken into account, nor did he leave out of account anything which he ought to have taken into account. He exercised his discretion and he did not exercise it in a manner which was plainly wrong. His decision [to discharge the injunction] is not one with which this court can interfere and we affirm it on that ground.'

16 Quasi-Contract

Aiken v *Short* (1856) 1 H & N 210 Court of Exchequer (Pollock CB, Platt, Martin and Bramwell BB)

- *Money paid under mistake – right of recovery*

Facts
The defendant lent one Carter £200, taking as security, inter alia, an equitable charge on some lands which the plaintiff bank subsequently purchased. When the defendant asked for the repayment of the money, he was referred to the plaintiffs who paid off the charge. It subsequently appeared that Carter had no title to the property so the plaintiffs sued for the recovery of the money paid.

Held
The action could not succeed.

Bramwell B:

'In order to entitle a person to recover back money paid under a mistake of fact, the mistake must be as to a fact which, if true,would make the person paying liable to pay the money; not where, if true, it would merely make it desirable that he should pay the money. Here, if the fact was true, the bankers were at liberty to pay or not, as they pleased. But relying on the belief that the defendant had a valid security, they, having a subsequent legal mortgage, chose to pay off the defendant's charge. It is impossible to say that this case falls within the rule. The mistake of fact was, that the bank thought that they could sell the estate for a better price. It is true that if the plaintiffs could recover back this money from the defendant, there would be no difficulty in the way of the defendant suing Carter ...
   I am of opinion they cannot [maintain this action], having voluntarily parted with their money to purchase that which the defendant had to sell, though no doubt it turned out to be different to, and of less value than, what they expected.'

Comment
In *Barclays Bank Ltd* v *W J Simms Son & Cooke (Southern) Ltd* [1979] 3 All ER 522, Robert Goff J said that a crucial fact here was that, the payment having been authorised by Carter, it was effective to discharge the debt which was in fact owed by Carter to the defendant; the defendant therefore gave consideration for the payment which was, for that reason, irrecoverable. See also *Morgan* v *Ashcroft* [1938] 1 KB 49 and *Larner* v *London County Council* [1949] 2 KB 683.

Craven-Ellis v *Canons Ltd* [1936] 2 KB 403 Court of Appeal (Greer and Greene LJJ and Talbot J)

- *Services rendered – quantum meruit*

Facts
In 1927 the plaintiff estate agent was employed by Parol Estates Ltd in connection with the development of an estate. The following year the defendant company was formed to purchase the estate and the plaintiff was one of its directors. Without any express agreement, the plaintiff continued his work. After two months, none of the directors having become qualified in accordance with the company's articles, they all became incapable of acting. The company subsequently purported to enter into a service agreement with the plaintiff as managing director, but the seal was affixed by resolution of the unqualified directors and for this reason was a nullity.

168

Held

The plaintiff was entitled to recover on a quantum meruit for all his services rendered to the defendant company.

Greer LJ:

'As regards the services rendered [before the purported agreement], there is, in my judgment, no defence to the claim. These services were rendered by the plaintiff not as managing director or as a director, but as an estate agent, and there was no contract in existence which could present any obstacle to a claim based on a quantum meruit for services rendered and accepted.

As regards the plaintiff's services after the date of the contract, I think the plaintiff is also entitled to succeed. The contract, having been made by directors who had no authority to make it with one of themselves, who had notice of their want of authority, was not binding on either party. It was, in fact, a nullity, and presents no obstacle to the implied promise to pay on a quantum meruit basis which arises from the performance of the services and the implied acceptance of the same by the company ...

In my judgment, the obligation to pay reasonable remuneration for the work done when there is no binding contract between the parties is imposed by a rule of law, and not by an inference of fact arising from the acceptance of service or goods ...

I accordingly think that the defendants must pay on the basis of a quantum meruit not only for the services rendered before the date of the invalid agreement, but also for the services after that date. I think the appeal should be allowed, and judgment given for such a sum as shall be found to be due on the basis of a quantum meruit in respect of all services rendered by the plaintiff to the company ...'

Comment

Distinguished in *Re Richmond Gate Property Co Ltd* [1964] 3 All ER 936 where there was an express contract for the payment of remuneration.

Larner v London County Council
[1949] 2 KB 683 Court of Appeal (Lord Goddard, CJ, Denning LJ and Birkett J)

* *Money overpaid by mistake – right to recover*

Facts

The defendants resolved to make up the difference between their employees' war service pay and former civilian pay. Although he knew that he had to inform the defendants of increases in his war service pay, the plaintiff employee did not do so: consequently, he was overpaid by the defendants.

Held

The defendants were entitled to recover the overpayments.

Denning LJ:

'The real question in this case arises on the counterclaim. Are the council entitled to recover from the plaintiff the sums which they overpaid him? Overpay him they certainly did. That is admitted. The overpayment was due to a mistake of fact. That is also admitted. They were mistaken as to the amount of his service pay. But it is said that they were voluntary payments which were not made in discharge of any legal liability, and cannot, therefore, be recovered back. For this proposition reliance was placed on the dictum of Bramwell B in *Aiken v Short* (1856) 1 H & N 210, but that dictum, as Scott LJ pointed out in *Morgan v Ashcroft* [1938] 1 KB 49, cannot be regarded as an exhaustive statement of the law. Take the present case. The London County Council, by their resolution, for good reasons of national policy, made a promise to the men which they were in honour bound to fulfil. The payments made under that promise were not mere gratuities. They were made as a matter of duty. Indeed, that is how both sides regarded them. They spoke of them as sums "due" to the men, that is, as sums the men were entitled to under the promise contained in the resolution. If then, owing to a mistake of fact, the council paid one of the men more than he was entitled to under the promise, why should he not repay the excess, at any rate if he has not changed his position for the worse? It is not necessary to inquire whether there was any consideration for the promise so as to enable it to be enforced in a court of law. It may be that, because the men were legally bound to go to the war, there was in strictness no consideration for the promise but that does not matter. It is not a question here of enforcing the promise by action. It is a question of recovering overpayments made in the belief that they were due under the promise, but, in fact, not due. They were sums which the council never promised the plaintiff and which they would never have paid him had they known the true facts. They were paid under a mistake of fact, and he is bound to repay them unless he has changed his position for the worse because of them.

It is next said, however, that the London County Council should not be allowed to recover the money because the plaintiff changed his position for the worse before the council asked for it back. He spent the money on living expenses – or his wife spent it for him – and he spent it in a way which he would not otherwise have done. This defence of estoppel, as it is called – or more accurately, change of circumstances – must, however, not be extended beyond its proper bounds. Speaking generally, the fact that the recipient has spent the money beyond recall is no defence unless there was some fault, as, for instance, some neglect or breach of duty or misconduct, on the part of the pay-master and none on the part of the recipient ... But if the recipient was himself at fault and the pay-master was not – as, for instance, if the mistake was due to an innocent misrepresentation or a breach of duty by the recipient – he clearly cannot escape liability by saying that he has spent the money. That is the position here. On the judge's findings the London County Council were not at fault at all, but the plaintiff was. He did not keep them accurately

informed of the various changes in his service pay. It does not lie in his mouth to say that, if he had done so, it would have made no difference. It might well have put them on inquiry and the mistake might not have been made at all. Many men did, in fact, fulfil their duty and were not overpaid. It would be strange, indeed, if those who neglected their duty were to be allowed to keep their gain.'

Comment

In *Barclays Bank Ltd* v *W J Simms Son & Cooke (Southern) Ltd* [1979] 3 All ER 522 Robert Goff J said that from a 'formidable line of authority' simple principles could be deduced as follows:

'1. If a person pays money to another under a mistake of fact which causes him to make the payment, he is prima facie entitled to recover it as money paid under a mistake of fact.

2. His claim may however fail if: (a) the payer intends that the payee shall have the money at all events, whether the fact be true or false, or is deemed in law so to intend; (b) the payment is made for good consideration, in particular if the money is paid to discharge, and does discharge, a debt owed to the payee (or a principal on whose behalf he is authorised to receive the payment) by the payer or by a third party by whom he is authorised to discharge the debt; (c) the payee has changed his position in good faith, or is deemed in law to have done so.'

Morgan v *Ashcroft* [1938] 1 KB 49 Court of Appeal (Sir Wilfrid Greene MR and Scott LJ)

• *Money paid under mistake of fact – right to recover*

Facts

Due to a mistake by the plaintiff bookmaker's clerk, the defendant customer was overpaid. The plaintiff sued to recover the amount of the overpayment.

Held

His action could not succeed, inter alia, because the amount of the overpayment could only be determined by examining accounts of gaming transactions and, by virtue of the Gaming Act 1845, this was a task the court could not undertake.

Sir Wilfrid Greene MR:

'But there is another ground, upon which the action ought, in my opinion, to have been dismissed, and, as we have had the benefit of a full argument upon it, I think it right to express my views upon it. The plaintiff's claim is for money had and received, and it is based upon what the county court judge found to be a mistake of fact. The question which arises is, can such a claim succeed in the circumstances of this case? In my opinion, it cannot ...

I come ... to the conclusion that the observations of Bramwell B [in *Aiken* v *Short* (1856) 1 H & N 210] supported, as they are, by much weight of judicial opinion, are, so far as regards the class of mistake with which he was dealing, in agreement with the more recent authorities, and I propose to follow them. It was said, on behalf of the respondent, that these observations do not correctly state the law. I do not agree, although I am disposed to think that they cannot be taken as an exhaustive statement of the law, but must be confined to cases where the only mistake is as to the nature of the transaction. For example, if A makes a voluntary payment of money to B, under the mistaken belief that he is C, it may well be that A can recover it. Bramwell B was not dealing with a case such as that, since he was assuming that there was no such error in persona. If we are to be guided by the analogous case of contract, where mistake as to the person contracted with negatives the intention to contract, the mistake in the case which I have mentioned ought to be held to negative the intention to pay the money, and the money should be recoverable. But it is not necessary to pursue this matter further. It is sufficient to say that, in my opinion, the present case falls within principles laid down by Bramwell B, and in the more recent authorities. In making the payment, the respondent was, it is true, under a mistake as to the nature of the transaction. He thought that a wagering debt was due from himself to the appellant, whereas in fact it was not. But, if the supposed fact had been true, the respondent would have been under no liability to make the payment, which, therefore, was intended to be a voluntary payment. Upon the true facts, the payment was still a voluntary payment; and there is, in my opinion, no such fundamental or basic distinction between the one voluntary payment and the other that the law can, for present purposes, differentiate between them, and say that there was no intention to make the one because the intention was to make the other.'

Comment

But see *Larner* v *London County Council* [1949] 2 KB 683.

Planché v *Colburn* (1831) 8 Bing 14 Court of Common Pleas (Tindal CJ, Gaselee, Bosanquet and Alderson JJ)

• *Literary work abandoned – author's entitlement*

Facts

The plaintiff agreed with the defendant publishers to contribute, for £100, a volume on costume and ancient armour for 'The Juvenile Library'. After the plaintiff had begun work, the defendants abandoned the series. The plaintiff sued for breach of contract and he was awarded £50 damages. The defendants appealed.

Held

This verdict would not be disturbed.

Tindal CJ:

'In this case a contract had been entered into for the publication of a work on costume and ancient armour in "The Juvenile

Library". The considerations by which an author is generally actuated in undertaking to write a work are pecuniary profit and literary reputation. It is clear that the latter may be sacrificed if an author who has engaged to write a volume of a popular nature, to be published in a work intended for a juvenile class of readers, should be subject to have his writings published as a separate and distinct work and, therefore, liable to be judged of by more severe rules than would be applied to a familiar work intended merely for children. The defendants not only suspended, but actually put an end to, "The Juvenile Library". They had broken their contract with the plaintiff and an attempt was made, unsuccessfully, to show that the plaintiff had afterwards entered into a new contract to allow them to publish his book as a separate work. I agree that when a special contract is in existence and open the plaintiff cannot sue on a quantum meruit. Part of the question here, therefore, was whether the contract did exist or not. It distinctly appeared that the work was finally abandoned and the jury found that no new contract had been entered into.

In these circumstances the plaintiff ought not to lose the fruit of his labour. ...'

Bosanquet J:

'The plaintiff is entitled to retain his verdict. The jury have found that the contract was abandoned but it is said that the plaintiff ought to have tendered or delivered the work. It was part of the contract, however, that the work should be published in a particular shape and if it had been delivered after the abandonment of the original design, it might have been published in a way not consistent with the plaintiff's reputation, or not at all.'

Comment

In *Thomas* v *Hammersmith Borough Council* [1938] 3 All ER 203 Slesser LJ cited this case as authority for the proposition that where an architect is engaged to build a town hall and, before the work is completed, the council, of its own volition, terminates the agreement, the architect would be entitled to reasonable remuneration for work done and damages for the remuneration which he had lost because the project was not completed.

17 Agency

Bolton Partners v Lambert (1889) 41 Ch D 295 Court of Appeal (Lindley, Lopes and Cotton LJJ)

- *Unauthorised acceptance – ratification*

Facts
Without its authority and purporting to act as agent on the company's behalf, the managing director of the company accepted an offer by the defendant to purchase the company's sugar works. The defendant then withdrew his offer, but the company ratified the managing director's acceptance.

Held
The defendant was bound. The ratification related back to the managing director's acceptance and the defendant's purported withdrawal was therefore of no effect.

Cotton LJ:

'... the acceptance by Scratchley [the managing director] did constitute a contract, subject to its being shewn that [he] had authority to bind the company ... when and as soon as authority was given ... the authority was thrown back to the time when the act was done by Scratchley, and prevented the defendant withdrawing his offer, because it was no longer an offer, but a binding contract.'

Comment
Although this decision was doubted by the Privy Council in *Fleming v Bank of New Zealand* [1900] AC 577, in *Lawson v Hosemaster Machine Co Ltd* [1966] 2 All ER 944 Danckwerts LJ cited it as authority for the proposition that, on ratification, the title of the ostensible principal dates back to the date of the contract adopted.

Keighley, Maxsted & Co v Durant [1901] AC 240 House of Lords (Earl of Halsbury LC, Lords Macnaghten, Shand, Davey, James of Hereford, Brampton, Robertson and Lindley)

- *Contract – ratification by third party*

Facts
Authorised to buy wheat at a certain price on a joint account for himself and the appellants, a corn merchant purchased wheat from the respondents at a higher price in his own name. Next day the appellants ratified the transaction but subsequently failed to take delivery of the wheat. The respondents sought damages for breach of contract.

Held
Their action could not succeed.

Lord Shand:

'The question which arises ... is whether, where a person has avowedly made a contract for himself – first, without a suggestion that he is acting to any extent for another (an undisclosed principal), and, secondly, without any authority to act for another, he can effectually bind a third party as principal, or as a joint obligant with himself, to the person with whom he contracted, by the fact that in his own mind merely he made a contract in the hope and expectation that his contract would be ratified or shared by the person as to whom he entertained that hope and expectation. I am clearly of opinion ... that he cannot. The only contract actually made is by the person himself and for himself; and it seems to me to be conclusive against the argument for the respondent, that if his reasoning were sound it would be in his power, on an averment of what was passing in his own mind, to make the contract afterwards, either one for himself only, as in fact it was, or one affecting or binding on another as a contracting party, even although he had no authority for this. The result would be to give one of two contracting parties in his option, merely from what was passing in his own mind, and not disclosed, the power of saying that the contract was his alone, or a contract in which others were bound to him. That I think he certainly cannot do in any case where he had no authority when he made the contract to bind anyone but himself'.

Penn v Bristol and West Building Society [1997] 3 All ER 470 Court of Appeal (Staughton, Waite and Waller LJJ)

- *Agent – warranty of authority – breach – causation of loss*

Facts
Mr and Mrs Penn owned a house as beneficial joint tenants. Their business having run into financial difficulties, Mr Penn and his partner decided to execute a mortgage fraud. To this end, the house was to be sold to a Mr Wilson (a party to the fraud) and the main aim was to obtain money in the form of a loan from the respondent building society. Although Mrs Penn knew nothing of what was taking place, the appellant solicitor believed that he was also acting for her and he purported to act for both her and her husband, but her husband had forged her signatures. The balance of the amount advanced by the respondent was used to discharge Mr Penn's business debts. On discovering the position Mrs Penn commenced proceedings and, in those proceedings, the respondent counterclaimed, inter alia, against the appellant for breach of warrant of authority.

Held
The appellant had given such a warranty and he was liable to the respondent for the loss which it had suffered by virtue of his breach of it.

Waller LJ:

'*Warrant of authority ...*

In truth, as I see it, the question of whether a warranty of authority has been given rests on a proper analysis of the facts in any given situation, and not on any preconceived notions as to what is essential as part of the factual analysis. Of course there is no issue that to establish a warranty of authority, as with any other collateral warranty, there must be proved a contract under which a promise is made either expressly or by implication to the promisee, for which promise the promisee provides consideration. But consideration can be supplied by the promisee entering into some transaction with a third party in a warranty of authority case just as it can in any other collateral warranty case. Furthermore, the promise can be made to a wide number of people or simply to one person, again all depending on the facts. It follows ... that the plaintiff, whether as one of the wide number of people to whom the offer is made or by virtue of being the only person to whom the offer is made, has to establish that the promise was made to him. There is also no doubt that what he has to establish is that a promise was being made to him by the agent, to the effect that the agent had the authority of the principal, and that he provided consideration by acting in reliance on that promise.

Application of the law to the facts
[The appellant] undoubtedly was representing throughout the negotiations with ... Gartons [the respondent's solicitors] that he was authorised to act for Mrs Penn. [The appellant] knew that Gartons, in their capacity as the solicitors for the building society, would be relying on his having the authority of Mrs Penn to bring the transaction to fruition, just as much as they were relying on the same as the purchaser's solicitor. What is more, [the respondent] through Gartons did rely on [the appellant] having the authority of Mrs Penn to bring the matter to fruition, in that having obtained from Mr Wilson execution of a charge, money was advanced and available for the purpose of completing the transaction. If at any stage

[the appellant] had said he did not have the authority of Mrs Penn the result would have been that [the respondent]would have proceeded no further.

There was a debate at the trial as to whether [the appellant] knew the actual name of the building society. The judge found that it did not matter whether he knew the actual name or not, but was of the view on balance that it was likely that the actual name had been given by [Gartons] to [the appellant]. I am clear that it matters not whether the actual name of the building society was known to [the appellant].

In my view, all the necessary ingredients are present for establishing a warranty by [the appellant] in favour of [the respondent] enforceable by [the respondent], that warranty being that [the appellant] had the authority of Mrs Penn.

Causation

The promise which on the above analysis was made, was that [the appellant] had the authority of Mrs Penn to negotiate and complete the transaction on her behalf. It was that warranty that was broken. If [the appellant] had actually obtained Mrs Penn's instructions, then either the transaction would never have gone as far as completion, and [the respondent] would not have advanced any money or (and not very likely) the transaction would have been completed properly without forged signatures and they would have had security for their loan. ...

The question is simply whether [the respondent] can establish that [the appellant's] failure to have the authority which he promised he had, caused them the loss they suffered. It seems to me clear on the basis outlined above that they can.'

Watteau v Fenwick [1893] 1 QB 346 Queen's Bench Division (Lord Coleridge CJ and Wills J)

• *Undisclosed principal – liability*

Facts

One Humble sold his public house to the defendants, but remained there as their manager. His name remained over the door and the licence continued to be in his name. Although he was forbidden by the defendants to buy cigars on credit, he bought some from the plaintiff who gave credit to him alone for them, not knowing of the defendants. After discovering that Humble was the defendant's manager, and being unable to obtain payment from Humble, the plaintiff sued the defendants.

Held

The plaintiff was entitled to succeed.

Lord Coleridge CJ:

'... once it is established that the defendant was the real principal, the ordinary doctrine as to principal and agent applies – that the principal is liable for all the acts of the agent which are within the authority usually confided to an agent of that character, notwithstanding limitations, as between the principal and the agent, put upon that authority. It is said that it is only so where there has been a holding out of authority, which cannot be said of a case where the person supplying the goods knew nothing of the existence of a principal. But I do not think so; otherwise in every case of undisclosed principal, or at least in every case where the fact of there being a principal was undisclosed, the secret limitation of authority would prevail, and defeat the action of the person dealing with the agent and then discovering that he was an agent and had a principal. But in the case of a dormant partner it is clear law that no limitation of authority as between the dormant partner and active partner will avail the dormant partner as to things within the ordinary authority of a partner. The law of partnership is, in such a question, nothing but a branch of the general law of principal and agent, and it appears to me to be undisputed and conclusive on the point now under discussion.'

Comment
Distinguished in *Jerome* v *Bentley & Co*
[1952] 2 All ER 114 (private individual
entrusted with a ring for sale not the owner's
agent in this sense).

Yasuda Fire & Marine Insurance Co of Europe Ltd v *Orion Marine Insurance Underwriting Agency Ltd*
[1995] 2 WLR 49 Queen's Bench
Division (Colman J)

• *Agency – records – principal's rights
after termination of contract*

Facts
The defendants were two associated underwriting companies who acted as underwriting
agents for the plaintiffs. The underwriting
agreements were terminated by the plaintiffs
in 1994, though the defendants continued to
manage risks already written on behalf of the
plaintiffs. Each underwriting agency agreement contained an express provision whereby
the plaintiffs were entitled to inspect and copy
or take abstracts from, all books records and
other documentation. The records were to be
the property of the defendants. On termination, which the defendants claimed was by
way of repudiatory breach, the defendants
refused to allow the plaintiffs any access to
the records or computer databases, claiming
that any obligation they had been under to
allow access ended with termination of the
agency contracts.

Held
The plaintiffs were entitled to inspect the
records generated under the agreements.

Colman J:

'Because the agent's duty to provide records
of transactions to the principal is founded on
the entitlement of the principal to the
records of what *has been* done in his name,
termination of the agent's authority to enter
into further transactions should have no
bearing on the continuance of the duty to

provide pre-existing records pertaining to
the period when transactions were authorised. Accordingly, in the absence of
express agreement to the contrary, the
agent's duty to provide to his principal the
records of transactions effected pursuant to
the agency must subsist notwithstanding termination of the agent's authority. That, as I
have held, is a duty that is imposed by law in
consequence of the existence of the agency
relationship and is not founded on the existence of a contract of agency.

If the agent's duty to keep and produce
accounts is attributable to the agency relationship as distinct from any contract of
agency, what happens to the duty where, as
in the present case, there is a contract of
agency? Particularly in a case where, like
the present case, there is express provision
in the contract of agency for the maintenance and production of agency records and
accounts? ...

There can be no doubt that the effect of
[the contract] was to exclude any obligation
on the part of the agents to deliver up to the
plaintiffs their original books, accounts and
records. The exclusion of title to the records
would not, however, have the effect of
wholly depriving the plaintiffs of the right to
inspect such material as related to their own
transactions – a general right arising from
the agency relationship reflected in the contractual right to inspect, extract and copy
reserved by the clause. The contract did not
therefore exclude the principal's right of
access to the contents of the agent's records
provided for in the clause. The principal
remained entitled to access to the material
information in the records, although he was
not entitled to delivery up of the records
themselves for they were not his property.

When the agency agreements were terminated for repudiatory breach ... what then
happened to the plaintiffs' entitlement to
inspect, extract and copy? Did it ... terminate with the contracts on the basis that it
was, as Lord Diplock put it in the passage
from his speech which I have already cited
from *Photo Production Ltd* v *Securicor
Transport Ltd* [1980] AC 827 an "unperformed primary function"?

In my judgment it did not so terminate ... the inspection facility ... was ... wholly ancillary to the subject matter of the agency agreements ... Therefore ... that part of [the agreements] which entitled the plaintiffs to inspect all the relevant records of the defendants at any reasonable time upon notice remained in full effect in spite of the accepted repudiation of the agency agreements.'

18 Sale of Goods, Consumer Credit and Supply of Goods and Services

Atari Corp (UK) Ltd v *Electronic Boutique Stores (UK) Ltd* [1998] 1 All ER 1010 Court of Appeal (Auld, Phillips and Waller LJJ)

• *Sale of goods – sale or return – notice of rejection*

Facts

The defendants ordered computer games and hardware from the plaintiffs and the contract provided 'Payment – 30 November 1995. Full SOR [sale or return] until 31 January 1996.' On 19 January 1996, the defendants wrote to the plaintiffs saying that they had reviewed the sales position of the goods in question and concluded that they would be 'no longer stocked within [the plaintiffs'] chain'. The letter continued:

> 'Our decision was made on performance, participation, gross profit earned from footage allocated to product, and general market analysis ... All stores have been requested to return all ... stock to our central warehouse and when this is all received we will submit to you a complete list of what you will need to raise RA [agreed to mean return authorisation] numbers against. This decision falls in line with our current trading agreement.'

The question was whether the defendants had given notice of rejection of the goods held by them on sale or return, particularly in the light of s18, r4, of the Sale of Goods Act 1979.

Held

The letter dated 19 January had been a valid notice of rejection.

Waller LJ:

'The point argued before the master and before the judge has simply been that the 19 January 1996 letter was not a notice of rejection because: (1) it postulated some future action being taken in order to exercise the right of rejection; (2) it failed to describe the goods which were being rejected with sufficient specificity; and (3) the defendants did not have the goods available when the notice was served. ...

The plaintiffs do not suggest that to exercise the right to return the goods the defendants had to physically return the goods to the plaintiffs' premises prior to 31 January 1996. It follows therefore that it is common ground that this is a notice case – ie what is required is some form of notice that the defendants are exercising their right to return goods the subject of the sale or return term. ...

My starting point is ... to define what was intended by the term "Full sale or return until 31 January 1996". ... In my view in the context of this contract where goods were spread out in various different outlets, it was open to give a notice exercising the right to reject with the sellers' entitlement to collect the goods arising only at a reasonable time after the notice. Whether the sellers were entitled to insist that that reasonable time could not extend beyond 31 January 1996 does not arise for decision.

Now to the terms of the letter of 19 January 1996. First, in my view it did give notice that the defendants were intending to exercise their right to return all unsold ... stock. Second, it was not saying that the goods were immediately available. That is clear from its terms because it was saying

178

that they were being collected from the stores. Third, ... it was permissible in the context of this contract, to give a notice exercising the right of rejection without the goods being immediately available, and the natural reading of the letter would indicate that the goods would be available within a reasonable time taking account of the time it would take to collect from the stores. Fourth ... the plaintiffs might have been entitled to insist that the goods should be available prior to 31 January 1996, but the point does not arise in this case. It also follows from what I have said previously, that I can see no necessity for identifying the goods with [precise] specificity ...

... on a fair reading of the letter of 19 January 1996, (1) the defendants were exercising their right to return unsold stock; in the result from the moment they wrote that letter the defendants had no right to continue to sell such stock as they had left; (2) the letter was saying that it would take a little time to collect the stock from the stores and that thus the plaintiffs could collect not immediately but a reasonable time after the notice; and (3) that to assist in the handover and in the accounting exercise that would take place, the defendants would prepare lists.

On receipt of that notice the plaintiffs would have been entitled to insist on being able to collect the goods within a reasonable time from the notice and possibly prior to 31 January 1996. ... In my view accordingly the 19 January letter was a good notice of exercising the right of return of the goods purchased by the defendants on sale or return.'

Comment
Applied: *Mannai Investment Co Ltd v Eagle Star Life Assurance Co Ltd* [1997] 3 All ER 352; distinguished: *Hardy & Co v Hillerns & Fowler* [1923] 2 KB 490.

Barber v *NWS Bank plc* [1996] 1 All ER 906 Court of Appeal (Kennedy, Peter Gibson LJJ and Sir Roger Parker)

• *Sale of goods – conditional sale agreement – prior interest in goods – recovery of money paid*

Facts
In October 1989 the plaintiff decided to buy a Honda Accord apparently owned by a garage (Kestrel). The garage sold the car to the defendant bank which then agreed to sell the vehicle to the plaintiff under a conditional sale agreement. Until the plaintiff had completed the agreed payments, the car was to remain vested in the defendants. The plaintiff paid the agreed instalments until May 1991. He then decided to sell the car, only to find that is was subject to a prior finance agreement on which there were moneys outstanding.

Held
The plaintiff was entitled to rescind the conditional sale agreement and recover all the moneys (ie his deposit and instalments) which he had paid under it.

Sir Roger Parker:

'Mr Barber [the plaintiff] sought the determination of five questions of law and construction. They were as follows:

"1. Whether it was an express and/or implied condition of the agreement that the Defendant was at the date of the agreement the owner of the motor car the subject of the said agreement. ...

4. Whether in the events that have happened the plaintiff was entitled, as he purported to do by letter dated 16 August 1991, to rescind the agreement and to demand repayment of all monies paid to the Defendant thereunder. ..."

Before us the dispute was narrowed in the course of argument when [counsel] for the bank accepted that the term set out in question 1 was an express term of the agreement. I regard this acceptance as being both correct and unavoidable ...

Although the express term is accepted, before an answer can be given to question 1 it has to be determined whether the term was a condition, breach of which would give a right to rescind ... or only a warranty or innominate term, breach of which would give only a right to recover proved damages ...

In my judgment there can be no doubt but that the term was a condition. It was fundamental to the transaction that the bank had the property in the Honda at the time of the agreement and would retain it until paid in full the moneys due under the agreement. Only on this basis could the agreement operate. My conclusion follows the decisions in *Karflex Ltd* v *Poole* [1933] 2 KB 251 and *Warman* v *Southern Counties Car Finance Corp Ltd (W J Ameris Car Sales, third party)* [1949] 1 All ER 711. These cases are not binding on us but in my view are plainly right. For the bank [counsel] relies principally on certain passages in the judgments in *Bunge Corp* v *Tradex SA* [1981] 2 All ER 513 and *Hong Kong Fir Shipping Co Ltd* v *Kawasaki Kisen Kaisha Ltd* [1962] 1 All ER 474 but in my view they do not avail him. This term is not one which admits of different breaches, some of which are trivial, for which damages are an adequate remedy, and others of which are sufficiently serious to warrant rescission. There is here one breach only. In truth the express term, in my view, puts the parties in the same position as if this was a sale rather than an agreement to sell. Upon a sale it is an implied condition that the seller has a right to sell the goods (s12 of the Sale of Goods Act 1979) and I can see no reason why, if there is any express term that the seller has and will retain the property in the goods, it should not have the same quality.

I would thus answer question 1, with the omission of the words "and/or implied", in the affirmative. This has the immediate consequence that questions 2 and 3 do not arise and require no answer. I turn therefore to question 4.

If in fact the bank had no title it must follow that Mr Barber was entitled to rescind and that the answer to the first part of the question must be in the affirmative. ... In the absence of evidence to the contrary the inescapable inference from [the] facts is that the bank did not have title to the car either at the date of the agreement or at any time thereafter prior to Mr Barber's letter of rescission. ... In the result I conclude that the bank were in breach of the fundamental term and, subject to one point, that Mr Barber was entitled to rescind the agreement. ...

For an answer to the second part of question 4 it is then necessary to determine whether Mr Barber is entitled to recover all money paid under the agreement notwithstanding that he had the use of the car for a considerable time without let or hindrance. On the established authorities he is so entitled but, for the first time before us, it was submitted that Mr Barber was not in any event entitled to recover the deposit ... on the ground that it had not been paid to the bank but to Kestrel and that any claim lay against Kestrel; alternatively that Mr Barber could only recover a like amount to that which the bank could recover against Kestrel (which is insolvent); further that the bank had changed its position and it would be inequitable for Mr Barber to recover any more than that. I reject all of these contentions. It is in my view plain on the documents that Kestrel received the deposit as agent for the bank. It is not inequitable in all the circumstances for Mr Barber to recover the full amount of the deposit and instalments from the bank.

In the light of my above conclusions question 4 should be answered [affirmatively] ...

The outstanding point, to which I have earlier referred, is a last minute contention on behalf of the bank that they have a complete or partial answer to the claim by virtue of the provisions of s27(3) of the Hire Purchase Act 1964. ...

In my judgment ... if, apart from the section, the bank is liable to refund all the moneys paid to Mr Barber, the section does not avail it. Its liability is unaffected. This accords with the clear object of the section, which is designed to protect private purchasers and those claiming under them, but not either the original hirer or buyer or any intervening trade or finance company from their full civil or criminal liabilities.'

Comment
A contention advanced by the bank in its skeleton argument that s25(1) of the Sale of Goods Act 1979 afforded a defence to the then alleged breach was abandoned during the hearing.

Beale v *Taylor* [1967] 1 WLR 1193 Court of Appeal (Sellers and Danckwerts LJJ and Baker J)

• *Sale by description – motor car*

Facts
The defendant advertised a car for sale as a 'Herald convertible, white, 1961, twin carbs'. The plaintiff answered the advertisement, went to the defendant's home, and having inspected the car there, bought it. Neither realised at the time that the rear half of the car was from a 1961 Herald convertible, that the front half was from an earlier model and that the two halves had been welded together. No one could see from an ordinary examination of the car that it was anything other than what the defendant had advertised it to be. On discovering the true position, the plaintiff brought an action against the defendant for damages under s13 of the Sale of Goods Act 1893 for breach of condition. The defendant contended that the plaintiff had seen the car before buying it and had then bought it on his own assessment of its value.

Held
The plaintiff was entitled to succeed.

Sellers LJ:

'The question in this case is whether this was a sale by description or whether, as the seller contends, this was a sale of a particular thing seen by the buyer and bought by him purely on his own assessment of the value of the thing to him. We were referred to a passage in the speech of Lord Wright in *Grant* v *Australian Knitting Mills Ltd*, which I think is apt as far as this case is concerned. Lord Wright said:

"It may also be pointed out that there is a sale by description even though the buyer is buying something displayed before him on the counter; a thing is sold by description, though it is specific, so long as it is sold not merely as the specific thing but as a thing corresponding to a description, eg woollen under-garments, a hot water bottle, a secondhand reaping machine, to select a few obvious illustrations"

– and, I might add, a secondhand motor car. I think that, on the facts of this case, the buyer, when he came along to see this car, was coming along to see a car as advertised, that is, a car described as a "Herald convertible, white, 1961". When he came along he saw what ostensibly was a Herald convertible, white, 1961, because the evidence shows that the "1200" which was exhibited on the rear of this motor car is the first model of the "1200" which came out in 1961; it was on that basis that he was making the offer and in the belief that the seller was advancing his car as that which his advertisement indicated.'

Comment
See now s13 of the Sale of Goods Act 1979. Applied: *Grant* v *Australian Knitting Mills Ltd* [1936] AC 85 (sale of woollen underwear across a retailer's counter a sale by description).

Charter v *Sullivan* [1957] 2 WLR 528 Court of Appeal (Jenkins, Hodson and Sellers LJJ)

• *Repudiation of contract – measure of damages*

Facts
The plaintiff dealer agreed to sell a Hillman

Minx motor car to the defendant. Subsequently he received a letter from the defendant refusing to complete the purchase, but seven to ten days later he resold the car to another purchaser (Mr Wigley) at the same manufacturers' fixed price. The plaintiff's sales manager said in evidence 'can sell all Hillman Minx we can get'.

Held

The plaintiff was entitled to nominal damages only for the defendant's breach of contract.

Jenkins LJ:

> 'The matter ... stands thus. If the defendant had duly performed his bargain, the plaintiff would have made on that transaction a profit of £97.15s. The calculation accordingly starts with a loss of profit through the defendant's default, of £97 15s. That loss was not cancelled or reduced by the sale of the same car to Mr Wigley, for, if the defendant had duly taken and paid for the car which he agreed to buy, the plaintiff could have sold another car to Mr Wigley, in which case there would have been two sales and two profits ...
>
> The matter does not rest there. The plaintiff must further show that the sum representing the profit which he would have made if the defendant had performed his contract has in fact been lost. Here I think he fails, in view of [the sales manager's] evidence to the effect that the plaintiff could sell all the Hillman Minx cars he could get.
>
> I have already expressed my opinion as to the meaning of this statement. It comes, I think, to this, that, according to the plaintiff's own sales manager, the state of trade was such that the plaintiff could always find a purchaser for every Hillman Minx car he could get from the manufacturers; and if that is right it inevitably follows that he should the same number of cars and made the same number of fixed profits as he would have sold and made if the defendant had duly carried out his bargain.
>
> Upjohn J's decision in favour of the plaintiff dealers in *Thompson (W L) Ltd* v *R Robinson (Gunmakers) Ltd* [1955] 2 WLR

185 was essentially based on the admitted fact that the supply of the cars in question exceeded the demand, and his judgment leaves no room for doubt that, if the demand had exceeded the supply, his decision would have been the other way.'

Comment

Distinguished: *Thompson (W L) Ltd* v *R Robinson (Gunmakers) Ltd* [1955] 2 WLR 185.

Forthright Finance Ltd v *Carlyle Finance Ltd* [1997] 4 All ER 90
Court of Appeal (Stuart-Smith, Pill and Phillips LJJ)

• *Sale of motor car – hire-purchase or credit sale agreement?*

Facts

The plaintiff finance company owned a Ford Sierra Cosworth and delivered the car to a dealer (Senator) under an agreement described on its face as a 'Hire-Purchase Agreement'. Under the agreement Senator had the option to purchase the car and it was deemed to have exercised this option when all instalments had been paid: title in the car would then pass to Senator unless it elected not to take it. Senator subsequently delivered the car to a Mr Griffiths under a conditional sale agreement financed by the defendant finance company to which it purported to transfer ownership. It was accepted that Mr Griffiths had a good title to the car, but the plaintiff was awarded damages for its wrongful conversion. On appeal, the defendant contended that the agreement between the plaintiff and Senator was one whereby Senator agreed to buy the car so that, having been placed in possession of the car, Senator was in a position to pass good title to the defendant under s25 of the Sale of Goods Act 1979 – and had done so. The crucial question, therefore, was whether that agreement had been a conditional sale agreement (as the defendant contended) or a hire-purchase agreement.

Held

It had been a conditional sale agreement and the defendant's appeal would therefore be allowed.

Phillips LJ:

'Senator were contractually obliged to pay all the contractual instalments until they had provided all the payments required by the contract as consideration for their right, inter alia, to become the owner of the car. At that stage, unless they had exercised the option to decline to receive title, it was to pass to them.

In my judgment, this contract has all the ingredients of a conditional sale agreement. The option not to take title, which would only expect to be exercised in the most unusual circumstances, does not affect the true nature of the agreement. It seems to me that it is incorporated simply to enable the supplier to advance the very argument that has been urged by [counsel for the plaintiff]. He has urged it most elegantly, but I remain of the view that is is specious. ... This agreement is, not merely in substance but in form, a conditional sale agreement. Whether ... contracts which differ from this one only in that they include a positive option to acquire title for a nominal payment also constitute conditional sale agreements I need not decide.'

Comment

In reaching this conclusion, the Court of Appeal was much influenced by the decision of the House of Lords in *Helby* v *Matthews* [1895] AC 471.

Glencore Grain Rotterdam BV v *Lebanese Organisation for International Commerce* [1997] 4 All ER 514 Court of Appeal (Nourse, Evans LJJ and Sir Ralph Gibson)

• *Fob contract – payment under letter of credit – repudiation for wrong reason*

Facts

The defendants (buyers) agreed to buy 25,000 tonnes of Turkish wheat from the plaintiff (sellers) and the contract stipulated fob shipment on a vessel chartered by the defendants. Payment was to be by an irrevocable and confirmed letter of credit, but the defendants subsequently said that payment was subject to the plaintiffs presenting bills of lading issued as 'freight pre-paid'. The defendants' vessel was a day late: on this ground the plaintiffs refused to load the wheat. Two issues of law arose: (i) were buyers under a sale contract on fob terms incorporating GAFTA Form 64 entitled to open a letter of credit in favour of the sellers which was restricted to payment against freight pre-paid bills of lading?; and (ii) if the buyers were not so entitled and were thereby in breach of contract, could the sellers rely on that breach to justify their own refusal and failure to ship the contract goods?

Held

The defendants had not been entitled to impose such a restriction and the plaintiffs had been entitled to rely on this breach of contract.

Evans LJ:

'The first issue ... is whether the buyers under a sale contract on what are described as normal fob terms are entitled to open a letter of credit which requires the seller to present "freight pre-paid" bills of lading if they are to receive payment from the buyers' bank. Absent any special agreement, the sellers are entitled to see a conforming letter of credit in pace before they begin shipment of the goods, and then their obligations is to ship the contract goods on board the vessel provided by the buyers, for carriage on whatever terms as to freight and otherwise the buyers have agreed with the shipowner. The sellers are expressly free of any obligation to pay freight (special terms apart, fob is the antithesis of c and f – cost and freight) and in the normal course they cannot be sure before shipment that the shipowner will issue freight pre-paid bills of lading, unless they are prepared if necessary to pay the amount of freight themselves, or unless some other guaranteed payment mechanism is already in place. I would put the matter broadly in that way, because it may be that an undertaking from the shipowner himself, or a third party guarantee of the payment of freight following due shipment of the goods, would suffice. It is unnecessary to consider that aspect further in the present case, because all that was offered by the buyers was their own assurance that the freight would be paid, by them or on their behalf. It is abundantly clear, in my judgment, that the buyers' own assurance cannot be enough to serve as a guarantee to the sellers that "freight pre-paid" bills of lading will be issued when shipment is complete. That would mean ... that the security of a bank guarantee for the payment of the price, which is what the letter of credit mechanism provides, would be destroyed. I therefore agree ... that the buyers' contention, that the letter of credit terms were in conformity with the contract, is contrary both to the underlying concept of the fob contract (subject always to what special terms may be agreed in a particular case) and to the essential commercial purpose of the letter of credit machinery. ... In short, the buyers cannot allege that there was a fresh agreement as regards this term of the letter of credit which had the effect either of supplementing or varying the requirements of the sale contract.

For these reasons ... in my judgment the buyers were not entitled to require the sellers to procure and produce freight pre-paid bills of lading in order to receive payment under the letter of credit opened by them. It follows that the buyers failed to open a letter of credit conforming with the sale contract and, subject to the question of waiver considered below, they were thereby in breach of contract. The second issue is whether the sellers can rely on that breach to of justify their own refusal and failure to ship on the contract terms. They did not assert that they were relying on it at the time.

Basic rule

"It is a long established rule of law that a contracting party, who, after he has become entitled to refuse performance of his contractual obligations, gives a wrong reason for his refusal, does not thereby deprive himself of a justification which in fact existed, whether he was aware of it or not." (See *Taylor* v *Oakes Roncoroni & Co* (1922) 127 LT 267 at 269 per Greer J.) ...

Conclusion

There was no finding ... of any unequivocal representation by the sellers that they relinquished or would relinquish their rights arising out of the buyers' failure to open a letter of credit in the form required by the sale contract. Nor in my judgment could any such finding be justified by the facts ... The buyers made their position clear ... saying that no further changes were possible. This was immediately over-shadowed by the ship's failure to meet the contractual eta ... and, in the event, to arrive and give valid notice of readiness before the amended loading period began ... The fact that the sellers made no further reference to the letter of credit issue ... cannot be said to have misled the buyers into believing that the "freight pre-paid" requirement was no longer important to them, nor so far as we know is there any evidence to that effect.

In my judgment, ... the sellers were [able] to rely upon the buyers' breach as a defence to the claim for damages for refusal and/or failure to load.'

Comment

While Evans LJ identified and considered various qualifications to the basic rule in *Taylor* v *Oakes Roncoroni & Co*, none was found to apply in the circumstances of the present case.

Harlingdon & Leinster Enterprises Ltd v *Christopher Hull Fine Art Ltd*
[1990] 1 All ER 737 Court of Appeal (Slade, Nourse and Stuart-Smith LJJ)

• *Sale of paintings – implied terms*

Facts

Mr Hull owned and controlled the defendant art dealers. In 1984 he was asked to sell two paintings which, in a 1980 auction catalogue, had been described as being the work of Gabriele Münter. He contacted the plaintiff art dealers and, after he had made it clear that he did not know much about the paintings and that he was not an expert in them, the plaintiffs bought one of them for £6,000. The invoice described the painting as being by Münter, but it was later discovered to be a forgery. The plaintiffs sought repayment of the purchase price alleging, inter alia, that there had been a sale by description within s13(1) of the Sale of Goods Act 1979. The judged dismissed the action: the plaintiffs appealed.

Held (Stuart-Smith LJ dissenting)

The appeal would be dismissed.

Slade LJ:

'... where a question arises whether a sale of goods was one by description, the presence or absence of reliance on the description may be very relevant in so far as it throws light on the intentions of the parties at the time of the contract. If there was no such reliance by the purchaser, this may be powerful evidence that the parties did not contemplate that the authenticity of the description should constitute a term of the contract, in other words, that they contemplated that the purchaser would be buying the goods *as they were*. If, on the other hand, there was such reliance (as in *Varley* v *Whipp* [1900] 1 QB 513, where the purchaser had never seen the goods) this may be equally powerful evidence that it was contemplated by both parties that the correctness of the description would be a term of the contract (so as to bring it within s13(1)).

So far as it concerns s13(1), the issue for the court in the present case was and is, in my judgment, this: on an objective assessment of what the parties said and did, ... and of all the circumstances of the case, is it right to impute to them the common intention that the authenticity of the attribution

to Gabriele Münter should be a term of the contract of sale? The proper inferences to be drawn from the evidence and the findings of primary fact by the judge are matters on which different minds can take different views ... However, I for my part feel no doubt that the answer to the crucial issue is, No ...

The form of the invoice subsequently made out in favour of the plaintiffs does not, in my judgment, assist the plaintiffs' case. By that time the contract had already been concluded. While the reference to Gabriele Münter in the invoice is quite consistent with the parties having made the origin of the picture a term of the contract, it can equally well be read as merely a convenient mode of reference to a particular picture which both parties knew to have been attributed to Gabriele Münter (and indeed both still though to be her work).

For these reasons, I agree ... that this was not a sale falling within s13(1) of the 1979 Act. In my view, one cannot impute to the parties a common intention that it should be a term of the contract that the artist was Gabriele Münter.

As to the claim based on s14 [of the 1979 Act], I hope that my opinion is not too simplistic, but it is very clear. The complaint, and only complaint as to the quality of the picture, relates to the identity of the artist. There is no other complaint of any kind as to its condition or quality. If the verdict of the experts had been that the artist was in truth Gabriele Münter, the claim would not have arisen. Having concluded that this was not a contract for the sale of goods by description because it was not a term of the contract that she was the artist, I see no room for the application of s14. If the plaintiffs fail to establish a breach of contract through the front door of s13(1), they cannot succeed through the back door of s14.'

Comment

Leaf v *International Galleries* [1950] 1 All ER 693 (painting innocently but mistakenly sold as a Constable) was a similar case, but there, inter alia, it was held that the purchaser would be deemed to have accepted the painting within s35 of the 1979 Act.

Lewis v Averay [1971] 3 WLR 603

See Chapter 8.

St Albans City and District Council v International Computers Ltd [1996] 4 All ER 481

See Chapter 14.

Slater v Finning Ltd [1996] 3 All ER 398 House of Lords (Lords Keith of Kinkel, Griffiths, Jauncey of Tullichettle, Slynn of Hadley and Steyn)

• *Sale of goods – implied conditions as to fitness – idiosyncrasy as to use of goods by buyer*

Facts

The appellants engaged the respondent marine engine suppliers to repair the engine of their fishing vessel Aquarius II. The respondents fitted a new type of camshaft but it (and two replacements of the same type) failed at sea. The appellants claimed damages for breach of the implied condition as to reasonable fitness for purpose contained in s14(3) of the Sale of Goods Act 1979. The trial judge found that the trouble had not lain in the camshafts themselves but in some external feature peculiar to the ship of which the respondents had not been made aware.

Held

The respondents were not liable for any breach of the implied condition.

Lord Keith of Kinkel:

'The argument for the appellants did not involve any challenge to the Lord Ordinary's findings in fact. It was accepted that the excessive torsional resonance which

resulted in damage to the camshafts was caused by some unascertained force external to the engine and the camshafts themselves. It was argued, however, that the condition to be implied by s14(3) of the 1979 Act was properly to be related to Aquarius II as a vessel having its own peculiar characteristics, including the possession of a tendency to give rise to excessive torsional resonance in the engine camshaft. The appellants had made known to the respondents that the camshafts were being bought for the specific purpose of installation in Aquarius II. The respondents therefore took the risk that Aquarius II might have some unknown and unusual characteristic such as would cause the camshafts to be subject to excessive wear. In the event, the camshafts proved not to be reasonably fit for use as part of the engine of Aquarius II.

Counsel for the appellants relied on *Cammell Laird & Co Ltd* v *Manganese Bronze and Brass Co Ltd* [1934] AC 402. In that case the defendants had contracted to supply for two ships under construction by the plaintiffs two propellers according to specifications provided, and to the entire satisfaction of the plaintiffs and the shipowners. On trials the propeller fitted to one of the ships made so much noise that the vessel could not be classed A1 at Lloyds, though it worked perfectly well on the ship. A second propeller was made for the first ship and proved equally unsatisfactory. A third propeller, however, worked quite silently. The plaintiffs sued the defendants for breach of contract, founding inter alia on s14(1) of the Sale of Goods Act 1893, the statutory predecessor of s14(3) of the 1979 Act. This House held that the defendants had been in breach of s14(1). There was an implied condition that the propeller should be reasonably fit for use on the particular ship for which it was required, and it was not.

The case does not however, in my opinion, assist the appellants. The propeller was not a standard part to be fitted to a standard propulsion plant. It was specifically manufactured for a specific ship. ...

In the present case the Lord Ordinary has

found that cause of the trouble did not lie in the camshafts themselves but in some external feature peculiar to Aquarius II.

Griffiths v *Peter Conway Ltd* [1939] 1 All ER 685 is closer to the point. There the plaintiff had purchased from the defendants a Harris tweed coat, which had been specially made for her. Shortly after she had begun to wear the coat she contracted dermatitis. She sued the defendants for damages, claiming breach of s14(1) of the 1893 Act in that the coat was not reasonably fit for the purpose for which it was supplied. It was proved that the plaintiff's skin was abnormally sensitive, and that there was nothing in the coat which would have affected the skin of a normal person. The defendants were not aware of the plaintiff's abnormal sensitivity, and the plaintiff herself was also unaware of it. Branson J dismissed the action and his judgment was affirmed by the Court of Appeal. Greene MR quoted the relevant findings of the trial judge and continued (at 691):

"That finding is, of course, that no normal skin would have been affected by this cloth. There was nothing in it which would affect a normal skin, but the plaintiff unfortunately had an idiosyncrasy, and that was the real reason why she contracted this disease. On the basis of that finding, which is not challenged, Mr Morris says: 'Take the language of the section, and the present case falls within it.' He says that the buyer, Mrs Griffiths, expressly made known to the defendants the particular purpose for which the coat was required – that is to say, for the purpose of being worn by her, Mrs Griffiths, when it was made. Once that state of affairs is shown to exist, Mr Morris says that the language of the section relentlessly and without any escape imposes upon the seller the obligation which the section imports. It seems to me that there is one quite sufficient answer to that argument. Before the condition as to reasonable fitness is implied, it is necessary that the buyer should make known, expressly or by implication, first of all the particular purpose for which the goods are required. The particular purpose for which the woods were required was the purpose of being worn by a woman suffering from an abnormality. It seems to me that, if a person suffering from such an abnormality requires an article of clothing for his or her use, and desires to obtain the benefit of the implied condition, he or she does not make known to the seller the particular purpose merely by saying: 'The article of clothing is for my own wear.' The essential matter for the seller to know in such cases with regard to the purposes for which the article is required consists in the particular abnormality or idiosyncrasy from which the buyer suffers. It is only when he has that knowledge that he is in a position to exercise skill or judgment, because how can he decide and exercise his skill or judgment in relation to the suitability of the goods that he is selling for the use of the particular individual who is buying from him unless he knows the essential characteristics of that individual? The fact that those essential characteristics are not known, as in the present case they were not known, to the buyer does not seem to affect the question. When I speak of 'essential characteristics', I am not, of course, referring to any variations which take place and exist within the class of normal people. No two normal people are precisely alike, and, in the matter of sensitiveness of skin, among people who would be described as normal their sensitiveness must vary in degree."

The reasoning contained in that passage was directly applicable to the facts of the present case. The particular purpose for which the camshafts were here required was that of being fitted in the engine of a vessel which suffered from a particular abnormality or idiosyncrasy, namely a tendency to create excessive torsional resonance in camshafts. The respondents, not being made aware of that tendency, were not in a position to exercise skill and judgment for the purpose of dealing with it. Nor were they in a position to make up their minds whether or not to accept the burden of the implied condition, a matter which Greene MR alludes (at 692). It is to be noted that Greene MR specifically mentions that the plaintiff was unaware of her abnormal sensitivity.

In *Ashington Piggeries Ltd* v *Christopher Hill Ltd, Christopher Hill Ltd* v *Norsildmel* [1971] 1 All ER 847, a firm of mink breeders had contracted with certain sellers for the supply of animal feedstuff. The feedstuff supplied caused thousands of mink to die because one the ingredients, Norwegian herring milk, contained a toxic chemical agent called DMNA. This House, reversing the Court of Appeal, held that the sellers were liable to the buyers inter alia for breach of s14(1) of the 1893 Act. It was proved that herring meal containing DMNA was deleterious to a wide variety of animals, not only to mink. On the other hand, mink were more sensitive to it than other animals. ...

As a matter of principle, therefore, it may be said that where a buyer purchases goods from a seller who deals in goods of that description there is no breach of the implied condition of fitness where the failure of the goods to meet the intended purpose arises from an abnormal feature or idiosyncrasy, not made known to the seller, in the buyer or in the circumstances of the use of the goods by the buyer. That is the case whether or not the buyer is himself aware of the abnormal feature or idiosyncrasy.

In the course of argument my noble and learned friend Lord Griffiths put the illustration of a new front wheel tyre being purchased for a car which, unknown to the buyer or seller, had a defect in the steering mechanism as a result of which the tyre wore out after a few hundred miles of use, instead of the many thousands which would normally be expected. In these circumstances it would be totally unreasonable that the seller should be liable for breach of s14(3). The present case is closely analogous. Aquarius II suffered, unknown to the respondents, from a defect in the shape of an unusual tendency to produce excessive torsional resonance in the camshafts, with the result that the camshafts became badly worn and unserviceable much sooner than would otherwise have been the case.'

Thompson (W L) Ltd v *R Robinson (Gunmakers) Ltd* [1955] 2 WLR 185
High Court (Upjohn J)

• *Repudiation of contract – measure of damages*

Facts
The defendants agreed in writing to buy from the plaintiff Hull dealers a Standard Vanguard motor car. Next day, they refused to accept delivery, the plaintiffs losing £61 profit as a result. At the time of the agreement, there was insufficient local demand to absorb all Standard Vanguards available there for sale.

Held
The plaintiffs were entitled to £61 by way of damages for breach of contract.

Upjohn J:

'It was, of course, notorious that dealers all over the country had long waiting lists for new motor cars. People put their names down and had to wait five or six years, and whenever a car was spared by the manufacturer from export it was snatched at. If any purchaser fell out, there were many waiting to take his place, and it was conceded that if those circumstances were still applicable to the Vanguard motor car, the claim for damages must necessarily have been purely nominal. But on the assumed facts, circumstances had changed in relation to Vanguard motor cars, and ... there was not a demand in the East Riding of Yorkshire which could readily absorb all the Vanguard motor cars available for sale. If a purchaser defaulted, that sale was lost and there was no means of readily disposing of the Vanguard contracted to be sold, so that there was not, even on the extended definition, an available market. But there is this further consideration: even if I accepted the defendants' broad argument that one must now look at the market as being the whole conspectus of trade, organisation and marketing, I have to remember that s50(3) [of the Sale of Goods Act 1893] provides only a prima facie rule, and, if on investigation of the facts, one finds that it is unjust to apply that rule, in the light of the general principles mentioned above it is not to be applied. In this case ... it seems to me plain almost beyond argument that, in fact, the loss to the plaintiffs is £61. Accordingly, however one interprets s50(3), it seems to me on the facts that I have to consider one reaches the same result.'

Comment

See now s50(3) of the Sale of Goods Act 1979. Distinguished in *Charter* v *Sullivan* [1957] 2 WLR 528 and *Lazenby Garages Ltd* v *Wright* [1976] 2 All ER 770 (second-hand car sold for more than contract price so no loss and no damages). Applied in *Interoffice Telephones Ltd* v *Robert Freeeman Co Ltd* [1957] 3 All ER 479 (hirers repudiated agreement for hire of telephone installation: owners placed in same position as if contract performed).

Wilson v *Best Travel Ltd* [1993] 1 All ER 353 Queen's Bench Division (Phillips J)

• *Holiday accident – tour operator's duty – Supply of Goods and Services Act 1982*

Facts

The plaintiff, while staying on holiday in Greece at an hotel featured in the defendants' brochure, tripped and fell through plate-glass balcony doors. He sustained serious injuries. He claimed damages against the defendants, alleging that they were in breach of a duty of care implied by s13 of the Supply of Goods and Services Act 1982. The doors satisfied the requirements of Greek, but not British, safety standards.

Held

The plaintiff's claim would fail.

Phillips J (after citing s13 of the 1982 Act):

'The nature of the services provided by a travel agent when arranging a holiday can vary enormously, depending on the nature of the holiday. I am satisfied, having read their brochure, that the service provided by the defendants included the inspection of the properties offered in their brochure. Such service is implicit from a number of passages in their brochure ...

In my judgment, one of the characteristics of accommodation that the defendants owed a duty to consider when inspecting properties included in their brochure was safety. The defendants owe their customers, including the plaintiff, a duty to exercise reasonable care to exclude from the accommodation offered any hotel whose characteristics were such that guests could not spend a holiday there in reasonable safety. I believe that this case is about the standard to be applied in assessing reasonable safety. ...

What is the duty of a tour operator in a situation such as this? Must he refrain from sending holidaymakers to any hotel whose characteristics, in so far as safety is concerned, fail to satisfy the standards which apply in this country? I do not believe that his obligations in respect of the safety of his clients can extend this far. Save where uniform international regulations apply, there are bound to be differences in the safety standards applied in respect of the many hazards of modern life between one country and another. All civilised countries attempt to cater for these hazards by imposing mandatory regulations. The duty of care of a tour operator is likely to extend to checking that local safety regulations are complied with. Provided that they are, I do not consider that the tour operator owes a duty to boycott a hotel because of the absence of some safety feature which would be found in an English hotel unless the absence of such a feature might lead a reasonable holidaymaker to decline to take a holiday at the hotel in question. On the facts of this case I do not consider that the degree of danger posed by the absence of safety glass in the doors of the Vanninarchis Beach Hotel called for any action on the part of the defendants pursuant to their duty to exercise reasonable care to ensure the safety of their clients.'

19 Assignment

Darlington Borough Council v Wiltshier Northern Ltd [1995] 1 WLR 68 Court of Appeal (Dillon, Steyn and Waite LJJ)

• *Contractual rights assigned to third party – whether assignee entitled to damages for breach of contract*

Facts
Wiltshier entered into two contracts with Morgan Grenfell, a finance house, to build a recreational centre in a partnership scheme with Darlington Borough Council who owned the site. Subsequently, Morgan Grenfell assigned to the council all rights and causes of action under the two contracts. Following this assignment, the council took action against Wiltshier for assorted alleged breaches of contract.

Held
The council was entitled to claim substantial damages in respect of foreseeable loss caused by Wiltshier's breaches of contract, should any such breaches be established.

Dillon LJ:

'We start ... with certain elementary propositions in the law as to damages for breach of contract which are binding on this court. Thus in the first place the general principle for the assessment of damages for breach of contract is compensatory – to compensate the plaintiff for the damage, loss or injury he has suffered through the breach: see *Johnson* v *Agnew* [1980] AC 367 at 400 per Lord Wilberforce and *British Westinghouse Electric and Manufacturing Co Ltd* v *Underground Electric Rlys Co of London Ltd* [1912] AC 673 at 689 per Viscount Haldane LC.

In the second place, though the doctrine has been much criticised, it remains the law binding on this court that a third party cannot sue for damages on a contract to which he was not a party: see the decisions of the House of Lords in *Dunlop Pneumatic Tyre Co Ltd* v *Selfridge & Co Ltd* [1915] AC 847, *Midland Silicones Ltd* v *Scruttons Ltd* [1962] AC 446 and *Beswick* v *Beswick* [1968] AC 58.

In the third place, the general position is that if a plaintiff contracts with a defendant for the defendant to make a payment or confer some other benefit on a third party who was not a party to the contract, the plaintiff cannot recover substantial damages from the defendant for breach of that obligation on the part of the defendant: see *Woodar Investment Development Ltd* v *Wimpey Construction UK Ltd* [1980] 1 WLR 277. The plaintiff can, prima facie, only recover for his own loss. ...

It has been recognised in the House of Lords, however, that there are certain exceptions to the general principles I have mentioned. One exception, recognised in the *Woodar Investment* case [1980] 1 WLR 277 at 284, 293 per Lord Wilberforce and Lord Russel of Killowen respectively, is where the plaintiff made the contract as agent or trustee for the third party, and was enforcing the rights of a beneficiary, there being a fiduciary relationship. This is recognised in the decision of this court in *Lloyd's* v *Harper* (1880) 16 Ch D 290, where it was held that the corporation of Lloyd's, as successors to the committee of Lloyd's, were entitled to enforce a guarantee of the liabilities of an underwriting member which had been given to the committee, which had itself suffered no loss for the benefit of all persons, whether members or not, with whom the member had contracted engagements as underwriting member.

A further exception is to be found, in the law as to the carriage of goods by sea, in the recognition by the House of Lords in *The Albazero, Albacruz (cargo owners)* v *Albazero (owners)* [1977] AC 774 of the continuing validity, in such a context, of the earlier decision of the House in *Dunlop* v *Lambert* (1839) 6 Cl & Fin 600.

It is unnecessary to go into details of the circumstances in *The Albazero* and *Dunlop* v *Lambert,* since what Lord Diplock referred to in *The Albazero* as the rule laid down by the House in *Dunlop* v *Lambert* was applied by the House in a building contract context in *St Martin's Property Corp Ltd* v *Sir Robert McAlpine & Sons Ltd,* reported with *Linden Gardens Trust Ltd* v *Lenesta Sludge Disposals Ltd* [1994] 1 AC 85.

The key passage giving the ratio in the *McAlpine* case is in the speech of Lord Browne-Wilkinson ...

"In my judgment the present case falls within the rationale of the exceptions to the general rule that a plaintiff can only recover damages for his own loss. The contract was for a large development of property which, to the knowledge of both Corporation and McAlpines, was going to be occupied, and possibly purchased, by third parties and not by Corporation itself. Therefore it could be foreseen that damages caused by a breach would cause loss to a later owner and not merely to the original contracting party, Corporation. As in contracts for the carriage of goods by land, there would be no automatic vesting in the occupier or owners of the property for the time being who sustained the loss of any right of suit against McAlpines. On the contrary, McAlpines had specifically contracted that the rights of action under the building contract could *not* without McAlpines' consent be transferred to third parties who became owners or occupiers and might suffer loss. In such a case, it seems to be proper, as in the case of the carriage of goods by land, to treat parties as having entered into

the contract on the footing that Corporation would be entitled to enforce contractual rights for the benefit of those who suffered from defective performance but who, under the terms of the contract, could not acquire any right to hold McAlpines liable for breach. It is truly a case in which the rule provides 'a remedy where no other would be available to a person sustaining loss which under a rational legal system ought to be compensated by the person who caused it'." (Lord Browne-Wilkinson's emphasis.)

The present case is, in my judgment, a fortiori since, so far from there being a prohibition on the assignment of Morgan Grenfell's rights against Wiltshier under the building contracts, the covenant agreement, of which Wiltshier was aware, gave the council the right to call for an assignment of such rights. The argument to the contrary, that Lord Browne-Wilkinson's decision depended on the prohibition on assignments in the building contract in the *McAlpine* case seems to be to lead to absurdity ...

[Counsel for Wiltshier] also sought to distinguish the decision in the *McAlpine* case on the ground that the present case Morgan Grenfell never acquired or transmitted to the council any proprietary interest in the Dolphin Centre. I do not see that that matters as the council had the ownership of the site of the Dolphin Centre all along. It was plainly obvious to Wiltshier throughout that the Dolphin Centre was being constructed for the benefit of the council on the council's land. ...

Accordingly, I would [decide in favour of the council] by direct application of the rule in *Dunlop* v *Lambert* as recognised in the building contract context in Lord Browne-Wilkinson's speech in the *McAlpine* case.'

Farrow v *Wilson* (1869) LR 4 CP 744 Court of Common Pleas (Willes and Montague Smith JJ)

• *Contract for personal service – death of party*

Facts

The plaintiff was Price Pugh's farm bailiff. Pugh died; his administrators dismissed the plaintiff without notice. The contract provided that, in such circumstances (ie, should the plaintiff be dismissed without notice), he was entitled to six months' wages. The plaintiff sued the administrators to recover this amount.

Held

His action could not succeed.

Willes J:

'The declaration alleges a contract between the plaintiff and the defendants' testator. The contract was for personal service, and it is not stated in the declaration that either party, either expressly or impliedly, contracted for his executors or administrators. The general rule of law is that, in the case of a contract for personal service, the death of either party puts an end to the contract unless there is a stipulation, express or implied, to the contrary. There being no such stipulation in the present case, the general rule must apply, and our judgment must consequently be for the defendants.'

Comment

See generally s1(1) of the Law Reform (Miscellaneous Provisions) Act 1934.

Investors Compensation Scheme Ltd v West Bromwich Building Society
[1998] 1 All ER 98 House of Lords (Lords Goff of Chieveley, Lloyd of Berwick, Hoffman, Hope of Craighead and Clyde)

• *Investment business – assignment of right of action – interpretation of contractual document*

Facts

Arising out of home income plans, investors sought from the defendants (WBBS), inter alia, damages for misrepresentation. The plaintiffs (ICS) made similar claims as assignees of the investors' rights. The underlying question was as to the validity, extent and effect of the assignment.

Held (Lord Lloyd of Berwick dissenting)

On the true construction of the assignment, the investors had validity assigned to ICS all claims for damages and such claims could therefore be made by ICS and not by the investors. However, the investors' right to claim rescission of their mortgages had not been and could not be assigned: an award could be made on such terms as the court considered just.

Lord Hoffmann:

'... I think I should preface my explanation of my reasons with some general remarks about the principles by which contractual documents are nowadays construed. I do not think that the fundamental change which has overtaken this branch of the law, particularly as a result of the speeches of Lord Wilberforce in *Prenn* v *Simmonds* [1971] 3 All ER 237 at 240–242, and *Reardon Smith Line Ltd* v *Hansen-Tangen, Hansen-Tangen* v *Sanko Steamship Co* [1976] 3 All ER 570, is always sufficiently appreciated. The result has been, subject to one important exception, to assimilate the way in which such documents are interpreted by judges to the common sense principles by which any serious utterance would be interpreted in ordinary life. Almost all the old intellectual baggage of "legal" interpretation has been discarded. The principles may be summarised as follows:

(1) Interpretation is the ascertainment of the meaning which the document would convey to a reasonable person having all the background knowledge which would reasonably have been available to the parties in the situation in which they were at the time of the contract.

(2) The background was famously referred to by Lord Wilberforce as the "matrix of fact", but this phrase is, if anything, an understated description of what the background may include. Subject to the requirement that it should have been reason-

ably available to the parties and to the exception to be mentioned next, it includes absolutely anything which would have affected the way in which the language of the document would have been understood by a reasonable man.

(3) The law excludes from the admissible background the previous negotiations of the parties and their declarations of subjective intent. They are admissible only in an action for rectification. The law makes this distinction for reasons of practical policy and, in this respect only, legal interpretation differs from the way we would interpret utterances in ordinary life. The boundaries of this exception are in some respects unclear. But this is not the occasion on which to explore them.

(4) The meaning which a document (or any other utterance) would convey to a reasonable man is not the same thing as the meaning of its words. The meaning of words is a matter of dictionaries and grammars; the meaning of the document is what the parties using those words against the relevant background would reasonably have been understood to mean. The background may not merely enable the reasonable man to choose between the possible meanings of words which are ambiguous but even (as occasionally happens in ordinary life) to conclude that the parties must, for whatever reason, have used the wrong words or syntax (see *Mannai Investment Co Ltd* v *Eagle Star Life Assurance Co Ltd* [1997] 3 All ER 352).

(5) The "rule" that words should be given their "natural and ordinary meaning" reflects the common sense proposition that we do not easily accept that people have made linguistic mistakes, particularly in formal documents. On the other hand, if one would nevertheless conclude from the background that something must have gone wrong with the language, the law does not require judges to attribute to the parties an intention which they plainly could not have had. Lord Diplock made this point more vigorously when he said in *Antaios Cia Naviera SA* v *Salen Rederierna AB, The Antaios* [1984] 3 All ER 229 at 233:

"... if detailed semantic and syntactical analysis of words in a commercial contract is going to lead to a conclusion that flouts business common sense, it must be made to yield to business common sense."...

The next question is whether ... the assignment of claims to compensation and damages against WBBS was valid. ...

My Lords, I agree that a chose in action is property, something capable of being turned into money. *Snell's Equity* (29th edn, 1990) p71 defines choses in action as "all personal rights of property which can only be claimed or enforced by action, and not by taking physical possession". At common law, for reasons into which it is unnecessary to discuss, choses in action could not be assigned. In equity, they could. Assignment of a "debt or other legal thing in action" was made possible at law by s136 of the Law of Property Act 1925. In each case, however, what is assignable is the debt or other personal right of property. It is recoverable by action, but what is assigned is the *chose*, the thing, the debt or damages to which the assignor is entitled. The existence of a remedy or remedies is an essential condition for the existence of the chose in action but that does not mean that the remedies are property in themselves, capable of assignment separately from the *chose*. So, for example, there may be joint or several liability; a remedy for the recovery of a debt or damages may be available against more than one person. But this does not mean that there is more than one chose in action. The assignee either acquires the right to the money (or part of the money) or he does not. If he does, he necessarily acquires whatever remedies are available to recover the money or the part which has been assigned to him. ...

Let us consider what rights the investor might have had when he signed the form. He may have had a claim for damages in respect of the loss which he had suffered on account of entering into the transaction. This may have included money which he had lost on the ill-advised investment in an equity-linked bond, fees which he paid to advisers to extricate himself from this predicament, high rates of interest paid to the building society, possibly even money spent under the impression that he could afford to do so. The persons liable for this loss might have been the financial adviser, the building society and his solicitor. ... The building society, for example, might have been liable for participating in misrepresentations made by the financial adviser in the course of a joint scheme for marketing home improvement plans, or in breach of its duties under the 1986 Act. I am not suggesting that any building society was actually liable on this basis, but only that the claim form contemplates this as a possibility. This right of damages would have been a chose in action, a right to recover money, which was capable of assignment in equity and under s136 of the Law of Property Act 1925.

The investor might in addition have had a right against the building society to rescission of his mortgage. Or he might have such a right without having any claim for damages. For example, he might have been able to show that the building society had actual or constructive knowledge of undue influence exercised by the financial adviser: compare *Barclays Bank plc v O'Brien* [1993] 4 All ER 417. This would entitle him to rescission but not damages. By itself, the right to rescission would have done little to solve the investor's problems because it would have been a condition of rescission that the investor should restore the benefits which he had received in return for the mortgage: the building society's advance and a reasonable rate of interest for having the use of the money. His real complaint was not merely that his house was mortgaged but that he no longer had the money to pay back the building society. Until he had obtained compensation or damages, he would usually be unable to do so. Nevertheless, one can imagine reasons why it would be more advantageous to the investor, even after obtaining his compensation, to claim rescission of the mortgage rather than simply paying it off. For example, the reasonable rate of interest which a court might fix as a condition of rescission might be less than the higher rate

due under the contract (some of which he had already paid) and so, on the taking of accounts for the purposes of rescission, there might be an abatement of what he would otherwise have to repay.

Now it is important to notice that a claim to rescission is a right of action but can in no way be described as a chose in action or part of a chose in action. It is a claim to be relieved of a mortgage, and such a claim can be made only by the owner of the mortgaged property. The owner cannot assign a right to rescission separately from his property because it would make no sense to acquire a right to have someone else's property relieved of a mortgage. Likewise, the possibility of an abatement of the debt as part of the process of rescission is not a chose in action which can be assigned. It is simply part of the process of rescission, which is a right attached to the ownership of the house itself. ...

It is of course true that there are ... links between the claim for damages and the claim for rescission. The facts giving rise to liability would have a great deal in common, so that if both claims were being made, by the ICS in the one case and the investor in the other, it would be sensible to try both cases together. But this can often happened when the same facts give rise to claims by different people and there are procedural means for dealing with the possibility of duplicated evidence and conflicting decisions. ...

My Lords, I think that if the rights of the investor are property analysed, it will become clear that ... the claim form is a complete and effectual assignment of the whole of the investor's claim to compensation and damages to the ICS.'

Comment

While the decision here was made ultimately in the light of the particular facts of the case, Lord Hoffmann's speech is significant for its concise statement of the principles now to be applied in construing contractual documents and for the explanation there given as to what is, and what is not, a chose in action.

Pan Ocean Shipping Co Ltd v Creditcorp Ltd, The Trident Beauty
[1994] 1 All ER 470 House of Lords (Lords Keith of Kinkel, Goff of Chieveley, Lowry, Slynn of Hadley and Woolf)

• *Time charterparty – assignment of receivables – recovery of advance hire*

Facts
The appellant company (Pan Ocean) sought to recover from the respondent company (Creditcorp) an instalment of time charter hire paid by Pan Ocean as time charterers of the vessel *Trident Beauty* to Creditcorp as assignee from the disponent owner of the vessel, Trident Shipping Co Ltd (Trident), of receivables due under the charterparty, such assignment having been made as part of an arrangement under which Creditcorp, on behalf of a group of investors, made finance available to Trident. Pan Ocean did not seek to recover the hire instalment from Trident, because it did not consider Trident worth suing. Instead, it sought to recover the money from Creditcorp on the ground of total failure of consideration, since the vessel was off hire for the whole of the period in respect of which the relevant hire instalment was paid.

Held
The claim could not succeed.

Lord Woolf:

"It is one thing to require the other party to the contract to repay if he does not provide the consideration which under the contract he was under obligation to supply, it is another to make the assignee, who was never intended to be under any obligation to supply the consideration, liable to make the repayment. It is conceded that there is no right to trace moneys which are paid to an assignee and there is never any question of their being any restriction on the assignee preventing him dealing with the money as his own. There is no justification for subjecting an assignee, because he has received a payment in advance, to an obligation to make a repayment because of the non-performance of an event for which he has no responsibility. ...

Pan Ocean are in exactly the same position as against Trident as they would have been if there had been no assignment to Creditcorp of the right to receive payment. The assignment occurred quite independently of Pan Ocean's contract with Trident. If Pan Ocean were entitled to recover from Creditcorp, the consequence would be that they would have two different parties instead of a single party from whom they could recover; on [counsel for the appellants'] argument, against Trident under the contract and against Creditcorp for money had and received. It is equally possible to frame a different fundamental question. Why should Pan Ocean have two alternative parties to whom to look for a repayment merely because Trident, as part of their own financial arrangements, have assigned their right to receive payment to a third party, Creditcorp?

I should also refer to the fact that [counsel for the appellants] criticises the reliance which Beldam LJ made in his judgment in the Court of Appeal on *Aiken* v *Short* (1856) 1 H & N 210 and *Barclays Bank Ltd* v *W J Simms Son & Cooke (Southern) Ltd* [1980] QB 677, which were apparently not considered in the course of argument. Those cases were dealing with payments made by mistake and I would not, myself, rely on them in order to come to the conclusion that this appeal has to be dismissed.'